Essentials of Group Therapy

Essentials of Mental Health Practice Series
Founding Editors, Alan S. Kaufman and Nadeen L. Kaufman

Essentials of Interviewing
by Donald E. Wiger and Debra K. Huntley

Essentials of Outcome Assessment
by Benjamin M. Ogles, Michael J. Lambert, and Scott A. Fields

Essentials of Treatment Planning
by Mark E. Maruish

Essentials of Crisis Counseling and Intervention
by Donald E. Wiger and Kathy J. Harowski

Essentials of Group Therapy
by Virginia A. Brabender, April E. Fallon, and Andrew I. Smolar

Essentials

of Group Therapy

Virginia A. Brabender

April E. Fallon

Andrew I. Smolar

John Wiley & Sons, Inc.

Dedication

Virginia: I dedicate this book to the memory of my cousin, Deborah Brabender Kissman, who lived her life with vibrancy and spirit.

April: I dedicate this book to my daughter, Marianna Gogineni, who has expanded my family group in a most joyful way.

Andrew: I dedicate this book to the Einstein hospice staff who taught me most of what I know about support groups.

Acknowledgments

The authors would like to thank Wiley editors Tracey Belmont and Isabel Pratt for their kind, gentle, and competent guidance throughout the writing process. The authors also wish to express their gratitude toward Susan Dodson of Graphic Composition, Inc., for her helpful editorial input. Carol Bricklin and Jeanne Nolan provided very able technical support. Dr. Geoffrey Marczyk provided extremely helpful input on Chapter 7, "Is Group Therapy an Effective Treatment?" Dr. Dennis Debiak offered invaluable suggestions on Chapter 9, "The Diversity among Members in a Therapy Group." Widener graduate students in clinical psychology, Amanda Charlton and Josh Kutinsky, competently aided the authors in library research and other tasks. Finally, the authors would like to express gratitude toward their families for allowing them the time to write this book.

CONTENTS

SERIES PREFACE

I n the *Essentials of Mental Health Practice* series, our goal is to provide readers with books that will deliver key practical information in an efficient and accessible style. The series features books on a variety of critical practice topics, such as interviewing, treatment planning, and outcomes assessment, to name a few. For the experienced professional, books in the series offer a concise yet thorough overview of a specific area of expertise, including numerous tips for best practices. Students will find here a prioritized assembly of all the information and techniques that must be at one's fingertips to practice knowledgeably, efficiently, and ethically in today's behavioral health environment.

Wherever feasible, visual cues highlighting key points are utilized alongside systematic, step-by-step guidelines. Chapters are focused and succinct. Topics are organized for an easy understanding of the essential material related to a particular practice area. Theory and research are continually woven into the fabric of each book, but always to enhance the practical application of the material, rather than to sidetrack or overwhelm readers. With this series, we aim to challenge and assist readers engaged in providing mental health services to aspire to the highest level of proficiency in their particular discipline by arming them with the tools they need for effective practice.

This text provides an overview of contemporary group therapy—a theoretically pluralistic, empirically based modality. This book is directed not only to students in introductory courses and fledgling group therapists but also to seasoned group therapists interested in updating their knowledge bases. The text revolves around the notion that group therapy, rather than being merely interventions made in a group, is a medium that capitalizes on the interactions among members to move them toward their therapeutic goals. The reader is assisted in seeing how, from different theoretical vantages such as psychodynamic, interpersonal, and cognitive behavioral, the therapist uses his or her professional skill to tap the therapeutic potential of these interactions.

This book has a number of distinctive features. First, it provides many practical tools for organizing and conducting a group. Special emphasis is given to the ethical and legal issues that often arise in group therapy practice. Second, this text allocates an entire chapter to the diversity present in the therapy group, a topic of particular importance given the increasingly multicultural character of our society. Third, a chapter is devoted to outcome research in group therapy including the efficacy of group therapy in relation to no treatment and individual therapy. The status of research on particular psychological problems such as anxiety and depression is described. Fourth, the book provides recognition that groups designed to help people are not confined to therapy groups. A chapter on support and self-help groups describes how they differ from, and are similar to, therapy groups.

Alan S. Kaufman, PhD, and Nadeen L. Kaufman, EdD, Founding Editors
Yale University School of Medicine

One

INTRODUCTION TO GROUP THERAPY

One of the principles most fundamental to group therapy is that an individual is affected by the system in which he or she functions. What applies to individuals also applies to the modality of group therapy: The sociocultural context in which group therapy is embedded has over the years critically influenced the course of its development. For example, group therapy was born in the United States at a time when the philosophical school of pragmatism was the dominant intellectual orientation. Pragmatism, espoused by such writers as Charles Pierce, William James (1907), and John Dewey (1900), put forth the principle that the practical value of our ideas of self, other, and the world is the measure of their truth. Whether an idea should be retained or discarded turned on its workability, its capacity to enable an individual to adapt to his or her environment. Pragmatism also emphasized how identity emerges out of one's relationships with others (i.e., having an identity means being in relationship to others). These notions were highly compatible with fundamental tenets of most theoretical approaches to group therapy. For example, if one's identity relates to how others see the self, then what could be more useful in consolidating one's identity than to ask others how one is perceived? If the test of one's concepts about self and others is whether they are adaptive and functional, then what could be more helpful than learning about the effects of one's conceptions on others? Some of the educational concepts of the pragmatists, especially Dewey, were directly applied to the therapy groups.

A thumbnail sketch of its history will introduce the reader to group therapy. However, rather than merely describing the evolution of this modality, we will consider those intellectual trends and historical events that most affected its course over time, and we will identify elements in past approaches that have reached fuller fruition in the present. Through this discussion, the reader will be led to the question: What is group therapy?

I

THE HISTORY OF GROUP THERAPY

The following sections note the significant events in the evolution of group therapy, broken down by developmental periods.

1900–1920: Practical Beginnings

At the beginning of the twentieth century, tuberculosis was a disease of epidemic proportions. A Boston internist, Joseph Pratt, after seeing patient after patient individually, developed a growing curiosity as to whether patients would provide solace to one another if given the opportunity to converse. His curiosity found fruition in groups that he organized and led, which he called "thought control classes" because they included didactic elements such as tips for how to cope with the illness. However, gradually he became impressed with the power of the interactional components of group. Pratt not only functioned as a trailblazer in establishing a path for this new modality but also anticipated many aspects of contemporary approaches. For example, his work foreshadowed the use of group treatment with many populations of individuals with physical problems such as breast cancer, irritable bowel syndrome, lupus, heart problems, and so on. He provided the first example of a homogeneous group that revolves around a difficulty shared by members. Especially prescient of later work was Pratt's clear recognition of the social component of physical illness, a component that made it very amenable to treatment through the group. Pratt was also attentive to the effects of group treatment. For example, he tracked members' weight changes because weight gains might be seen as one positive consequence of treatment. His data collection effort was typical of rich empirical tradition in the practice of group therapy in America.

In the next decade, L. Cody Marsh published an article describing a group treatment format he developed for a psychiatric population. Marsh's approach was multidimensional, relying upon lectures, art, music, and dance. Marsh recognized that members could act altruistically toward one another, find common ground in their thoughts and feelings, experience acceptance, and enjoy an esprit de corps, all of which would ameliorate suffering. Marsh, who is credited with the founding of milieu therapy, is remembered for his dictum "By the crowd they have been broken, by the crowd they shall be healed," an optimistic view that is very much at odds with some dominant theoretical positions of the next decades.

In the work of L. Cody Marsh we see two elements that were drawn from the broader American culture (Van Schoor, 2000). The first was a religious inspirational component. In a country that was populated by the descendants of immigrants who were escaping persecution, religious ideas had a fundamental importance and were expressed in many mediums, including group therapy. Marsh was a former minister and introduced inspirational elements into the group sessions. Connected to this religious value is a belief in education. As Van Schoor (2000) notes, it was the great religious groups of the United States that founded so many of its educational institutions. There was a belief of unlimited self-improvement through education. This value is seen in the work of Marsh, Pratt, and other pioneers in their emphasis on group therapy as an educational experience.

In 1919 and into the next decade, psychiatrist Edward Lazell developed a group approach for the treatment of schizophrenic and manic-depressive individuals at St. Elizabeth's Hospital in Washington, D.C. His method consisted of presenting patients with basic psychoanalytic concepts. Lazell believed that once individuals see that their symptoms are understandable, those symptoms are likely to abate. Like Pratt, Lazell believed it was important to track members' progress to see if in fact the group experience was beneficial: He had nursing staff note changes in patients' need for nightly sedatives over the course of their group experience (Fuhriman & Burlingame, 1994a). This empiricism exhibited by early practitioners was highly congruent with the philosophy of pragmatism given the latter's emphasis upon the testing out of ideas.

The accomplishments of group therapy's first decade are summarized in Rapid Reference 1.1.

1920–1930: Theoretical Beginnings

The next decade distinguished itself by its theoretical developments, many of which took place in Europe. At the beginning of the 1900s, Europe was in a state of disarray, a spirit of nationalism held sway, and many countries sought to extend their borders. Europe's great powers such as France, Great Britain, Austria-Hungary, and Germany were fiercely

≡ *Rapid Reference 1.1*

Achievements from 1900 to 1920

- The first therapy group was conducted with individuals with physical illness.
- A therapy group format was developed for psychiatrically hospitalized patients.
- Psychoeducational techniques were developed for therapy groups.
- The pioneers of group therapy demonstrated interest in tracking members' progress.
- Therapists began to identify therapeutic mechanisms such as universality, hope, and altruism.

rivalrous with one another. The Ottoman Empire, including the Balkan region, was in a state of rapid decline. Europe was a veritable land mine, whose ignition led to World War I.

Given these circumstances, scholarly interest was naturally drawn to group psychology and the dangers inherent in group life. A theorist who had some rather provocative ideas on group life was Gustav LeBon, a scholar of the French Revolution. Although LeBon published his seminal work, The Crowd, in the late 1800s, it was not until its republication in 1920 that it achieved scholarly attention. Because his ideas were so provocative, he succeeded in creating some intellectual interest in the problem of how large groups affect the mental lives of individuals within them. LeBon held that when individuals come together in a large group, they exhibit, in aggregate, a kind of group mind or collective mentality wherein participants show a willingness to engage in behaviors that they would never exhibit when operating individually. This lack of inhibition is rooted in a sense of invincibility: Being in a crowd enables individuals to feel that they can escape both external punishments and their own consciences. The large group or crowd is highly suggestive and vulnerable to the manipulations of charismatic but un-scrupulous leaders. Members are also subject to contagion or the readiness to take on without reflection the psychological elements manifested by those around them. For example, one person's fear can easily lead to an entire group's becoming fearful. The reader will see in Chapter 7 that, like LeBon, new members of therapy groups often believe that the symptoms of other members are contagious (e.g., saying, "I don't want to catch their depression"; MacKenzie, 1990).

Also interested in collective mental life was William McDougall (1923), who shared many of LeBon's views of the primitive functioning of the large group. However, McDougall made a distinction between the organized and unorganized group, with the former having a capacity for work and the latter being dominated by its own impulse life. The differences between LeBon and McDougall antici-pated differences among later theorists concerning whether group life brings greater peril or promise (Ettin, Cohen, & Fidler, 1997).

DON'T FORGET

Contagion, identified by Le Bon, is the readiness of members to take on the psychological elements manifested by those around them.

Sigmund Freud's 1921 text *Group Psychology and the Analysis of the Ego* set forth important notions about group life that would be used and fur-ther developed by psychodynamic group scholars in later decades. In this classic text, Freud raised the basic question of what is a group. He distinguished a group from a mere collection of individuals and held that the key element for a group was the presence of a leader with whom members could identify and with whom they could form an attachment. Out of members' common re-

> **DON'T FORGET**
> ···
> Freud believed that members' relationships with one another in a group are forged out of their relationship with the leader.

lationship with the leader comes their identification with one another. This identification sets the stage for empathy, whereby members can participate in one another's psychological lives. Freud's ideas about the primacy of members' relationships with authority have been incorporated into group developmental theory (see Chapter 7), which holds that members can grapple with their relationship with one another only after they have dealt with their impulses and feelings about the leader. Also influential was his delineation of the role of identification and empathy in producing change.

Triggant Burrow integrated the theoretical notions of his former mentors, Freud and Carl Jung, in his approach to group work (Fried, 1972). Burrow organized experiential groups with students, patients, and colleagues, which were held in the Adirondack Mountains in upstate New York. Here he endeavored to foster a group process whereby members would be freed from their everyday social images or masks. He felt that underneath the social masks lay the defensive patterns described by Freud. Once the defenses were stripped away, what remained were experiences that were rooted in a phylogenetic substructure. This latter notion was inspired by and congruent with Jung's postulation of the existence of archetypes as knowledge passed through the species. Although Burrow's search for the evolutionary undergirding of group process was one that did not take hold, what was of interest to group practitioners was his emphasis on the usefulness of examining contemporary experience. Burrow was the first theorist to use the term *group as a whole* and one of the first to recognize that group phenomena exist beyond behaviors and reactions of any individual member of the group (Burrow, 1928; Ettin, 1997). Scheidlinger (2003) noted that it may have been Burrow's work on groups that discouraged Freud from pursuing them beyond his initial publication. Burrow's claims about the success of his groups were quite extreme and his scientific explanations of their workings highly speculative. These factors may have led Freud to want to distance psychoanalysis from group practice lest the former be discredited by the manner in which the latter was being practiced.

Rapid Reference 1.2 summarizes some of the accomplishments of this period.

1930s–1945: The Age of Integration

The next 15 years saw the integration of the theoretical and applied efforts of the prior 2 decades (see Rapid Reference 1.3). Louis Wender came to the practice of group therapy with a strong psychoanalytic background. He had attended Freud's seminars in Vienna and was analyzed by one of Freud's associates. Wender is credited with conducting the first psychoanalytic group, at Hastings Hillside Hospital in New York (Anthony, 1972b). He viewed his groups as employing four types of process, the first of which he referred to as intellectualization. Wender wrote, "a synthesis of intellect and emotion dominates every phase of our lives and is the basis of all social adjustment" (p. 44). This notion of the importance of cognition alongside affect anticipated the concept of interpersonal learning (Yalom, 1995) and also led Wender to intervene in ways consistent with the strategies of contemporary cognitive therapists. The second element, patient-to-patient transference, recognized that elements of members' relationships with one another can be derivative of earlier relationships.

Wender's last two elements are those that are special aspects of the group experience. The third element, catharsis in the family, was based on his awareness that the group as a whole may be evocative of each member's early family unit and elicit reactions that the individual had to that earliest of relationship configurations. The last element is one that will figure prominently in our definition of group therapy. For Wender, the interaction among members was key to their improvement. Con-

≡ *Rapid Reference 1.2*

Achievements from 1920 to 1930

- Large-group phenomena, such as contagion, were identified.
- Preliminary formulations on the role of the leader, especially in relation to group development, were made.
- The roles of identification and empathy were elucidated.
- Aggression in groups was explored.

≡ *Rapid Reference 1.3*

Achievements from 1931 to 1945

- The term *group therapy* was coined by Jacob Moreno.
- Group therapy was first used with children and adolescents.
- The American Group Psychotherapy Association was founded.
- The American Society for Group Psychotherapy and Psychodrama was founded.
- Psychoanalytic approaches to group treatment were developed.
- Action-oriented approaches to group treatment, particularly psychodrama, emerged.

sistent with the philosophy of pragmatism, Wender felt that one's view of self is socially based. In order for it to be altered, a social experience is required that has greater richness and variety than what individual therapy can provide.

Samuel Slavson in New York developed group therapy applications for the treatment of children. His notion was that children, rather than sitting and talking like adults, need to act out their conflicts within the sessions. For younger children, the medium for action was play therapy; for older children (up to about age 15), activity therapy involving the planning and execution of projects of various sorts was the preferred method. In both formats, younger people were offered an environment in which they were "free to express a wide range of wishes, fears, and fantasies without endangering themselves, their peers, or the therapists" (Schamess, 1993, p. 562). The nonjudgmental and permissive stance of the therapist encouraged a healthy regression that constituted a corrective emotional experience for participants (Lomonaco, Scheidlinger, & Aronson, 2000).

Slavson's notion that children must be treated differently from adolescents, who in turn must be treated differently from adults, highlights an aspect of his understanding of the therapeutic process in groups. Slavson believed that it was always crucial to make the individual the target of intervention rather than the group as a whole. In fact, Slavson took the unusual position that group cohesion is not an asset to the group because it obscures the needs and reactions of the individual. The value of individualism and the freedom of the individual to engage in full, unfettered self-expression runs deep in the American ethos and is manifest in the writings of later American group theorists (Van Schoor, 2000).

Slavson recognized not only the importance of the individual but also the power of individuals' working together. In 1943, Slavson founded the American Group Therapy Association (renamed in 1952 the American Group Psychotherapy Association [AGPA]) and served as its first president. Initially, the organization bore the stamp of Slavson's own theoretical allegiance in that it was wholly Freudian and embraced the goal of personality reorganization as the aim of treatment. Slavson effectively worked to ensure that psychiatrists dominated the organization in its early years and lobbied to have strict requirements for membership criteria, requiring, for instance, supervision by a psychiatrist for entrance. Today the AGPA is an umbrella organization that includes all mental health disciplines and dominant orientations.

Also pursuing a psychoanalytic approach to group treatment was Alexander Wolf. He recognized that psychoanalysis conducted on an individual level presents an economic demand that many could not afford. He believed that psychoanalysis conducted in a group provided a more affordable alternative. Other psychoanalysts, such as Slavson, did not regard the group situation as amenable to psychoanalysis because they believed that members are not able to achieve the same depth of transference as in the individual situation. Wolf's perspective asserted that members are able to achieve an even deeper transference in the group because the members are supported in their explorations by a group ego (Anthony, 1972). Wolf believed that members' representation of the group as a whole provides containment for those contents members find difficulty tolerating. His notion anticipated object relational notions about the function of the group.

Pioneering another type of movement altogether within group therapy was Jacob Moreno, who regarded the traditional psychoanalytic methods of Slavson and others as producing passivity and rigidity and as focusing on the past to the neglect of the present and future (Moreno, 1940). He believed that more action-oriented methods were necessary to enable group members to reach goals that he saw as worthwhile, such as developing the capacity to live creatively and spontaneously. Moreno viewed improvisational drama or psychodrama as a medium by which participants could pursue these goals in an active way. In 1942, he founded the American Society for Group Psychotherapy and Psychodrama, dedicated to the exploration of action-oriented group methods. In Chapter 2, psychodrama will be discussed in some detail. Here, we will merely note that the differences between Slavson and Moreno gave rise to a split within the group therapy field. From Slavson's vantage, the only legitimate type of group treatment was psychoanalytically informed. He claimed that psychodrama was of benefit to psychotic patients only (Scheidlinger, 1993). Moreno perceived himself to be the father of group therapy, not Joseph Pratt. He claimed that he coined the term group psychotherapy in 1931 (Moreno, 1959). Moreno also coined terms that have had usefulness in various types of group therapy, terms such as *hic et nunc* (or here-and-now) and acting out. The friction between Slavson and Moreno set the stage for a more long-standing rift between psychodramatists and other types of group therapists, most especially those with a psychoanalytic orientation. The distance between these different types of group therapy reflected other conflicts—for example, the conflict between passivity and activity. Today, group therapists who differ on levels of activity and structure show far greater collegiality and collaboration than they once had. As the reader will see, group therapists of many orientations use classic psychodramatic techniques such as role playing.

1945–1960: The Age of Expansion

The historian E. James Anthony (1972b) noted that whereas World War I was good for the development of group psychology, World War II catalyzed the growth of group therapy. British and American military hospitals were overflowing with psy-

chiatric casualties, far disproportionate to the number of professionals
available to treat them. Group therapy
provided a solution to this problem.

These groups functioned as labo-
ratories for some of the greatest theoreticians on group life in the history
of group therapy. A few of these theoreticians include

DON'T FORGET

Whereas World War I created an interest in group psychology, World
War II precipitated the establishment
of group therapy as a major treatment
modality.

- *Wilfred Bion.* This British theoretician examined the unconscious life of
  the group through the lens of the object relational theory of Melanie
  Klein. Throughout this text, we will be discussing Bion's basic assumptions, which are group-as-a-whole patterns or cultures based on their
  unconscious needs. Bion believed that the therapist should interpretively
  attend not to individuals but to the dynamics of the group as a whole.
- *Henry Ezriel.* While accepting of many of Bion's notions about the unconscious lives of groups, Ezriel saw it as important that the therapist
  attend not only to the group as a whole but also to the individuals' dynamics as they interfaced with the common group tension at any period
  within the group's life. He believe that the individual dynamics could
  best be understood through the therapist's identification of the relationship the member felt compelled to assume in the group, the relationship for which the member longed, and the catastrophe that the
  member feared would occur if the sought-after relationship were realized (Horwitz, 1993).
- *S. H. Foulkes.* Like McDougall, Foulkes saw in groups tremendous potential for good (Ettin et al., 1997). Foulkes was a German-Jewish psychoanalyst who fled to England in 1933. Foulkes understood group life
  as involving the creation of a network of communication that he referred to as the group matrix. The group matrix consists of the foundation matrix, which is the background members share by virtue of their
  humanity and their participation in common or overlapping cultures,
  and the dynamic matrix, which is their set of unique experiences of this
  particular group. Psychological health is the capacity for members to
  communicate clearly and directly. Psychopathology is the presence of
  significant blocks to communication. At the outset of a therapy group,
  members cannot tolerate communicating directly with either themselves
  or others. The increasing sense of safety derived from an ever-growing

fund of experience with the other members enables each member to behave in ways that reveal rather than protect themselves. The role of the therapist, whom Foulkes (1975/1986) referred to as the conductor, is to work to "broaden and deepen the expressive range of all members, while at the same time increasing their understanding of the deeper, unconscious levels" (p. 120). The conductor, nonauthoritarian and nondirective, attends to both the group matrix and the individuals within the group with the understanding that changes at the level of the group influence the individual and the individual's growth alters the group matrix. However, in the main, the conductor intervenes in a fashion that permits the group ultimately to treat itself.

- *Kurt Lewin.* A Jewish émigré to the United States in the 1930s, Lewin came with a background not as a psychotherapist but rather as a social scientist. Lewin developed a metatheory of group life. Although many prior thinkers had embraced the assumption that the whole of group life represents the accumulation of individual members' contributions, Lewin's position was that the group possesses properties that transcend those of any individual (Agazarian & Janoff, 1993). He saw the individual and group as working toward a mutual state of adaptation. Lewin's concepts about the group as a system, expressed in his field theory, have had a seminal influence on group-as-a-whole and social systems perspectives (discussed in Chapter 2).

Practitioners tended to apply these newly emerging theories in a strict, purist way. For example, psychoanalytic group therapists would generally not consider using psychodrama. Moreover, practitioners largely assumed that others practicing in a different way were misguided. Consequently, the atmosphere among unlike-minded practitioners was contentious and adversarial. See Rapid Reference 1.4 for the main advances during this period.

Rapid Reference 1.4

Achievements from 1946 to 1960

- Group therapy saw widespread use in providing treatment to World War II psychiatric casualties.
- Many theoretical approaches to group treatment were developed.
- The unique properties of groups and the existence of group dynamics received greater recognition.

1960–1970: Group Therapy Enters the Community

The community mental health movement of the 1960s effected the more widespread use of this modality. In response to the Community Mental Health Center Act of 1963, over 500 mental health centers sprang up, requiring both services and human service professionals to provide those services. Group therapy was considered a cost-efficient means of providing treatment. However, often the human service professionals who were called upon to lead groups had little specific training in group therapy (Scheidlinger, 1994). The difficulties that ensued led to an awareness of the importance of group therapy training. The community mental health movement also gave rise to group approaches directed toward goals more immediate than personality structuring and a greater diversity of methods accommodating individuals at various points along the continuum of ego functioning.

The Vietnam War also stimulated the development of nontraditional group methods. Along with the mistrust of authority evoked by military involvement and the draft was a value individuals placed on self-exploration in an egalitarian setting. In this environment, the growth group movement was spawned. These groups had various names, including T-groups (T for training), sensitivity groups, encounter groups, and marathon groups. Rather than being directed toward the diminishment of psychopathology, these groups were aimed at the enhancement of members' well-being and the realization of members' potential. The growth group movement, dominant in the United States, flourished in an environment in which the creative self-expression of the individual was viewed as being of paramount importance and was catalyzed by the growth of a middle class that had the resources for such an endeavor (Van Schoor, 2000). These groups were often led by persons other than professionally trained group therapists; rather, leadership was drawn from a variety of disciplines, including education, business, and the social sciences (Reid & Reid, 1993). These groups, primarily focused on the here and now, used a variety of experimental techniques, some of which have become incorporated into mainstream group therapy. However, because of the report of some individuals who had not benefitted but had even been harmed by encounter group experiences, they also had the negative effect of creating some suspicion about the modality of group therapy. See Rapid Reference 1.5 for the main advances during this period and the next.

≡*Rapid Reference 1.5*

Achievements from 1961 to 1985

- The community mental health movement enhanced the popularity of group therapy.
- The development of the growth group movement gave rise to many new techniques.
- Interpersonal theory was introduced by Irvin Yalom.
- A research base accumulated that showed that group therapy is at least as effective as other modalities.
- The need for training for group therapists met with increased recognition.

1970–1985

In 1970, Irvin Yalom published the first edition of *The Theory and Practice of Group Psychotherapy*, a text many consider to be the bible of group treatment. In this seminal work, Yalom described an interpersonal approach to group treatment. This model posits both goals and methods that have an interpersonal character. The overarching goal of an interpersonal group is to enable the individual to improve his or her capacity to have positive relationships with others. The method is to address the member's manner of relating to other members in the group within the here and now of the sessions. The interpersonal approach is considered to be one of three dominant approaches to group therapy (Dies, 1992b). It has stimulated a fund of studies on therapeutic factors—that is, the mechanisms within group responsible for positive change. In Chapter 2, this model will be more fully explicated and illustrated.

Although a good deal of outcome research occurred in the 1960s, much of it was methodologically flawed. In the 1970s, outcome studies possessed far greater methodological rigor (Fuhriman & Burlingame, 1994a). Control groups, random assignment, and therapists adequately trained in the approach being examined were more characteristic than not of the research of the day. In general, research findings supported the value of group therapy, independently and relative to other treatment modalities.

1985–Present

In the beginning of the 1980s, the mental health field in the United States and many other countries experienced the emergence of managed care systems that attempted to place controls on reimbursement for health care services. The managed care industry positively regarded group therapy because it enabled the provision of cost-effective treatment (MacKenzie, 1994). At the same time, group therapy needed to adapt to economic changes. The greater inaccessibility of long-term therapy necessitated the construction of approaches that could be used in short time frames. Through the eighties and nineties, such short-term models did indeed appear for a great variety of populations, problems, and settings. Some of these models will be featured in Chapter 10. Cognitive-behavioral interventions, which have historically been applied within a short-term time frame, increased in popularity.

A related trend has been the practitioner's greater accountability for the usefulness of his or her interventions. No longer can group therapists establish for members vaguely defined goals pursued through unspecified processes and measured in impressionistic ways. Third-party payers require clear treatment plans. Goals must be operationalized, methods clearly detailed, and outcomes explicitly identified. Group therapists are expected to use validated approaches. Fortunately, research questions in the eighties and nineties and through the present have become much more specific (Fuhriman & Burlingame, 1993), so that therapists have data to buttress their decision making. Rarely do researchers ask "Does group therapy work?" but rather "Does Approach X work with this problem in this time frame in this setting?" Still, some approaches are far better studied than others. For example, cognitive-behavioral group treatments have been validated far more substantially than interpersonal approaches.

The accumulation of research showing not only that group therapy is effective but also that different approaches have value that depends on the characteristics of the group member, the time frame, the setting, the characteristics of the therapist, and so on has led to the emergence of a pluralistic value in the group therapy community of professionals (Scheidlinger, 1993). No longer do practitioners adopt an adversarial attitude toward other practitioners using different theoretical approaches. Rather, an awareness that a multiplicity of approaches may benefit clients has led to a rise in a more collegial atmosphere. Moreover, there is a greater tendency than existed in the 50s and 60s for practitioners who pay allegiance to a given theory to borrow concepts and techniques from others. For example, psychoanalytic group therapists working in a short-term time frame occasionally use the cognitive-behavioral technique of assigning homework between sessions.

At the same time, there is a stronger recognition than there was in earlier decades that group therapists need to be well trained and that training must be a lifelong endeavor. Professional organizations devoted to group therapy such as AGPA have taken greater responsibility for this training by developing educational programs for the new therapist and credentialing opportunities for the senior individual. There is also greater attention to the legal and ethical aspects of group therapy. For example, there have been many more contributions to the literature on the problems of confidentiality and privacy in therapy groups. Organizations have also provided educational offerings to support group therapists in conducting their practices in a legal and ethical way, such as the training course in the area of ethics that AGPA has developed.

As part of being an ethical and competent practitioner, the group therapist must understand individual differences and how the various attributes of group members affect how they are likely to participate in the group and benefit from it. This recognition has given rise to a burgeoning literature on diversity and group therapy. The 1990s saw a dramatic increase in the number of articles on such topics as group therapy and race, culture, and gender, an increase that con-

≡Rapid Reference 1.6

Achievements from 1985 to the Present

- Short-term applications are necessitated by greater economic controls on mental health treatment.
- Group therapists respond to the demand by third-party payers for greater accountability for members' progress.
- Greater specificity of research findings is obtained about what approaches are successful in what conditions.
- Theoretical pluralism, theoretical integrative work, and collegiality characterize the community of group therapy professionals.
- There is increased focus on training and credentialing of group therapists.
- There is increased attention to ethical and legal issues.
- There is increased attention to diversity topics.

tinues in the present decade. We will cite many of these contributions in Chapter 9 but also note that there are certain areas of diversity such as religion that have still been only scantily explored.

Increasingly, group therapists recognize the power of group therapy to help members respond adaptively to challenges presented by the environment, even those of the most extreme sort. For example, group therapists working with children have developed crisis intervention formats for children who have experienced natural disasters, suffered the death of a teacher, or witnessed episodes of violence between divorced parents (Lomonaco et al., 2000). Group therapists conducted crisis groups for the victim-survivors of the September 11th attack upon the World Trade Center in New York (see Roth, 2002, for a description of such groups with members who were in the vicinity of Ground Zero on the day of the attack). As did the participants in many crisis groups before them, these individuals found that discovering how their reactions to this horrific occurrence were both the same as and different from those of others enabled them to bear those reactions and to marshal their resources. See Rapid Reference 1.6 for the main advances during this period.

THE DEFINITION OF GROUP THERAPY

Group therapy is a treatment modality involving a small group of members and one or more therapists with specialized training in group therapy. It is designed to promote psychological growth and ameliorate psychological problems through the cognitive and affective exploration of the interactions among members, and between members and the therapist. There are three elements of this definition that require commentary.

- *"Group therapy is designed to promote psychological growth and ameliorate psychological problems."* This element distinguishes therapy groups from self-help and support groups. Whereas group therapy seeks to effect psychological change, self-help and support groups have the more limited goal of assisting members in coping with their immediate problems. Nonetheless, all of these groups have in common great potential to alleviate psychological suffering. Further discussion of the differences and similarities among these three types of groups will occur in Chapter 11.
- *". . . through the cognitive and affective exploration of the interactions among members, and between members and the therapist."* Imagine a group situation in which a therapist came in, gave a brief lecture on a mental health topic, and went around the circle of members, individually speaking with each one about his or her difficulties. Such a circumstance might be therapeutic, but it would not be group therapy. Over the years of the study of this modality, it has been learned that unless members are given an opportunity to interact with one another, and unless the interactions are a focus of study, the potential benefits of members' being in a group together are not realized (Fuhriman & Burlingame, 1993).
- The group therapist must be a mental health professional skilled in intervening both within the group and on an individual level. Why must a group therapist be a mental health professional? Although the history of group treatments includes the long-standing facilitation of various types of groups by laypersons and paraprofessionals, group therapy necessitates professional-level training. Group therapy is a powerful modality, which in most cases produces positive effects. However, like most powerful instruments, it is capable of producing negative consequences for certain participants (Roback, 2000). From

---

DON'T FORGET

Therapy groups must be conducted by mental health professionals with specialized training in group therapy in order that they may minimize the risk of negative outcomes, respond appropriately to emergency situations, and access the therapeutic processes that are specific to group therapy.

their interviews of senior group therapists Dies and Teleska (1985) estimated the adverse outcome rate to be 10 percent. Training in psychopathology that has both breadth and depth is needed to ensure that the group leader can recognize these negative effects and intervene appropriately. Furthermore, included in therapy groups are individuals who may have mental health emergencies. Professional-level training is needed for intervention that is efficient and effective. The reason specialized training is needed in group therapy is implied by the former two points in this list. If there are processes unique to the therapy group, then it is not sufficient for a therapist to be knowledgeable about other forms of therapy, such as individual therapy. The group therapist must have training that is specific to this modality (see Chapter 12 for a description of such training). That group therapists do in fact respond differently from less-trained individuals was seen in a study of participants in child group therapy. Leichtentritt and Schechtman (1998) observed that group therapists and trainees decrease and increase respectively their verbalizations over the course of the group. The behavior of the therapists was more congruent with the developmental trend that members became more self-sufficient in the group as the group progressed.

Nonetheless, there is a place for nonprofessionals in group treatments other than therapy groups. These types of groups will be discussed in Chapter 11.

SUMMARY AND CONCLUSIONS

This chapter presented a brief history of group therapy. The relationships between advancements in group treatments and the sociocultural context were described. For example, as Anthony (1972b) noted, World War I provided a context for the development of group psychology, whereas World War II created the environment for group therapy to emerge as a major treatment modality. We also saw how the value of self-liberation created a context in which the encounter or growth group movement in the United States could occur. Today, group therapy is a treatment modality that is widely used across different psychological problems, populations, and settings. Its effectiveness has been well established by many outcome studies. Although there are currently many types of therapy groups, all of them have in common (1) the direct involvement of a mental health professional trained in group therapy and (2) the use of interactions among members, and between the therapist and members, to advance the goals of the group.

🐟 TEST YOURSELF 🐟

1. **How was Joseph Pratt important to the evolution of group therapy?**
   (a) He was the first to use group treatment with a psychiatric population.
   (b) He was the first to have patients use the group format to converse about the difficulties they shared.
   (c) He recognized the social component of physical illness.
   (d) b and c only

2. **During the first two decades of the twentieth century, the pioneers of group therapy did not worry about whether their methods worked.** True or False?

3. **What is the meaning of Gustav LeBon's term** *contagion?*

4. **Which component of Louis Wender's four group processes most strongly resonates with the definition of group therapy provided in this chapter?**
   (a) The idea that one's view of self is socially based
   (b) Patient-to-patient transference
   (c) Catharsis in the family
   (d) Intellectualization

5. **In what way did the differences between Samuel Slavson and Jacob Moreno (during the 1930–1945 period) set the stage for a split within the group therapy field?**

6. **The expansion of new psychological theories in the post–World War II era gave rise to many practitioners' applying theories in a strict, purist manner and an adversarial atmosphere among practitioners who differed in opinion.** True or False?

7. **The community mental health movement of the 1960s had which effect?**
   (a) It helped to alleviate tension among practitioners with opposing viewpoints.
   (b) It decreased the demand for group therapists.
   (c) It underscored the need for training of group therapists.
   (d) It showed that group treatments could not be applied to highly dysfunctional populations.

8. **Dr. Spin organizes a group format in which he converses with each member on a one-on-one basis. Members have no opportunity to interact. Is this group therapy?**

9. **How did the group therapy field adapt to changes in the health care environment and sociopolitical environments since the emergence of managed care in the early 1980s?**

(continued)

10. What distinguishes group therapy from self-help and support groups?

    (a) Cognitive and affective exploration of the interactions among members

    (b) Cognitive and affective exploration of the interactions between members and the therapist

    (c) The promotion of psychological growth and amelioration of psychological problems

    (d) One or more therapists with specialized training in group therapy

Answers: 1. d; 2. False; 3. The readiness of members of a group to take on without reflection the psychological elements manifested by those around them; 4. a; 5. The strong opposition between Slavson (psychoanalytic) and Moreno (psychodramatic) set a precedent for the later conflict between psychoanalytic/psychodynamic orientations and action-oriented orientations and also between passivity and activity; 6. True; 7. c; 8. No; 9. Construction of short-term group therapy, validation and increased specificity of treatment plans, increased focus on training, and greater attention to legal, ethical, and diversity issues; 10. c.

Two

THEORETICAL APPROACHES TO
GROUP PSYCHOTHERAPY

One of the most important decisions a therapist makes early in the process of designing a group is what theoretical orientation will inform the group. There are a number of reasons why a therapist should operate from a clear theoretical perspective.

- A theoretical orientation offers a view on what is a psychological problem. This contribution assists the therapist in identifying possible goals toward which group work might be directed. For example, one popular theory holds that psychological problems are fundamentally interpersonal problems. This theory would direct the group therapist to set as a goal assisting members in improving their relational abilities.
- Theories offer a conceptual framework for understanding the meaning of events that occur in the group. That is, a theory helps the therapist to make sense out of what he or she is observing during the session. Yalom (1983) noted, "By developing a cognitive framework that permits an ordering of all the inchoate events of therapy, the therapist experiences a sense of inner order and mastery—a sense that, if deeply felt, is automatically conveyed to patients and generates in them a corresponding sense of clarity and mastery" (p. 122).
- A theory points to the processes that are activated in a group setting to help members move toward their goals and the therapist interventions by which the processes can be activated. Stated simply, theory directs the therapist's actions in the group.

Within the field of group therapy, a wide array of theoretical orientations exists. In this chapter, we identify those theories that are most commonly used in today's practice. In comprising this list, we first considered the results of a survey (Dies, 1992b) in which senior group therapists, all members of the American Group Psychotherapy Association, were asked to list what they saw as the major orientations. Second, we surveyed the literature to see what theoretical emphases

≡Rapid Reference 2.1

Seven Theoretical Approaches to Group Psychotherapy

Approach	Major Contributors
Interpersonal	Yalom, Leszcz
Psychodynamic	Bion, Scheidlinger, Alonso, Rutan, Stone
Social systems approaches	Agazarian, Borriello, H. Durkin, J. Durkin
Cognitive-behavioral	A. T. Beck, J. Beck, Rose, White
Psychodrama	Moreno, Blatner, Kipper
Redecision therapy	R. Goulding, M. Goulding, Gladfelter
Existential therapy	Yalom, Mullan

currently exist in books and articles on group therapy. Third, we tapped our knowledge of different settings in which group therapy is practiced and the theoretical models commonly employed in those settings. From these sources, seven theoretical orientations emerged, which are listed in Rapid Reference 2.1 along with the names of major contributors to these approaches.

We've provided a description of the theoretical underpinning, goals, and methods of each of these orientations along with case examples. It is crucial that, in order to use any of these approaches competently, the practitioner have not only substantial exposure to the literature on the model but also supervision from someone who has extensive experience in its application.

CAUTION

A group therapist attempting to use a new theoretical approach should learn to use it under supervision.

THE INTERPERSONAL APPROACH

The interpersonal orientation to group therapy is one of the most popular approaches used today. For any mental health professional interested in practicing group therapy, familiarity with this approach is essential, because most other existing theoretical models have borrowed elements from this approach. The interpersonal orientation is based on the theories of personality and psychopathology of Harry Stack Sullivan (1953). Sullivan saw the yearning to form secure relationships with others as a fundamental motivational base of human behavior. Early in life, the child will accentuate those behaviors in his or her repertoire that bring acceptance and approbation by the parents and other important figures and will de-emphasize those that appear to be negatively received. Through this selection process, personality is fashioned. Later in life, an adult may perceive the environment in a way that is consistent with the past but inconsistent with present realities. Sullivan labeled such misperceptions *parataxic distortions*. The behaviors that proceed from these distortions are ones that may have led to satisfaction and the avoidance of discomfort in the past but are unlikely to be effective in the present because they are out of synchrony with the environment. For Sullivan, psychopathology occurs when a person's experience is highly influenced by parataxic distortions, distortions that inevitably lead to rigid and outdated patterns of response rather than flexible, environmentally sensitive behaviors (Sullivan, 1953).

The antidote to psychopathology, then, is the opportunity for a person to identify and correct parataxic distortions as they are occurring in the present so that the person is able to enjoy fulfilling relationships, a goal that Sullivan considered the desired outcome of psychotherapy (Gotlib & Schraedley, 2000). Irvin Yalom, synthesizing many of the ideas of interpersonal theories, advanced the notion that the therapy group is the ideal environment for the modification of dated assumptions about the self in relation to others (Yalom & Vinodagrav, 1993). Unlike the individual psychotherapy situation in which there is only one other person with whom to relate, in the group there is a range of personalities. Moreover, within the group there are different types of relationships. For example, members within the group have a relationship with an authority figure in the person of the therapist. The relationships with other members are peer relationships. Because of the diversity of relationships present, the group provides a microcosm of members' social worlds outside the group. In this microcosm, members' typical ways of seeing themselves in relation to others, and the behaviors that are integrally connected to these perceptions, will be revealed. Through a process of interpersonal learning, members can obtain feedback on the positive and negative aspects of these perceptions and behaviors. This feedback is a prerequisite for change in members' relational styles. Feedback occurs with respect to members' here-and-now experiences with one another. The "here" refers to in-the-room events; "now" pertains to present rather than past or future happenings. The group also offers a laboratory in which members may experiment with new behaviors associated with more accurate perceptions of themselves and in which they have the opportunity to receive feedback on these behaviors. In order for interpersonal learning to be maximally effective, members must be affectively engaged in the process and be provided with a cognitive framework for organizing their experiences with one another.

Although interpersonal learning serves as the cornerstone of the interpersonal approach, many other factors come into play. Group cohesion is a factor that enables members to realize the benefits of group participation in two ways (Leszcz, 1992). First, the feelings of acceptance and belonging that cohesion entails are crucial experiences for those group members accustomed to alienation and isolation in their lives. Second, for all members, group cohesion is a requirement for, and potentiator of, the operation of the other therapeutic factors, especially interpersonal learning. For example, in a cohesive group in which members commit themselves to promoting one another's well-being, they are more likely to perform the difficult task of giving one another constructive feedback. Universality is another important therapeutic factor because when members realize that many of their affects and impulses are shared, they are more likely to take risks in expressing feelings. Such affective expression is the first step of interpersonal learning. Self-disclosure is necessary because it is through this revelatory process that the person's maladaptive notions about him- or herself are revealed. Self-disclosure also occurs when members share how they have been affected by a given member. As members see improvement in themselves and others, the therapeutic factor of hope is fostered. As they experience themselves as being vehicles of others' change, the therapeutic factor of altruism is brought into play. This listing of how the various therapeutic factors assist a member in undergoing interpersonal change is only a partial one. The reader may see others illustrated in the following Putting It into Practice.

The interpersonal approach requires a therapist who is active in developing group cohesion, helping members to identify with one another, and supporting them in seeing one another as resources in moving toward the goals of the group (Leszcz, 1992). The interpersonal therapist assists members in engaging in interpersonal learning by doing the following:

- Encouraging members to stay within the here and now of the group. This leader activity helps the group to build a microcosm from which data can be obtained on interpersonal styles and stimulates members' affective involvement (heightened emotional engagement) in the group.
- Fostering interpersonal learning by identifying opportunities for members to provide one another with feedback.

Putting It Into Practice

Interpersonal Vignette I

Ingrid had been in a time-unlimited group for 6 months. This grade school teacher and department head had entered the group because her principal had informed her that if she did not learn to work more cooperatively with the other teachers she would request that Ingrid be transferred to another school despite her evident talent as a teacher. Of particular concern to the principal was Ingrid's domineering and insensitive manner toward other teachers in her department, especially the junior faculty. For example, upon walking into the classrooms of these other teachers, she would reprimand their students for trivial offenses. She would allow teachers within her department very little latitude in developing curricula and would harshly correct them for deviating from her methods of choice.

In the group, the tendency of her early participation was to give advice to those members who asked for direction from others. Over time, however, she became more overtly critical of the immediate feedback members gave to other members. For example, in one session, Dick told Adrian that when she spoke in such low tones that he had to strain to hear her, he felt irritated. Ingrid responded testily that a person's way of speaking is an inborn thing and should simply be accepted. Dick threw his hands up in the air and said, "Well, pardon me if I was doing what we came here to do!" One very senior member, Germaine, suggested to Ingrid that she was reacting out of her own fear that she (Ingrid) might be given feedback. Germaine acknowledged how frightening it was for her when she first came into the group to realize that she eventually would learn about others' impressions of her. Ingrid categorically and indignantly rejected the idea that her response to Dick was based on her own apprehension.

Despite Ingrid's defensive posture, she was receptive to hearing others talk about their negative reactions to her judgmental demeanor in the sessions. On her own, Ingrid was able to see the link between her difficulties with other teachers at work and the negative responses to group members. Ingrid made an effort to monitor her evaluative tendency and to be more expressive when she had positive responses to others' contributions. Members recognized this shift and articulated to her their appreciation of it. Considerably later in her tenure in the group, Ingrid came to understand that when she was unable to control other people, she felt an abject terror that she and those around her would be thrown into a state of chaos. Her achievement of this insight was followed by a more optimistic perspective on her ability to have more enjoyable relationships with both the group members and her colleagues. She gradually became more tolerant of the chaos and messiness (as she experienced them) of her own and other members' feelings. This tolerance freed her from needing to monitor her reactions to ensure that they were balanced; she found she could do so spontaneously.

Teaching note: Ingrid engaged in interpersonal learning when she obtained feedback on both her judgmental stance toward others and members' reactions to it. Her interpersonal learning was furthered by the positive feedback she received when she altered her behavior. She also used the factor of self-understanding as she recognized the connection between her fear and her effort to control others. The therapeutic factor of hope was brought into play as Ingrid saw that her progress in the group could have significant positive consequences for her interpersonal functioning and ability to derive fulfillment from relationships.

- Shaping feedback so that it is maximally helpful. The leader helps members to frame their observations so that they are balanced (inclusive of behaviors eliciting both positive and negative reactions), specific, and as nonjudgmental as possible.
- Providing a cognitive framework for organizing members' affective experiences. For example, suppose members Roberto and Andre express anger toward one another because each thinks the other is trying to monopolize the group. For these members to simply express anger is not necessarily therapeutic. Additionally, they need to achieve an understanding of both their anger and how it is instigated by certain social stimuli. For example, Roberto may come to recognize that seeing another person secure the attention of a group vexes him because he has doubts as to whether he can command others' interest. Perhaps he could learn alternatives to responding to this doubt, such as getting feedback on how to engage others or discovering different ways to obtain attention.

The following Putting It into Practice provides a more extended example of the therapist's role in fostering interpersonal learning.

Although *mass group process commentaries* or group-as-a-whole statements are not relied upon heavily, they are used when members in concert with one another launch a group-level resistance to tackling their interpersonal issues (Yalom, 1995). Such resistances are especially likely when members confront an issue that is highly threatening to many members. Mass group commentaries are also helpful when the group has developed an antitherapeutic group norm—for example, when the group develops an interactional format of intensively and invasively questioning a single member. The goal of the mass group commentary would be the resumption in the group of the process of interpersonal learning.

The interpersonal approach distinguishes itself from some of the other therapeutic approaches presented in this chapter in that it allows for a moderate level of self-disclosure on the part of the therapist. The interpersonal therapist makes judicious self-disclosures (Yalom, 1983), especially those that concern the group process. For example, the therapist might reveal feelings of concern or worry that a particular member was overwhelmed by the amount of feedback she received. By avoiding a presentation of

CAUTION

Within the interpersonal approach, mass group process commentaries are made very selectively: when the therapist senses that a group-level resistance is interfering with interpersonal learning or when an unhealthy norm is being established in the group.

Putting It Into Practice

Interpersonal Vignette II

Josefina opened the group session complaining angrily about one of her coworkers who obtained all of the attention from the supervisor by being helplessly incompetent. She said that she, Josefina, carried the office but failed to get any recognition because her supervisor was too focused on propping up the coworker, whose deficiencies were accepted because she had such a winsome manner. Several other members chimed in about similar inequities they had experienced in their office settings, with the more competent persons receiving fewer resources than the less competent.

The therapist wondered aloud whether such inequities existed in the group, especially in recent sessions. Frank asked Josefina if he spent too much time talking in the last session. She replied, "No, it wasn't *you* who was bothering me."

Rachel, a member who had identified with Josefina's irritation, said, "It's Catherine, isn't it?"

"But I didn't take up that much time last week," Catherine protested. "I talked about a few things, but ..."

Josefina interrupted. "It's not the time. It's that when you speak you have this fragile delicate thing going.... Everyone just wants to make it all better for you.... Even I did, and then later I felt cheated because I just never get that response. And it made me furious at you when I thought about it."

The therapist said, "*Made* you?"

"Well, yeah, it's still there."

Catherine began to tear up. Josefina, noticing this, added with irritation, "That's what I mean! Everyone now is going to rush to your defense."

"I'm not," said Rachel. "It gets on my nerves, too." Turning to Josefina, she added, "It's like through her tears, she controls things."

The therapist noted, "It seems that Catherine evoked a negative response in you just now. What could she have done that might have been more helpful?"

Josefina responded, "If she had just shown more interest in how I was feeling. I'm as much talking about how I can't get people to respond to me with the kind of caring she gets. I mean, maybe she could have asked me about my own reaction more. But instead, I felt it was all about her vulnerability. I could accept better the fact that Catherine takes so much from the group if only she would give a little!"

Teaching note: In this brief segment, the therapist moves the group to the here and now by using Josefina's complaint as a reflection of some members' feelings about events in the last session. Although one may never be able to establish the objective accuracy of the therapist's inference, it nonetheless serves a function in leading the group into that realm in which its work is likely to be most productive (Yalom, 1995). Once the group is within the here and now and affects have been aroused, the therapist helps members to reflect on their experiences in order to arrive at an understanding of them. In this interaction, the therapist's query about what alternate behaviors on the part of Catherine might have produced a different response allowed Josefina to refine her observations. However, there is no one correct intervention for any given process event.

inscrutability, the therapist discourages members from a preoccupation with the therapist and encourages their engagement with one another, a necessary condition for the complete use of the microcosmic aspect of the group.

The interpersonal approach can be applied in a wide range of settings, including outpatient, inpatient, and day treatment, and with individuals with a broad array of presenting problems. Although historically group therapists have applied this approach on a long-term basis, more recently Yalom (1983) and others have developed formats for its short-term use. These latter formats generally entail narrowing the range of interpersonal problems members can pursue in the group. Although there is a small empirical literature showing that participation in an interpersonal group produces positive changes in relationships, much more work is needed to discover what types of changes can occur in different time frames. For example, Budman, Demby, Solde, and Merny (1996) found that, after participation in 18 months of an interpersonally oriented group, members showed marked improvement in interpersonal functioning as reflected in scores on an inventory of interpersonal problems. Yet the same investigators found that certain types of interpersonal problems (e.g., satisfaction in relationships with friends and intimates) remained unchanged.

PSYCHODYNAMIC GROUP THERAPY APPROACHES

Psychodynamic group therapy encompasses a set of approaches to group work. These approaches distinguish themselves from one another in the goals set and the techniques used. Yet all of them share a common set of principles by which human functioning is understood and methods by which change is instigated (Pine, 1990; Rutan, 1993).

- According to the principle of *psychic determinism,* all elements of experience and behavior occur for a reason. No matter how random or bizarre an element of intrapsychic life or behavior may appear, it is fundamentally purposive in that it occurs to serve the needs of the person. The motivational base of experience and behavior confers upon each an orderliness that can be recognized with investigation. The psychoanalytic group therapist enters the session with the conviction that all aspects of members' activity within the sessions have a coherence and meaningfulness that can be uncovered through exploration.
- The dynamic unconscious exists and continually exerts an influence upon experience and behavior, both healthy and otherwise. Unconscious contents—such as thoughts, feelings, and impulses—are kept

outside of conscious awareness by defense mechanisms that function to preserve some aspect of a person's well-being. The operation of the defenses in relation to these contents highlights the dynamic character of the unconscious: Different elements, structures, and processes can and do come into conflict with one another. How these conflicts are resolved will greatly affect a person's ability to function effectively, have satisfying and stable relationships, and achieve and maintain a sense of well-being. Therefore, a goal of psychoanalytic treatment in groups and elsewhere is to obtain insight into these unconscious forces to enable the individual to achieve new, more adaptive resolutions of conflict.

- Thinking has both primary and secondary process aspects, with the latter being an adult's rational, logical cognition and the former being more primitive content "based on symbol and metaphor, on 'irrational' connections among ideas and that does not heed the rules of reality and social communication" (Pine, 1990, p.18). Although conscious cognition often (although not invariably) conforms to the laws of secondary process thinking, unconscious contents often have a more primary process character. The group therapist must create an environment in which primary process can emerge and be understood.

- Personality is formed through a developmental process in which events, achievements, and difficulties within one stage influence the individual's progress through subsequent stages. Relationships with significant figures in the earliest stages are highly influential in determining the character of relationships within the present. Yet, as Rutan (1993) writes, "Psychoanalytic theory is optimistic about human development in that it assumes that flaws in early stages of development can be repaired if that stage is recalled, relived, and affectively re-experienced correctively in the here and now" (p. 141). Psychodynamically informed group therapy provides such opportunities through the stages of group development described in Chapter 6. Each group stage invites the emergence of a set of issues, themes, and conflicts that may be associated with a member's current difficulties. Although each type of psychodynamic group therapy has its own distinctive set of goals for the group member, for all of them it entails addressing those blocks in the individual's developmental process that are having a detrimental effect on his or her current functioning.

The technical approach of the psychodynamic group therapist follows from the preceding four principles. The therapist encourages a regressive process by adopting a *nondirective stance* in the group. The only instruction the therapist provides members is to share spontaneously their thoughts and feelings. When the therapist neglects to steer the group, members experience frustration, which is born out of their natural longing for approval from the authority figure, the therapist. This frustration induces regression. Members move to a developmentally earlier mode of experiencing themselves and others. Regression brings to the surface elements related to members' core areas of difficulties, elements that are usually hidden. These elements will manifest themselves in transferences to the therapist and transferences of members to one another. These transferences are a reliving of an early situation with contemporary figures (Waelder, 1960). As these transferences develop, the group can explore them within the here and now of the session.

As transference elements appear, the therapist practices neutrality: refraining from siding with any elements or splits in each member's psychological life. The therapist avoids overtly or subtly reinforcing particular reactions of the members but maintains an evenhandedness that conveys the notion that all elements can be manifested, tolerated, and subjected to exploration. The therapist also abstains from disclosing information about him- or herself that might restrict the members' associations or fantasies about him or her (Rutan & Stone, 2001).

Although the psychodynamic group therapist does not actively direct the group, he or she performs a number of important functions. The therapist creates a holding environment in which members have the confidence that all of their reactions will be contained and understood. The therapist also establishes consistent boundaries and conveys empathy for members' reactions, most particularly those that are threatening or painful. However, the activity of the therapist that is regarded as mutative—that is, most contributory to members' change—is the *interpretation*. Piper, McCallum, and Azim (1992) defined an interpretation as a type of intervention in which the therapist makes "a statement that reveals one or more aspects of the dynamic equation of the context of a conflictual situation" (p. 73). Through the interpretation, members gain awareness of repressed contents and see their connection to their experiences and behaviors, which renders the latter more meaningful. The major foci of the therapist's interpretive efforts are the transferences that develop in the group and emerge on various levels (see Rapid Reference 2.2). Members can form (1) vertical transferences to the authority figure in the group, the therapist; (2) horizontal or member-to-member transferences; (3) transferences to a subgroup of members including or excluding the therapist; and (4) transferences to the group as a whole. Each transference provides the opportunity for members to rework an early conflict in a manner that will serve that member's intrapsychic growth.

The therapist's interpreting activity relies on his or her capacity to assimilate a great deal of information that is present in a group from a multiplicity of sources. The therapist attends to both verbal and nonverbal communications. The therapist is attuned not only to the manifestations but also to the content of members' behavior. Because of the operations of the defenses, members frequently speak in symbols or derivatives. For example, when members feel dissatisfaction with the therapist, they may talk in negative terms of other authority figures, onto whom they displace their negative feelings. The therapist listens to the material in the group with

≡*Rapid Reference 2.2*

Transferences That Develop in Group Therapy

Vertical transference: reactions to authority figure.

Horizontal transference: member-to-member reactions.

Subgroup transferences: responses to two or more members who are perceived as sharing some physical or psychological characteristic.

Group-as-a-whole transference: a response to the entity of the group apart from that to any specific member.

the aim of ascertaining the latent content of members' communications. Especially when members talk about issues external to the group, the therapist asks what the significance of the material may be for the internal concerns of members.

Among the types of information used by the therapist is his or her *countertransference*. Freud's classical view of countertransference was the notion that the therapist can have reactions to the patients (in this case the group members) that are due to his or her own neurotic conflicts. These reactions pose obstacles to effective treatment because they limit the therapist's capacity to respond optimally to the patient. Object relations theory, a branch of psychodynamic thought that examines how individuals represent their experiences of self and other, provided the insight that the therapist as a participant in the treatment relationship will inevitably be affected by the dynamics of the other participant. So too is the group therapist affected by the dynamics of the group and those of the individual members.

The object relational theorist Wilfred Bion, using the ideas of Melanie Klein in relation to groups, described the mechanism of *projective identification* as a key means by which the dynamics of the group influence the therapist. Projective identification is a three-step process:

- In Step 1, a member unconsciously projects his or her unwanted impulses and feelings onto another. For example, if Mary finds her anger unacceptable, she may project it onto Bill. She will thereby see Bill as angry and herself as devoid of anger.

- Step 2 entails behaving toward that person in a manner designed to co-erce him or her to act in accordance with the projection. That is, Mary will induce anger in Bill.
- In Step 3, the projection is taken back by the projecting person in the form in which it is manifested in the person who is the target of the projection. What is taken back is that psychological element as it appears to have been experienced by the person who is the target of the projection. Mary not only projects her anger toward Bill and gets him to feel anger and behave angrily: She also continues to observe him to see how he is bearing with her anger. If Bill expresses his anger in a more mature, controlled way than Mary would have, Mary can make Bill's expression part of her own psychological structure and thereby develops intrapsychically. If, however, he expresses it in a less mature way than Mary might have, Mary will nonetheless internalize this more primitively expressed version of her anger. See Rapid Reference 2.3 for a listing of the steps in projective identification.

Although group members establish projective identifications with one another, often the therapist serves this role, for two reasons. Early in group life, members are highly focused on the parent-child relationship, in which the therapist serves as the contemporary parent figure. Second, throughout many of the developmental stages, members are likely to experience the therapist as having a sturdiness that inspires a confidence that the therapist will merely contain rather than acting out the content projected upon him or her. In fact, this containment is a most important function of the group therapist. The therapist contains members' disturbing reactions until such time that the members can re-own them. Ultimately, members introject, or make part of their psychological structures, the therapist's containing function (Billow, 2000). Further, because the content of the projected identifications is those very psychological elements against which members are defending, the therapist through his or her own self-awareness can gain access to an otherwise hidden layer of group life. How the therapist uses countertransference as well as the other sources of information available to him or her will be seen in the following Putting It into Practice.

Rapid Reference 2.3

Steps in Projective Identification

- Placement of unwanted impulses onto another
- Coercion of the person to act in accordance with projection
- Identification with the person who is the target of the projection

Putting It Into Practice

Psychodynamic Vignette

"Now with the money you're going to save, you can buy a new car" was Dick's greeting to Lisa on the occasion of her second-to-last group meeting. Lisa, a long-standing group member who had carefully planned this termination, reddened. Billie Jo retorted, "No way would these monthly payments be enough for a car; the best she can do is have a dinner out—maybe once a week."

A few more members speculated on what Lisa could do with the saved fees. The therapist noticed that she was feeling an admixture of apprehension and irritation but was not sure why.

In a more serious tone, another member said she wouldn't use a windfall just to acquire something new: That was more her sister's style. She then described going to a party at her sister's house where everyone was admiring her sister's art collection. She felt it was all for show on the part of her sister. Although she appreciated art more than her sister and had more knowledge about it, her sister got the credit because she was the great collector.

Cynthia said she knew how Billie Jo felt. At her high school, her brother had received academic recognition for his high grades even though she was the more serious, intellectually curious student.

A brief discussion of the culture's valuation of style over substance followed. Geraldine then asked Lisa what she thought her biggest challenges would be in leaving the group. Members permitted Lisa to respond only minimally. They proceeded to exaggerate some of her vulnerabilities that had been identified over the course of the group that might surface in various future situations. Cynthia said her own difficulties were so enormous she doubted she could move forward in therapy. The atmosphere became gloomy as members resonated to Cynthia's claim of having unsolvable problems.

The therapist noted that members seemed to be very affected by Lisa's leaving the group. She suggested that it led them to feel that she had good things that they lacked, good things that enabled her to take this big step of leaving. She then said, "To not feel the lack of the good things, you feel an impulse to either take them away from her or make them less than what they are. But then, once you've done this, you feel kind of sad about it."

Cynthia said, "Yeah, like if we're not ready to leave, she can't be either. It's hard for me because we came in at the same time. It makes me wonder what's wrong with me."

Geraldine responded, "Nothing that we can't figure out in here. I've seen a lot of changes in you since I came into the group. But it's still hard to see someone leave. To Lisa, she added, "I know that after you leave I'll miss you, but right now I just feel envious. I know I felt better to think that the money you'd save wouldn't even cover your meal at a good restaurant."

Teaching note: In this vignette, the therapist uses various sources of information to make an interpretation about members. She considers the caustic humor that members exhibited and their gloomy attitude toward Lisa's ability to fare without the group's support. The therapist listens to material symbolically. Resentment toward relatives receiving credit may be derivatives for their feeling toward the departing group sibling. Finally, the therapist's own reaction must be weighed. Her apprehension may have been a reaction to members' disguised aggression and her irritation a projective identification with that aggression.

≡ *Rapid Reference 2.4*
....

**Activities of the
Psychodynamic
Group Therapist**

- Maintains a holding environment
- Contains members' disturbing reactions
- Manages boundaries
- Conveys empathy
- Collects data based on members' reactions, countertransference, and other data
- Clarifies and interprets members' reactions at various levels of group process

In the psychodynamic group, interpretations can be made at various levels. In the prior event, the therapist made a group-as-a-whole interpretation, identifying an element of a conflict whose influence extended beyond any individual member, an element that affected the work of the entire group. Although different psychodynamic approaches may place different degrees of emphasis on this type of interpretation, most if not all would recognize the existence of group-level phenomena that at times bear identification (usually by the therapist but at times by other members) and the group's exploration. Psychodynamic therapists also intervene at the interpersonal or dyadic level. Here they may oftentimes appear to function much like the interpersonal therapist, helping members to provide feedback on one another's behavior and also to understand the forces driving those behaviors. Interventions also occur at the individual level. At this level, the therapist may help an individual member to examine aspects of the conflict that may be unique to him or her. For example, in the vignette, the therapist might proceed to assist members in exploring their individual defenses against envy or their reactions to the emergence of their envy. (See Rapid Reference 2.4 for an overview of activities performed by the psychodynamic group therapist.)

SOCIAL SYSTEMS APPROACHES

Social systems approaches to group therapy are rooted in the notion, proposed by Ludwig von Bertalanffy in his open systems theory (1950) but anticipated by a variety of other writers, that a system is a configuration of elements each of which affects and is affected by all other elements. Each system is hierarchically and dynamically related to other systems. The hierarchical feature refers to the notion that each system is embedded in progressively larger and more complex systems and has embedded in it smaller and progressively simpler systems. Isomorphies exist within the systems of a hierarchy. Isomorphies are structural or functional features that all systems within a hierarchy have in common. For example, a particular family may have conflict over the pursuit of individual goals versus pursuit of the goals of the group. Although on the surface members of a family (subsystems of the family system) may appear polarized on this issue, at an unconscious level each family member may be beset by this conflict. Furthermore, this conflict may be found to exist not merely in a particular nuclear family but also in the broader relation (suprasystem) in which a given nuclear family is embedded.

The dynamic aspect of systems is that there are exchanges of information among the systems within a hierarchy. A consequence of such an exchange is that changes in one system can effect changes in others. The extent to which information is exchanged depends upon the porousness of the boundary between a given system and the other systems to which it is related. A boundary separates a system from all other systems. In a system with a permeable boundary, information is readily transferred from it to other systems and from other systems to it. For example, in an office in which boundaries are permeable among employees (with each employee constituting a separate system), what happens to one employee is likely to affect others. If it is widely known that an employee was fired because of insubordination, then other employees are likely to take note of this and monitor their behavior in relation to their supervisors. On the other hand, if a system is closed—if the business of that employee is known only to him or her—the effect on surrounding systems will be negligible.

Such writers as Helen Durkin, Jim Durkin, and John Boriello readily applied the notions of general systems theory to the workings of the therapy group. From the systems theory perspective, the therapy group is a system with a boundary separating it from the external environment. The group comprises the members of the group, each of which is a separate system and a subsystem of the group. Each member is constituted of various subsystems. Primary among these subsystems is the ego, which regulates the boundary between the member and the external world (A. K. Rice, 1969; Skolnick, 1992), which in this case is the therapy group. The relationship between the group as a whole and its member is one of a constant exchange of information. Members, as subsystems of the group, continually receive input that transforms the member and provide output, which transforms the group.

Social systems therapists integrate the aforementioned boundary concepts with the psychodynamic notions described earlier in this section to describe how change occurs in members. Projective identifications require a permeable boundary between self and another member, a subgroup of members, the therapist, or the group as a whole such that the former can export intolerable affects and impulses to the latter. Once the projection is received, it can be contained until such time as it can be safely re-owned, a process that also necessitates permeability of boundaries. Through this exchange of information, each system becomes more differentiated and complex. For example, the member re-owning the affect of rage after having projected it on another member not only reclaims that affect but also takes in the member's way of bearing the affect. As members internalize these new inputs, their old archaic ways of seeing the self gradually give way to more current models that are in greater synchrony with the environment.

Another notion that systems theory incorporated from psychodynamic theory is that human difficulties are rooted in psychological conflicts. Like other psychodynamic therapists, systems therapists believe that these conflicts may occur at the level of the group as a whole across the course of the group's development. Systems theorists believe that the permeability of members' boundaries to the group environment enables members to share any progress that the group makes in resolving the conflicts it addresses. This same permeability enables individual members or subgroups of members to influence the group as a whole. When an issue arises in a group, members will take on different positions in relation to it based on a variety of factors, including the preexisting personality features as well as the psychological difficulties with which they entered the group. In expressing a position on a conflict, a member is performing a function or role for the group insofar as conflict resolution necessitates that the elements of conflict be brought to the fore. For example, one member may serve the role of expressing hostility toward the leader, and another may take on the role of expressing the wish to respond compliantly toward the leader. Members who have a similar position on an issue join to form a subgroup (Bennis & Shepard, 1956). Members' residency in a subgroup provides them with a measure of safety and comfort so that they are able to explore the defensive aspects of their positions (Agazarian, 1997). For example, a subgroup of individuals who share a desire to be compliant with the wishes of authority can discover how their compliance is a defense against that part of themselves that wishes to rebel against authority. In the following Putting It into Practice, we see an example of another subgrouping structure. As defenses are identified, their strength diminishes. Such learning that occurs in the subgroup is exported to the broader group environment and leads to growth in the group as a whole.

The therapist's role within systems theory approaches is to be a boundary manager. Skolnik (1992, p. 336) described the systems therapist as having the following boundary management responsibilities:

• Defining and monitoring the task
• Selecting and taking in members

Putting It Into Practice

Systems Theory Vignette

Members of an inpatient group spent the first several minutes of the session joking with one another about a new psychiatric resident whom they deemed handsome. Jessica sat quietly during this time, and one member made a cutting comment about her acting "hoity-toity." She responded that she was feeling sad and their giddiness was making her feel worse. Members rolled their eyes and said that Jessica was being a "downer" and should "lighten up."

Nia objected, "If Jessica is feeling sad, we should make an effort to understand her feelings rather than just dismissing them." The therapist asked Nia if she could relate to Jessica's sadness. She admitted that even though she joined in the joking around, when Jessica said she felt sad, it struck a chord. Yet, she said, she could not pinpoint why she too might be feeling somewhat unhappy.

One member joked, "Maybe you feel Dr. T. just isn't paying enough attention to you." The therapist reminded the group that this was the first session in which Jared, a longstanding male member of the group, had been absent. The therapist wondered if the merry members and the sad members were expressing two aspects of the loss—the grief associated with it and the effort to manage the grief through joking and playfulness.

Teaching note: The systems therapist works to allow the diverse reactions to the group's loss to be expressed and tolerated. One method used by the therapist was to show members that both sets of responses were reasonable reactions to events in the group. The capacity of the group to accept the coexistence of these different emotional elements in the group system is a first step in the direction of their integration. Subsequent interventions might assist members in re-owning psychological elements projected onto one another. For example, members may see how Jessica was used as a container for their sadness. As subsystems of a broader system, individual members can participate in whatever achievements are made by the group as a whole.

- Delineating intragroup boundaries (roles, ground rules, culture, and contract)
- Delineating and managing his or her own role/person boundary
- Delineating and managing the group/environmental boundary
- Serving as catalyst and protector
- Processing and interpreting information

Although some systems approaches entail the assumption of a passive, interpretive posture, others involve a more active stance. An example of the latter is *systems-centered therapy,* which was founded by Agazarian (1997) and colleagues. In this application, the therapist actively encourages the formation of subgroups based upon members' similar positions with respect to a group-level conflict on the premise that subgroups provide a supportive structure in which psychological work is maximized. To do so, the therapist might point out a similarity to various members' expressed positions or may forthrightly ask a member with which subgroup he or she feels greater affinity. Once subgroups are formed, members in a subgroup can proceed to examine the differences among their positions, a task facilitated by the relatively open boundaries that exist among members of a subgroup. With the acknowledgment of differences, the subgroup moves to a less polarized position, and members therein are better able to identify with the positions of members of other subgroups, which may represent forces that they previously sought to deny within themselves. Throughout this process, the therapist works to ensure that the boundaries between members and between subgroups and the group as a whole remain open so that members as systems unto themselves, and the group as a system, continue to become more fully integrated and complex (Brabender, 1997).

COGNITIVE-BEHAVIORAL APPROACHES

The basic premise of cognitive-behavioral group therapy is that the meaning an individual assigns to events determines how he or she feels and behaves. The psychological problems that members bring into treatment such as anxiety, depression, dissatisfaction with interpersonal relationships and so on exist because the person makes an internal cognitive response to his or her life situation that is not adaptive. The goal of any cognitive-behavioral treatment, including group treatment, is to enable the person to acquire and sustain a system of meaning that will enhance well-being rather than fostering symptoms.

Cognitive-behavioral therapy groups, unlike most applications of the theoretical approaches previously presented, are relatively short-term (approximately 14 to 18 sessions) and often occur within a closed-ended format. Also, unlike the previously described approaches, the group sessions are structured. Although the format of the sessions is relatively consistent throughout the life of the group, there is some variation depending upon whether members are in the beginning, middle, or terminal phases of participation.

In early sessions, members learn the principles of cognitive-behavioral theory. This learning does not require that the group therapist lecture to members while they remain passive. The term that characterizes the relationship between group therapist and members is collaborative empiricism. Members and therapist function as co-investigators joined in the effort to understand the interrelationships of each member's cognitions, affects, and behaviors. Establishing this type of relationship encourages responsibility-taking rather than answer-seeking on the part of the member (White, 2000a). In the early phase of treatment, the therapist launches the collaboration using a Socratic method wherein a line of questioning enables the member to discover how systems of meaning influence feelings and behavior in the problems emerging in his or her life. The systematic exploration of members' experiences shows them that troublesome reactions in situations are preceded by barely discernable and fleeting automatic thoughts that give rise to the painful feelings. Members become skilled through the use of thought records in analyzing their experience into thoughts, feelings, and behaviors. To sharpen this skill, members are given homework in which thought records are completed in relation to problematic situations that arise in the members' lives.

Members begin to acquire the skills they will hone over the rest of the group. Among these skills are those described in the following sections.

Self-Assessment

In order to determine whether an intervention is having a desired effect, members must learn to measure the behaviors and reactions that are the targets of change. Mood monitoring occurs when members assign numerical values to particular mood states based upon intensity. For example, zero may represent the absence of anxiety and 100 may signify the peak of anxiety. Members may also count the frequency of behaviors, such as by counting the number of times that a person interrupts his or her conversational companion in a 5-minute interval. The emphasis on assessment of change is a major theme of cognitive-behavioral treatment (CBT) and is manifested by the relatively large corpus of outcome studies on CBT groups.

Cognitive Restructuring

This skill lies at the heart of CBT. It entails group members' learning to identify their dysfunctional cognitions, recognizing the negative consequences of those cognitions, testing them, and supplanting them with more adaptive cognitions. All of the elements of cognitive restructuring tap the resources of the group. To identify cognitions, members present troublesome situations (occurring both inside and outside the group) and analyze them to identify the thoughts that the situation evoked. Because members can frequently identify with situations presented, they can assist the member in capturing a fleeting thought, by saying, for example, "I know that when my boss reprimands me at work, I say to myself, 'I just can't do anything right.'" Other members, too, can assist with the discovery of the consequences of a cognition. The prior member may add, "Yeah, and when I have a thought like that, I just get paralyzed and then I make more mistakes." See Putting It into Practice on the next page for an illustration of this process.

The testing of a cognition may range from a simple and brief process to one that is extended and complex. Oftentimes the mere identification of an irrational cognition leads to its rejection by the member (Rose, 1993). In the process of examining the cognition, the therapist may be able to point out to the member a pattern of thinking that leads to the production of such distortions. For example, a member may exhibit all-or-none thinking, in which the member fails to see the shades of gray that are present in most situations. In a given situation, a member may think, for instance, that he or she will be a complete success or a total failure. In other cases, the testing of a cognition, particularly if it concerns a member's view of him- or herself, entails comparing it with other members' perceptions of that individual. More elaborate still is the *behavioral experiment*. The therapist might give an assignment such as the following:

> Your belief is that if you take a position different from that of most of the people you are with, they'll see you as "out of it" or "strange." Some time during this session, I want you to share an opinion that may be at least a little bit at odds with what others are saying. Let's see how it affects what others think of you.

In the group, the member experiments and then gets feedback from the other members on both his or her behaviors and their reactions to it.

Problem-Solving Training

Cognitive theory holds that members' ability to function effectively is contingent not only on the content of members' thoughts but also on how well members organize and process their thoughts. Especially with certain populations such as youths with conduct disorders, members may enter the group with difficulties in being able to identify problems, gather relevant information concerning a problem, and devise an appropriate solution. Some cognitive-behavioral groups will incorporate a problem-solving training component. Members learn a particular approach to problem solving that entails the following steps:

1. Developing a positive *problem orientation* in which the member perceives a problem as being inherent in living and amenable to solution.
2. Defining the problem.
3. Generating solutions using brainstorming in which quantity of solutions is emphasized. In this step, judgment about the quality of the

Putting It Into Practice

Cognitive-Behavioral Group Vignette

The CBT women's group was in its eighth session. At the beginning of the session, Kirsten reported that she had had difficulty completing a homework assignment in which she attempted to assert her wishes with her fiancé when the issue arose of how they would spend their weekend evenings. When she reported that she "just could not get up the nerve," the therapist suggested that a fuller exploration might be warranted and asked her to establish this topic as an agenda item for the session. Later, the therapist invited Kirsten to give a fuller description of the event in which she drew back from communicating her preferences, and the following interaction ensued:

Kirsten: I had written down what I was going to say to him—you remember, about wanting to go to a baseball game, and I practiced it in front of the mirror, but when he told me we were going to the movies, I just went along. There just wasn't an opening to say anything.

Reggie: An opening? You can't wait for an opening! He's one of those take-charge personalities.... He'll never give you an opening.

Thomasina: But I know what it's like to have to push your way in.... You just think ... [She drifts off.]

Therapist: What *do* you think? What goes through your mind ... maybe very fleetingly ... right before you decide to remain quiet?

Thomasina: Well, I suppose I think I don't want to be rude.

Reggie: Who cares about that?

Thomasina: But I also think the person wouldn't like it. Maybe he'll be angry.

Kelly: I always figure maybe he'll be so angry he just won't want to be with me.

Therapist [to Kirsten]: Are some of your thoughts like Kelly's and Thomasina's?

Kirsten: It's funny ... when they said the anger part, I realized that I would be happy if Jack would be angry. In fact, what I worry about is that he will be indifferent. Maybe he would say, "Okay, sweetie, you go to the baseball game and I'll go to the movies and I'll see you next weekend."

Therapist: So the thought is, "If I express a preference, I may find out that he doesn't care."

Teaching note: In this brief exchange, the reader can see how the process of the group enables members to learn about how their systems of meaning underlie their dysfunctional behaviors and upsetting feelings. The therapist encourages members to explore their common struggles, in this case the struggle of communicating directly to get their needs met. However, in this process, members also differentiate their experiences from one another, which allows them to identify their automatic thoughts in precise terms. Kirsten's later work in the session might involve reality testing her thought (the therapist might say, "What basis do you have from your past interactions with Jack to believe he might be indifferent?"), considering what catastrophe might ensue if the thought were found valid ("What if you did discover that he is indifferent?"), or exploring her perceptions of self and other within the here and now of the group. For example, Kirsten could reflect upon times when she might have thought members of that group were responding indifferently toward her and obtain feedback on the accuracy of that inference.

solution is suspended. The multiplicity of members increases the variety of solutions.

4. Evaluating solutions by considering both short-term and long-term consequences of their implementation.
5. Executing a solution and evaluating the results.

Members of the group can practice the steps of problem solving by identifying problems emerging either inside or outside the group.

Although problem-solving training is discussed here as an element of the cognitive-behavioral approach, it can also be a treatment method in its own right or can be integrated with a psychodynamic approach (Brabender, 2002; see Chapter 13).

Social Skills Training

Members in cognitive-behavioral groups will show difficulties making full use of the treatment because the individual is not adequately equipped to respond appropriately to complex social situations, leading the person to obtain feedback that may confirm dysfunctional thoughts. Therefore, a part of a cognitive-behavioral group therapy may be focused on training in the microskills needed to reach treatment goals. For example, Radomile (2000) notes that the treatment of obesity often necessitates the inclusion of assertiveness training because obese group members frequently have histories of being accommodating in interpersonal situations and have difficulty setting boundaries (e.g., asking someone not to bring a certain type of food into the home). Members would be trained in assertiveness skills and spend group time practicing them.

Like problem-solving training, social skills training can also be used independently of cognitive-behavioral therapy as an independent therapeutic approach (see Brabender & Fallon, 1993, Chapter 9).

In the middle phase of treatment, group members continue with the structure that has been established in the earlier sessions. However, as members become more adept at catching automatic thoughts and as their banks of identified automatic thoughts build, they may be able to identify those thought patterns that undergird the automatic thoughts. These thought patterns or *schemas* (Young, 1990) function as lenses through which current situations are experienced. For example, Radomile (2000), describing the group format for the treatment of obesity mentioned earlier, notes that common schemas for individuals in this patient population are "I've always been fat, I'll always be fat, and nothing can change it"

(p. 118). Schemas are then subjected to the cognitive restructuring process that has been implemented in relation to automatic thoughts. During this phase, members are also facilitated in identifying cognitive biases that may support the development of dysfunctional thoughts. For example, a member may be inclined toward all-or-none thinking (A. T. Beck, 1976). This bias might lead the person to declare him- or herself a winner or loser rather than recognizing intermediate levels of success.

In the final phase of treatment, work on schemas continues as members receive preparation to terminate from the group. *Relapse prevention* involves the acquisition of a set of skills with which to manage the inevitable return of symptoms in times of stress. Members are assisted in recognizing that the reemergence of old problems does not mean that treatment was a failure: It merely signifies that the member must make an especially vigorous effort to utilize the skills acquired in the group (White, 2000b). *Booster sessions* are commonly used to enable members to maintain the skills acquired in the group (see Rapid Reference 2.5 for a sampling of activities performed by the cognitive-behavioral group therapist).

Cognitive-behavioral groups have been found to be effective for the treatment of a wide range of symptoms, including depression (e.g., Bright, Baker, & Neimeyer, 1999; Kush & Fleming, 2000), bulimia (e.g., Gray & Hoage, 1990), Social Phobia (Hope & Heimberg, 1993), and obsessive-compulsive symptoms (McLean et al., 2001). Evidence also exists that cognitive-behavioral groups are helpful in fostering more effective social behaviors. For example, college students participating in a CBT group showed greater emotional control than partici-

≡Rapid Reference 2.5

Commonly Utilized Cognitive-Behavioral Techniques

Technique	Function
Cognitive restructuring	Modifies dysfunctional thoughts.
Behavioral experiments	Enable members to test automatic thoughts.
Mood ratings	Assist therapist and members in monitoring affective changes.
Homework	Provides opportunities to practice and strengthen skills between sessions.
Booster session	Enables skill maintenance after treatment has ended.

pants in other treatment groups (Deffenbacher, Thwaites, Wallace, & Oetting, 1994).

PSYCHODRAMA

Psychodrama is one of a number of approaches that are distinguished by their emphasis on action. These approaches are based on the view that action is a precursor to intrapsychic and interpersonal change. That is, by acting in a new way, an individual can think and feel in new ways. Action is also important because when a person is bodily engaged he or she has access to psychological elements that otherwise would not be available (Blatner, 1996). Many of these elements have roots in childhood but are repressed as individuals mature. Action is inherently interpersonal: Because others can witness action, it invites a response from them. Psychodrama is chosen to represent this set of approaches because it is the prototype of an action-oriented approach. Jacob Moreno, who founded psychodrama in the early 1920s, believed that group treatment should not only alleviate psychopathology but also advance the person toward his or her dreams. Achieving these goals requires the capacity to live a more spontaneous and creative existence. Such an existence entails the ability both to be aware of one's internal, immediate state and to respond to the demands of reality appropriately and flexibly but not stereotypically (Shaffer & Galinsky, 1974).

Jacob Moreno believed that theatre is an especially powerful medium and enables an individual to move toward both the alleviation of problems and the actualization of his or her potential. In a psychodrama, a person develops his or her situation into a play. The psychodramatic experience has a number of characteristics that are absent in the real-life situation. The situation in the person's life that created difficulties may be one that occurred many years ago. The psychodrama brings it into the here and now, where it can be dealt with actively and creatively. In a psychodrama, the individual has an opportunity to act a role and reenact it. With each reenactment, the person moves toward a way of responding to the situation that is more adaptive. The individual can give expression to those elements that normally would be present only on a covert level. For example, the person can put into words a commentary that in real life would be silent. Psychodrama creates a space between reality and fantasy, which permits the individual to try out new ways of responding to a situation with the guarantee of safety. For example, a person who never expressed anger toward a parent out of fear that the parent will terminate the relationship can do so in the psychodrama with the assurance that the feared consequence will not be realized. Acting allows for not only what is in the present but also what might be: In that way it provides standing for one's dreams and hopes. A psychodrama also permits a stopping of the action and a processing of what has occurred. In this way the individual can not only experience a situation but also understand his or her experience more fully.

To see how these potential resources of psychodrama are tapped, we will consider an actual session itself. In the psychodrama session, participants must be provided with a clear differentiation between fantasy and reality, and therefore an area (even if only a rug) that is clearly demarcated as a stage is a necessity. Beyond the stage, there must be room for the audience, members of the group who although not currently on stage must witness the action and participate in its processing. The following sections provide the format of a psychodrama session (see Sacks, 1993, for a more detailed description) that is relatively characteristic.

Warm-Up

This period prepares members to work psychodramatically and is more extended when members are beginning a new psychodrama group. Members participate in a succession of exercises that progressively engage them in the types of activities that will take place in the psychodrama itself. An initial exercise might be a simple go-around in which each member reveals to the group a pleasant memory from childhood. Progressively, the exercises become more emotionally challenging. For example, after the group's dividing into pairs, members would utter to one another an idea or reaction that they could not share with their parents.

Transition to Drama

Now that members have had some experience with a psychodramatic way of working, the therapist, referred to as the *director,* prepares them for the drama itself. A major task of this step is choosing the *protagonist,* the group member whose situation will be enacted. The choice of the protagonist is based on a variety of factors, including the compatibility of a particular member's predicament with a theme that the director has established, the acuteness of a member's distress in a given session, a member's wish to be the protagonist in that session, and so on. The protagonist works with the director to develop the drama by specifying the scene of an event, what led up to it, and how it unfolded. Typically, the protagonist identifies other members, or auxiliaries, to serve as actors in the drama, although sometimes volunteers or trained auxiliaries (for example, a staff member or the cotherapist) are selected to play particular roles (Blatner, 1996). The director works with the protagonist to provide direction to other actors on how they should play their roles, by asking, for instance, "Now, would your father have made that comment gruffly or indifferently?"

Drama

This phase includes enacting the troublesome circumstance, clarifying dynamic elements of the enactment, and searching for solutions or alternative means of solving the problem at hand (Kipper, 1992). As the enactment of a scene is occurring, small clues in the form of hidden emotional elements will emerge. For example, the protagonist may have a facial expression, such as a grimace, or an association that points the way to elements whose identification would provide the protagonist with a fuller understanding of his or her internal workings. Frequently, additional role plays that are tributaries from the main role play are designed by the director to illumine such barely perceptible elements.

For example, suppose Ellie, the protagonist, is enacting a scene in which she expresses to her mother a desire to be closer to her. When the younger sister (played by another member) enters the room during this interaction, Ellie glowers. Her change in expression alerts the director to a possible negative element in the relationship between the sisters: Does Ellie feel a resentment that the sister trespasses on her relationship with her mother? At this juncture, a *connecting scene* must be created in which the protagonist delivers a *soliloquy* that explores and expresses her feelings toward the sister. The opportunity to have a *catharsis,* the unbridled expression of feeling leading to relief, is regarded as having therapeutic value. This connecting scene could lead to another *key scene* in which Ellie interacts with the sister and expresses her need to have her own special time with their mother. The director throughout all of these dramatic interactions functions as an *action-analyst,* helping actors to discover the meanings of their behaviors (Kellermann, 1992).

There are a variety of techniques in which the dramatic work is enriched. These techniques capture *surplus reality,* "the intangible, invisible dimensions in the reality of living, not fully experienced or expressed" (Moreno, 1992, p. 57). For example, the director may employ *role reversal,* in which an auxiliary plays the protagonist and the protagonist plays another figure in the drama. The role reversal can be used both to provide information to the auxiliaries on how a certain role should be played and to enable the protagonist to gain insight into the reactions of the other figures in the drama. For instance, while playing her mother, Ellie might realize that her mother, rather than lacking loving feelings toward her, is encumbered by an inhibition in expressing her love.

A *double* is used as an auxiliary who gives voice to a certain aspect of a protagonist's experience. For example, if Ellie were having difficulty expressing her yearning that her mother would be more emotionally responsive, the double would articulate this wish. The use of a double helps protagonists learn to express their reactions and also facilitates their recognition of aspects of their response that may have been hidden. For example, a double's asking "Why do you have to show up just when I was trying to tell mother something important and private?" may help Ellie recognize her resentment toward her sister.

The skill of the director is in orchestrating these and other techniques (see Rapid Reference 2.6) to create a compelling drama. In some instances, the therapist may enter into the drama, typically by serving as a double so that the protagonist's ability to gain insight from the drama is enhanced.

Sharing and Closure

After the psychodrama is over, a thorough processing of all reactions, those of participants and members of the audience, occurs. As a first step, actors are assisted in transitioning out of their roles, a gradual process that still permits the

≋ Rapid Reference 2.6

Commonly Utilized Psychodrama Techniques

Technique	Definition and Function
Warm-up exercises	Group members perform structured interactions designed to prepare them to enact a psychodrama.
Role playing	Group members enact a problem or situation to achieve insight into a role, clarify feelings, and/or experiment with different types of solutions to problems.
Soliloquy	The protagonist talks to him- or herself out loud to clarify feelings.
Double	An auxiliary plays some part of the person's internal life to enable the person to identify feelings and barely conscious thought.
Role reversal	The protagonist plays the part of figures in his or her life to gain access to their points of view.
Behavioral Practice	The protagonist tries out new behaviors and obtains feedback from other members.
Catharsis	This release of feeling is accompanied by relief.

group to hold onto the feelings stimulated by the role play. To accomplish this, the actors describe and explore their feelings in playing their roles. Through this process, auxiliaries can gain in self-understanding (Blatner, 1996). For example, a woman assigned to the role of Ellie's mother may confide that she had difficulty being as withholding as she thought Ellie's mother was. By pursuing this line of thought further, she may realize that she is highly expressive of her feelings and nurturing of others, sometimes beyond the demands of the situation, in order to distinguish herself from her mother, who, like Ellie's, was also constricted and withholding. Then all participants share how each of them in his or her own life identifies with the different issues addressed in the psychodrama.

Psychodrama developed as an alternative treatment to the dominant paradigm of the day, psychodynamic therapy. Whereas the latter involves a thoroughgoing focus on transference, psychodrama entails an immersion in *tele* or "the full range of conscious, unconscious, cognitive, and emotional communication between people in any genuine human contact or encounter" (Sacks, 1993, p. 215).

The influence of psychodrama on group therapy has been both direct and indirect. Although some group practitioners are psychodramatists and implement on a wholesale basis many of the ideas of Moreno, others have integrated psychodramatic techniques such as role playing into other theoretical approaches (Kipper, 1998). Still others have stayed true to many important psychodramatic notions while integrating the concepts of other approaches (see Putting It into Practice below). In fact, a meta-analysis (Kipper & Ritchie, 2003) of outcomes from the application of the major psychodramatic techniques such as role rever-

Putting It Into Practice

Purism Discarded; Integrationism Embraced

A recent survey of psychodramatists reveals the tendency of group therapists to borrow concepts of other approaches in their application of a particular model. Kipper and Matsumoto (2002) had senior psychodramatists rank 44 concepts describing elements that might be used in the working-through phase of group therapy. They found that the most highly ranked concept was that of transference, followed by nonverbal behavior and countertransference. Role playing and identifying underlying process themes tied for the next position. The authors point out that in almost all contemporary textbooks on psychodrama, transference and countertransference have minor roles. Apparently, practice differs from descriptions of practice. At the same time, psychodramatists maintain some adherence to classic notions in their use of role playing, a technique not commonly emphasized by group therapists who use alternate approaches such as psychodynamic and interpersonal approaches.

sal and doubling shows that they individually possess demonstrated usefulness, which enables their incorporation into other theoretical approaches.

REDECISION THERAPY

This theoretical approach, developed by Robert and Mary Goulding, distinguishes itself from many others presented in this chapter by its focus upon the individual rather than the process of the group. Because of this, many of the phenomena that are of critical interest to interpersonal, psychodynamic, and social systems are of relatively low interest to those using the redecision approach. For example, transference is not regarded in this approach as an essential resource in the treatment. Although the existence of transference is recognized, the therapist's interventions are largely geared to ensure that it does not emerge as an impediment to the members' working toward goals. Because of the individual focus, group cohesion is also not seen as an essential commodity for the group to do its work. However, the redecision therapist does emphasize the criticalness of the cultivation of a safe and trusting atmosphere. The therapist also does not use stages of development. Although the redecision therapist has a developmental perspective, it is the individual's development that is of central interest.

Many of the features that distinguish redecision therapy from other approaches to group treatment qualify it for application in settings that are less amenable to process-oriented approaches (Roller, 1997). Redecision therapy is useful when the group lacks the time to develop and become cohesive, thereby enabling the flowering of a full transference. This approach can be implemented within the course of a single session. Often participants in redecision therapy attend only one or two marathon sessions, which often last 4 to 8 hours or even several days. Redecision therapists see it as more productive to create an intensive rather than extensive environment (i.e., briefer meetings distributed over time) for change (Goulding & Goulding, 1979). This approach can also be used when there is a need to accommodate a number of members beyond the size of a typical psychotherapy group. Because sessions are structured in a way that each member is the focus for a limited period, the format guarantees that each member will receive an allotment of group time.

Redecision therapy is an integration of Eric Berne's (1972) transactional therapy, which provides the cognitive framing for members' exploration of their experiences, and Gestalt techniques developed by Frederick Perls (1969), which instigate intense affective expression. It focuses on critical decisions that a person makes in his or her life. These decisions are ones that are frequently made very early in life and may have been adaptive at that time but at the current time undermine the individual's well-being. Consequently, the therapy provides the person with the opportunity to revisit the decision—that is, to make a decision suitable for the present rather than the past. Goulding and Goulding (1979) describe redecision therapy this way: "In redecision therapy the client experiences the child part of self, enjoys his childlike qualities, and creates fantasy scenes in which he can safely give up the constricting decisions he made in childhood" (p. 9). The reader can most readily obtain a picture of how redecision therapy works by considering the unfolding of a typical session. The session format that we present is only one possibility, however—redecision therapists use different formats based on such factors as member characteristics, typical presenting problems, the setting, and the time frame.

The redecision therapy session begins with a focus on a single member of the group. The therapist is likely to begin with a group member who has already been in the group before so that newer members obtain a model of how redecision therapy works. The therapist begins by asking, "What specifically would you like to change about yourself today?" (Lennox, 1997, p. 3). This query leads to the creation of a contract between therapist and group member that serves as the basis for their work in that session. Suppose a female member were to say, "I want to feel like I don't always need to put on a performance to have people like me." The therapist might then ask the member to talk about both the behaviors and feelings associated with this perceived need to put on a performance. Suppose further that the member said, "I continually feel apprehensive . . . because I don't know if I'll put on a good enough performance to win their love." The therapist might then direct the member to think about that time in her life when she made the decision to use performing as a way of garnering others' affection. For example, the therapist might say, "Do you have an early memory of a time when you felt that same apprehension, a time when someone made his or her love or caring dependent upon your performing?" The member would then share a memory that is likely to be affectively charged. To continue our example, the member might say, "I can recall a time that my mother wanted me to perform in a dance recital. I was frightened to do so and I refused. She didn't speak to me for three days." The therapist would encourage the member to provide as much detail as possible so that the event is vivid in her mind. The therapist would also invite the emergence of the feeling that that recollected event evokes in the present, perhaps by asking, "How are you feeling as you describe this memory?"

In helping our hypothetical member to explore this material further, the therapist then assists her in identifying injunctions that she received in the situation. An *injunction* is a command that the person received over time that exerts an influence, typically unconscious, over the individual's experience and behavior. Injunctions are the result of interactions between different *ego states*. These are the basic psychological positions a person takes on that organize the way he or she experiences the self and the world. In transaction theory, such injunctions emerge in the interactions between the Child ego and the Parent ego states. The *Parent ego state* is the voice of authority that can be nurturing or critical. The *Child ego state* has two aspects: the Natural or Free Child and the Adapted Child. The former is able to be freely expressive, whereas the latter is constricted by the demands of the adult world. A third ego state, the *Adult ego state,* is responsible for processing information about the world. The therapist and member would consider what injunction is implicit in the message that the Adapted Child receives from the Parent Ego State. For example, the injunction might be "Don't be yourself—just perform to glorify me." Goulding and Goulding (1979) provide the more general list of injunctions: "Don't; Don't be; Don't be close; Don't grow; Don't succeed; Don't be you; Don't be sane; Don't be well; Don't belong" (p. 35). Because these messages are implicit rather than explicit, their elucidation is a major achievement for the group member.

Often, the crystallization of the injunction provides the member with a heightened access to the feelings that relate to both the injunction and the fact that the Adapted Child chose to obey the injunction. For example, the member we have been considering may have feelings of anger as she sees that she was expected to be a narcissistic extension of the parent. With the identification of the injunction and the related feelings, the therapist might then use a Gestalt empty chair technique of having the member speak to a significant figure—in this instance, the mother. The therapist could say, "Face this chair. As you do, you are facing your parent. What is she like?" The member provides as much detail as possible in order to create a picture both for herself and for the entire group. The member then can carry on a dialogue with her mother in which she reveals her feelings to her mother. It is at this juncture that the member can experience the original decision and make a redecision, as follows:

Member: I just feel frightened that I cannot perform well enough for you to have your approval.
Therapist: How does your mother respond?
Member: I just can't think. I'm blocking.
Therapist: You can't think or you won't? [Here the therapist is demonstrating an important feature of redecision therapy—attendance to the language of the group member to find subtle manifestations of the member's effort to undermine therapeutic goals. Here the confrontation of her own denial encourages the member to take responsibility for her work in treatment.]

Member: She says, "I don't know what you're talking about. I want you to do well for yourself, so you can have the good things in life."

Therapist: How are you feeling now?

Member: It makes me furious that she won't acknowledge that it's not for me; it's for her.

Therapist: So what do you want to say to her? Do you want to tell her that that's fine—that it is all right with you to perform just to keep her happy with you and to pretend it's for you and not for her? [Here the therapist is giving the member language to express the original decision. These words are likely to evoke discomfort in the member.]

Member: I can't do that! That's what I've done and my life is a mess and I never feel that what I get from people is real! They like a me that is fake and showy. And that's what she loved . . . someone other than who I have always been!

Therapist: So what *do* you want to say to her?

Member: I want to tell her, "I am sick and tired of being who you wanted to be. I can no longer push myself into the limelight just to please you because when I do I sacrifice getting affection that I can trust. I'm going to do only what I want to do and no more, and if that's not enough for you, if you can't love me as I am, I will just have to accept it."

Therapist: That was a great piece of work! [Here the therapist is using the re-decision technique of *stroking,* in which the therapist gives positive recognition to the work done by the member; the assumption is that if the therapist models this behavior, eventually the member will be able to stroke him- or herself.]

We see here the point of redecision: The member has found and experienced a new and presumably more adaptive way of responding to the injunction from the Parent ego state. The therapist would continue to work with the member to explore the feelings associated with this redecision. The technique of *anchoring* is used here, wherein positive affects are anchored to the new decision (Gladfelter, 1992) and supplant the painful affects associated with past ineffective decisions. To further reinforce the redecision, the therapist would invite other members of the group to offer their support for the redecision and explore the meanings of the member's work for themselves. In later sessions, the member may want to grieve for the limitation of the parent in taking joy in her child only when she was performing (O'Hearne, 1993). The therapist views a member as having completed his or her work on a contract when he or she makes changes both within and outside of treatment (Gladfelter, 2000; Lennox, 1997; see Rapid Reference 2.7 for the stages of redecision work).

As could be seen from the illustration, when work begins with a member, other members are not encouraged to enter the dialogue until redecision has occurred: that is, until the member has moved beyond his or her impasse. Such interruptions could break the crescendo that is so crucial to the member's sustaining the Child ego state and reaching a point at which the old decision can be recognized and the new decision embraced. Once an individual member has broken through an impasse and reached redecision, he or she is encouraged to savor the triumph of the moment, and another member is accordingly directed to work on a contract. If the member is unable to break through an impasse after a certain duration, such as 30 minutes, the therapist will move to another group member (Baird, 1997). Typically during the course of a session, all members get the opportunity to work on their contracts. This approach, like psychodrama and cognitive-behavioral group therapy, assumes that while one member is working with the therapist, other members are drawing useful connections to their own lives.

Redecision therapy is recommended for relatively high-functioning and highly motivated individuals who are able to tolerate well the regression that the approach entails (Roller, 1997). Despite this limitation, this approach can accommodate a wide variety of problems, and members within the same group can have heterogeneous complaints. Redecision therapy can also be used in the treatment of older children and adolescents (Allen & Allen, 1997). The format of the group allows members to make progress within a very brief period of time; thus, this approach is suitable for individuals who lack the temporal or financial resources to pursue long-term group therapy. A limitation of this approach is that relatively little empirical work has been done to test its effectiveness. However, the fact that the contract so clearly specifies what work is to be done during the course of group participation makes this model quite amenable to outcome evaluation.

> ≡ **Rapid Reference 2.7**
>
> ## Stages in Redecision Work
>
> 1. The contract: agreeing on a circumscribed piece of work.
> 2. Reliving the critical scene: re-evoking the memories related to the contract and the accompanying feelings.
> 3. Redecision: making a decision that is more adaptive than the original decision.

EXISTENTIAL GROUP THERAPY

As Walter Kaufman (1975) wrote, "Existentialism is not a philosophy but a label for several widely different revolts against traditional philosophy" (p. 11). In part, existentialism emerged as a reaction to the position of logical positivism that absolute knowledge is possible. Existential writers such as Søren Kierkegaard, Jean-Paul Sartre, and Karl Jaspers contended that knowledge is always relative to one's position in the world—it is always fundamentally subjective. Moreover, certain core questions such as Martin Heidegger's query "Why is there being rather than nothing?" must necessarily remain unanswered. The consequence of these ideas is that the subjective realities described above are inherent to being human: One lives and dies alone without understanding why.

An existentially oriented group acknowledges and helps members to approach constructively the realities that characterize the human plight. Among the features of this plight are the inevitability of suffering and death, the fundamental isolation of the human being who must face life—and eventually death—alone, and the meaninglessness of existence. To an even greater extent than psychodrama, the emphasis is not on eliminating a disease or providing a cure but on offering an exploration that will lead to growth. Although relatively few group therapists describe themselves as existentialists, this perspective has influenced practitioners of diverse orientations who have found ways to integrate the existential perspective into their own approach. The existential approach also has important historical ties to new theoretical perspectives such as the intersubjective approach.

From the vantage of existentialism, satisfaction in living is limited by the common tendency to deny the realities just described. Yalom (1995) points out that such facts as the inevitability of death are painful and people are therefore motivated to minimize such realities or ignore them altogether. Such avoidance leads to an absorption in trivial concerns. This strategy, too, founders when individuals encounter circumstances, such as the loss of a loved one, that make avoidance impossible. However, it also fails when an individual experiences existential guilt over "a failure to become, a failure to be authentic, a failure to meet his potentials" (Frankel, 2002, p. 224). Alongside existential guilt is a profound alienation from self, for one has denied that which is core to one's humanity.

Existential group therapy seeks to assist members in diminishing existential guilt and their estrangement from themselves and in achieving meaningfulness in life, despite the inevitability of death. To assist members in moving toward these goals, the therapist must be present fully and authentically. Therapist neutrality and detachment have little place in the existential group: These qualities entail the therapist's compartmentalizing and denying in the group aspects of his or her humanity. Members' engagement in these very behaviors led to the creation of lives filled with anxiety and despair. The therapist allows him- or herself to confront the same issues with which members grapple, and a confrontation may lead to therapist self-disclosures if they serve the needs of the group.

The therapist also strives to develop a group environment that lends itself to the exploration of existential themes. Specifically, the therapist cultivates members' subjective involvement with one another by focusing on their raw affective interactions and avoiding cumbersome or lofty intellectual constructs that would distance them from one another and the therapist (Mullan, 1992). What is important is not for members to find meaning in their experience (a concept that assumes absolute truths) but to create their own individual meanings (Rosenbaum, 1993).

The creation of a group atmosphere in which subjectivity reigns will allow members to appreciate those elements of experience that are inherent in their humanity. Frankel (2002) identifies these interrelated elements as finiteness, aloneness, guilt, and responsibility. Finiteness is the awareness of one's own and other's mortality, and the possibility of making active choices about how one uses one's limited time on earth. Attention to finiteness in the group provides a model for this awareness of temporal limitations and the opportunity for choice throughout one's life. The existential group therapist emphasizes the temporal dimension of the group. For example, termination from the group is typically irreversible; once members leave they cannot return. This policy leads members to take more seriously both their time in the group and their decision to leave.

Aloneness is the awareness not only that we die alone but also that our experiences are our own, and others' understanding of them (or ours of theirs) can never be complete. In group, members learn how to achieve relatedness to one another even in the midst of the awareness of aloneness:

Susan: I honestly have been trying to understand what you've been telling us for three weeks and I'm still confused.

Michelle: I know that I haven't found words to do justice to the panic, but I have felt you have been here with me anyway because you've let me talk and you've really listened.

The concept of *existential guilt,* the third element, has already been described as the awareness of not fulfilling one's potential either in one's relationships with others or in one's individual pursuits. In the sessions, opportunities exist to face head on disappointment and guilt due to such failures. This process enables the members to harness guilt so that it need not overwhelm other, more positive feelings. Facing guilt also leads members to take greater advantage of the opportunities and choices that life continually presents. Often, members reckon with existential guilt in the here and now through an acceptance of the missed opportunities of deepening their relationships. This awareness activates the fourth element, *responsibility,* as members recognize that the relationships they achieve are of their own making—a knowledge that can contribute to transforming relationships in positive ways.

Selecting an Approach

The array of approaches covered in this chapter is not comprehensive. Although we have outlined a number of the major models used in the practice of group therapy today, there are many others. Given this abundance, how does the therapist go about selecting his or her particular approach? The following are some of the factors to be considered in this decision.

- *The training of the group therapist.* Certainly therapists should practice only those approaches in which they have been thoroughly trained. A therapist seeking to utilize an approach unfamiliar to him or her should be prepared to make a substantial commitment to acquiring the knowledge base and skills associated with the approach through both didactic opportunities and supervision.
- *The personality of the therapist.* Therapists are naturally drawn to certain approaches by virtue of their personality characteristics. For example, outgoing individuals may be drawn to active, directive approaches, whereas contemplative individuals may be drawn to interpretive approaches. Compatibility between an approach's technical demands on the therapist and the therapist's interpersonal style is desirable because it may enable the therapist to be more effective in delivering the approach and will enhance the therapist's enjoyment in doing group work.
- *The empirical support for the approach with a particular population in a given setting.* Therapists have an obligation to ensure that any approach they select actually works. To satisfy this obligation, the therapist may be knowledgeable of the empirical literature on the approach he or she selects. Because local conditions may differ from those in which outcome studies were conducted, the therapist must have the means to evaluate whether a selected approach is effective in his or her setting and be prepared to make another decision if it is warranted by the data the therapist collects.
- *The time frame available.* Some approaches have been devised specifically with a certain time frame in mind. For example, we saw earlier how redecision therapy was designed to be conducted in a small number of sessions, as few as one. Each approach entails the pursuit of particular

types of goals, and the therapist must ensure that the time available is adequate to accomplish the goals of the approach. Oftentimes, time frame does not so much determine whether but how an approach is applied. For instance, whereas early applications of the psychodynamic approach were long term, recently, this approach has been adapted to shorter-term time frames.

- *The context of treatment.* The therapist is well advised to think about the characteristics of the environment in which the therapy group is to be situated. For example, on an inpatient unit, the therapist will want to take note of the dominant theoretical orientation of the treatment team or the institution at large (Brabender & Fallon, 1993). Suppose there is a unit in which staff members embrace a psychoeducational approach that entails the containment of affect. In this case a psychodrama group emphasizing the expression of feelings may obtain very limited support.

Selecting a given approach does not make other approaches irrelevant to the group therapist. Each theory captures some aspect of group life that the therapist should recognize even while applying an alternate approach (Lonergan, 1994). For example, psychodynamic approaches direct the therapist's attention to those countertransference and transference reactions that emerge regardless of what theoretical orientation is being employed. The cognitive-behavioral group therapist who stays abreast of developments in psychodynamic theory on countertransference is more likely to make good use of his or her reactions as they emerge in the group sessions.

SUMMARY AND CONCLUSIONS

There exists a rich array of group therapy models, of which this chapter provides a mere sampling. Although these models are highly variable in their goals, they share important commonalities. Perhaps the most crucial is their use of the process of the group to move members toward their goals. For some models, such as cognitive-behavioral group therapy, the focus upon group process is a more recent development. These approaches differ from one another in terms of their degree of empirical support. For example, the effectiveness of the cognitive-behavioral model is well established for a variety of symptom conditions. Other models, such as psychodrama and psychodynamic group therapy, have a more limited base of empirical support, largely because a thoroughgoing investigation of effectiveness has yet to be undertaken.

🖋 TEST YOURSELF 🖋

1. **The interpersonal approach is the only approach to place emphasis upon here-and-now explorations.** True or False?

2. **The following orientation often requires that members complete homework assignments between sessions:**
   (a) Interpersonal
   (b) Cognitive-behavioral
   (c) Existential
   (d) Object relations

3. **Common assumptions of psychodynamic approaches to group therapy are the following:**
   (a) The importance of the use of highly formatted sessions
   (b) The existence of a dynamic unconscious
   (c) The centrality of the relationship between members and between members and therapist
   (d) b and c only

4. **Two approaches that entail a high degree of interaction between the therapist and individual group members are**
   (a) existential and interpersonal.
   (b) psychodrama and redecision therapy.
   (c) cognitive-behavioral therapy and psychodynamic therapy.
   (d) systems theory and psychodrama.

5. **Proponents of action-oriented groups see what benefits in the emphasis on action?**

6. **"The role of the existential therapist is to help members discover absolute truths." What is wrong with this statement?**

7. **"Subgrouping is always detrimental to a group's functioning." What is wrong with this statement?**

Answers: 1. False; 2. b; 3. d; 4. b; 5. Brings problems into the here and now; creates the possibility of reenacting solutions; makes the covert, overt; creates a space between reality and fantasy, thereby creating safety; 6. The existential therapist emphasizes that members must create their own meaning; 7. Subgrouping can create a structure in which members can explore similarities and differences.

Three

BUILDING A GROUP

This chapter will address how to select appropriate members for the group and prepare them for the experience in such a way that they will derive maximum benefit from being in the group. These tasks can be undertaken only when the therapist has identified group goals and processes by which the goals will be pursued. These elements will inform who is selected and how they are prepared for the group. The final section of the chapter will consider some of the important structural features that the therapist establishes in building the group, such as location, time, and size of the group.

SELECTION OF MEMBERS

In selecting group members, the therapist should ask two questions. First, is the member likely to benefit from the group experience? Second, is the member likely to make a positive contribution to other members? For the most part, the therapist in evaluating a prospective member considers these criteria together because an individual who can benefit from the group is likely to be someone who can contribute to the group. Selection of the individual member is also predicated on the therapist's vision of the entire group composition, which will also be addressed. Finally, we will look at how the selection process occurs, that is, both the content and method by which information is garnered about the prospective member.

Exclusion Criteria

There is such an abundance of group formats that there is probably a group that could serve the needs of virtually anyone. At the same time, there are some characteristics of individuals that would disqualify them from many if not most groups (see Rapid Reference 3.1). Moreover, some characteristics may preclude the individual's group participation at present but not necessarily in the future. If

≡Rapid Reference 3.1

Criteria for Group Therapy

Exclusion criteria:
- Unwillingness or low motivation to participate
- Extremely high level of distress
- Noncompliance with rules
- Incapacity for connection

Inclusion criteria:
- Goal compatibility
- Ability to use group processes

an individual possesses one of these characteristics, the format of the group must very explicitly take it into account so that it does not stand as an insurmountable obstacle to the candidate's progress or to that of other members.

Unwillingness or Low Motivation to Participate

Generally, individuals benefit from group therapy when they wish to be in a group. When they do not, group therapy is only likely to be of benefit if the therapist carefully takes this attitude into account and builds the group around it. For example, suppose in a captive population, such as a prison population, many prospective members state their unwillingness to be in group therapy because they mistrust the other members. If mistrust, rather than being situational, is a major dimension of their stance toward others, then increasing the members' capacities for trust might be established as a major and early group goal.

Another important aspect of the candidate's attitude is the expectation that the group will be helpful to him or her. The majority of studies on expectation (see Dies's 1994 review) show a positive relationship between favorableness of anticipation and outcome (gains made in the group), possibly because the former leads to more constructive behaviors in the group (Caine & Wijesinghe, 1976). In a recent survey (Riva, Lippert, and Tackett, 2000), group therapists indicated that this variable is one they most commonly use to make selection decisions. Furthermore, the authors found that failure to consider this factor was most frequently identified as being responsible for selection errors relative to other possible factors.

The therapist should distinguish between the candidate's view of the group at the beginning of the evaluation and the perspective he or she has once the therapist has helped the candidate to learn about group therapy and how it might address his or her needs. Many candidates enter the evaluation for group therapy with considerable trepidation about this enterprise. Most commonly, the idea of pursuing group treatment was someone else's rather than the client's. If the candidate continues to feel negatively about being in the group as the evaluation process is nearing completion, then he or she is unlikely to be someone who will thrive in the group.

Level of Distress

Most people have had some negative life experiences that are so intense and all-consuming that for a brief time it is difficult to attend to anything or anyone else. Individuals who are in the throes of an immediate crisis (Alonso & Rutan, 1990; Salvendy, 1993) may not find the group setting to be an optimal environment because of the demands it places on the person to attend to others and to have attention deflected from themselves. The exception to this point is a group that has been organized specifically to help individuals deal with trauma. For example, Herman (1992) describes a three-tiered system for the group treatment of individuals who have undergone trauma: The first level is organized as a crisis group that provides coping strategies for dealing with the trauma, leaving exploration of the trauma for higher-tiered groups. However, even within this system that carefully takes into account the psychology of the trauma survivor, it may be necessary to treat individuals who require a detailed examination of the trauma first in individual therapy.

Noncompliance with Rules

Every group has rules that safeguard the rights and safety of the members and that create an atmosphere in which the goals of the group can be pursued. Maintaining confidentiality, putting feelings into words rather than actions, attending the sessions regularly, and making timely payments are among the most common rules that group therapists establish. When individuals provide evidence that they are unable or unwilling to observe these rules, they are not appropriate for a group (see the following Putting It into Practice).

Capacity for Connection

Group therapy in most of its forms requires that members have some rudimentary ability to attend to, identify with, and form a relationship with one another. Much that occurs in the group that is beneficial is made possible by these abilities. For example, the therapeutic factor of universality entails individuals' recognizing that they are not alone in their suffering (Yalom, 1995). Universality occurs naturally as a member hears other members talk about feelings and impulses that to some degree resemble his or her own. In order for universality to work, however, the member must have a readiness to identify with the other members who are sharing their struggles, because without it, he or she will fail to see commonalities in experience no matter how clearly they are presented.

DON'T FORGET

There is probably no human attribute that prevents a member from deriving benefit from group therapy, provided that the group approach is designed to take the attribute into account.

Putting It Into Practice

Incompatibility with a Group

Darren's physician had referred him to the group. He had been a member of a motorcycle gang and had been jailed repeatedly for assaulting the members of other gangs. When the therapist probed, it seemed that Darren had a fairly low threshold for getting into a physical imbroglio. The therapist asked Darren how he would respond if someone in the group aroused his anger. Darren said, "I can assure you I would never hurt a woman, but with a man . . . I can't make any promises." Based on this statement and other evidence related to Darren's physical controls, the therapist decided that group therapy in a mixed diagnosis group would not be an appropriate placement.

Teaching note: Although Darren's aggression difficulties would disqualify him from most groups given that he would pose a threat to other members, this feature would qualify him for a group built around the theme of anger control. Such groups establish mechanisms to protect members from one another, such as the presence of staff members who are able to restrain members if necessary (see Kellner & Bry, 1999, and Snyder, Kymissis, & Kessler, 1999, for examples of effective group formats for the treatment of anger expression).

Individuals who have profound and pervasive mistrust of others as a long-standing personality feature fare poorly in group therapy. Being present in the group is an extremely stressful experience for such individuals, and their group participation may lead to a deterioration in functioning. Beyond this risk factor, however, is the reality that such persons have little wherewithal to take advantage of what the group can offer because all of their energies are allocated to defending against genuine contact with the other group members.

Cognitive Limitations

Group therapy makes cognitive demands on members. It requires that they be able to listen to one another, respond appropriately, and concentrate in a sustained way on the events of the session. Members are expected to be able to remember the events of the group, typically from session to session or at the very least from the beginning of the session to the end. Members with marked cognitive limitations are best placed in a group that takes these limitations into account rather than in a group with members who are more cognitively able.

Inclusion Criteria

The exclusion criteria provide a general screening during which individuals who would be unlikely to benefit from the group or benefit others are disqualified from the group. The next level of assessment entails the application of criteria that are specific to a particular group. With respect to inclusion criteria, two broad areas will be discussed: (1) goals and therapeutic processes and (2) composition. Whereas the former involves evaluating the candidate in relation to the plan for the group or the *group design,* the latter entails the assessment of the candidate's characteristics in relation to those of other members of the group.

Goals and Therapeutic Processes

The quintessential criterion for including a member in a therapy group is that the member's goals are compatible with the goals of the group. Of course, to make this determination, the interviewer must enter the evaluation of the candidate with an explicit understanding of the group goals within the context of a well-crafted group design. The group design includes the goals, the therapeutic processes leading to fulfillment of the goals, the therapist interventions that instigate the therapeutic processes, and the rules and structural features that support the emergence of the therapeutic processes. Through the evaluation, the interviewer must achieve a clear recognition of the individual's goals. Especially for long-term groups, the individual's goals crystallize in the therapist's awareness over one or more interviews and may be quite different from the individual's initially stated goals. For example, a candidate may come into the interview with the stated goal of anxiety alleviation. In the course of that discussion, both the interviewer and the candidate clarify that the anxiety emerges primarily in social situations and is connected to the individual's self-perception that he or she lacks the skills to navigate complex social situations. The goal that the candidate and interviewer settle upon may have more emphasis on interpersonal than on symptomatic change. In some short-term therapy settings, the priority may be getting candidates into groups as rapidly as possible. Having an extended discussion of goals over several sessions that will lead the interviewer to ascertain hidden or subtle goals may not be possible. Nonetheless, even in a briefer time frame, attention to the fit between what the candidate wishes to accomplish and what change the group fosters is crucial to the candidate's successful participation.

The interviewer must determine whether the candidate can use the processes emphasized by his or her group format. For example, psychoanalytically oriented groups provide members with the opportunity first to gain awareness of psychological conflicts and then to resolve them. Piper, McCallum, Joyce, Rosie, and Ogrodniczuk (2001) found that the variable *psychological mindedness* was positively related to obtaining benefit (in the form of symptom reduction) from a short-term interpretively oriented loss group. They defined psychological mindedness as the ability to recognize both the elements of one's psychological life (one's own or another's) and their connection to the person's struggles (e.g., symptoms, lack of satisfying relationships, and so on). In an earlier study (Piper, McCallum, & Azim, 1992), higher levels of psychological mindedness were found to be associated with remaining in a psychoanalytically oriented group. Therefore, this variable would be one that therapists running a psychoanalytically oriented group might consider when evaluating members. Therapists employing other theoretical orientations may identify other member capacities and characteristics that would be at least as important as psychological mindedness and then use them as a basis for member selection.

Composition

In selecting a member, the therapist should have a picture of the overall composition of the group. This picture encompasses an idea of the extent to which members will be variable from one another on important dimensions related to the group's functioning. Whether a group should be composed of members who are homogenous or heterogenous for any given quality depends on many factors. Yalom (1995) identified two theoretical notions that are especially likely to inform decisions about cohesion: cohesion and microcosm. As he has noted, arguments for homogeneity of members revolve around the cohesion theory, which posits that "attraction to the group is the intervening variable critical to outcome, and that the paramount aim should be to assemble a cohesive, compatible group" (p. 662). The argument for heterogeneity, based upon the social microcosm theory (Yalom, 1995), is that the group consists of members who, like people in the world outside the group, possess a great range of characteristics. The theory holds further that this diversity enables members to acquire the repertoire of skills needed to cope with the interpersonal variety of the external world. This position would direct the therapist to have as much diversity as possible along a wide variety of variables in composing the group. In the factors discussed here, we will see that for many groups both cohesion and microcosmal factors play a role in decision about composition. However, from group to group, there is often a differential weighting of these factors.

Goals and processes. Decisions about goals have implications for composition because, once the goal is established, the population for whom that goal is appropriate will be delimited accordingly. If the goal, for instance, is to reduce members' levels of anxiety, this goal would have pertinence only to those individuals for whom anxiety is a significant complaint. Hence, upon formation, the group will be relatively homogeneous in terms of levels of anxiety.

Consider the following two examples.

- Group A: The therapist designed a brief therapy group (6 sessions) for survivors of terrorism. The therapist intended for members to benefit through the realization that many of their feelings are shared.
- Group B: A therapist designed a long-term group to help members improve their relational abilities. The mechanism fostering such change is interpersonal learning, one aspect of which is members' exchange of feedback about one another's style of relating.

In Group A, the therapist would wish to create the conditions that would enhance the use of the factor of universality. This mechanism works best when members can readily see themselves as similar to one another. Therefore, in this type of group, the therapist will want to minimize member heterogeneity, especially in relation to those member characteristics that are likely to be most evident to members early in the development of their relationships with one another. For example, identification among members may be promoted by some similarity among the types of terrorist events members had experienced, or whether or not they sustained significant physical injuries or lost loved ones. In this application, the cohesion notion is emphasized over the microcosmal notion (see Putting It into Practice below).

In Group B, the therapist aims to create an atmosphere in which members can provide one another with accurate feedback. When members see themselves as highly similar to one another, it can be difficult for them to summon the detach-

Putting It Into Practice

Group Composition and Goals

Just as goals have implications for group composition, compositional considerations may affect how goals are delineated. For example, Vannicelli (2002) argues that with the population of individuals abusing alcohol, a distinction should be drawn between problem drinking and alcoholism because, in her view, each subpopulation has distinctive characteristics. Problem drinkers, she holds, are more likely to "have not developed a physiological dependence on alcohol, can reliably commit to not driving under the influence of alcohol, do not have an existing health problem that would be exacerbated by drinking," and so on (p. 197). Because of these differences, she regards drinking in moderation as an appropriate goal for problem drinkers and abstinence as more suitable for alcohol-dependent people. A therapist subscribing to Vannicelli's conceptual framework concerning the two subpopulations would then design a group geared to the goal appropriate for it. Members would then be chosen who were homogeneous for the type of alcohol abuse they exhibited.

ment required to provide accurate feedback. To maximize member-to-member exchange, diversity in relational style, point of view, and presenting complaint can be helpful. In this context, cohesion would by no means be ignored (because members are most likely to heed feedback in a cohesive group), yet the micro-cosmal aspect is also crucial.

In deciding upon group composition, the therapist must ask to what extent subpopulations within a targeted population may make differential use of the therapeutic processes identified by a group model. For example, Samide and Stockton (2002) describe a model for the treatment of bereaved children. This model excludes those children for whom the loss is extremely recent (occurring as few as 4 months ago) because individuals in this group have not yet reached the point of putting experiences into words. Good composition decisions require that the therapist making design decisions be extremely knowledgeable about the nuances of those psychological problems that are the objects of treatment.

As MacKenzie (1990) notes, certain therapeutic processes make more de-mands on the capabilities of members. Group A could include members who are quite diverse on a host of variables such as level of ego functioning, psychologi-cal mindedness, and so on. Hence, although members may need to be homoge-neous in relation to the presenting problem, the group could otherwise tolerate a good deal of heterogeneity. In contrast, Group B would require that members have the ability to make observations, identify their own reactions, and engage in a number of other processes. Hence, members may need to be relatively homo-geneous on certain dimensions.

Temporal factors.   Groups A and B differed from one another on the basis of not only goals and processes but also the length of the existence of the group. Tem-poral factors interact with therapeutic processes. If Group A were long term, members would have more extended opportunity to learn about their similarities even amid apparent differences. Such a group would be able to emphasize the mi-crocosmal aspect of composition. In a short-term frame, the therapist interested in capitalizing on the factor of universality must create the conditions in which similarities are evident to members, and a way of doing so is to create a group of members who are homogeneous with respect to a problem area.

The participant pool.   The therapist can attend to composition only to the extent that there are sufficient group members to accommodate whatever composi-tional decisions the therapist makes. Suppose, for example, that a therapist be-lieved that the group would be able to work most productively toward its goals if only members with green eyes were accepted in the group. Use of this notion would require a sufficient number of green-eyed members to enable the group to get off the ground.

In many settings, attention to composition is an unattainable luxury. In settings such as psychiatric units of hospitals, day hospitals, and partial hospitals, the group members are drawn from the participants in the broader program. In some cases, all or most of the participants in the broader setting will participate in the group. Establishing strict limitations on composition may result in two negative consequences. First, there may be too few members to enable the group to be formed. Second, the therapist will not be able to accommodate the expectation of other staff that the group will include most or all of the clients in the setting. Failure to fulfill such an expectation may undermine the therapist's cultivation of a *progroup climate,* an atmosphere in which group therapy is perceived to be a valuable modality (Rice & Rutan, 1981).

Sometimes the therapist is in the position of considering whether to include someone in a group who would represent a unique category. What if the person were to be the only male, the only person of color, the only gay individual? Especially early in the life of the group, such demographic differences are extremely salient to members and are often used to give expression to the psychological force operating within the group for members to remain separate from one another. Group members may act on this force by isolating the individual, hindering him or her from establishing effective identifications with the other group members. Difficulty in identifying with the other members of the group is likely to diminish the isolated member's comfort in being in the group as well as his or her sense of commitment to the group and willingness to remain in the group (Dugo & Beck, 1984). Because being a singular representative of a group may compromise early group participation, only with careful consideration should individuals be accepted who would solely represent a given demographic category. For the most part, the therapist should operate according to the Noah's ark principle: Each member should have someone with whom he or she can readily identify (MacKenzie, 1990). Among the considerations is the degree of structure in the group. In a highly structured group, members' identifications may be more directed and there may be less openness to processes such as scapegoating.

Final Comment

When the constraints of the setting (or any other practical factor) create a composition that is less than optimal, outcomes need not be adversely affected. What the therapist must do in this instance is to compensate for this compositional feature in the group

> **DON'T FORGET**
>
> To whatever extent possible, the therapist should apply the Noah's ark principle (MacKenzie, 1990) in establishing composition: Each member should have another member with whom he or she can readily identify.

design. For example, it is not uncommon in inpatient settings to have members who vary in their capacities to do psychological work (i.e., identify feelings and recognize connections among different psychological elements). In order for the therapist to ensure that every member thrives in the group (i.e., obtains maximal benefit), the therapist should adopt an approach that offers the flexibility for different members to do different types of work in the group. For instance, Yalom's (1983) interactional agenda approach, developed for inpatient groups, provides members considerable latitude to work at their own levels.

SELECTION METHODS

Once the therapist has in mind clear criteria for membership, from both an individual and a group compositional standpoint, he or she is ready to begin evaluating the appropriateness of candidates for the group. There are three procedures that can be employed for selection, all of which can be used in tandem with one another.

Interviewing

Particularly in outpatient settings, interviewing is an extremely common method of determining the appropriateness of a candidate for a particular group. In this format, the interviewer (typically the therapist) sits with the candidate and has a semistructured exchange of information. Several goals are typically established for the interview:

1. The interviewer's learning about the candidate by observing his or her interpersonal behavior in the interview.
2. The interviewer's discerning the compatibility between the candidate's motivation for seeking group and the group's goals.
3. The interviewer's assisting the candidate in learning about the group through presentation of goals, processes, rules, and so on.

Goals 1 and 2 serve an important role in providing informed consent (see Chapter 8) so that the candidate has sufficient information to make a decision about joining the group. The interviewer should keep in mind that during the selection process both parties are making a selection decision. Also, how the candidate responds to the presentation of information about the group may reveal the candidate's appropriateness for it. For instance, a candidate who feels overwhelmed by anxiety at the prospect of receiving feedback from other members may find a

group that emphasizes this activity too threatening to be beneficial. Yet, therapists should not give undue weight to the candidate's behavior. Possibly because
of the differences between the dyadic situation of the interview and the multiperson aspect of the group, the candidate's interview behavior has not been
found to be an especially good predictor of group behavior (Piper, 1994).

In recent years, some tools have been developed to obtain more information
from the interview. Piper and McCallum (1994) describe the development of the
quality of object relations scale, which is defined as "a person's tendency to establish certain kinds of relationships with others. It refers to the quality of a person's lifelong pattern of relationships, not just current or recent relationships" (p.
25). Although the terminology that Piper and colleagues use is psychodynamic,
the information is of potential usefulness to virtually any theoretical approach
that establishes interpersonal change as a goal. Employment of this scale requires
two semistructured interviews, separated by a few days to 1 week. The interviewer engages the candidate in a discussion of a variety of types of relationships
(e.g., with parental figures or friends), which yields material to classify the person
in one of five levels of relationship development ranging from the primitive to the
mature. Therapists can use this scale not only for selection but also for setting
goals and planning interventions. In a setting in which many candidates must be
placed in groups, this scale may be used to organize potential members into
groups based upon different levels of object relations. Piper et al. (2001) found
that members with higher scores on this scale obtained more favorable outcomes
in the interpretive group, whereas members with lower scores made greater gains
in a supportive group.

Group Screens

A particularly helpful source of data concerning a member's capacity to benefit
from group therapy is a small group experience in which the member's behavior
is directly observed. This method entails organizing a group of four or so members who are given enough structure that anxiety is kept at a moderate level but
accorded sufficient leeway that typical interpersonal behaviors emerge. Research
shows that group behaviors provide extremely useful information in making
selection decisions. Connelly and Piper (1989) found that ratings of members'
on-task behavior and degree of participation were positively related both to members' behavior in the group and to the benefit they derived from the group. Despite the usefulness of this method, a survey by Riva et al. (2000) suggests that
only a small proportion of therapists (10.7 percent in their sample) use this

method, possibly because it requires the simultaneous availability of several group therapy candidates.

Psychological Assessment

Psychological tests provide information that can round out the picture of the candidate in terms of both personality features and symptom patterns. Cognitive-behavioral group therapists have long used symptom measures such as the Beck Anxiety Inventory (A. T. Beck & Steer, 1990), the Beck Depression Inventory (A. T. Beck & Steer, 1987), and the Beck Hopelessness Scale (A. T. Beck, Weissman, Lester, & Trexler, 1974) to establish a candidate's appropriateness for group, to obtain evidence of psychological problems for third-party payers, and to obtain baseline data to measure the effects of treatment.

Personality assessment tools can provide information on various aspects of personality relevant to a member's functioning in the group. Among these are the ability of the person to perceive reality, the presence or absence of thought disorder, the capacity of the person to modulate affect, the person's sensitivity to affective cues, and the ability of the person to modify existing cognitive schemas based on new input.

Results on the use of psychological assessment measures have been mixed. From a review of available studies, Piper (1994) concludes that those psychological test scores that have implications for a person's group behavior show particular promise. For example, a study by Kedden, Cooney, Getter, and Litt (1989) with a 2-year follow-up by Cooney, Kedden, Litt, and Getter (1989) highlights a psychological feature having relevance for group behavior. Research participants were drawn from an inpatient alcoholism treatment program. The investigators measured sociopathy using scores on the Socialization Scale of the California Personality Inventory. Members with little sociopathy had lower relapse rates in an interactional aftercare group, whereas highly sociopathic members performed better in a coping skills aftercare group. Sociopathy was a variable highly pertinent to members' participation because it relates to members' capacities to form attachments to other members. Such a capacity is of greater importance in an interactional group than in a coping skills group. Additionally, the coping skills group developed anger management skills, an especially important area for people with sociopathic tendencies.

There are many well-validated psychological tests that provide information relevant to likely group behavior that have remained uninvestigated. For example, Morey (1999) notes that the Personality Assessment Inventory (PAI;

Morey, 1991) has a number of scales that are pertinent to group behavior and provide information on such interpersonal personality features as social awkwardness, social anxiety, need for interpersonal control, failure of empathy, and so on.

Piper (1994) notes that, overall, psychological test scores focusing on interpersonal behavior appear to be more useful than behavioral observations taken in the interview situation. However, psychological testing is not currently a highly utilized method for selecting members, possibly because of the specialized and extensive experience required to administer, score, and interpret many psychological tests (Riva et al., 2000).

PREPARATION OF NEW MEMBERS

There are very few major life commitments that do not require a good deal of preparation, and group therapy is no exception. As many have noted (e.g., Yalom, 1995), a good preparation can often compensate for a less-than-ideal composition.

Components of Preparation

Preparation should fulfill two purposes: (1) to give the individual an accurate picture of the group and (2) to insure member behavior that is supportive of the group goals.

Achieving an Accurate Picture of the Group

In the preparation, members must receive basic information about the group, such as the time the group meets, the length of the sessions, the location, the fee arrangement, and some basic facts about group process. Entering members are often interested in knowing the number and gender of the members in the group. The new member may have questions that have underlying significance: For example, a member may ask what will happen if he knows someone in the group has a deep-seated fear of exposure. Nonetheless, at this time, what is appropriate is to respond to the manifest content of the question (Agazarian & Peters, 1981) and allow the exploration for the group itself unless, of course, the concern stands in the way of the member's entering the group. In a later section, we will address the situation in which an individual therapist is preparing a client for group therapy participation. (See Rapid Reference 3.2 for an overview of information commonly provided during preparation for a group member.)

≡Rapid Reference 3.2

Common Types of Information Given in the Preparation for Group Therapy

- Time of the group meetings
- Address of the group meetings
- Number of members
- Length of time the group has been in existence
- Fee arrangement
- Group rules

Individuals typically contemplate the prospect of entering a group with a good deal of trepidation. Often, the idea of joining a group is not theirs but someone else's. Not atypically, the individual has certain irrational thoughts and feelings about the group. These ideas often center on some negative experiences or even harm that group participation might bring. For example, patients admitted to an inpatient psychiatric hospital often undergo a significant amelioration of symptoms. Being presented with the option of participating in group therapy arouses the fear that they will "catch" other members' difficulties ("I was just beginning to feel better and these other people will bring me down again"). Another common fear is that other members will psychologically assault the member if he or she exposes his or her weaknesses. If such beliefs are left unchallenged, the individual risks entering the group with such a high level of anxiety that he or she is too paralyzed to begin the process of engaging with other members.

In the preparation, the therapist can acknowledge the patient's realistic concerns (Dies, 1994; Yalom, 1995). For many of the misconceptions entering members have, the notion of *balance* provides a necessary correction. For example, the prospective member concerned about being attacked will be helped by recognizing that both positive and negative feedback occurs in a group and that there are many supportive elements (Vinodagrav & Yalom, 1989). The concept of balance broadens the entering member's perspective rather than discounting it.

Although allaying an entering member's anxiety by dispelling mistaken ideas about the group is crucial, the therapist should also apprise him or her of the risks of the group, which include the likelihood of periods of discomfort (see Chapter 8 for further discussion of risks). For example, when a new member enters an ongoing group, he or she is likely to have some difficult moments due to the group's response

DON'T FORGET

The notion of balance often helps members to correct misconceptions about group treatment.

to the entrance. Among the common ways a group responds to a new member are interrogating or ignoring the member, devaluing the group, engaging in internal warfare (Rosenthal, 1992), and attacking the therapist. All of these patterns are likely to be disconcerting to the new member, who may internalize them to form expectations of his or her long-term experience. Assisting the new member in realizing that a mutual adjustment process will take place is likely to encourage greater tolerance of the feelings stimulated by other members' responses. Particularly for a long-term exploratory group, the member should also be helped to realize that at times he or she, along with other members, may feel confused, upset, or frustrated and that these states are a normal part of a productive group process (Brabender, 2000).

Promotion of Healthy Norms

Behaviors that become characteristic for any given group are defined as the *norms* of the group. Preparation is a time during which the therapist can promote healthy group norms: that is, norms that serve group and individual goals rather than undermining them. The therapist can endorse these norms by discussing with the new member the rules of the group and the rationale for the rules, as well as salutary behaviors in the group (see Putting It into Practice below).

The second way to encourage helpful behavior is through training in the behaviors that facilitate group work. For example, a therapist may provide specific small group experiences to cultivate members' abilities to observe others, provide

Putting It Into Practice

Providing a Rationale for Good Attendance

"It is extremely important that you be present for all sessions unless you are absolutely unable to do so. Of course, if you were extremely ill, I would not expect you to be in the group that evening. Your faithful attendance is crucial because only if members are reliably present can we work through the problems that emerge in the group. Say, for example, you give a member a piece of feedback at the end of a session. If the member is absent the next week, you won't know how the feedback was received. You also won't have an opportunity to clarify for the member what you meant. By the time the member returns, the group will have moved on to other concerns and it may be difficult to return to your exchange."

Teaching note: The rationale for good attendance assumes that the therapist has already explained certain essential concepts to the incoming member, such as interpersonal learning and microcosm. The explanation of group-specific processes should occur relatively early in the preparation for group therapy because it is germane to many of the operating procedures of the group.

feedback, make observations of themselves, engage in self-disclosure, and so on. The therapist might demonstrate these skills by modeling them him- or herself or through playing videotapes in which the skills are demonstrated and by then giving members opportunities to practice these skills with one another.

Research Findings on Preparation

Research has demonstrated three major benefits of preparation (see Rapid Reference 3.3).

- *Decreased dropout rate.* Prepared members are less likely to leave the group precipitously. For example, members presented with a 4-hour pretraining program that included cognitive and experiential elements had a lower dropout rate than members who did not receive preparation (Piper, Debbane, Garant, & Bienvenu, 1979). This finding has significance for both members who leave and those who remain. Members terminating precipitously are denied the treatment they need; members remaining are subjected to the disruptive effects of others' brief periods of participation in the group.
- *Improved attendance.* A number of studies (e.g., France & Dugo, 1985; Piper et al., 1979; Piper, Debbane, Bienvenu, & Garant, 1982) find that pretrained members have significantly higher attendance rates. For example, outpatients who received a preparatory interview had better attendance records than those obtaining a placebo interview (Garrison, 1978).
- *A greater incidence of the types of behaviors that move members toward their goals.* Piper and Perrault (1989) reviewed seven studies that investigated 80 process variables. For 25 of the variables, pretraining altered the group process in a favorable direction. For 58 of the variables there was no difference between pretraining and non-pretraining conditions.

Rapid Reference 3.3

Positive Effects of Preparation

- Decreased dropout rate
- Improved attendance
- Increased goal-directed behavior

One variable favored the non-pretraining condition. More recently, Palmer, Baker, and McGee (1997) provided written cognitive pretraining to one group of individuals being treated for incest-related issues and not to another. The pretraining group was given reading material that explained the importance of openness in the group. The authors found that the pretrained group exhibited a higher level of self-disclosure during the course of the group than the group that did not receive the reading material.

Research is mixed on the issue of whether pretraining leads to more positive outcomes. For example, in one study inmates at a medium-security penitentiary who received pretraining in the form of a videotape presentation and guided performance experience prior to group made more progress toward individual goals than members who did not receive preparation. On the other hand, in another study (Piper et al., 1982), members who received pretraining highly relevant to the group (presentation of reading material to group members, followed several days later by structured group exercises involving an emphasis upon here-and-now processes, the role of the leader, and group dynamics) had outcomes similar to those of other members given less relevant information, and similar to those of still other members who received no information.

Even though prepared and unprepared members do not always show different outcomes, the importance of preparation in diminishing premature dropouts, increasing attendance, and providing an informed consent justifies this step. The issue, then, is not whether to prepare members but how to prepare them. Indeed, many formats are available, including interviewing, reading written instructions, participating in experiential opportunities, viewing videotape presentations, and having members read synopses of prior group meetings (Yalom, 1995). Research does not clearly point to the relative usefulness of one method over another. Individual differences in receptiveness to different methods were demonstrated in a study showing that some group members responded more favorably to written material and others to a video presentation (Muller & Scott, 1984).

Another issue to consider is when to give the preparation. Kivlighan, Mc-Govern, and Corazzini (1995) performed a study that varied the point in the group at which different preparatory materials were given to members. Their results suggested that the therapist should keep developmental stages in mind by giving members information that they are likely to use to address the developmental issues on the group's horizon. Finally, whether the entering member has had or is currently receiving individual psychotherapy is a relevant consideration. Research suggests that such therapy itself constitutes a form of pretraining. For example, MacNair-Semands (2002) found that participants receiving group therapy at a university counseling center showed better attendance and had more positive expectations about group treatment if they had had prior therapy. Therefore, when a member is entering group therapy as a first therapeutic experience, the

Putting It Into Practice

Preparing a Group for a New Member

Not only do individual members require preparation for groups, but an ongoing group needs to be prepared for the new member. The following are some tips on the preparation of the group.

- In general, a new member should be added only when the group has had the opportunity to explore members' reactions to any recently departed member. In a long-term group, preparation should begin well in advance of the new member's entrance.

- The therapist, having made the announcement about the new member, should remind the group of the impending event regularly if the group is not addressing this membership change.

- Often, the anticipation of the entrance of a new member spawns a variety of reactions, both positive and negative. Negative reactions include envy of the new member's special status as baby of the group, fear of the new member's usurping one's role in the group, and anxiety over the emergence of dependency wishes (a consequence of identification with the new member). Positive reactions include hopefulness and excitement over the resources brought by a new member.

- The therapist should recognize that because of the threatening character of many of the reactions toward the arrival of a new member, these reactions may be expressed indirectly. For example, anger toward the therapist for enlarging the group may be expressed by tardiness or absences. Alternatively, members may discuss irritation in relation to events that are symbolic of the expansion of the group (e.g., the hiring of a new employee at work).

preparation phase bears more of a burden than if the member has some experience as a therapy participant (see Putting It into Practice above).

STRUCTURAL FEATURES OF THE TREATMENT PACKAGE

Group therapy frequently occurs in the context of other interventions. It is not unusual for an individual to come to group therapy after having participated in another therapeutic modality—most commonly, individual therapy. If an individual's goals can best be pursued through a combination of modalities, the question arises as to how that treatment should be organized. This section will consider the options available with a special consideration of how each option affects selection and preparation. In Chapter 8, the discussion of this topic will be continued as we address the ethical and legal issues arising when a person receives a combination of treatments of which group therapy is a component.

Concurrent Therapy

Group and individual therapists can work together synergistically. For example, in the group setting, clients may obtain feedback on their difficulties with relating to others. In individual therapy, they can achieve insight into the underpinnings of these difficulties in their early family experiences. Possessing the knowledge of relational problems and their roots, the individual is well equipped to use the group to experiment with new and progressively more effective ways of relating.

The simultaneous occurrence of individual and group therapy is called *concurrent therapy*. Concurrent therapy can take two forms. In *combined therapy*, the same therapist conducts the individual and group therapies. In *conjoint therapy*, different practitioners administer each treatment. The special features of each arrangement will be considered.

Conjoint Therapy

Conjoint therapy provides the client with a treatment team of professionals who can share with one another their unique perspectives on the client. For clients who find dependency on a single therapist intolerable, a conjoint arrangement provides a measure of dilution. With two therapists, the patient may feel less vulnerable and thus more able to be open and work actively within each modality. The patient can risk expressing negative feelings toward one therapist knowing that the positive tie with the other therapist remains. Conjoint therapy allows for continuity in treatment because when one professional is away, the client may continue to have access to the other (Ulman, 2002). This is no small advantage in working with those severely disturbed clients for whom a minor interruption disrupts in a major way their sense of well-being. Conjoint therapy is also a stimulus-rich environment. The patient is provided with two individuals who inevitably vary along a range of dimensions. This variability invites a diversity of reactions on the part of the patient that are available for exploration.

A primary disadvantage of conjoint therapy is that it places on the therapists a tremendous burden of communication (see Caution). Effective treatment within each modality requires that each therapist know what is occurring in the other modality. Hence, communications must be regular and frequent rather than occasional. Imagine a group in which eight patients are all in therapy with a different individual therapist. Were the group therapist to have a weekly phone exchange with the individual therapist, this would entail at least several hours of professional time. Oftentimes, individual therapists are not knowledgeable about group therapy, which means that a burden falls on the group therapist to educate the individual therapist about the goals and processes of the group. Other problems that have ethical or legal implications will be described in a later chapter. An-

> ## CAUTION
> ....
> Conjoint therapy places a heavy bur-
> den of communication upon the ther-
> apists.

other potential source of difficulty in conjoint therapy occurs when the two therapists disagree about the direction of the case (Porter, 1993) or when one therapist does not value the contribution of the other modality. Both the group and individual therapists may have countertransference reactions to one another that must be managed and understood so that these reactions can be resources rather than hindrances to the treatment (Ulman, 2002).

Combined Therapy

In combined therapy, the same therapist conducts the individual and group aspects of the treatment. Although some conceptualize the two modalities as being distinct and separable, other practitioners see them as two facets of a single indivisible modality. In combined therapy, the therapist is in the most advantageous position to see the client in a multidimensional way (Caligor, 1990). Within the group, the therapist can see what relational difficulties the person has in a variety of types of relationships. In individual therapy, the therapist can most fully explore the underpinnings of those difficulties. In the following Putting It into Practice, this strength of combined therapy is illustrated. For many individuals the idea of entering a therapy group is a frightening one indeed. Some patients would have an utter unwillingness to enter a group and could not use their positive tie with the therapist to create some measure of safety as they did so. Combined therapy can be a deterrent to a member's precipitously leaving a therapy group, however (Porter, 1993). For example, if a member storms out of the group with the intent not to return, the therapist, having full knowledge of the circumstances giving rise to the member's feelings, can help the member explore and understand them in such a way as to make them more manageable.

One disadvantage of combined therapy that has been cited in the literature (Taylor & Gazda, 1991) is that the patient's involvement with the therapist in two modalities could create excessive dependency. Such dependency may lead the patient to avoid expressing any feelings that he or she would see as endangering the relationship. This disadvantage is most likely to be realized when dependency upon the therapist does not become a matter for exploration in either therapy. A second disadvantage is that the therapist's extensive knowledge of the client's developmental history could hinder the therapist from being fully and freshly present in the here and now of the group (Bernstein, 1990). A third disadvantage is that if the patient-therapist relationship sours in one modality, the patient's par-

Putting It Into Practice

Combined Therapy: The Case of Maud

Maud, a 22-year-old woman who lived with her parents, had been in individual treatment for 8 months when her therapist began to speak with her about the possibility of her being in a therapy group. Maud had been extremely timid and often reported that her mind "went blank" once she got into the session. Her presenting difficulties included a lack of relationships in her life except for a few female friends who themselves appeared to have an extremely constricted lifestyle. The notion of group was extraordinarily intimidating to her, but eventually she said she would try it.

The members of the group found Maud to be a winsome figure and went out of their way to foster her identification with their experiences. They questioned her about her relationship with her parents, made suggestions about how she could broaden her social connections, and expressed positive feelings for her. For her part, Maud took a lively interest in all that was said. Often, in individual therapy, she used another member's situational difficulty as a point of departure for talking about a problem of her own that she perceived as similar.

As time passed, members were sometimes less indulgent with Maud than they were when first she entered the group, although they continued to encourage her participation. It was easy for Maud to feel rebuffed. The therapist noted Maud's difficulty in tolerating this shift. Within the individual treatment, an exploration of her feeling of being neglected led to some very productive explorations of how her parents showed indifference to Maud when she behaved more independently and to the recognition that this pattern seemed to take hold in her early childhood. Maud was eventually able to articulate a fear that group members' treatment of her as one of them was the harbinger of being ignored altogether. Having articulated this expectation, she could test it out in members' actual behavior toward her.

ticipation in both may be jeopardized. The ethical and legal complexities of combined therapy will be explored in Chapter 8.

Selection and Preparation for Conjoint Versus Combined Therapy

In making the decision whether a client would benefit from combined or conjoint treatment, the individual therapist should ask a variety of questions, such as the following:

- Does the therapist have a group that would be appropriate for the client? The individual therapist who also conducts group therapy knows the dynamics both of the group and of the potential member and can use this knowledge to determine whether the candidate is likely to be compatible with the group.
- Is the candidate likely to benefit from an intensification of transference

or its dilution? For many clients, conjoint therapy will lead to a dilution of transference, and combined therapy to its intensification. For example, the safety a highly vulnerable patient might feel in having two authority figures toward whom to direct feelings might facilitate both the individual and group work.

- Will there be particular reactions evoked by combined or conjoint therapy that limit or spur work in treatment? For example, should a patient who is already in individual treatment be assigned to a group in which the therapist sees only some of the members in individual treatment? This configuration can readily lead the client to see him- or herself as a favorite child. The therapist can use knowledge of the patient derived from individual treatment to answer the question posed by Alonso and Rutan (1990, p. 8): "Is this a victory that helps put into better perspective whatever envy or yearnings are felt by that member, or, on the other hand, is it a victory that generates so much anxiety that it gets in the way of exploration and the development of intimacy with other peer members?" The answer to such a question can enable an optimal assignment of a patient to conjoint or combined therapy.

Both conjoint and combined therapy are variable in whether the individual and group components begin simultaneously or sequentially. Which format applies to a given case affects how the preparation for the group treatment is conducted. When individual therapy precedes group treatment, a much more exploratory approach to the entrance into the client's group is possible. Relative to an interviewing situation, individual treatment often affords the time to conduct an in-depth exploration. More important, however, the establishment of a trusting relationship between therapist and client creates the atmosphere for greater openness about fears and fantasies. This opportunity may be one reason that individuals who have been in individual therapy are less likely to leave the group precipitously (MacNair-Semands, 2002). This is a great advantage given that the mean dropout rate in many clinical settings is roughly 35 percent. Whether group and individual treatments begin simultaneously or successively, it is useful if the preparation involves helping the client to understand the differences between the (1) goals, (2) processes, and (3) roles of the therapist in the two modalities.

STRUCTURAL FEATURES OF THE GROUP

In designing the group, the therapist must consider not only the group composition but also other defining features of the group, such as location, size, and temporal characteristics (e.g., length of sessions, frequency of sessions). As we will see, each of these areas bears in important ways upon the group's capacity to meet its goals.

Spatial Characteristics of the Group

The spatial characteristics of the group concern where the group is held and the physical features of the group room itself. For groups of all types, an important feature of the room is that the physical structure safeguards the confidentiality of communications made in the room and protects the group from intrusions from the outside. (See Putting It into Practice below.)

Many other aspects of the physical environment warrant the therapist's careful attention. Examples of these are the configuration of the chairs, the level of il-

Putting It Into Practice

Spatial Characteristics of the Group

In one inpatient group, the room in which the group met did not serve its function. The group sessions were held in a room in the center of a psychiatric unit in near proximity to the nursing station and the patient lounge. During the session, members were privy to conversations between patients and the nursing staff, which were often loud because the staff members spoke from the station and the patients spoke from the lounge. The group members would partake in a conspiratorial titter, knowing that the parties outside the room were unaware that their exchanges were being overheard. Occasionally, they responded to issues raised by the exchanges. At least once during any given session, a physician would tap on the window of the door, point to a member, and beckon that member outside. The group would stop their conversation and watch as the member would depart. When the sessions ended, other patients in the unit would be waiting outside and would make such comments as, "Were you having a séance in there? You weren't as noisy as you usually are!" or "What were you guys laughing about?"

Teaching note: The group described in the vignette is not an unrepresentative depiction of some treatment settings. Because of the location of the group and the physical characteristics of the room, the boundary between the group and the environment was exceedingly porous: Information was passed fairly constantly between the group and the broader environment. This arrangement is not altogether without benefit: If a problem arose in the group, such as a member's becoming physically aggressive, help would be proximate. On the other hand, members would have difficulty feeling secure in sharing personal material, recognizing how easily it could be exported. The therapist faced with such an arrangement should strive to cultivate the environment so that it maximally supports the group's work. Some modifications will be directed toward the physical environment (e.g., perhaps the therapist could use a white noise generator or place a curtain over the window). However, the cultivation of the environment also entails working with staff members to understand how it functions and what behaviors of theirs might affect the group's ability to pursue its goals. Such an investment on the part of the therapist is a component of establishing the progroup environment (Rice & Rutan, 1981) described earlier in this chapter.

lumination, the size of the room, the noise level, and the temperature. The furniture in the room should be organized so that each member of the group can see all of the other members clearly. For this reason, furniture is typically arranged in a circle. Members are seated at a sufficient distance so that they can easily see the participant to each side and maintain their personal space. The latter may vary over the course of the group as members achieve a greater sense of intimacy in their relationships and tolerate greater physical closeness (Hall, 1966).

Illumination is typically kept at a moderate level. Harshly bright lighting might intensify members' sense of exposure and have an inhibiting effect on the sharing of personal material. A low level of illumination might hinder members from picking up subtle visual cues in each other's reactions or create a kind of nightclub atmosphere that could detract from the group as a working system. If the room is exceedingly small for the number of occupants, members' negative affects are more likely to emerge (Marshall & Heslin, 1975). Other variables such as temperature and noise have been shown to be very influential in the kinds of behaviors in which members engage (Forsyth, 1990). For example, extremes in temperature can result in increases in aggressive behavior (C. A. Anderson, 1989), and a high level of noise can increase distractibility (Cohen & Weinstein, 1981).

TEMPORAL VARIABLES

Time is one of the group's most valuable commodities, and whether the available time is great or small, it constitutes a special resource to the group. When available time is extremely limited, it creates a pressure upon members to work with focus and intensity. Time-limited groups can symbolize many other limits in life and ultimately the limit of life itself. Groups in which time is ample and even unlimited (that is, the member has considerable decision-making power over the length of his or her tenure) allow members to achieve great depth and breadth in the issues they explore, provided they use the time wisely.

In some cases, the therapist can set the level of one or more of the temporal variables we will describe; in other cases, they are preset, either by the setting or by some other constraining force. Whatever circumstance avails, the therapist serves the group well by actively using time as a tool, establishing it as a core rather than incidental feature of the group design.

Frequency and Length of Sessions

How does the group therapist know how many sessions are needed for a member to accomplish the goals of the group? Two variables the therapist must consider are the intended format of the sessions and the desired level of affective intensity. *Format* is a variable that is relevant to both frequency and length but especially to the latter, because when the session entails a multiplicity of steps, sufficient time must be available for members to proceed through each step. For example, Toner et al. (1998) describe a cognitive-behavioral group for patients with irritable bowel syndrome. Each session entails 10 different steps. Many of the steps (such as members' reports on significant events during the week) require that time be allocated to each individual member. In calculating the total time needed for the group, the therapist must think about the format in terms of how many members are likely to be in the group. Format may also be relevant to frequency of sessions because one way for the therapist to accommodate a relatively larger number of members in this kind of structured group is to have frequent sessions (i.e., more than once a week) and have members alternate the spotlight.

The more frequent the sessions, the more intense members' affective experience is likely to be. Consider, for example, the situation in which two members at the end of the group have an argument in which one accuses the other of being a sycophant in relation to the therapist. If the group were to meet two days later, the likelihood that members could hold onto the thoughts and feelings associated with the event would be much greater than if the group were to meet a week later.

Duration of Participation

One of the most significant decisions a therapist must make in designing a group is how long each member is expected to remain in the group. There are two ways duration of participation can be organized. In a closed-ended group, the group meets for a set period and all members begin and end at the same time. In an open-ended group, members enter and leave the group continuously.

How does the therapist determine how long a group experience should be? The therapist should consider many factors in making this decision, but primary among these is the group's goals. Treatment goals may be distinguished from one another by type and breadth. The types of goals pursued in group therapy include symptomatic change, skill acquisition, interpersonal change, and intrapsychic change. Symptom alleviation goals can sometimes be achieved within a short-term and even brief time frame. For example, research studies have shown that participation in a short-term group (20 or fewer sessions) leads to the amelioration of depression in adolescents (Clarke, Rohde, Lewinsohn, Hopson, & Seeley, 1999) and adults (Bright et al., 1999). Short-term group treatment of anxiety (Mendlowitz, Manassis, & Bradley, 1999; Wagner, 2001), of mixed symptoms of anxiety and depression (Kush & Fleming, 2000), bulimia (Gray & Hoage, 1990), and aggression (Feindler, Ecton, Kingley & Dubey, 1986) has also proven effective.

Skill acquisition of certain kinds has also been shown to be possible over a brief period of group therapy. For example, studies on groups aimed at improving members' abilities to solve problems have shown that after only 12 sessions, members have demonstrated an increased ability to define a problem, generate alternate solutions, and decide among the various solutions (Arean et al., 1993). In only six sessions, members have been shown to have an increased ability to identify the intermediate steps in solving a problem (Jones, 1981).

Groups targeting interpersonal and intrapsychic change have tended to be longer term than groups directed toward symptom alleviation or skill acquisition. Because interpersonal and intrapsychic patterns are aspects of personality that have crystallized over long periods of time, they are less easily modifiable. Budman et al.'s study (1996) in which personality-disordered individuals proceeded through an 18-month period of interpersonally oriented group therapy demonstrates this point. The investigators tracked four therapy groups over an 18-month period. They found that over the course of therapy, and even at termination, positive interpersonal changes were continuing to take place.

For all types of goals, the more focal the goal, the shorter the period required for its achievement. The fact that groups directed toward interpersonal and intrapsychic change have generally been long term is in part due to the breadth of the goals commonly established in these types of groups. Members address not merely a particular problem, interpersonal concern, or behavior but a range of interpersonal patterns and conflicts. When goals for interpersonal and intrapsychic groups are sharply delimited, members can show progress over relatively brief intervals. For example, Kilmann et al. (1999) developed a short-term group format for treating persons with attachment difficulties that manifest themselves in interpersonal insecurity. The treatment focused on four elements: dysfunctional relationship beliefs, childhood factors influencing partner choices and relationship styles, relationship skills training, and relationship strategies. Female group members participated in a 3-day weekend (17 hours). The investigators found that, relative to the controls, the group members showed more effective interpersonal behaviors, more satisfactory relationships with family members, more functional relationship beliefs, and less fearfulness in their attachments both at the end of the group and at a 6-month follow-up.

In deciding upon the length of group treatment, the therapist is well served by considering any available research on his or her particular model. Unfortunately, available data on length of treatment and outcome are scarce. An example of a useful study is that of Wood, Trainor, and Rothwell (2001), who investigated the effects of group treatment on self-harm in adolescents. Group members proceeded through a course of treatment incorporating elements of problem-solving therapy, cognitive-behavioral treatment, psychodynamic group psychotherapy, and dialectical behavioral therapy (Linehan & Wagner, 1990). Members were permitted to remain in the group as long as they desired. The investigators found that group treatment, although not affecting depressive symptoms, did reduce incidents of deliberate self-harm relative to the control group. They also found that the greater the number of group sessions (in a range from zero to 19), the less the likelihood of self-harm behaviors. Active manipulation of the number-of-sessions variable would provide even more helpful information.

SIZE OF THE GROUP

Most therapy groups range from 5 to 10 members. There are compelling reasons why therapists do not typically go above or below this number. To the extent that a group goes beyond 10, the following factors may deter members' work:

- Each individual member's opportunity to participate actively in the group and receive input from other members is unduly limited.
- Groups beyond 10 members may have greater difficulty achieving cohesion, a finding suggested by research on nontask groups. For example, Marshall and Heslin (1975) compared groups of 4 versus 16 undergraduate students who were asked to reconstruct paragraphs from component phrases. They found that members of the large group expressed a lower level of attraction to the other members of the group than did members of the small group. In another study, (Schroeder, Bowen, & Twemlow, 1982) in which alcoholism groups ranged in size from 5 to 23 veterans, larger groups were associated with higher dropout rates.
- With some therapy models, it may be impossible to implement the model if there are more than 10 members (in some cases, 10 may be too large). The example was given earlier of a cognitive-behavioral model (Toner et al., 1998) for the treatment of irritable bowel syndrome. The reader in which the therapist developed for each member an individual agenda for the session helped the member to review the agenda. The addition of each member adds a significant temporal interval to the needed session length. Beyond a certain point, the session length may not be capable of extension to accommodate additional

group members because of limits in members' attention or other practical factors.

Extremely small groups (below five) also have significant limitations:

- Groups with low membership may not be conducive to the full emergence of those therapeutic factors that are unique to group therapy. For instance, with interpersonal learning, members benefit from having access to a range of perspectives on their social behaviors. Groups with only three or four members provide each member with more limited feedback opportunities. Group dynamics emerge with less clarity in a smaller group, which creates an impediment to the application of those theoretical approaches that revolve around their exploration.
- Members in small groups may have a heightened sense of exposure (Roller, 1997), which fosters constriction rather than openness.
- Smaller groups may be so focused on survival (Rutan & Stone, 2001) that members may avoid those interactions that will lead to growth, such as confronting one another on interpersonal difficulties.

These relationships between size of the group and member reactions and behaviors may not apply to all groups. Factors such as the maturity of the group may neutralize the effects of size. For example, a mature group that has seen members come and go may be less reactive to these variations.

SUMMARY AND CONCLUSIONS

How the group therapist sets up the group is crucially important to its success. Attention to all of the structural features of the group, such as the number of members in the group, the spatial characteristics, and the temporal factors in the group design, ensures that a good environment will be created for work. Of paramount importance is the selection of members who have the qualities to benefit from a particular type of group and personal goals that are aligned with the group goals. Preparation for the group is necessary to provide informed consent, to diminish unproductive anxiety, to foster accurate conceptions about the group, to increase the likelihood of good attendance, to active therapeutic processes, and to discourage premature terminations.

☙ TEST YOURSELF ☙

1. **Positive expectations about the value of group are associated with positive outcomes.** True or False?

2. **The theoretical notion of cohesion can be used to explain why a therapist would seek to compose a group of members with different interpersonal styles.** True or False?

3. **The best predictor of a prospective member's group behavior is the person's**

   (a) behavior in the interview.

   (b) performance on psychological tests.

   (c) behavior in a small group situation.

   (d) all prior methods have equal predictive value

4. **A disadvantage of large groups (more than 10 members) is**

   (a) opportunities for active individual participation are too limited.

   (b) the group may have difficulty achieving cohesion.

   (c) certain models requiring a multistep session could not be implemented.

   (d) all of the above

5. **The value of preparation in enhancing outcomes has consistently been established across studies.** True or False?

Thought Question

6. **How might the process of preparation be different for individual therapy than for group therapy?**

Answers: 1. True; 2. False; 3. c; 4. d; 5. False

Four

W hat occurs within a therapy group that is helpful to members? This question has been given a great deal of thought by students of group therapy and has also been the topic of a considerable body of research. In the mid-1950s, Corsini and Rosenberg surveyed 300 articles on group therapy to identify what factors mediate change in group treatment. From this work, they constructed a list of 10 recurring factors. Since that time, many clinicians, including Berzon, Pious, and Farson (1963), Yalom (1970), and Bloch and Crouch (1985), have performed much additional research. Based on these and other writings, this chapter will provide an overview of the primary therapeutic factors as they are currently understood and will consider how these factors can be activated.

A *therapeutic factor* is an element of the group that potentially benefits one or more group members. The qualification "potentially" is made because any of the factors in a given circumstance could have a negative or neutral effect. For example, one factor we will discuss is *catharsis,* or a venting of feelings. Although many theoreticians have cited catharsis as a therapeutic factor, there is some research evidence that catharsis that is too intense or unaccompanied by an understanding of the feelings being expressed can have negative effects. The important point is that a group therapist must not assume that any particular factor cited here is therapeutic but must investigate its influence upon the capacity of the group to help its members.

CLASSIFYING THERAPEUTIC FACTORS

In this chapter, we shall use MacKenzie's system (1990) for classifying therapeutic factors. Although other systems exist, this one is useful in its applicability not only to therapy groups but also to self-help and support groups (see Chapter 11). MacKenzie's schema also is helpful because it has a developmental aspect, with sets of certain factors emerging prominently in the new group and others operating more conspicuously as the group gains maturity. According to MacKenzie's system, there are four types of factors: supportive factors, self-revelation, learning from others, and psychological work factors, with each having two or more subtypes, which will be described. We will also explore the connection between the therapeutic factors and group cohesion, a commodity essential to the group's work.

Supportive Factors

Across different theoretical approaches, the supportive factors are especially crucial early in group treatment. When members enter a group treatment, often they have recently suffered a decline in self-esteem and a sense of futility about their situation. The supportive factors target these negative experiences. They cultivate in the member the kind of positive outlook both about the group involvement and about the future that is likely to contribute to the member's willingness to engage with other members in the ways necessary to derive benefit from the group. The operation of the supportive factors should increase a member's feeling of effectuality or ability to find constructive approaches to his or her difficulties. The supportive factors are elements of treatment that appear prominently in self-help and support groups. (See Rapid Reference 4.1 for an overview of supportive factors.)

Instillation of Hope
Hope is a crucial element throughout group treatment. In the beginning of group participation, hope spurs the member to be involved with other members be-

Rapid Reference 4.1

Supportive Factors

Factor	Definition
Instillation of hope	Positing goals, recognizing pathways to reach the goals, and regarding the self as capable of sustaining effort.
Acceptance	Experiencing oneself as positively esteemed by the other members of the group.
Altruism	Responding in a helpful way to another member.
Universality	Recognizing that one is not alone with one's difficulties.
Cohesion	Experiencing a sense of togetherness in the group.

cause he or she expects such an engagement to lead to an enhancement in the member's well being. In the middle of treatment, hope motivates a member to persist even in the face of difficult emotional experiences that may be stimulated by the group. Toward the end of treatment, hope helps the member to grapple with difficult feelings associated with terminating from the group in order to make constructive beginnings following group life.

Although we all have a general notion of hope as a positive outlook about the future, recent research offers the group therapist a deeper understanding of its fabric. Research by Snyder and colleagues (Snyder, Cheavens, & Sympson, 1997) shows that several distinct processes underpin hope. Hope entails an individual's positing goals, recognizing that there are feasible routes by which the goals can be achieved, and perceiving the self as able to sustain an effort to reach the goals. Prior to group treatment, the process of sculpting a set of goals and seeing how processes that occur in the group sessions might advance these goals is a hope-bolstering step. Often members begin group therapy with considerable trepidation but find initial sessions to be disconfirming of at least some of their fears. This reassurance instigates the third element of hope, the conviction that "I can do this; I can see this effort through."

Group therapists can intervene in a variety of ways to nurture hope in members:

- In interviewing prospective group members, therapists can share with candidates the positive outcome findings concerning group therapy. They can also express their belief (without making unwarranted promises) that group participation will benefit the potential member. The fact that the individual has taken a constructive step in addressing his or her life difficulties by inquiring about group treatment can be underscored.
- During the group sessions, the therapist can create a culture in which members point out to one another success in reaching microgoals. For example, a highly intrusive member might be given positive feedback on an occasion on which she allows another member to finish speaking before she responds. The awareness of his or her progress strengthens the member's belief that putting forth additional effort will be worthwhile.
- The therapist might point out to members occasions when they have shown a willingness to tolerate negative feelings, conflicts with other members, and new, potentially surprising insights about themselves in order to grow.

- At termination, therapists can encourage remaining members to offer the departing member their views on how the member has changed over the course of the group. For both parties, this step is hope bolstering. For the departing member, it fortifies his or her sense of personal agency—that is, the confidence of possessing the wherewithal to transform one's life in a positive way. For the remaining members, this taking stock underscores the existence of viable means by which members can pursue their goals; in this case, the viable means are the processes the group uses to do its work.

Research on the influence of hope on performance reveals that hope is a valuable commodity. Individuals with high hope are in fact more likely to meet their goals than low-hope individuals even when the effects of other factors such as intelligence and ability to perform the task are removed (Curry, Snyder, Cook, Ruby, & Rehm, 1997). Although hopefulness appears to be a personality feature with some stability, future research should be directed to the question of the extent to which an individual's level of hopefulness can be modified when it is established as a target of intervention.

Acceptance

When individuals are interviewed for group therapy, one of their greatest fears, inevitably, is that they will be slighted or shunned by the other group members. This worry is even more acute when a rejection precipitated the need for treatment. Entering members are thereby heartened and relieved when they find both their persons and contributions welcomed rather than spurned.

Acceptance is experienced at various levels during the course of the group. Early in the life of the group, members will exhibit a politeness and respect for conventionality that leads them to avoid behaviors that are outwardly rejecting of one another. Most members feel accepted at a modicum level. Later, the acceptance that emerges is more fully grounded in members' awareness of each other's strengths and weaknesses. Consequently, it disconfirms in a more powerful way members' negative anticipations about others' responses to them. Ideally, the member is able to say, "They know who I am, and they still accept me."

The therapist can promote acceptance by:

- Showing a nonjudgmental attitude toward all of the material shared by members, an attitude that members can model.
- Helping members to give feedback to one another in ways that are concrete and noncondemnatory, and helping those who receive feedback to register it accurately.

- Responding to any acts of rejection with curiosity about such events, with the goal of understanding them further. Often, rejections serve a need of which the rejecting person is unaware. For example, the rejecting party may be seeing in the other person qualities that also reside within him- or herself and cannot be tolerated. By imagining that only the rejected party owns the quality, the rejecting individual can feel, for the moment, liberated from the unwanted presence. As this defensive process is understood, not only can the rejected person feel greater acceptance, but also the rejecting person can move toward a more stable self-acceptance.

Altruism

In group therapy sessions, the opportunities members have to be helpful to one another are many. A member may offer a soothing comment to another member who is experiencing psychological pain (see the following Putting It into Practice). Members may suggest a solution to another's problem. Members may put other members' emotions into words, thereby helping the latter to feel understood. A member may refrain in a given session from introducing a topic concerning him- or herself so that other members in greater need can receive the group's attention.

Altruism pertains to both the motives and the effects of members' behaviors. In some cases, the member may make an active decision to respond in a fashion that could be useful to another group member. However, in other instances, a member may be unwittingly helpful. For example, a group member whom we will call Flora may express anger toward the therapist. Another member, Ken, who possesses similar feelings, may express gratitude to Flora for inspiring him to be more communicative about his negative feelings. Although Flora may not have intended to provide a model for other group members, the fact that she did so can be an esteem-lifting realization.

The extent to which members value altruism varies across populations. For example, in one study (Kapur, Miller, & Mitchell, 1988), although acute care inpatients rated altruism as one of the factors most influential in their capacity to derive benefit from the group experience, outpatients perceived it to be a relatively unimportant factor. This contrast highlights the power of altruism to be especially useful to individuals who, because of recent life events, have come to doubt their coping capabilities. Altruism also figures prominently in support and self-help groups. Marcus and Bernard (2000) noted that in such groups altruism provides a vehicle by which individuals can transition from giving to receiving help. They described the case of a woman who had been treated for 15 years for breast

Putting It Into Practice

An Illustration of the Supportive Factors

A open-ended outpatient men's group was meeting for its third session. Howard said he had found the group helpful the prior week and had done better in confronting his supervisor at work. Marty said he was glad to hear that, because he had wondered about Howard during the week. Stanley said he had as well. Marty said he had noticed before the session that Colin was sitting in his car, staring ahead of him, and he looked "bummed out." Colin, who had been fairly active and upbeat in the prior session, didn't respond.

Howard persisted, "Did something happen, or are you just in a different space?" In an ornery tone, Colin said that he felt he couldn't talk about it. Members asked what could be so awful that he couldn't mention it. Colin said that it wasn't that it was so awful . . . it was the fact that it was affecting him so much that was awful. He felt weak. Howard said that he felt weak on a daily basis—he was accustomed to feeling weak and almost didn't mind anymore. Other members, some joking, some seriously, talked about their acceptance of feeling or being weak.

The therapist questioned, "But might it also have something to do with *looking* weak . . . looking weak in *here?*" Colin admitted that he worried about looking weak to the other group members. He said that he realized the other members hardly know him. They might think he is this way all the time. That he's a real loser.

Marty laughingly responded, "You think we'll look down on you? Not a chance!" Colin then said that he felt boxed in: He would never get peace in the group until he said what was bothering him. Members agreed. Colin said that he had had a relationship, only a short-term one. He had been feeling despondent ever since the woman told him that while she was seeing him, she was dating another man also. She had decided to have an exclusive relationship with the other man. Colin said he couldn't stop thinking about it and was feeling far more miserable than he would have expected. The funny thing was, he realized he didn't have a strong interest in the woman.

Marty responded by describing several prior situations involving competition with other men that were very similar. He revealed that he, too, was astonished to find how strong his feelings were after he had lost a woman to another man. Howard said that although he had had a strong reaction after losing his partner Jerome to a competitor, he wondered whether the strength of the feelings were rooted more in jealousy than deep affection for the partner, and he suggested that perhaps this was what was occurring for Colin. Howard noted, "It's humiliating to be the vanquished."

(continued)

cancer. At the beginning of her participation in a group for breast cancer patients, she stated that her intention in joining the group was to help the other group members. Buoyed by the other members' appreciation of the information she had to share, she gradually moved into the exploration of personal topics, thereby enabling others to assist her.

Colin laughed the laugh of recognition. He said, "You mean it's more about being a sore loser than anything else?" Both Colin's and Howard's comments elicited disclosures from other members about circumstances in which they had difficulty admitting to themselves that they were engaged in a competition with another man. Marty said, "Well, at least we don't have to compete in here."

Howard ruefully responded, "Don't be so sure," and other members laughed.

Teaching note: The supportive factors were very much in operation in this session, as is generally the case early in group life. Howard's report that he applied learning from the group to a problem outside was a *hope*-fostering comment. The implicit message was "This group is going to be effective in helping us to deal with our difficulties." Marty's and Stanley's declarations that they had thought about Howard's situation over the week involved the factor of *altruism*. It was also a manifestation of the burgeoning cohesion in the group: In a cohesive group, members carry the group with them between the sessions. Altruism was also seen in Marty's observation about Colin and his effort to get him to reveal the source of his distress. *Universality* was established in relation to members' shared feelings, first in relation to rejection, but later on a deeper level, in relation to competitive strivings and related feelings such as jealousy. Note that Howard, by establishing a personal connection with Colin, was able to make an interpretation that Colin accepted, namely the notion that the seeming sadness over a romantic disappointment masked jealousy and humiliation in relation to competitive strivings. *Acceptance* was demonstrated in the group's reaction to Colin's revelation of his feelings of vulnerability. All of these factors operated to increase the level of *cohesion* in the group. The group humor at the end of the sequence is one manifestation of cohesion.

Universality

When misfortunes arise in our lives, we are drawn to others who are facing or have faced similar circumstances (Forsyth & Corazzini, 2000). Through this contact comes the soothing awareness that we are alone neither with our situation nor with the feelings attached to that situation. The recognition of shared experience is referred to as *universality,* a factor present in virtually every form of group treatment. It is also a factor that group members identify as being key to the benefit they derive from the group experience.

Although universality operates in most therapy groups, the type of universality that is emphasized depends upon the nature of the group. In self-help and support groups, members establish universality with respect to feelings and impulses that they can easily access. When an external event such as a death or some other calamitous occurrence has precipitated the need for treatment, the feelings are ones that most people would have in this circumstance. For example, in a support group for stroke survivors, members share extreme feelings of helplessness and grief over loss of functions. In short-term therapy groups, universality covers a broader terrain. Typically it includes feelings and impulses that pose a challenge to the individual's capacity to maintain self-esteem but are not so objectionable that they lie outside a person's awareness. For example, in a short-term group, members may commiserate over their inability to be assertive with demanding people in their lives. Although the lack of assertiveness may be a quality that brings shame to the person, it is not so abhorrent as to be banished from awareness altogether. In long-term groups, especially those run from a psychodynamic perspective (see Chapter 2), the feelings and impulses that are recognized as being shared are so intolerable that often individuals lack awareness of them when they enter the group. For example, if the unassertive individuals described here were in a long-term group, they might learn that underlying the lack of assertiveness is some other element (such as anger) that is so wholly objectionable to them as to be inadmissible to consciousness.

Cohesion

The therapeutic factor of cohesion has a special status. It is both a condition for the operation of the other therapeutic factors and a therapeutic factor in its own right. *Group cohesion* has been defined in great variety of ways. Among the definitions are those emphasizing group-level phenomena (e.g., cohesion is the sense of togetherness in the group), the member-to-member phenomena (e.g., cohesion is members' levels of attraction for one another), and individual-member phenomena (e.g., cohesion is the individual's level of felt commitment to the group). Rather than attempting to select one definition, we must make best use of this concept by regarding all of these elements as reflecting aspects of group cohesion (Burlingame, Fuhriman, & Johnson, 2001). Group cohesion has also been regarded as the group counterpart to the therapeutic alliance in individual treatment.

Groups that have achieved high levels of cohesion are more likely to reach their goals than groups that are less cohesive. Many studies on both therapy and nontherapy groups demonstrate this point. For example, one investigation of therapy groups lasting 15 sessions showed that the level of cohesion established early in the group is positively associated with both global and problem-specific change (Budman et al., 1989). In another study, high levels of cohesion in interpersonally oriented groups for individuals with borderline pathology led to positive outcomes in terms of social adjustment and symptomatology (Marziali, Munroe-Blum, & McCleary, 1997).

How might cohesion be nurtured in a therapy group? Burlingame et al. (2001) identified six empirically supported principles by which cohesion can develop in the group:

- Members should be thoroughly prepared for the group experience. The reader will recall that preparation diminishes the frequency of premature terminations, absences, and lateness. In addition, preparation contributes to the establishment of cohesion, particularly if the preparation contains material relevant to cohesion. Santarsiero, Baker, and McGee (1995) randomly assigned participants in an interpersonal learning group to cohesion pretraining and general pretraining conditions. The cohesion pretraining consisted simply of the provision of written material on how group therapy works, with specific information on roles, processes, and behaviors that would assist members in forging stronger bonds. Individuals in the cohesion pretraining group were given a comprehension quiz on the material, and all reached criterion. Individuals in the general pretraining group (the control group) were given reading material on the history of group therapy and also completed a quiz. The investigators found that the experimental group achieved a higher level of cohesion than that of the control subjects.

- Early in the group's life, identifying the processes that are deemed useful will promote cohesion. One way in which structure promotes cohesion is by stimulating self-disclosure. When therapists say explicitly, "These activities are the ones you should be pursuing," members are less anxious in the early sessions and more willing to take risks. One form of risk taking is the disclosure of personal information. The sense on the part of each member of "I know who these people are" stimulates cohesion. Consistency in the temporal and spatial features of the group also enhances structure: Starting and ending the group on time and meeting in the same location establish a predictability that sets the conditions for the emergence of group cohesion (see Chapter 5 for further discussion of the leader's role in maintaining structure).

- The leader should foster member-to-member interaction. High levels of interaction contribute to trust, which in turn contributes to cohesion. Early in the life of the group, members are likely to focus on the therapist. At this time, there is much the therapist can do to help members forge helping relationships with one another. For example, frequently in early sessions members will pose questions to the therapist. When this happens, the therapist can redirect those questions to the group as a whole or to specific members.

- The therapist should consider feedback as a cohesion-building factor. This principle will be discussed further in the section on interpersonal learning.

- The therapist should be aware of, and manage, how his or her bearing in the group contributes to the emotional atmosphere of the group. For example, therapists who manifest warmth and caring are likely not only to increase the comfort level of individual group members but also to contribute to a nurturing group atmosphere.

• An atmosphere should be fostered in which members relate to one another in positive ways. Suppose, for example, that Joe enters the group in a distressed state. Madeleine talks with Joe in a way that increases all members' understanding of Joe's situation and capacity to support him. If Madeleine were to receive feedback on her interaction with Joe, members would be likely to emphasize her sensitivity. Such feedback would contribute to establishing such caring ways of interacting with other members as normative.

Self-Revelation Factors

Two factors that often (but not invariably) occur together are *self-disclosure* and catharsis. They both involve a member's conveyance of personal or private information to other members. Whereas self-disclosure involves primarily factual or cognitive information, catharsis entails affective material. (See Rapid Reference 4.2.)

Self-Disclosure

When members begin to feel a sense of trust in other members, self-disclosure, or the communication of private information about the self, occurs. Self-disclosure is important in several ways. First, unless members feel that others know them, a genuine experience of acceptance is impossible. Second, the act of disclosing provides the opportunity to test fears about being known. Group members, like most people, harbor the notion that "Sure, they like me now, but if they only knew. . . ." Whereas most people rarely get to test this belief of likely rejection with self-revelation, group members do. Even when a particular disclosure does not evoke a positive reaction, the negative reaction is likely to pale in relation to the anticipated response. Most of the time, disclosures beget additional disclosures. When a member finds that sharing

≡Rapid Reference 4.2

Self-Revelation Factors

Factor	Definition
Self-disclosure	Revealing oneself to the group in a cognitive way.
Catharsis	Revealing oneself to the group in an affective way that is accompanied by a sense of relief.

parts of the self leads others to communicate similarly, the member realizes that such risk taking is more likely to strengthen than to undermine relationships. Third, self-disclosures are often necessary in order for members to obtain helpful feedback from the group. Often, self-disclosures communicate information about a member's self-perception. Once they possess this knowledge, other members can agree, disagree, or elaborate on that member's view of him- or herself. A woman who believes that she conveys only positive sentiments to others can benefit from realizing that others pick up on her hostility toward them.

The therapist seeking to create the conditions in which helpful self-disclosures can occur should consider the following:

- The therapist can underscore a member's use of self-disclosure by encouraging other members to respond not only to the content of the self-disclosure (which they are likely to do spontaneously) but also to the fact of the disclosure. For example, the therapist might say, "How do you feel that Tanya shared with us her distress over being teased at school today?"

- The therapist should consider the timing of self-disclosures. Tschuschke and Dies (1994) found that self-disclosures were associated with positive outcomes when members made them in the beginning or middle of the group's life, but that self-disclosures made at termination were associated with negative outcomes. There are at least two reasons for this finding. When members make disclosures early in the group, they have the time to explore them thoroughly and obtain others' reactions to the disclosures. When self-disclosures are made at termination, the member may be left with the fantasy that other members were silently and harshly critical of the self-revealing member. Another possibility is that late disclosures may interfere with the termination process and may even be a defense against the feelings associated with it. In fact, it may be the interruption of the termination process and not the disclosure per se that adversely affects the group's work. Although the therapist cannot control when members will disclose, the therapist can subtly work to make the atmosphere more or less conducive to disclosures. Especially at termination, the therapist can present the group with the possibility that the new material is brought in to derail the termination process if this hypothesis seems to be a viable one.

- The therapist should include in the composition of the group individuals who are likely to be moderately to highly self-disclosing. Once one member engages in self-disclosure, others are likely to follow. For example, Leichtentritt and Schectman (1998) observed that it is useful to have both girls and boys in a therapy group together because the former model self-disclosure for the latter.

- When working with a population that is known to have difficulty with self-disclosure, it may be useful to incorporate a self-disclosure exercise or ritual (Horne, Jolliff, & Roth, 1996).

Catharsis

Whereas self-disclosure pertains to a *cognitive* sharing of information about the self, catharsis is an *affective* sharing. *Catharsis* is a release of feeling that brings about relief. Often the experiences that are discharged are ones that have been pent up over a long time. Although catharsis can be of benefit to particular members at moments in the group's life, the research has provided limited support for its usefulness across settings and populations.

Catharsis has not only potential benefits but also possible costs. When group members experience the release of strong feelings for which they are not provided some cognitive frame, disorganization and distress may ensue rather than symptom relief.

Learning from Others

One of the strengths of a group is the opportunity it provides members to benefit from the example or the wisdom of another group member. These factors summarize different facets of the group as an arena of learning. Although all of them can operate within any psychotherapy group, they are especially useful in self-help, support, and psychoeducational groups (see Rapid Reference 4.3).

Modeling

Whatever a member or therapist does in the group can provide an example to other members of how to behave in relation to one another. For some members, the *modeling* may provide an example of a response that is not even in their repertoire, or perhaps one they did not contemplate would be possible in a given situation. For example, Mary may not realize that it is possible to express dissatisfaction with an authority figure until she sees Jill do it. For other members, the refinement of a response can be

CAUTION

Members who experience a catharsis in the group should be assisted in cognitively framing their intense emotions (e.g., a cognitive-behavioral therapist might help a member to identify automatic thoughts in relation to sadness over a rejection).

≡Rapid Reference 4.3

Factors in Learning from Others

Factor	Definition
Modeling	A member's copying a particular behavior or set of behaviors exhibited by another member.
Vicarious learning	A member's privately applying knowledge gained from the behaviors of one or more members, or interactions between them, to his or her life.
Guidance	Advice given to a member by another group member or the therapist.
Education	Didactic information presented to the group members.

achieved through modeling: Sam may discover that one can express anger in an intensive way and still not raise one's voice or use expletives.

Modeling typically implies the direct copying of a given behavior. Within some approaches, the therapist may design modeling events. For example, in a social skills training approach, the therapist may model for members how to end a conversation. The members will then be directed to emulate the therapist's behaviors and obtain feedback on their success in doing so.

In many cases, the effect of modeling is simply to convey that it is acceptable to engage in a given behavior. As noted in the discussion of self-disclosure, once one member breaks the ice, others are likely to follow.

Vicarious Learning

For other members, the learning is not so much in establishing the response in one's range of responses but in recognizing that some anticipated outcome does not always occur when that particular response is made. Although Mary, our earlier example, may have had some experience in expressing dissatisfaction with authority figures, she may only do it when pushed against a wall. Because her way of expressing dissatisfaction is so raw, authority figures do respond negatively. However, when she sees the therapist accepting Jill's more modulated expression of dissatisfaction, she realizes that it is only her particular way of expressing herself that produces the unwanted effect. The phenomenon of members' relating group events concerning other members to their own lives is *vicarious learning*. The first step of vicarious learning is *identification*. For Mary to benefit from Jill's experience in the group, she first must see part of herself in Jill. Later, we may see Mary copying Jill. Over time, if Mary incorporates into herself the learning she obtained from Jill's experience and approaches authority figures differently, then she has *internalized* this new response.

Some theoretical approaches are predicated on vicarious learning. In redecision therapy (see Chapter 2), members take turns working with the therapist on a dilemma or difficult issue. However, during the time that members are not working with the therapist, the presumption is that they are identifying with the work in which the actor is engaging and drawing applications for their own lives. Within some approaches such as psychodrama, vicarious learning is cemented by creating a segment in the group in which members can share the associations they made during the earlier portion of the group when they were vicariously partaking in the actor's experiences.

Guidance

Guidance occurs when members receive advice or direction from either the therapist or the other group members. In groups in which members have an opportunity to engage in spontaneous interaction, advice will be especially common early in the group's life. Members will often hear suggestions that they have received from friends, family, and other persons outside the group. Although the content of the advice is often not highly useful, the fact of its occurrence is. The therapeutic factor of guidance pairs nicely with that of altruism: Members experience the pleasure of showing the care for another that advice often implies even if other motives are present, such as the wish to place oneself above another group member. Members are often appreciative of advice early in the group's life even when they have received the same input previously. The gratitude derives from the recognition of the positive feelings that attend this gift. For both givers and receivers alike, advice is useful because it lessens the anxiety that accompanies entrance into the group. Members have a job: They work to solve one another's problems. In fact, one inpatient model, Maxmen's educative approach (Brabender & Fallon, 1993), systematically entails that newer members of an ongoing group give older members advice so that the former are eased into the group. Later in the group, members realize that the group has other, more unique offerings. Such awareness leads to a diminished use of this therapeutic factor.

Education

All groups provide some level of *education* to their members. As we have seen, in the preparation for group therapy, members are educated on how to be group members. They learn about the processes that are available and the rules that must be observed in order for them to obtain benefit from participation. In some groups (often aptly referred to as "psychoeducational groups") the educational component is foremost. These types of groups are often theme-oriented and composed of members who share a common psychological problem. For example, Honey, Bennett, and Morgan (2002) describe an 8-week psychoeducational group for women suffering from postnatal (postpartum) depression. The format of the group entailed the delivery of three educational components. First, the women were provided with education on postnatal depression as well as strategies for dealing with challenging child care situations and for cultivating social supports. Second, the women were taught cognitive-behavioral techniques for modifying dysfunctional thoughts about motherhood and strategies for managing anxiety. Third, the women learned relaxation techniques. The investigators found that this approach produced significant amelioration in depression immediately after the termination of the group and at a 6-month follow-up. However, it did not produce a change in psychosocial outcomes.

Homework is a technique that is used in connection with the therapeutic factor of education. Members are directed to complete assignments between sessions to strengthen learning from the session. Key elements to the success of a homework assignment are (1) the careful planning of the homework assignment so that the group member knows what specifically is to be done, (2) the anticipation of obstacles to performing the assignment, and (3) the opportunity for the member to report back to the group on the successes and failures in relation to its execution. Homework is especially useful in short-term groups as a way of intensifying the therapeutic experience. Cognitive-behavioral therapists and therapists using other highly structured formats have long used it. However, with the flowering of short-term approaches within virtually every theoretical orientation, homework is likely to be used more broadly, even with the less structured formats (Spitz, 1997).

Psychological Work Factors

Interpersonal learning and self-understanding are the two psychological work factors, and they represent two sides of one psychological coin (see Rapid Reference 4.4). *Interpersonal learning,* which was briefly characterized under the interpersonal model in Chapter 2, is the experience of (1) being engaged in the here and now of the group in an affective way and (2) cognitively processing the data emerging from this engagement. In interpersonal learning, members discover through the

> # DON'T FORGET
> A good homework assignment is specific and understandable to the group member, incorporates an anticipation of likely obstacles to its completion, and is reviewed in the following session.

≡Rapid Reference 4.4

Psychological Work Factors

Factor	Definition
Interpersonal learning	Achieving a cognitive and affective awareness of one's interpersonal style and the effects it produces on others.
Self-understanding	Gaining insight into the internal processes and psychological elements that give rise to aspects of one's interpersonal style.

medium of their present group experience how they relate to others. They have opportunities to amend dysfunctional ways and receive feedback on their new attempts. *Self-understanding* involves the resurrection of the internal templates of relationships, which influence one's interactions with others and their correction based upon interpersonal learning experiences.

An ingredient crucial to interpersonal learning and self-understanding is feedback. Feedback can potentially include any information a member chooses to share about another member. However, research (Flowers & Booraem, 1990a, b) suggests that the most useful type of feedback is observations of a member's interpersonal behaviors and the observer's reactions to those behaviors. Less useful are inferences about the historical underpinnings of the interpersonal behaviors. Another important dimension is whether the feedback is positive (highlighting strengths or behaviors that have an agreeable effect on the observer) or negative (identifying weaknesses or behaviors that are negatively regarded). Research suggests that positive feedback should be plentiful and should precede negative feedback (Jacobs, 1974; Pine & Jacobs, 1991). Finally, the usefulness of feedback in the world outside the group may be augmented if an aspect of the feedback is the establishment of connections between the members' in-the-group and out-of-the-group behaviors (for example, "You made a good start telling Fred how you feel, but you gave up quickly, just like you tell us you do at work. I feel frustrated that you didn't hang in there a little longer").

A primary means by which members learn how to give appropriate feedback is through modeling. Members emulate how the therapist provides feedback in the group. Morran, Robison, and Stockton (1985) found that over time members' feedback became more similar to the therapist's. The consequence of this shift is

DON'T FORGET

....

Negative (or constructive) feedback is most successful when preceded by positive feedback.

that members perceived the other members' feedback to be as helpful as that of the therapist.

To varying extents, most contemporary approaches to group therapy entail interpersonal learning and self-understanding. Those approaches that do not—approaches, for example, in which the therapist works with members one at a time with no opportunity for member-to-member interaction—should not be considered group therapy, because they do not use those processes that are unique to the group modality. Rather, these alternate models might be thought of as individual therapy in a group setting. However, among approaches that do use these factors there is great variability in the extent to which they are employed. Interpersonal learning and self-understanding flourish in approaches in which there is a great deal of spontaneous interaction among members, as often occurs in interpersonal, psychodynamic, and systems approaches. Formats involving a highly structured session in which member interactions are choreographed provide less of an opportunity for these factors to emerge. However, even therapists using highly structured formats are increasingly seeking ways in which interpersonal learning can occur in the sessions (Rose, 1990).

There are various means by which the therapist can foster interpersonal learning:

- In the preparation, educate prospective members on the value of interpersonal learning and its successor, self-understanding.
- Consistently focus the group on the here and now. In the following Putting It into Practice, the reader will see how the therapist assists a member in moving from an external or there-and-then focus to an internal focus by asking about a possible parallel between external and internal events. The therapist can also focus on the *structure* of members' interactions rather than the *content*. For example, if two members are talking about problems with their in-laws, the therapist can wonder aloud why it is that only two members are participating in the conversation or ask members how it feels to be listening to the exchange and not actively participating. The therapist can also focus on affect and nonverbal behaviors.

> **Therapist:** I noticed that when Sabrina was speaking with you, you moved your chair a little closer to her.
>
> **Erin:** You're right. . . . I didn't notice but I did.

Putting It Into Practice

Illustration of Psychological Work Factors

Bertie had arrived in the geriatric facility 3 weeks ago, and because she had been having difficulties establishing new relationships, she was put into an ongoing therapy group. She was in the midst of her fifth session when another member, Esther, said that she was going to be leaving. She indicated that her family could no longer afford her residency in the facility and she would be moving in with her daughter and son-in-law. For the latter she had little regard. Other members talked about their sadness over her impending departure. Various members said how she had helped them.

"Well, can't you say anything at all?" Bill demanded of Bertie. "You're the only one who hasn't spoken!"

"I don't really know Esther," Bertie responded. "I have nothing I can say to her."

"That's okay," Esther said. "Don't put her on the spot."

"It just annoys me that she can't just wish you good luck or something," said Bill.

Letitia chimed in, "Yeah, it bothers me, too. Like you just don't care."

"That's not it," Bertie exclaimed. "But that's what most people think." The therapist asked Bertie to elaborate.

"I know when I came here, everybody was already in their own little groups, and I understand it. No one really asked me to join them for anything. At the senior center I use to go to, people thought I was a snob or like you said, that I don't care. Really, I'm just afraid."

"Is that how you've felt in the group, too?" asked the therapist.

"Well, that first time I was here, the people here asked me a lot of questions. I know I didn't answer them very well. My answers were too short. And since that time, no one has asked me anything."

Bill asked her, "But what stops you from speaking up? Do we have to ask?"

"I have that same feeling that all of you know each other and have your friendships," Bertie answered. "It's like I would be cutting in . . . placing myself where I don't belong."

"When you gave short answers, I thought you didn't want to be questioned," said Letitia. "I thought you needed to take your time and that you would speak when you wanted to. In fact, I did want to hear from you. I thought maybe you were around my age and I noticed you have a big family like I do. I figured maybe we have some common ground."

"Yeah, I do have a big family with big problems. And maybe sometime later I can talk about all of the problems, but right now I need people to ask me questions."

"We can sure do that," said Bill, "but can you try asking a question once in a while, or saying something about what we've said? I can try to remember that you feel afraid, but it still would help if you would try to jump in here and there so we don't think you're stuck up."

Bertie tentatively responded, "I . . . I had a question for Esther. . . . I was wondering if there was anything that you've learned in here that will help you with your

(continued)

daughter's husband's temper. When you talked about that I listened real well because my husband ... he's dead ... well, it was sort of the same way with him. I hope you can go home and not cower like I did every time something made Jack unhappy."

Teaching note: Critical to *interpersonal learning* is affective engagement, and we see that ingredient in both Bill's annoyance at Bertie's lack of responsiveness and Bertie's distress over being misread. As the session proceeds, each party has an opportunity to learn a bit more about the other's position and the cues to which the other is responding. Bill and the rest of the group learn how difficult it is for Bertie to feel welcomed and how tentatively she approaches social situations. They also receive information from Bertie concerning how they might help her to be more forthcoming. Bertie learns how other members respond to her reticence. She also is given the responsibility of taking fledgling steps. This processing of one another's reactions provides a kind of cognitive scaffolding for the affect-laden events of the group. As Bertie learns more about the expectations she takes into interpersonal situations (for example, that others are already ensconced in relationships and have no need for her), she can modify them in an adaptive direction. This greater awareness of one's internal workings is *self-understanding*.

> **Therapist:** I wonder what you were feeling toward her when you did that?
> **Erin:** I guess I just really felt moved that she understood what I was saying.

Regardless of what may have been the content, the group is now focusing on a here-and-now issue: the affective tie between two members.

• As noted previously, the therapist can model for members how to give feedback.

SUMMARY AND CONCLUSIONS

This chapter explored the processes that are available in the therapy group to move the members toward their goals. Therapeutic factors have been studied by a number of group therapy scholars, including Corsini and Rosenberg (1955), Yalom (1995), Bloch and Crouch (1985), and others. In this chapter, we have used MacKenzie's (1990) system for cataloguing therapeutic factors specifically because this scheme works well to characterize the workings of, and the differences among, all of the types of groups we discuss in this text—therapy groups, self-help groups, and support groups. MacKenzie's system posits four categories of therapeutic factors. The supportive factors alleviate anxiety, build self-esteem, and help the member gain access to the psychological skills he or she possesses. These four factors are acceptance, instillation of hope, universality, altruism, and cohesion. The latter factor is an outcome of the presence of the former three working together. The self-revelation factors involve the sharing of emotional information and they include self-disclosure (cognitive) and catharsis (affective). The group is a prime place to experience learning from others, and the factors in the third category are modeling, vicarious learning, guidance, and education. The fourth category probably better than any other captures the unique features of group life, the intertwined factors of interpersonal learning and self-understanding. We saw that the therapeutic factors emphasized in any one group format depend upon the patient population, goals of the group, setting, time frame, and a host of other contextual variables. We also reviewed the means by which the therapist can activate the therapeutic factors.

 TEST YOURSELF

1. **Research suggests that**
   (a) negative feedback should precede positive feedback.
   (b) positive feedback should precede negative feedback.
   (c) all negative feedback is injurious.
   (d) negative feedback should always include interpretation of motives.

2. **The more lasting type of psychological change is**
   (a) imitation.
   (b) vicarious learning.
   (c) internalization.
   (d) identification.

3. **For a brief time, members of the group believe that everyone in the group was selected because of a difficulty with anxiety. The members' belief relates to the operation of the therapeutic factor of**
   (a) hope.
   (b) altruism.
   (c) vicarious learning.
   (d) universality.

4. **Hope, altruism, and acceptance are likely to be primary factors in which type of group?**
   (a) A six-session therapy group
   (b) A long-term, dynamically oriented group
   (c) A self-help group
   (d) A support group
   (e) a, c, and d only

5. **What are the characteristics of effective homework?**

(continued)

6. **Interpersonal learning requires some level of spontaneous interaction among members.** True or False?

7. **Research suggests that self-disclosures made as a group is approaching its end are more helpful than self-disclosures in the midlife of the group.** True or False?

8. **Self-disclosure is an affective sharing and catharsis a cognitive sharing.** True or False?

Answers: 1. b; 2. c; 3. d; 4. d; 5. A specific assignment; anticipation of obstacles and how to surmount them; and an opportunity to report back to the group in the next session; 6. True; 7. False; 8. False

Five

GROUP LEADERSHIP

Now that we have considered what therapeutic processes are available to move a group toward its goals, we will consider the role of the therapist who seeks to activate these processes. Certainly, therapists vary from one another tremendously in the type of group they are conducting, their training, their intellectual and personality features, and a variety of other factors. Yet we would contend that among effective therapists there is a core of attributes that characterize their bearing and activity in the group. For some therapists, the features we outline are ones they bring to the enterprise of group therapy. For others, the features must be carefully cultivated through the training. Although the roads vary, the destination must be the same in order for the therapist to facilitate a constructive experience for members.

At the same time, it is important to understand the differences among group therapists in how they define their roles and, in a related issue, how they intervene in the group. With a recognition of differences, the therapist can be aware of the vast number of alternatives available in group treatment, an awareness that will enable the therapist to make the best match of his or her activities to the requirements of a particular group. An acknowledgment and identification of differences is also necessary for the empirical investigation of what styles are associated with better outcomes. Finally, a delineation of differences is useful in referring an individual to group treatment so that the characteristics and needs of the client can be matched with the nature of the group, including the therapist's style of conducting the group.

COMMONALITIES AMONG THERAPISTS

Using both the research and the clinical literature, we have identified core characteristics of effective leadership of a therapy group. For those who would like to begin doing group work or who have been assigned the task of running a group, we encourage a candid self-evaluation of these factors. Through such an evaluation, the individual can make a more informed decision about whether to embark on this project, and he or she can also identify personal work that should be accomplished in preparation for it.

Attitudes and Styles of Relating of Successful Therapists

When a therapist possesses the qualities described in the following sections, a group is catalyzed in its work.

Belief in Group Therapy as a Legitimate and Effective Treatment

A review of the outcome literature has taught us that belief in a particular treatment or modality is more likely to ensure its success with clients (see Chapter 7). It is difficult to run an effective treatment group if the enthusiasm and belief in its legitimacy as an effective treatment are not present. Yet each year when we begin our group classes and seminars and canvass students and trainees, most of whom have elected to take the class, on their attitudes and preconceptions, they almost unanimously express a preference for individual treatment over group treatment. Such a preference is likely to allow clients to maintain their resistance to joining or using group therapy to the fullest extent. For example, if in the course of an interview with a client for a group the client expresses a lack of interest because he or she feels that group is a second-rate treatment compared to individual therapy, this bias is likely to go on unexplored if the therapist maintains the same attitude. Clearly the therapist must regard group therapy to be of value in order to run a group effectively. The therapist need not have a particular belief in terms of its standing relative to other modalities. However, the therapist's awareness of whatever bias he or she has will enable its modification if the therapist acquires data at odds with it. A careful survey of the many possible beliefs and biases that a therapist maintains about the value of group therapy will enable the therapist to then be more aware of these same ideas and attitudes held by the client. Rather than taking them at face value, the therapist can then explore them more fully.

Optimism

Related to the belief in the effectiveness in group treatment is the therapist's overall optimistic attitude about the ability of the group to achieve the goals that individual members establish. The therapist's initial optimism activates one of the therapeutic factors that Yalom (1995) has found to be most essential to the effectiveness of group: the instillation of hope in clients, hope that help and amelioration of pain and suffering are possible. As the group progresses, the therapist's continued optimism fortifies group members' internal strength to handle their negative emotions and therapeutic setbacks without plummeting into despair.

CAUTION

Groups in which the therapist does not convey caring do not thrive.

Capacity for Empathy and Caring

Rogers (1957) and later Truax and Carkhuff (1967) discussed the importance of empathy, unconditional positive regard, and genuineness as being essential for the success of all therapies. Lieberman, Yalom, and Miles (1973) in their seminal work with encounter groups found that one of the most important factors that directly correlated with the successful group experience was members' perceptions of the therapist as being genuinely kind and concerned. A warm and caring therapist provides a role model for the group members in their interactions toward each other. Compassion on the therapist's part helps create a safe environment in the group and is the first step in the establishment of trust among members necessary for group work. Although other attributes that promote effective leadership functioning can be learned or improved upon as the group progresses, the absence of this characteristic is likely to doom the group experience from the beginning. This is not a behavior that is easily faked. This characteristic is so essential to successful group therapy that it is suggested that therapists unable to project this trait should consider delaying conducting groups until they are able to understand in greater detail the origins of their interpersonal stance and develop a plan for how they might develop this capacity.

Awareness of the Self

In addition to biases about the group modality, and knowledge of one's internal workings, an understanding of one's interpersonal functioning is important in running a group. Unlike individual therapy, which involves a dyadic relationship, group therapy involves multiperson relationships that are experienced in the here and now. Good interpersonal skills are helpful but not sufficient. An honest assessment of their interpersonal strengths and weaknesses will enable therapists to anticipate the kinds of groups in which they might function most effectively and where they might have more difficulties and require help or supervision. For individuals desiring to achieve competency in group work some experience of therapy as a patient, especially group therapy, is recommended. Further, an evaluation of his or her functioning, relationships, and roles in all sorts of groups—friendships, classes, committees, team meetings, and family of origin—will help the therapist garner an accurate portrait of his or her interpersonal functioning. Such knowledge will help the therapist anticipate his or her functioning as a leader in a group therapy situation (see Putting It into Practice below).

Ability to Deal with Narcissism and Shame

A certain amount of healthy narcissism, which aids in the regulation of self-esteem, is necessary and even desirable for successful functioning as a leader. Therapists who learn to care for their personal needs as well as remaining attuned to those of their clients model a healthy respect for the self. When training begins, there usually is a substantial gap between the therapist's idealized and real selves. With the accrual of experience and supervision, the grandiose professional ideal (desiring to be all knowing, all powerful, and all loving) is replaced by more realistic professional goals and a more accurate assessment of one's clinical acumen. The therapist's continued expectation of unrealistic control, power, and benevolence, however, can interfere considerably with the functioning of the group and with clients' growth and achievement of goals. In the Lieberman et al. (1973) study mentioned earlier, casualties related to the group experience were carefully analyzed. A disproportionate number of them came from a subset of the therapists. Each of these casualties reported the experience of being attacked by the leader. These leaders were charismatic but confrontational: They appeared to be supportive when members made progress but became derogatory when members failed to do so.

When clients do not progress as the therapist has envisioned, it is potentially injurious to the therapist's self-esteem, as the therapist must reflect upon his or her own contribution to the lack of progress. Criticism, devaluation, and ridicule

Putting It Into Practice

Therapist Style and Venue

A soft-spoken therapist who successfully ran a high-functioning outpatient group became disheartened when she attempted to conduct inpatient groups. Observation of her functioning as a member of the inpatient team mirrored her presentation in the inpatient group. She was silent both as a team member and as a therapist. The silence abetted the team in pushing inappropriate referrals into the group. The group was composed of members who were unable to contain their feelings. Their strong affective displays in the midst of the therapist's passivity made it an unsafe environment in which members could not establish the trust necessary for them to pursue their goals. The therapist began to question whether this was an optimal venue for her group work.

Teaching note: Therapeutic venues make different demands upon the therapist's personality and style of leadership.

by members are also potential as-
saults to the therapist's sense of competence and efficacy. Possible responses of therapists who struggle
with narcissism include encouraging
members to idealize them, being excessively critical or confrontative,

CAUTION

The manifestations of the therapist's
unresolved narcissistic issues are varied; all should be explored because
they limit the therapist's effectiveness.

withdrawing emotionally, discouraging negative feedback toward them, fostering
early negative feedback toward other group members, boasting about personal
accomplishments, and preferring to provide feedback rather than supporting
members' contributions to each other (Horowitz, 2000).

Therapist narcissism often plays a significant role in whether the therapist can
acknowledge that he or she is wrong or fallible. All challenges to the therapist's
narcissism have in common the tendency to beget shame, an affect state that entails a view of the self as worthless and inadequate (Weber & Gans, 2003).

Attempting to avoid both narcissistic injuries and shame is merely human, yet
an acknowledgment and acceptance of both one's narcissism and one's fallibility
are first steps in keeping these tendencies in check. Billow (2001) suggests acknowledging the contributions of both individual clients and the group, with a
statement such as, "I didn't see that quality in our relationship, but I do now,
thanks to our group" (p. 237). Weber and Gans (2003) note that shame can be
mitigated by the therapist's recognizing that he or she is bound to make mistakes,
that learning about oneself is part and parcel of the group process, and that peer
supervision provides a holding environment for all of the difficult affects therapists experience so the therapist in turn can create a holding environment for
group members.

Capacity to Be Aware of Multiple Levels of Interaction

Group therapy is unique in that multiple levels of interaction take place at any
given moment, as well as numerous dynamics occuring within levels (see Chapter 2). The talent to track these levels and dynamics at the same time is both a gift
and a skill to be cultivated. The choice of which level toward which to direct an
intervention, and when and how to direct it, is the essence of effective leadership
(Pollack & Slan, 1995). However, making that decision can be an overwhelming
task, even to an experienced clinician. In addition to a solid grounding in theory,
which informs intervention, group leadership requires flexibility, spontaneity,
creativity, and tolerance for ambiguity and its accompanying tension, as well as
the fortitude to resist trying to control the interaction. Developing a comfort with
complexity and the multiple levels of possible understanding and intervention is

a lifelong effort for most enthusiastic and devoted therapists and is the subject of most of this chapter.

Ability to Manage Fear and Anxiety

In a discussion on preparation for leaders, Lonergan (1982) states, "I have never met a group leader, new or experienced, who was not nervous before starting a new group" (p. 78). Indeed, there are many aspects of group therapy that can create anxiety in the therapist. Exposure of the self; being ganged up on by a group of angry clients; members' needs for power, control, and dominance; long silences; dealing with clients who monopolize; public humiliation and criticism; rejection—these are just a few of the common scenarios that group therapists dread. Experience helps to attenuate some of these fears and exacerbate others, as some of these fears may become reality. Self-reflection is necessary to begin the process of managing these fears. Courageous acknowledgment and acceptance of needs (for omnipotence and dominance, power and control), desires (for acceptance), and fears (of aggression and rejection) further the goal of managing these anxieties. These, too, require lifelong monitoring and can often be most effectively managed by personal therapy and supervision.

Creating a Therapeutic Frame

We will now consider those activities pursued by all group therapists that require considerable training in the use of this modality. The first is the creation and maintenance of an effective therapeutic frame. Specifically, group therapists must form an adequate structure in which the group can thrive; apply that consistent structure to the setting; draw and maintain the group boundaries; and foster an emotionally safe environment in which members can begin to trust the therapist and each other.

Group Structure

The single most important task of the leader prior to beginning group meetings is to create an adequate structure in which the group work can take place. This includes formulating the purpose and function of the particular group, providing an appropriate space in time and place, deciding upon group composition (size, gender, and type of client), selecting clients for membership, preparing potential members for the group experience, and aiding participants in forming appropriate individual goals (see Chapter 3).

Once the group begins to meet, the consistent application and reinforcement of the structure becomes a task essential to the successful functioning of the group. Paramount in completion of this task is the therapist's own reliability.

Much like a good parent, the therapist must be a dependable presence. When alert and on time, he or she is an exemplar of appropriate, responsible group behavior. Therapist adherence to group rules and maintenance of the group contract (as previously articulated in the preparation session) models what is necessary for members to achieve their goals. Deviation from the contract or rules by the therapist is likely to lead to confusion and possible acting out on the part of group members.

Norms for effective group interaction develop early in a group's life and are often difficult to modify later. The leader is involved in shaping these norms directly or indirectly. Some therapists harbor the naive view that they are not influencing the development of norms unless they verbally comment on a particular behavior. On the contrary, both subtle and obvious social reinforcements are easily perceived by group members. For example, the therapist's leaning forward when members talk about a particular feeling state, such as anger, or the therapist's unresponsiveness when a member comes into the group late sends a message about what behaviors are acceptable or unacceptable.

Boundary Maintenance

Several aspects of boundary maintenance are essential to creating a positive group environment that allows the furtherance of individual and group goals. The external boundaries include membership boundaries, time boundaries, unhealthy alliances both inside and outside the group, and informational boundaries. Internal boundaries of importance include the boundary between the therapist and group members. The therapist alone is responsible for the creation and maintenance of the membership boundaries. He or she alone chooses appropriate members for the group, invites them to join, and ultimately encourages their continued attendance. Despite the leader's best efforts at screening, even experienced leaders occasionally admit a member who can neither benefit from the group nor assist others in doing so. Helping that member to leave a therapeutic involvement that is not beneficial to him or her and find other means to address his or her needs is an important ethical responsibility.

Likewise, respect for the temporal boundary of the group is important. Beginning and ending on time helps to draw an unambiguous boundary around the session. Agazarian makes this boundary explicit as she articulates the idea that "we are crossing a time boundary." A clear spatial demarcation often helps members to recognize group time. This demarcation might be concretized by allowing entrance into a separate group room at the appointed time rather than allowing members to enter in their own time. Some therapists allow members to collect in the group room up to 15 minutes prior to the commencement of group but delineate the time boundary by shutting the door at the appointed time. A leader who is not settled in his or her seat at the appointed time provides a confusing message about temporal parameters and sets the stage for members' use of tardiness as a means of expressing various reactions (see Putting It into Practice below). Therapists who violate the temporal boundaries they establish should seek to discover the reasons (both obvious and subtle) for such violations. For example, is the therapist avoiding some feeling or impulse that might be stimulated by the group? Might the temporal violation be a way of punishing members for some perceived transgression? Often, until the therapist understands such issues, violations continue and the group fails to progress.

Informational boundaries refer to the safeguarding of material that both group members and therapists collect in the course of their interactions with each other in the group and in the pregroup exchanges, as well as during contact with other professionals involved in members' care. The leader's ability to manage the informational boundary influences the degree to which members can begin to trust other participants. As part of the group contract leaders must specify the extent to which the group proceedings are confidential, including the boundary of their own communications. Therapists must address questions such as the following: Does the therapist keep confidential individual meetings that group members request and knowledge acquired from individual sessions? Does the

Putting It Into Practice

Setting Temporal Boundaries

One hospital-based therapist began an outpatient group 10 minutes late for the first two sessions. Even though she acknowledged her tardiness to the group and explained that it had been due to unforseen circumstances that arose from her other responsibilities at the hospital, group members thereafter would wander in late. Initially, she did not address their lateness. However, after six sessions, fashionably late attendance appeared to be more the norm than punctuality. She attempted an exploration of the meaning. Tardy members of the group defended their lateness by stating that it could not be helped: Buses were late, and other aspects of their lives interfered with strict adherence to the time boundaries of the group. Although there was certainly some truth to their explanations, just as there was a real reason for the therapist's lateness, this unfortunate and inauspicious beginning put the therapist at a considerable disadvantage in reinforcing the group norm of punctuality and the importance of group as a priority.

Teaching note: This example illustrates both the importance of the norms the therapist establishes in the beginning of the group and the importance of the therapist's owning up to a violation of the group rules.

leader share group proceedings with outside individual therapists? Are there any other limits of confidentiality, such as when danger to self, other, or child is present? Therapists must give considerable thought to the informational boundaries they wish to establish and elicit prospective members' commitment to honoring these boundaries before they enter the group.

Maintaining clear boundaries between members and between therapist and member are equally important tasks for the leader. For a person to be a productive and comfortable member of society (and a group), he or she needs to respect the distinction between individuals but be open to learning and exchange from others. Self boundaries, if too loose, lead to loss of self and psychotic dissolution, but those that are too restricted do not allow for the benefits of a give-and-take relationship. An acceptable range allows for growing and learning as well as protection from psychological harm. The leader must be aware of and comfortable with the boundary between him- or herself and other people. Leaders must be role models for this self-awareness and be role models for the acknowledgment and acceptance of others who may be different from them. In addition, the therapist must be keenly aware of the ways in which the roles of leader and member are different. The therapist does not have the luxury of trying to resolve his or her issues in a group in which he or she agrees to take on the leadership function. Empathic attunement is essential, but the therapist is not one of the boys. To some extent the group's setting, goals, composition, and theoretical orientation will dictate therapist disclosures and transparency. However, a leader who shares too many personal anxieties or who regularly participates in the personal exchange of information will be less likely to be seen as an authority figure for transferential purposes, will create anxiety about safety, and will place an unnecessary burden on members. On the other hand, a therapist who is completely undisclosing, humorless, and noncommittal will encourage group members to develop norms of guardedness.

In summary, the leader must monitor informational, time, and membership boundaries in order to preserve the group framework and promote the achievement of the group goals. Above all else, in order to maintain adequate internal and external boundaries, a therapist must be extremely dependable, consistent, and nondefensive in acknowledging when the framework that he or she has established has been shaken in major or minor ways. As Rutan and Stone (2001) assert, "This task may be deferred but never ignored" (p. 182).

Creation of a Safe Environment

The third leader task related to providing an adequate framework is the creation of an emotionally safe environment in which members can begin to trust the therapist and each other. A safe haven is created when the therapist manages the boundaries, provides the appropriate structure for the group, and reinforces such group rules as a ban on physical violence or a method for indicating that a member does not wish for further input or discussion on a personal matter. Creation of an adequate framework also involves achieving a balance between nonjudgmental acceptance of each member and a dissatisfaction with the problem areas that precipitated referral to the group. This is more difficult to achieve in a group environment than in individual therapy, because each member is likely to have a somewhat different level of narcissistic sensitivity. Although application of different standards among individual therapy clients will generally be undetected by clients, in a group it will be recognized and will evoke a variety of reactions in members, including envy, anxiety, and anger. Group safety also involves members' achieving a balance between interpersonal honesty and spontaneity, and appropriate restraint. When the therapist models behaviors that combine these elements, members follow suit and intuitively adjust their behaviors toward each member based on their perceptions of his or her fragility or robustness.

Providing a safe environment also means striking the appropriate balance between frustrating and gratifying members. Therapists frustrate and gratify group members for good reasons. Therapists gratify members because members come to the group with legitimate needs that only the therapist can fill. For example, a member's need to receive acceptance rather than disapproval from a figure of authority is one that the therapist routinely fills in the group. Members' need for safety is another legitimate need. Needs that therapists typically gratify are those whose fulfillment leads the member closer to the goal he or she established upon entering the group. Therapists may frustrate members when the gratification of a need would hinder the member's work in the group. For example, if the goal is for members to become more self-sufficient in solving problems and the therapist provides solutions to every problem, then the goal of the group will be compromised. Furthermore, the psychological experience of frustration itself can be seen as having a catalyzing effect on members' growth. For example, frustration can increase a member's motivation to address a problem. Because frustration is endemic to living, when frustrated in the group, the member displays his or her customary way of responding to this psychological challenge, a way that may hinder the member's adaptation outside the group. Having recognized a maladaptive response to frustration, the member can experiment within the sessions on the development of a new, more serviceable response.

Providing the appropriate level of frustration or gratification requires considerable discernment on the part of the therapist and a tolerance for occupying various positions on the frustration-gratification continuum. Some therapists, depending on their backgrounds and personalities, may have difficulty either gratifying or frustrating a particular need of members. For example, some therapists experience their failure to answer a direct question as a rejection of members. By recognizing the meaning the therapist attributes to certain types of gratifications and frustrations, the therapist achieves greater freedom in basing a decision to gratify or frustrate in a given moment on what would serve the member's long-term goal.

Cognitive Framing

All group therapists must help members to find meaning in their group experiences. Often they do so by conducting their groups along the lines of a particular theoretical orientation. As noted in Chapter 2, theories provide a framework in which to organize social and affective experience. Each supplies a world view for understanding problems and a model that encompasses a series of interventions that attempt to ameliorate the difficulty. In their seminal study of encounter groups, Lieberman et al. (1973) found that those groups conducted by leaders who emphasized meaning attribution had more successful outcomes than leaders who did not. Members' finding meaning in their experiences and behavior, particularly the problem behaviors, is accomplished when the therapist regularly and consistently aids members in framing their experiences into a coherent world view.

Cognitive framing can be further broken down into a number of specific methods. These techniques cut across the various orientations and include education, reflection, clarification, confrontation, and interpretation.

Education

The theoretical orientation and its accompanying model for intervention provide the therapist with a system of meaning. This system of meaning identifies the types of events that members should pay attention to and indicates how events are related to each other. For some leaders this remains the same no matter what the group composition or setting is. For other leaders, the system of meaning is specifically chosen for the identified group. The leader is not forced to choose a single framework. For example, a therapist utilizing an interpersonal framework might occasionally use a role play to help mem-

CAUTION

If the leader does not provide members with a consistent cognitive frame, the group is likely to falter in its efforts for individual members to achieve their goals.

bers prepare for interactions outside the group. However, to the extent that the framework is clear and consistent and can readily be taught to the participants, it will be easier for other members to become partners in the teaching and implementing of the framework. Moreover, switching systems without warning—or even with warning—is likely to impede members in their learning about how to organize their reactions.

The leader must educate the members about what aspects of their reactions they should be focused upon—thoughts, feelings, or behavior. Therapists teach the relationship between these aspects of their reactions. For example, within the cognitive framework, members learn that automatic thoughts lead to feelings, whereas within the psychoanalytic system participants learn that their actions are often motivated by elements outside their awareness. The leader teaches members how to focus upon these reactions. In social skills training, members are encouraged to review, role play, and practice a specific set of behaviors in order to improve their interpersonal skills.

The methods for educating members about the system of meaning vary. Some leaders provide minilectures within the group on various aspects of the system of meaning, such as a brief lecture that includes various notions about the meaning of dreams and their use within therapy. At the less directive end of the continuum, the leader can educate members about the cognitive framework by showing attention to and interest in specific remarks or comments made by a group member. For example, in the interpersonal framework, members are encouraged to share their unspoken reactions to each other. In the cognitive-behavioral framework, members are directed to identify the fleeting thought that occurred prior to a feeling of being overwhelmed.

Reflection

All successful leaders, regardless of their affinity with a particular cognitive framing, are capable of empathic attunement and the articulation of that sensitive connection to the other. It is the ability to feel what another feels and then simply acknowledge, verbally or nonverbally, the member's feeling state. A therapist's saying "I see that you are hurting today" is a common example. In addition to empathic sensitivity, reflection may also involve putting into words what a member might previously have experienced but could not articulate. Reflection entails identifying and labeling various aspects of the members' reactions: "Your face is flushed and you describe feeling unable to concentrate when you meet a new person; it sounds like you are anxious." Note that this reflection pointed to the evidence for a feeling and then named it. As members emulate the therapist in reflecting on their own and others' experiences, the group becomes a more coherent and thereby a safer environment.

Clarifications

Clarifications are questions or statements that help individuals further understand the connection between the cognitive framework that they embrace and their reactions. Clarifications help the individual differentiate and crystallize that understanding of the distinction between two thoughts, feelings, or behaviors. Examples of clarifications are "Is it a thought or is it a feeling?"; "Were you feeling angry, or were you feeling afraid?"; "Is that a distorted cognition, or does that represent reality?"; and "In learning the social skill of greeting another, do you look at the individual first, or do you wait until after you have spoken?" Clarifications also assist in identifying additional elements of the system of meaning (e.g., "What was the thought that occurred just before your feeling of utter helplessness?").

Confrontation

Leaders encourage members to challenge their views of themselves. Confrontation involves letting members know they need to recognize, explore, or change despite not wanting to do so. Effective leaders realize that confrontation of members must be done with care and delicacy, for several reasons. First of all, this type of intervention can cause extreme anxiety in the member being confronted. Second, it can encourage the scapegoating of the particular member. Third, it can create anxiety in members who are not the immediate target of the intervention in that they may recognize that they, too, could be confronted. With particular populations, confrontations must be administered with even greater caution. The lower the functioning of the individual members, the more detrimental confrontation can be in terms of self-perception. Confrontations that are poorly timed, harshly stated, or too frequent can be humiliating and result in a decrease in self-esteem for individuals, both in their own eyes and in their views of what others think of them. Some orientations, such as social skills training, are not in favor of confrontation. Instead the leaders encourage individuals to focus upon their successes and place only minor emphasis on what needs improvement.

Interpretation

Interpretation involves bringing into awareness thoughts, feelings, or impulses that the member may not have previously recognized. Making an interpretation presumes that there has previously been a discovery of a pattern of behavior. Interpretations can make a significant contribution in rendering experiences meaningful because they help members see that those behaviors and reactions that seem irrational or bizarre are understandable and coherent when they are related to hidden psychological elements. Nonetheless, interpretations can increase members' anxiety because they entail bringing into awareness elements that members may find objectionable. Therefore, interpretations should be approached with care: They are often reserved for relatively mature groups and for groups with healthier members.

Not every model of treatment makes use of interpretations. For instance, underlying motivations are generally not focused upon in social skills training or in interpersonal problem solving. Of all the frameworks, the psychoanalytic approach makes perhaps the most frequent use of this technique. Within this framework, conflicting behavior is linked to underlying motivations. In cognitive-behavioral group therapy, interpretations are more superficially defined; they involve preconscious activity and link automatic thought to the resulting affects.

In summary, therapists have a variety of tools at their disposal to help members find meaning in their group experiences. What is crucial is not how meaning is achieved but that it be achieved.

Putting the Leadership Structure to Good Use

There are two leadership structures commonly used in group therapy: solo therapy and cotherapy. Each format has strengths and challenges, the awareness of which permits the therapist to use each format to its best advantage. No one format has been empirically demonstrated to be better than the other (McRoberts, Burlingame, & Hoag, 1998), although in particular clinical contexts one format may be preferable.

In solo therapy, one therapist single-handedly conducts the group. This format has the advantages of clarity and simplicity. *Clarity* occurs in several ways. First, when one therapist conducts the group, that one therapist is responsible for all that occurs or does not occur in the group session. There is no possibility of diffusion of responsibility. Second, members' reactions to the therapist often emerge more clearly in the solo therapy situation. When members have all of their dependency longings tied up with a single figure, those longings are likely to be felt in a more acute way than when they are distributed. Suppose member A asks the therapist for advice about a difficult situation and the therapist demurs. The member cannot, as in the cotherapy arrangement, hold out hope that another figure of authority will be more responsive. Furthermore, expressing negative reactions is likely to be less intimidating when those reactions are directed toward a single figure rather than a cotherapy team. Because member reactions are often stronger toward a single therapist and therapist reactions are a response to member reactions, therapist reactions are often stronger in the solo therapy format. We will see how therapist reactions can often be used in order to learn more about the group in the next section.

Simplicity, too, is multifaceted. The simplicity of the solo therapy situation is that the therapy need not partake of the complex negotiation process that occurs in the formative stage of any cotherapy team. The solo therapist can design the group taking into account only his or her perspective. The advantages of solo therapy are summarized in Rapid Reference 5.1.

Cotherapy also has a unique set of benefits (see Rapid Reference 5.2). Many of the benefits can be seen as aspects of a *richness* factor. One aspect is the duality of perspectives that each

Rapid Reference 5.1

Advantages of Solo Therapy

Clarity
- Lack of diffusion of responsibility
- Greater manifestation of member reactions toward the therapist
- Greater manifestation of therapist reactions toward members

Simplicity
- Ease of establishing features of group design
- Freedom from having to manage the relationship
- Efficiency

Rapid Reference 5.2

Advantages of Cotherapy

Richness
- Duality of perspectives
- Greater range of interpersonal stimuli offered to members
- Greater opportunity for therapists to obtain feedback and process reactions

Continuity
- Fewer interruptions of the group due to such events as therapist vacations and illness
- Shared responsibility for recruiting new group members

Safety
- Greater security in expressing anger toward one therapist due to the availability of the other

therapist offers. Each cotherapist by virtue of his or her unique personality, background, and training can see dimensions of the group the other cotherapist cannot. For example, one therapist may have a special attunement to dependency issues, while another may be better able to detect the early manifestations of authority issues. As cotherapists blend their perspectives, they achieve a much more comprehensive view of all of the events that occur in a session. Sometimes cotherapists access these different dimensions through their reactions to occurrences in the group. Putting It into Practice (below) illustrates how two therapists' distinctive reactions each illuminated different dimensions of members' experiences in the group.

The variety of the stimuli offered to members is another facet of richness. Each cotherapist will differ from the other physically, behaviorally, and often demographically. These differences will evoke different reactions in the group members. If, for instance, one therapist is considerably older than the other, members may respond to the more senior member as an authority figure and the more junior member as a peer. The junior cotherapist may elicit more competi-

Putting It Into Practice

Cotherapy Vignette: Two Points of View

Two psychiatry residents, Fatima and Drake, had been leading an outpatient group with a fairly stable membership for 9 months. They had only 2 more months of residency, after which time the group would come to an end. After one particular session, Fatima was particularly annoyed with Drake, saying that he had been too responsive to Richard, a group member who was about the same age as Drake. Drake initially contended that Fatima was imagining a differential response, but she persisted in her belief.

Drake finally admitted that he had recently noticed that he and Richard were alike in certain ways, although it had not struck him earlier. He did not see himself as pairing off with Richard, but in the last session it had occurred to him that there were several other members who were responding intensely to one other member and minimally to anyone else. This recognition led the therapists to ponder why, at this time, members would form themselves into dyads.

Fatima, who had not paired off, had noted that she was feeling sad in the sessions. She puzzled over whether she saw herself as being left out. She quipped, "You know, it's like the end of the dance and you're alone." When she made mention of the end, both cotherapists recognized that in fact it might have been the impending ending that was the stimulus for both of their reactions in the group. Fatima felt sadness but dissociated it from the upcoming loss. Drake, like others, shielded himself from his reactions by focusing on the newness of his connection with the group member. Possessing these insights, both cotherapists were able to better assist members with the ending of the group.

tive responses; the senior cotherapist may evoke disappointment or anger in relation to frustration of longings for nurturance. When cotherapists differ from one another in gender, the idea of the group as a family is evoked and transferences to maternal and paternal figures are stimulated.

A third aspect of richness is the opportunities it provides members to observe the interactions between the cotherapists. As Roller and Nelson (1993) noted, "Patients in group therapy can learn as they watch their cotherapists[,] equal in power and self-esteem, model how to behave in a relationship" (p. 307). Finally, cotherapy provides many opportunities for members to understand their own reactions to the group. Cotherapists can share their observations of how the other member of the dyad is responding in the group and explore with one another the bases of these responses (again, see the previous Putting It into Practice).

Another benefit of cotherapy is its capacity to safeguard the *continuity* of the group. The group can continue to meet even when one of the therapists is unavailable. This continuity nurtures group cohesion, allows for the uninterrupted pursuit of whatever themes and interpersonal issues have become established in the group, and permits the group to explore within the here and now their reactions to the absence of the therapist. The presence of a cotherapist can be especially helpful when one therapist has an emergency.

Safety is a third benefit. In a cotherapy format, members enjoy the knowledge that if they were to disappoint, anger, or in any other way negatively influence their relationship with one therapist, the other therapist would remain available. This safety promotes risk taking in the group, particularly with respect to the full range of reactions members have toward therapists.

The challenges of solo therapy and cotherapy correspond to the strengths of the alternate format. In solo therapy, the therapist shoulders all of the responsibility not only for performing the full array of tasks associated with conducting a group but also for recognizing, understanding, and constructively using reactions that are stimulated during the course of the sessions. Because no one practitioner's perspective is comprehensive, it benefits the solo therapist to have some form of supervision wherein other viewpoints can be considered. Another challenge of solo therapy is in managing the intensity of member reactions to the therapist. For some types of group members, extremely strong reactions to a given therapist may lead to the client's disorganization. Some members may benefit from being in concurrent therapy (see Chapter 3), in which they participate in individual therapy with one therapist and group therapy with another. Such an arrangement can diffuse transference reactions so that their level of intensity is tolerable to the group member. Finally, solo therapists must exercise particular

CAUTION

Solo therapists should
- use supervision to achieve a more comprehensive view of the group, and
- fulfill their obligation to safeguard the group by developing an emergency plan for an unexpected extended absence.

CAUTION

Unaddressed conflicts between cotherapists may be played out within the group to the detriment of the group members. Therefore, cotherapists should
- make sure they reach agreement about such important matters as goals and therapeutic processes before the group begins, and
- allot processing time before and after the group meets.

care to plan for their group should any emergency requiring a long-term or permanent absence befall them.

Cotherapists, on the other hand, must agree on goals, methods, levels of self-disclosure, and numerous other issues concerning the group and make a great investment in their own relationship. To the extent that unaddressed conflicts exist between the members of the cotherapy team, the risk exists that the conflicts will be played out in the group to the detriment of the members. Some writers claim that groups cannot advance any further than the developmental level of the cotherapy relationship (Beck, Dugo, Eng, & Lewis, 1986). Cotherapy places great demands upon the therapists for negotiating with one another on the establishment of the group, processing the group session, and addressing conflicts in their relationship with one another. The best friend to the cotherapy team is time for these activities. Also beneficial is a consistent structure for the types of explorations that are necessary. Cotherapists, too, should have a readiness to enter into supervision when they are not able to resolve differences in a way that forwards their work as a team. According to Weinstein (1971), the three characteristics that are important for the success of a cotherapy relationship are cotherapists' trust in one another, acceptance of one another's personality characteristics, and equivalence in terms of therapeutic ability (unless the relationship is one that is explicitly a training situation). These are areas that should be explored before individuals decide to commit to one another as cotherapists.

Therapist Self-Monitoring

All group therapists benefit from self-awareness as they are conducting the therapy group. Self-awareness is crucial for two reasons. The first reason is that whatever reactions the therapist has that escape his or her awareness could be acted out in the group. In some cases, these reactions could be the consequence of the therapist's own conflicts. For example, Dr. Palt may become angry when members express dependency wishes in relation to him because their manifestations stimulate his own dependency urges, which he finds intolerable. This type of therapist reaction has been identified as *subjective countertransference* (Ormont, 1991) in that it is determined by the particular psychology of the person experiencing the countertransference, in this case Dr. Palt. In other words, Dr. Palt's reaction has more to do with his own psychodynamics than with this group. When Freud introduced the notion of countertransference, it was this type of countertransference that he had in mind. On the other hand, Dr. Palt may become angry because of the group's passive-aggressive way of handling dependency impulses: When he tries to help, members reject his efforts. This reaction is typical of how many if not most therapists would respond. This reaction is labeled *objective countertransference* in that it pertains more to the object or entities evoking the response, in this case the group members (Ormont, 1991).

These two types of countertransference call for different responses on the part of the group therapist. Subjective countertransference should lead to exploration, particularly in personal therapy (either group or individual). For example, it could be very helpful to Dr. Palt to understand why he is intolerant of his own dependency wishes. On the other hand, objective countertransference leads to a full exploration of the group itself, by no means excluding the therapist, but seeing the therapist as pointing to the group dynamics. In other words, the group therapist uses objective countertransference as a clue to hidden layers of group life.

By examining the different types of objective countertransference, the therapist can learn even more about his or her group. Racker (1972) points out that the therapist is always poised to identify with the group members—that is, to experience as a part of him- or herself some aspect of members' psychological experience. Racker goes on to distinguish between concordant and complementary identifications. *Concordant identifications* occur when the group therapist experiences an aspect of another's way of representing the self. For example, if the therapist achieves empathy for a member's intense self-dislike, this would be a concordant identification. A *complementary identification* is when the group therapist experiences an aspect of another's way of representing others. If the therapist were to feel disdainful in the way a member thinks about her mother as being disdainful, this would be a complementary identification. Both types of identification are important because they point to different dimensions of members' internal lives that otherwise might not be accessible to the therapist. In the following Putting It into Practice we see how a cotherapy team's exploration of a

Putting It Into Practice

Cotherapy Vignette: Identification

Letitia and Marge were two social work practicum students who were leading a therapy group at a community mental health center. The purpose of this 16-session psychodynamically oriented group was to help members identify and address relationship difficulties. Because all members had been given a very elaborate preparation for the group, in which they not only had goals and relevant processes identified but also had an opportunity to practice using the processes, the therapists had intended to be relatively nondirective in the first session. For the first 45 minutes, the therapists adhered to the plan. However, as the session progressed through the next 45 minutes, Marge noticed that she was becoming completely passive and inactive while Letitia was becoming both more directive and more dramatic in her way of speaking to the group. Marge thought, "She seems to want to call attention to herself and let them know that she's going to be the one who is important in here."

Letitia and Marge went into supervision feeling somewhat annoyed at one another. Each privately doubted that the cotherapy arrangement would work. The supervisor quickly homed in on the fact that as the session went on, the therapists became increasingly different in their behaviors in the group. She wanted to know what each therapist had been feeling. Marge said that in the early part of the session she experienced herself as incompetent. She sensed that members were floundering, yet she had no idea how to help them. Letitia also felt that the group was drowning in a sea of uncertainty, and she feared that no one would return. But she also had confidence that if she directed them with a strong hand, they would be reassured and would continue to attend. Each therapist found the other to be acting in a way that was at odds with the group's needs: Letitia felt that Marge's total passivity required her to be more active than she wished to be, and Marge felt that there were no openings for her because Letitia was all-present in the session.

The supervisor pointed out that both Letitia and Marge were responding to the same behaviors of group members and both had anxiety in relation to a perception of the group's floundering. With exploration, both supervisor and cotherapists realized that each member of the cotherapy team was giving expression to some aspect of the member's own experience. Marge was experiencing and manifesting the helplessness that each member felt, their representations of themselves as unable to pursue a course of action that would be consonant with the goals they established in joining the group. By taking on this part of members' views of themselves and the discomfort associated with this view, she provided a containment function. Letitia became that figure for whom the members longed, the leader on whom they could depend to relieve them of the anxiety that group membership brought. Recognizing how the group dynamics gave rise to their experiences and behaviors during the group session, the cotherapists were able to reestablish their alliance and go into the next session with a greater understanding of their group.

Teaching note: The cotherapists were aided in their work as leaders through the exploration of their *objective countertransference,* their reactions that are not idiosyncratic to themselves but are precipitated largely by the dynamics of the group and hence are more universal (Ormont, 1991). The responses of Letitia and Marge illustrate the differences between concordant and complementary identifications. Both therapists were identifying with aspects of the members' experiences, albeit different aspects. Marge, identifying with members' self-representation at that moment in group life, formed a *concordant representation*. Letitia, identifying with members' object representations (or, in this case, idealized object representations), formed a *complementary identification*. Why did one therapist form a concordant identification and the other a complementary identification? The answer to this question may lie in their *subjective countertransference*, those aspects that are unique to them. Whereas in supervision the exploration of objective countertransference is very useful, in their own private therapies the investigation of subjective countertransference could contribute immeasurably to their personal and professional growth.

concordant identification and complementary identification within supervision enabled the team to understand the underpinnings of members' behaviors at one point in the group's life. However, these identifications, like all countertransference responses, are helpful only when the therapist summons the level of self-reflection that enables these responses to be identified and then understood in the light of group members' behaviors. When therapists fail to grapple with these countertransference responses, they are at risk for acting upon them in a way that could be detrimental to the group's work. If Dr. Palt from our earlier example were to reject members for their expression of their dependency wishes rather than understanding his inclination to reject, then members would internalize the belief that dependency wishes are unacceptable, at least within the forum of the group.

Historically, the examination of countertransference has been the province of psychoanalytic and psychodynamic group therapists. Increasingly, however, therapists from all schools of thought are recognizing that reactions of the therapist within the treatment are important. Although the system that was described made use of psychodynamic concepts, the language of any orientation can be used to capture the therapist's reactions. For example, within cognitive-behavioral treatment, the therapist could look at his or her automatic thoughts during the course of the session. However, many approaches to group fail to distinguish between objective and subjective countertransference and limit the exploration of the therapist's reactions to the discovery of issues that might interfere with treatment rather than cues that might forward the treatment.

DIFFERENCES IN THERAPIST STYLE

Despite the many commonalities in the leadership demands placed on all group therapists, significant differences exist also. Many group theorists have developed schemes to account for differences in leadership. For example, Rutan and Stone

(2001) have developed an elegant and useful scheme of nine dimensions to capture how psychodynamic therapists might differ from one another or even differ from themselves at various points in time. Based on their research with encounter groups, Lieberman, Yalom, and Miles (1973) described four dimensions on which leaders vary: caring, emotional stimulation, meaning attribution, and structure. Dies (1985) identified three dimensions differentiating leaders: introduction of structure, support/confrontation, and openness/deception. These and other classification systems will be used here to describe how leaders differ from one another. We will delineate eight dimensions of the leadership role (see Rapid Reference 5.3).

Directive versus nondirective style is one of the major differentiators among group therapists. Therapists who are nondirective allow the material to emerge from the group itself. They avoid giving instructions or setting the course of the group. For example, a therapist who enters the room, sits quietly as members speak with one another, and then articulates the theme members have been exploring is nondirective. A directive therapist, in contrast, might establish an agenda for the group and give members instructions, in some cases throughout the session, on how to fulfill the agenda. Both approaches have benefits. Direction is also provided in giving homework assignments. The nondirective approach enables members to take responsibility, encourages them to form relationships with one another rather than the leader, provides an arena in which they can show their characteristic modes of relating, and allows for the emergence of material previously outside of their awareness. The directive approach permits the efficient use of time, ensures that a greater number of members are going to participate, and encourages the group to stay on whatever track the therapist has laid down for the group.

Transparency versus opaqueness, the second dimension of the therapist's role, concerns the extent to which the therapist shares information about him- or herself,

≡ *Rapid Reference 5.3*

Dimensions of the Leader Role

Directive versus nondirective	Content/process
Transparency versus opaqueness	Understanding/corrective
Group as a whole/subgroup/interpersonal/individual	Emotional experience
Past/present/future	Confrontation/exploration versus support
Inside/outside the group	

including aspects of the therapist's background and his or her experiences of being in the group. At one end of this continuum is the therapist who is completely transparent, willing to share any personal data. Highly transparent therapists do not necessarily wait for the members to request information about them but volunteer it frequently. At the other end of the continuum is the therapist who shares virtually nothing about his or her own life. The only aspect of the therapist to which members are privy is that which they can directly observe in the sessions. Of course, therapists can assume various positions along the continuum. Although therapists differ from one another in the frequency of sharing personal information, or self-disclosure, they also differ in the type of information they are willing to share. For example, some therapists may share only reactions that they have within the sessions, as in the following exchange:

Therapist: I was deeply moved when I saw how tenderly the group supported Mimi in her time of loss.

or

Therapist: Right now, I feel torn—as I think others are—between whether to respond to Margaret or Jim.

Other therapists may make self-disclosures that involve their personal history:

Therapist: Billy, I, too, had a very difficult time after I lost a pet, so I know something of what you're going through and don't think your reaction is silly at all.

The reader may notice that in all of these examples, the therapist is disclosing material that is within the scope of everyday experience and is potentially supportive of one or more members. More questionable are those disclosures in which the therapist attests to experiences suggesting weakness or pathology on his or her part or those communicating strong negative feelings toward a member of the group. Research suggests that the latter types of communications are not only unusual (McNary & Dies, 1993) but also of little therapeutic value to members (Dies & Cohen, 1976).

Therapist disclosures can have both risks and benefits. Potential risks include members' loss of confidence in the therapist, worries about the therapist's degree of self-preoccupation, or the creation of a pressure on members to self-disclose prematurely. To the extent that some of these member concerns lead to their departure from the group or, more generally, a disillusionment with therapy, the risk becomes more severe. The benefits include encouraging members to self-disclose through modeling, validating their reactions (e.g., acknowledging anger when the therapist is feeling it), and showing a caring attitude. Rachman (1990) has noted that self-disclosure can be a good way to establish an empathic connection with members. Yet, in order for a disclosure to produce this benefit and others, it must be *judicious self-disclosure,* which is predicated on the therapist's grasp of his or her motives for a given disclosure and its likely effects on this group of members at this time in the group's life.

In Chapter 2 we talked about the different layers of group life available for the group's exploration. Which layer the therapist emphasizes— *group as a whole, subgroup, interpersonal,* or *individual*—is a major distinguishing feature among therapists. As Rutan and Stone noted, a therapist focus on the dynamics present at the level of the group as a whole is especially common "when members are responding to the same stimuli, such as when the group's framework is affected—for example, when the group is forming, a new member is being introduced, a member is terminating, or the therapist's vacation is imminent" (2001, p. 164). A *subgroup* focus occurs when two or more members coalesce into subunits of the group and explore the similarities and differences among them as a means of engaging in conflict resolution (Agazarian, 1997). For example, all of the members who take an oppositional stance in relation to authority may form a subgroup and explore how they are similar to and different from one another. An *interpersonal* focus is when specific relationships among members are the target of intervention, such as when the therapist focuses on how Mimi is competing with Cecilia or how Tom and Dwayne are exchanging hostile communications. The *individual* level is when the therapist directs the group to examine one member's issues (e.g., the group considers why Margaret has had a string of failures in her romantic attachments).

The fourth and fifth dimensions concern the *temporal* (past, present, future) and *spatial* focus of interventions (here versus there). These dimensions seen in relation to one another yield a matrix of possible arenas of exploration. For example, the group could focus on the past in terms of the group's history ("I remember when I first came here . . .") or the members' individual history outside the group ("My mother was a strict disciplinarian as I was growing up"). Similarly, the therapist can establish a focus on present happenings within the group ("I am feeling angry right now") or outside the group ("My father and I have been fighting a lot lately"). Finally, a future orientation can be established concerning the group itself ("I hope that at some point we will be able to argue without putting one another down") or members' lives outside the group ("Down the road, I hope I can apply what I've learned in this group").

These foci are not mutually exclusive, and many types of group therapies will employ all of them, albeit to greater or lesser degrees. At times, the therapist may relate these realms to one another. Research suggests that members' openness to observations about their behaviors in the group (i.e., here) increases if parallels are identified to their difficulties outside (i.e., there; Flowers & Booraem, 1990a, b). The therapist might say, "Jeremy, you've been talking about feeling embarrassed during this session in response to members' arguing with one another. I'm reminded that several sessions ago, you described responding in a similar way when your parents argue." Such an intervention can help the members to recognize the relevance of the here and now to their lives outside therapy.

The sixth dimension, *content versus process,* involves a contrast between the "what" or overt meaning of communications versus the "how" or covert meaning (Yalom, 1995) For example, very often in the beginning of group life, members will articulate the beliefs that they are very similar to one another and have achieved a high level of rapport with one another. However, the astute observer will notice that members make very little genuine contact with one another. When answering the question of another member, they may look at the therapist. When members express strong affect, other members may ignore them. Here we see a contrast between what members are saying—that is, the content of communication—and the form of communication, or the process. Process and content are examined in relation to one another because when each layer is examined alone, it provides only a limited picture of the group. For example, if we simply considered that members are making only superficial contact with one another early in the group, we might conclude that they do not truly wish to be group participants. If we only recognized that members are expressing positive sentiments about the group and one another, we might infer that members had unbridled enthusiasm about being in the group. Seeing content and process in concert with one another enables the realization that members have conflicting feelings about group membership.

Variation exists in the extent to which content and process disparities become a focus of the group. Therapists may avoid a strong emphasis on process for good reasons. As noted, a process focus typically involves an identification of unconscious psychological elements. Some members may respond to the awareness of such elements with a regression that may not be helpful to their overall adjustment. For example, individuals who are participating in a discharge group from the hospital may be less rather than more fortified by such explorations. For some types of members, attention directed toward process leads them to feel vulnerable and even violated. If the therapist comments on nonverbal behaviors, as often occurs in process observations, the hypervigilant person is likely to feel far more anxious. This member would find the recognition that he or she is not in full control of his or her self-presentation quite disturbing. Hence, although a process focus is necessary for the full realization of the power of group therapy, therapists must nonetheless exercise sensitivity in how and to what extent this tool is used.

The seventh dimension is *understanding versus corrective experience*. Are group members helped by achieving insight into conflicts and difficulties, or is help to be had in experiencing a new type of relationship, one with positive features that early important relationships may have lacked? Therapists who view understanding as key emphasize reaching an accurate appraisal of what is occurring in the group, in terms of both members' reactions to one another and the internal phenomena that accompany these reactions. Therapists who emphasize corrective experiences concentrate on the quality of relatedness among members and between therapist and members as well as the behaviors members are exhibiting. Although the term *corrective emotional experience* is common within the psychodynamic literature, the corrective experience can also involve those situations in which the focus is getting the patient to acquire some new skill, the manifestation of which will lead to the member's having a different type (presumably more positive) of experience with others. For example, in social skills training, a technique often used with a low-functioning population, the member may learn how to greet others without overwhelming them. The member's more effective greeting behavior is likely to elicit a more favorable response from those who are greeted.

Whether a given therapist emphasizes the insight or corrective aspect of the relationship often depends on that therapist's philosophical view of psychopathology (Kibel, 1987). Those therapists who emphasize the value of corrective emotional experiences typically view psychopathology as due to one or more deficits. More specifically, psychopathology is rooted in developmental arrest that prevents the person from gaining the capacity to develop the internal structures necessary for the maintenance of a stable sense of well-being. In contrast, group therapists who emphasize insight view psychopathology as deriving from conflict.

The eighth dimension is *confrontation/exploration versus support*. The therapist continually makes a determination whether to raise the level of emotional stimulation, and hence anxiety, or whether to diminish it and to bolster members' coping resources. Consider the following interactions:

Therapist: Mary, when you spoke, you looked at everyone but Derek.

versus

Therapist: I noticed that many of you were nodding when Mary spoke as if you could clearly relate to what she is saying.

Both of these statements may be true. However, the second statement is likely to diminish anxiety by leading Mary to recognize that her comments are not only understandable but also emotionally accessible to other members. The first comment raises question about whether there is some unacknowledged conflict in the group that is manifested nonverbally, and thus it is likely to raise the anxiety level in the group. High levels of anxiety paralyze members and induce cautious behavior; low levels of anxiety breed detachment. Moderate levels of anxiety stimulate members to work.

Although confrontation and support can be seen as being in opposition to one another, in fact, it is important that confrontations occur in as supportive a way as possible in order to be effective in encouraging group members to do a certain piece of psychological work. Dies's (1994) guidelines for making supportive confrontations appear in Rapid Reference 5.4.

Factors That Influence Therapist Differences

The differences in therapists' styles are attributable to a wide range of factors, but here we will examine only three that have particular importance: the therapist's

≡*Rapid Reference 5.4*

How to Make Supportive Confrontations (drawn from Dies, 1994)

1. *Therapists should avoid interpreting or labeling the behavior and should attempt to remain as descriptive as possible.* Saying "you interrupted Mary several times in a short period" is more descriptive and less pathologizing than saying, "You're kind of immature at times, aren't you?"

2. *Confrontations should come from a position of therapeutic neutrality.* A therapist who lashes out at a member in anger is not likely to be seen as working from a stance of neutrality.

3. *The self-defeating nature of the problematic behavior should be sensitively highlighted.* When members can see that certain behaviors are at odds with the achievement of the goals to which treatment is directed, their motivation to address them is likely to increase. On the other hand, sometimes the difficulty is not motivation but the absence of knowledge of other modes of response. In this case, the group can assist the member in identifying other possible responses: "Can we think of other ways that Ari could let the group know that he needs the group's attention?"

4. *Therapists can share and invite other clients to reveal their feelings about the specific client's problematic behaviors.* Doing so conveys that a behavior is not inherently negative or bad but merely detrimental to one's good relationships with others (e.g., "How did others feel when Louise and Larry were raising their voices at one another?").

theoretical orientation, the length of the group's life, and the developmental status of the group.

Theoretical Orientation

In Chapter 2, we identified some of the predominant theoretical orientations that are used today. These orientations require different therapist behaviors, largely determined by the goals of the model and the processes needed to reach the goal. Let us consider the therapist's role with its two dimensions of therapist directiveness and level of transparency in light of some of the theoretical models we encountered in Chapter 2. If we contrast a psychoanalytic approach with a cognitive-behavioral approach, we will find differences along both of these dimensions. Within the psychoanalytic approach, the therapist is interested in facilitating the emergence of unconscious material to enable its integrations with conscious elements of the person's self. A high level of therapist directiveness would interfere with the development of spontaneous associations. Consequently, the therapist is likely to assume a more passive posture. In contrast, the cognitive-behavioral therapist is teaching members to reorganize their thinking in the direction of what will be more adaptive. This therapist is likely to be much more directive than the psychodynamic therapist in coordinating members' contributions.

On the whole, the psychodynamic therapist maintains a low level of transparency because this permits the greatest leeway for members' own fantasies about the therapist to emerge. The cognitive-behavioral therapist, however, enters into a relationship with the group members described as one of a collaborative empiricism. Within this relationship, the therapist relates to members more as a consultant who has some special expertise. To encourage the members to take responsibility, the therapist de-emphasizes the authority aspect. Part of this de-emphasis involves relating to the member as a real person. For example, if the therapist had an example of the application of a principle from his or her own life, he or she would share it. Generally, the cognitive-behavioral therapist will have a higher level of transparency than the psychodynamic therapist.

If we take therapist focus and continue to compare the psychodynamic and cognitive-behavioral approaches, we also recognize differences in the temporal and spatial dimensions. Within the psychodynamic group, the here and now has great importance in that it is through members' immediate behaviors that their conscious and unconscious feelings, impulses, fantasies, and attitudes are most available for exploration. Transference reactions to the therapist and one another are a primary focus of the psychodynamic group therapist. Experiences external to the group, particularly those of a historical nature, have some value in elucidating present reactions. However, when members become preoccupied with concerns external to the group, this behavior will generally be regarded as defensive. Of course, there are times when such a focus is not appropriately considered to be resistance. For example, when a member has been traumatized by some external circumstance, it is fitting that members in a given session have a fairly protracted external focus.

On the other hand, cognitive-behavioral therapists make more extensive use of material generated out of the room. At several points in the structured cognitive-behavioral session, members are likely to be directed to focus outside the group. Often, the agendas they form for a given session are based on difficulties they encountered outside the group, perhaps since the last group session. Later in the session, members may consider those external situations in some detail as they work toward the identification of the automatic thoughts occurring in these situations. Later still, members will be given homework assignments, which they then report on in the subsequent session. Although members are frequently directed to look outside the group in a cognitive-behavioral group, the here and now can become part of the group's explorations. For example, a member may notice feeling distressed in the group. The member may establish as an agenda item finding out what automatic thoughts are stimulated in the group to evoke the negative feeling. Sometimes members may perform a behavioral experiment in the group and reflect on the thoughts and feelings stimulated by a new way of interacting with others. Cognitive-behavioral therapists have not historically placed as much emphasis on what is occurring in the room, but this emphasis, due perhaps to the influence of other theoretical approaches, is increasing.

Length of the Group's Life

How long the group lasts is likely to play a role in determining the way the therapist in charge conducts the group. For example, the briefer the group, the more active the therapist is likely to be, because a group working in a short-term time frame does not have the luxury of languishing. The therapist must be extremely active in moving the group toward its goals. In our last section, we noted that psychodynamic therapists are frequently not as active as therapists in certain other orientations. However, this difference occurs primarily when the psychodynamic group is long term, as many are. Short-term psychodynamic group therapists will be more active than their long-term counterparts. The short-term group therapist will deliver an interpretation with a lesser accumulation of evidence of its accuracy and will be much quicker to point out members' defensive activities (Piper, McCallum, & Azim, 1992).

The temporal and spatial dimensions also differentiate short- and long-term group therapists. The excursions into each member's past are not unusual in a

Putting It Into Practice

Is the Therapist the Only Leader?

Although members entering a group would by and large identify the therapist as the leader, what they rarely realize is that they and a number of other members may be called upon to perform crucial leadership functions. A good deal of research has pointed to the distributed property of group leadership: The leadership of most groups is shared and does not reside wholly within the person of the designated leader, in this case the therapist. Dugo, Beck, and colleagues have identified four critical leadership functions that emerge over the course of a group:

- *Task leader.* This role requires the completion of organizational tasks. Individuals occupying this role help to establish the group boundaries and the group norms—the behaviors that will be typical of members. For example, if Jacob comes late to the session and Vijay says, "You're five minutes late. What happened to you?" Vijay is responding as a task leader. Particularly early in the group's life, the therapist executes many responsibilities of the task leader. Relatively quickly, however, one or more members will come to the fore to assist the therapist with these tasks. Members perceive a task leader as an authority figure.

- *Emotional leader.* This role involves establishing a positive emotional climate in the group through the manifestation of caring, the identification of elements that unite rather than divide members, and the diffusion of tension and conflict through humor and other devices. For example, Carol says to Dmitri, "I know you've been quiet in this session, but it's clear that you're following everything that is going on and have a great deal of compassion for other members." Carol's action of pulling in a withdrawn member and making that member feel comfortable is part of emotional leadership. The activities of the emotional leader in tandem with the task leader contribute to group cohesion. The task leader creates the framework and the emotional leader the positive affect among members for cohesion to develop.

- *Scapegoat leader.* This leader engages in behavior that protects individualism within the group. Because of this member's tendency to set him- or herself apart from the group, other members' hostilities will be projected onto him or her. For example, in a group that had been meeting for 3 months, members were expressing some question about whether a given member should be permitted to continue to speak at length in the group. Another member suggested that the group have a go-around so that everybody would have a chance to speak. Scott said that the group members were a bunch of "dumbbells" because they couldn't see that it was the therapist's job to interrupt the member. He went on to say that the idea of a go-around was preposterous and designed to get the therapist off the hook but that he wasn't going to let that happen. Often the members who occupy this role are fairly robust and eager to be in the limelight. Nonetheless, they generate great conflict, and if the group finds the tension unbearable, members may attempt to scapegoat this member, casting him or her out in an effort to rid the group of the conflict.

- *Defiant leader.* This individual enters the group with tremendous distrust and is hypervigilant to any encroachment on his or her personal boundaries. Because he or she sees interpersonal involvement as being fraught with danger, this member acts self-protectively, avoiding a high level of activity, self-disclosure, and intimacy. One group had met for a year and had been through many struggles but recently had been in a period of great productivity, in which members were receiving highly specific feedback on their interpersonal styles. This member had been quiet as usual, and Hilde said, "Dylan, I feel you are even more withdrawn than usual." Dylan said, "I was thinking maybe I should take a break from the group. It just seems like things are getting too personal in here, and I leave wondering who's going to get hurt." Hilde responded, "You think you are?" Dylan observed, "It's a possibility … and I don't spring back too easily." Dylan in this session is a voice for both autonomy and the importance of recognizing the dangers in interpersonal relationships. Because the defiant leader is more comfortable with separation than other members, he or she can be especially helpful at termination.

The importance of these different leadership roles is that they all constitute resources for the therapist. At different times in the life of the group, the fulfillment of one or more of these roles is essential. As Roller (1997) suggested, "Group therapists must be careful not to take the initiative away from leaders as they start to carry out tasks appropriate to their nascent role" (pp. 168–169).

long-term group, especially those that are run according to a psychodynamic orientation. In a short-term time frame, journeys into the there and then are too inefficient because they entail only a single member's working actively at a time. In short-term groups a focus on the here and now makes sense because all members are involved. Short-term groups also tend to place greater emphasis on the future. As we will see in Chapter 10, one of the tools of a short-term group is the limit in time. To use this tool fully, members need to be reminded throughout the group that the end is in sight. That is, the fact of a future life after the group is always kept at the forefront of their awareness.

Developmental Status of the Group

As the reader will learn in Chapter 6, the interactional patterns among members, and between the members and the therapist, change as the group progresses. These changes reflect differences in group members' needs. That is, in order for them to ultimately fulfill their group goals, they need different types of therapeutic commodities, because the group develops in much the same way that children do in needing different provisions from the parent over time. Early in the life of the group, members feel uncertain about how they should conduct themselves, and they look to the therapist for structure. Consequently, at this time therapists are likely to be directive in cultivating the behaviors that will enable members to reach the group goals. Later in the course of the group, when members have a much clearer idea of what helpful processes are and how to access them, the therapist can accord to members greater independence.

Early in the life of the group, members see the therapist as an all-knowing, all-powerful authority figure. Although the therapist need not engage in behaviors to attempt to support this fantasy, dispelling it prematurely can lead members to flee the group or engage in behaviors that are not supportive of the group's development. One way in which the therapist might lead members to precipitously discard this needed fantasy is to engage in self-disclosures, particularly ones that might suggest that the therapist is more of a peer than a leader. Imagine the therapist saying at the outset of the group, "I'm not sure how this is going to go. I'm pretty new at it." Surely such a statement would not intensify members' enthusiasm for the group therapy enterprise. Hence, early in group life, therapists tend to be fairly opaque. Later, when members have a more complex idea of the therapist and know the ropes of the group, the therapist can make judicious self-disclosures without unsettling the group unduly. For example, were the therapist of a mature group to say "I'm not sure what's happening here right now," this disclosure might have a beneficial effect in stimulating members' curiosity. Therapists tend to be more transparent once the group has some significant history.

Although only a few examples have been given of how our three variables—theoretical orientation, length of the group, and developmental status—are likely to affect the therapist's decision making in regard to his or her position on the different axes, these variables are likely to affect the therapist's behavior with respect to most if not all of these axes. Furthermore, there is a host of other variables we might have considered, such as group venue (e.g., inpatient versus outpatient), level of functioning of the group members, and members' symptom profile. The important point to extract is that the therapist must show what Hersey and Blanchard (1977) term *situational leadership*. That is, the leader must adjust his or her style according to the consideration of a wide range of contextual factors. The more comprehensive the therapist's awareness of context, the more effective his or her group leadership is likely to be.

SUMMARY AND CONCLUSIONS

This chapter has reviewed the therapist's role within the therapy group. Those features that characterize good leadership in all types of groups were delineated. These include an optimsitic attitude about group, healthy ways of relating to others, the capacity to develop a stable therapeutic frame, skill in helping members find meaning in their reactions, an ability to use their own reactions, and optimal use of the leadership format (solo or cotherapy). Nevertheless, therapists are very different from one another. A number of dimensions on which group therapists differ were identified. Some of the factors that are associated with differences on these dimensions were discussed, including directive versus nondirective; transparent versus opaque; group as a whole, subgroup, interpersonal, or individual; temporal (past, present, future); spatial (here, out there); content-oriented versus process-oriented; providing understanding versus a corrective emotional and behavioral experience; and providing support versus confrontation. Several features that may influence leadership style include theoretical orientation, time frame, and developmental status.

 TEST YOURSELF

1. **The therapist recognizes that the members have induced in him the desire to be a leader who can take away all of the members' problems. This therapist reaction is most likely a**
   (a) concordant identification.
   (b) complementary identification.
   (c) objective countertransference.
   (d) subjective countertransference.
   (e) a and c only
   (f) b and c only

2. **Self-disclosures by the therapist may hamper the group's work if**
   (a) they suggest that the therapist has severe psychological problems.
   (b) they involve the expression of intense negative feelings toward one or more members.
   (c) they occur early in the life of the group.
   (d) all of the above
   (e) none of the above

3. **Neither cotherapy nor solo therapy has been empirically demonstrated to be a more effective leadership structure.** True or False?

4. **List some of the benefits of cotherapy.**

5. **Define situational leadership.**

6. **Members' recognition of parallels between their behavior inside and outside of the group increases their receptivity to feedback.** True or False?

(continued)

7. The therapist notes that three of the members of an eight-member group share a yearning to get closer to other members. This therapist is working at what kind of level?

   (a) Individual

   (b) Interpersonal

   (c) Subgroup

   (d) Group as a whole

Answers: 1. f; 2.d; 3.True; 4. A fuller picture of the group, the opportunity to process reactions of the group together, the presentation to members of more varied interpersonal stimuli, and the recreation of the family situation; 5.The position that factors within a group call for different leadership activities at different times; 6.True; 7. c

Six

GROUP DEVELOPMENT

One of the most fundamental features of the life of the group is its capacity for growth or development. To the new group therapist observing a singular group, changes will be evident from one moment of group life to another. These changes may seem random or a function of changes in membership or perhaps of outside events bearing on the group. However, if a new therapist were to have the very instructive experience of following a series of closed-ended (all members beginning and ending simultaneously) short-term groups, one after the other, the therapist would notice a kind of similarity among the groups in how events unfolded. That is, the therapist would see that themes emerge in a systematic way and that members' relationships to one another and to the therapist change in an orderly way. The therapist would begin to anticipate that members act subserviently with the therapist before they challenge the therapist's authority. Moreover, these changes would appear progressive in that what members did at a later period in group life would build upon what had taken place earlier. To capture the periods in a group's evolution, observers of group life have used the term *stage*. In any given stage, members experience the group and behave toward one another and the therapist in a way characteristic of that stage.

A group therapist's sensitivity to the developmental status of the group—that is, the group's level of maturity—can benefit the group in at least two ways. First, each stage of development provides a set of therapeutic opportunities for members in that it puts the spotlight on a set of issues that have relevance to all members and special significance for some. The therapist's recognition of the opportunities that the stage presents will enable him or her to intervene in such a way that members will be able to take fullest advantage of them. The use of developmental concepts is most pertinent to therapists conducting expressive, exploratory groups. Second, a developmental perspective can help a therapist in any orientation or format understand and thereby respond appropriately to the ways in which members are behaving at any point in the life of the group. For example, if members come to the group late (tardiness being a potential behavior in most types of groups), the therapist will respond to this behavior differently if he or she perceives it as a flight from intimacy with the other members as opposed to an attack upon the therapist's authority. To use developmental concepts to enhance the effectiveness of group treatment, the therapist must have an understanding of both the characteristics of a stage and the relationship of the stages to one another.

DEVELOPMENTAL STAGES: CONCEPTUAL UNDERPINNINGS

As noted in Chapter 2, Wilfred Bion (1959) observed that groups commonly exhibit three different patterns of emotionality when placed under stressful conditions. Underlying each pattern is a particular assumption that members share about the group. This *basic assumption* is a belief that the group could enable members to get their needs met without having to do any work—that is, without having to put forth a conscious effort to engage in those activities consistent with members' goals. The three basic assumption groups that Bion delineated were as follows (see the following Putting It into Practice):

- *Basic assumption dependency.* Members act in accordance with the belief that they will be rescued and cared for by a powerful parental figure.
- *Basic assumption fight/flight.* Members behave consistently with the expectation that their survival will be ensured by following a leader who will direct them to flee or fight.
- *Basic assumption pairing.* Members develop a culture that revolves around the belief that the interaction (particularly sexual) among members (or subset of members) will produce a messianic figure who will rescue them.

These basic assumption states have been observed to occur in many types of groups, psychotherapy and nonpsychotherapy groups alike. They exist in contrast to the *work group,* in which members, rather than being influenced by powerful unconscious beliefs that violate reality, engage in behaviors that are based on orderly and logical processes directed toward the goals of the group. For example, if a group of high school students who had convened to assist one another in solving a group of math problems stayed on task and worked systematically toward that goal, they would constitute a work group. Their engagement in some alternate activity, such as joking about the limited math proficiency of their instructor, might suggest that a basic assumption state had taken hold.

Bion saw the basic assumption states as occurring episodically whenever stress in the group increased. Later investigators Bennis and Shepard (1956), who based their work on their observations of individuals in an experiential group, began to

Putting It Into Practice

Are There Other Basic Assumption States?

When Bion (1961) wrote about the basic assumption states, he did not claim that his list was exhaustive. Other theoreticians have speculated that there may be basic assumption states beyond the three that Bion identified. Edward Hopper (2001) described a fourth basic assumption state, *incohesion: aggregation/massification*, which is especially likely to emerge in the large group. According to Hopper, the large group stimulates the fear of having one's person annihilated. Against such a challenge, members can turn inward, protecting themselves from assault by relating to one another minimally. Members preserve their identities by relating no more to one another than would an aggregation. The other side of the defensive coin is massification, which means that members function as a mass. Although members in such groups may appear to have achieved a high level of cohesion, they are warding off annihilation by bonding together in a way that obliterates all differences. In fact, in such transitory and fragile groups, the levels of cohesion are extremely low. Because complex tasks require use of members' individual resources and thereby the implicit or explicit acknowledgment of differences among members, the group that functions as a mass is unable to work effectively.

Hopper's work is important in suggesting that the unconscious processes that characterize different types of groups vary. Although the small group has historically been the object of greatest interest, recently there has been considerable focus on the therapeutic potential of medium-sized groups of 20 or so members (or *median groups;* see de Mare, 1989) and large groups. Tapping such potential requires a recognition of not only the features that these groups share with smaller groups but also those that make them unique. In Chapter 11, we describe support and self-help groups that often are considerably larger than the psychotherapy groups that have been our primary focus in this text.

see that the basic assumption states have a developmental character. That is, early in the group, members engage in behaviors characteristic of the basic assumption *dependency* state. With the frustration of expectations for gratification that accompany this state, members appear to transition to a basic assumption *fight/flight* mode in which they address conflicts related to authority. Once the group has achieved some resolution of its differences in relation to authority, members move toward the establishment of more intimate connections with one another, and some of the phenomena of the basic assumption *pairing* group are evident. Passage through these stages can also bring the group to a closer approximation of a *work group,* in which members take responsibility for their own progress in the group and engage in activities that will ensure such progress.

From their observations, Bennis and Shepard proposed that groups develop in stages, much as do individuals. These investigators and others have noted that the stages of group development have several characteristics:

- The order of stages is invariant. Somewhat akin to the way that a child must learn to crawl before walking, so too must groups address certain psychological issues before others.

   The time different groups require to pass through a given stage is variable. For example, researchers have noted that a group composed of lower-functioning members requires a longer period to pass through the earlier stages of development than groups of higher-functioning members. Situational factors also influence development. For example, when a group experiences frequent membership turnover, development is slower than when there is constancy of membership.

- Groups can regress to earlier stages of development or become fixated at a present stage of development. The factors that can lead a group to proceed slowly through a given stage of development can also lead the group to either become fixated at a given stage or regress to an earlier stage. At times, regression is useful to the group, as when it helps the group to rework in a more adaptive way the conflicts of earlier stages. For example, the entrance of new members into the group frequently leads members back to the earliest stage of development in which they have an opportunity to address once again issues related to needs and deprivation. However, they will do so with the benefit of their work in the later stages of development. In this sense, regression is never complete: Members return to earlier points in time altered by their newer experiences in the group, a notion termed *recycling* by Erik Erikson (1994) in relation to individual development.

   Some groups manifest behaviors that suggest that the group's agenda, typically unconscious, is its own destruction. Nitsun (2000) referred to these as *antigroups*. The *pathological antigroup* occurs when the forces within members resisting connection completely overwhelm those forces propelling members toward involvement. Although in all groups the antigroup waxes and wanes, in its pathological form it gains a stronghold over the group, making development impossible.

- Groups do not exclusively reside within a given stage. Careful observation reveals the remnants of earlier stages and the harbingers of stages to come.

A Five-Stage Model

The stage sequence presented here is a distillation of many developmental schemes that have appeared in the literature. There is variability among developmental models in both the number and the content of the stages. This variability is attributable to many factors, including the setting in which the group took place, the length of the group, the population from which members were drawn, and the theoretical lens through which group behaviors were observed; nonetheless, these models overlap greatly. These stages can most vividly be seen in closed-ended short-term groups, but they also occur in ongoing groups.

Stage 1: Forming a Group

Members enter Stage 1 as a mere collection of individuals and leave this stage as a group. In order to make this transition, members must successfully resolve the conflict between the wishes to affiliate with others and to remain apart. The longing to forge relationships with others is deeply rooted in the social nature of human beings and our dependency on each other for survival and growth. Group members enter the group because they expect that through their relationships with one another and the therapist something positive will occur in their lives, whether it be short-term relief from loneliness or the achievement of particular therapeutic goals. The other side of the conflict is often manifested when the therapist first suggests the idea of group therapy to the individual. At this moment, the patient may articulate various fears about group members (e.g., "the group members will tell me about all my flaws"; "the group will bring me down and make me even more depressed"; "someone in the group will make me really furious and I'll let them have it"). Involvement with others, members realize, is fraught with dangers, and there is some safety in solitude. Although members may have very particular fears about the group, a shared concern is the loss of autonomy, individuality, and privacy that accompanies connection with others. As Nitsun (2000) wrote, "Most people wish to preserve a part of their inner selves inviolate and intact. . . . The group is felt to constitute a threat to this fragile inner self" (p. 462).

Members' behaviors during this stage express each side of the conflict. These behaviors are illustrated in the following Putting It into Practice. The wish to affiliate is seen in members' decision to join the group and attend the initial sessions. Members' communication of information about themselves and their expressions of curiosity about one another are also manifestations of the wish to be involved with group members. However, members also engage in a variety of behaviors to ensure that their engagement with one another remains on a superficial level. For example, members studiously avoid focusing on the here and now. The content of initial sessions frequently focuses on those member concerns that lie outside the group, and a high level of externalization will be evident ("She is the one who doesn't know how to control her temper, but I'm the one who is in therapy"). Members will often complain about others in their lives whom they see

Putting It Into Practice

An Illustration of Stage 1

Rosemary and Clyde opened the session, talking about relatives who said they were so glad that they were finally in therapy, as if the relatives had nothing to do with the problem. Ella told Rosemary that she must learn to be more assertive in pointing out to others their part of the problem. Rosemary looked puzzled and said that she had always been known among all of her acquaintances as an especially assertive person. Alissa said that no measure of assertiveness would be enough for her family. She referred to herself as the "identified patient" of the family and said that because others used her to hide their difficulties, her family would do whatever was necessary to keep her in the sick role. Frances asked Rosemary if she had tried medication.

As if Frances had not spoken, Ronnie said that what most helped people was to move far away from family members. The group briefly discussed appealing places to live. One member said she had thought of moving to San Francisco rather than joining this group. If the group didn't help her, she said, that's what she would do. Terence said that would be just running away from problems. Several members agreed, and Rosemary again said that she wished her family members would take responsibility for what they were doing to her just as she was taking responsibility for what she did to them.

Clyde said, "Yeah, we're the really courageous ones doing the hard work in here."

Teaching note: Many classic Stage 1 behaviors are seen in this vignette. Group members reveal an effort to establish the group by drawing contrasts between those inside and outside the group. These contrasts also serve the function of externalization, a means to avoid working on the difficulties that brought members into the group. A variety of other mechanisms are evident. Intellectualization was evidenced by the member who chose to use the technical language of mental health professionals when she referred to herself as an "identified patient." Embracing a somatic cure (i.e., medication) for problems was another means. Avoidance by fantasizing about a perfect place to live was still another means.

Members also showed a very low level of attunement to one another. Ella gave Rosemary highly concrete advice without knowing her. Ronnie ignored Frances's question. Yet some members were ready to point out members' defensive maneuvers as such. What we see is a tension, very characteristic of Stage 1, between the wish to be cured without any exertion and the recognition that progress requires work by members.

as responsible for their misery. Also common is advice giving, in which members offer solutions to problems that they understand at a very superficial level ("Just forget about him: You'll be fine!").

In fact, rarely during this stage are members able to listen to one another with close attention. They avoid asking questions or making requests of one another. Members take refuge in conventional forms of behavior. For example, a member may say that another's advice was helpful whether it is or not. Competing with their interest in other group members is a substantial focus on the therapist. Members function as a basic assumption dependency group in which their connection with one another is born out of their common wish that the therapist will provide the fulfillment of any and all needs. In fact, even when ostensibly speaking to the members of the group, they primarily reserve eye contact for the therapist. Members operate in a manner akin to that of children who are waiting for parents to come home from the supermarket with dinner: They will relate to one another as a means of waiting until they receive the needed provisions from the parent. The notion that they could fulfill their needs through their interactions with one another is at this time out of the scope of their awareness.

Although at this early stage of development members are not yet able to utilize all of the resources of the group, their interactions with one another and the therapist can nonetheless lead to important accomplishments:

- They begin to develop a sense of membership in the group and a rudimentary degree of cohesion, an essential element in enabling them to move to the next stage of development. As members share their stories with one another, they recognize commonalities, a factor described in Chapter 4 as *universality*. Attending this discovery of common ground is a sense of relief at not being alone with suffering and difficulties.
- Members obtain some practice in the processes on which their progress will depend later in the group, such as giving feedback to one another. Often the feedback that occurs very early in the group is of limited usefulness because members have yet to fully attend to one another. Still, members learn how to work within the here and now so that at a later point they are able to take full advantage of the potential of this medium.
- The group can develop healthy norms that will nurture the group's growth. Through the therapist's reinforcement and education of members (some of which occurs in the preparatory phase), the group can acquire habits, such as regular member attendance and promptness, and putting feelings into words rather than actions, that will be conducive to the members' work.

Stage 2: Authority and Power Issues
Members can wait for the therapist to relieve them of their troubles for only so long. Members increasingly notice that their expectations of what would be derived from the group are not being fulfilled. Often, the initial irritation is with the other members of the group as members perceive others as in some way hindering them from what they had wanted to accomplish in the group. Implicit in the

criticisms that members make of one another is the notion that the group is not working as it ought. This negative evaluation, which initially is hidden, becomes progressively more explicit as members feel freer to acknowledge their disappointment with this experience. Members eventually more openly identify the object of the discontent: the therapist. The therapist, members realize, has failed to deliver what they expected. Although some members may ally themselves with one another in the verbal expression of dissatisfaction with the therapist, others will express their feelings behaviorally by coming late to group, being absent, and violating group rules. However, the therapist is likely to have defenders: Some members may point out that the therapist is doing his or her best or may argue that in fact the therapist is helping the members. As members assume these polar positions, tensions will rise.

Through these diverse behaviors, members express their conflicts toward authority and the power wielded by authority, as embodied in the figure of the therapist. The members who voice dissatisfaction with the therapist use their anger as a defense against feelings of dependency on this authority figure. Those members who take on a more compliant stance are unable to tolerate feelings of anger toward authority, lest the expression of anger lead to some negative consequence, such as the therapist's losing interest in helping them or maybe even retaliating against them for expressing anger. See the following Putting It into Practice for an illustration of the emergence of these Stage 2 subgroups.

In some cases, only a single member will be a voice for one side of the authority conflict. This member is at great risk for being scapegoated by the other members, who project upon that person their own unwanted psychological contents. They coerce the individual into manifesting them in such an extreme way to discourage others from identifying with this member. To ensure that they are fully rid of the unwanted element, members will silence, attack, or otherwise reject him or her. When this circumstance arises, it is important that the therapist intervene, both to protect the scapegoated member and to address a defensive pattern that could limit the group's capacity to grow.

Although groups vary in how they do the work of this stage, for many groups the intensification culminates in an attack upon the therapist's authority, an occurrence referred to as a *barometric event* (Bennis & Shepard, 1956). At this time, the group exhibits the fight mode of Bion's basic assumption fight/flight group. For some groups, this attack may be extremely muted and couched in pleasantries. For others, it may be raw and intense. Still other groups may express their disaffection symbolically—for example, by sitting on the floor rather than their usual chairs. Although for new group therapists this event can be extraordinarily threatening, he or she will be aided by recognizing how conducive to growth such an event can be for members. As MacKenzie (1990) notes, what is espe-

Putting It Into Practice

An Illustration of Stage 2

Six adolescents in a school-based therapy group for the treatment of self-esteem problems had convened when the therapist walked in to begin the session. Horace belched loudly, and Severine, with some fierceness, said, "That was incredibly rude!" Horace responded, "Yeah, well, you only thought that when the therapist walked in." Severine responded, "That's right. It's one thing to do it in front of us, but you should give the therapist more respect."

"Why should I?" said Horace. "Why is the therapist any different from the rest of us?"

"He has a point," said Marty. "Should we act like he's ... better than us? I mean, it's not like he's some sort of god!"

"No," said Cherise, "but he knows more than we do and so he deserves our respect. That's what you"—to Horace—"do that makes all of the teachers annoyed with you all the time. And you're not going to get one of them to write a letter of recommendation for you for college."

Zachary said, "She's right. Even if you feel like you don't owe these people respect" (here he turned to the therapist) "and I'm not talking about you, you should at least pretend that you do."

Horace replied, "I'd have to pretend, because none of them are cool enough to really earn my respect."

Teaching note: We see in this vignette early Stage 2 behavior in which members are engaging in internecine warfare and beginning to organize themselves into subgroups of those who are ready to defy authority and those who will assume a more compliant stance. As is characteristic of this period, members direct their hostilities toward figures outside the group, authority figures who symbolize the therapist but are safer targets for the members' hostilities. As the stage progresses, members will more and more directly focus on the therapist, a progression that the therapist might hasten by interpreting the members' symbolic expressions. We also see articulated one of the fears that may constrain members in fully expressing their dissatisfaction with the therapist: their fear of retaliation. When this fear is made explicit, members are able to test it out in their actual interactions with the therapist.

cially helpful to members is for the therapist merely to stay calm throughout this stage. This posture conveys the message that the issues that members are raising are important, legitimate ones and that nothing calamitous will come of their explorations and expressions. Through

DON'T FORGET

The barometric event is a group-as-a-whole challenge to the leader's authority that enables the group to progress to the more advanced stages of development.

their challenge to the therapist's authority, members can experientially test their catastrophic fantasies about the consequences of expressing anger. They can also have a fledgling experience in collaborating with one another, a skill that will be utilized heavily in ensuing stages. The collaboration also gives rise to a deeper level of cohesiveness.

Stage 3: Intimacy

The emotional atmosphere that follows members' passage from Stage 2 is very positive. Members enjoy exhilaration and triumph at having challenged the authority figure, which to many seemed impossible. There also is the satisfaction of having worked with one another successfully. As Garland, Jones, and Kolodny (1965) wrote, "There is a growing awareness and mutual recognition of the significance of the group experience in terms of personality growth and change" (p. 47). Members are sufficiently free of their fixed focus on the therapist to be able to focus on one another, yet they are not able to see in a highly precise way the behaviors, attitudes, and personality characteristics of the other members. Members are caught in the sway of their rapture with each other and the group as a whole and imagine that simply through their closeness with one another their difficulties will vanish. In this cultlike phase of group life, members' regard for one another provides no room for an awareness of the perils of relationships. Because of the climate of acceptance and warmth, members will often engage in a deeper level of self-disclosure than they had achieved in prior stages.

The push toward intimacy in this stage can be associated with behaviors that challenge the boundaries of the group. Members may abrogate the boundary between social relationships and group relationships by having contact with one another outside of sessions. Sometimes the contact is sexual. Members may seek to replace outside relationships with relationships with group members (MacKenzie, 1990). In some groups, there may be an effort in the session to partake of gratifications that violate the rules the therapist has established, the norms members have developed, or both. For example, members may bring food to the group to share with other members.

This stage is most important in the preparation it affords members in doing the work of Stage 4. In Stage 3, members achieve a new level of cohesion in which they feel very tangibly the high value they place on their relationships with one another. It is this investment that enables relationships to function as therapeutic instruments in the succeeding stage.

Stage 4: Dealing with Differences

Stage 3 is relatively brief because members have a difficult time sustaining the extreme level of denial characteristic of this stage. Evidence accrues that members have different opinions on matters, experience reactions toward one another that are not wholly positive, and offer relationships with not only benefits but perils as well. For some members, progressively greater discomfort accompanies the perception that their individuality is being challenged. These members will verbalize the dangers associated with intimacy and the need for a modicum of self-protection. All of these factors can be instrumental in moving the group into Stage 4, in which there is a greater awareness of each member's uniqueness and the fact that differences abound in the group.

Although Stage 4 often begins with members taking a more distant stance toward one another, over the course of this stage members learn to achieve intimacy while preserving individuality. Along with this achievement emerges a developing capacity to acknowledge both negative and positive feelings toward other members. A consequence of both of these achievements is that members are now able to use the mechanism of interpersonal learning more productively than they have in the past. Because members are more attuned to other members, they can offer more precise, accurate observations and reflections on each member's behavior than they could earlier in the group's life. By accessing their own feelings as events unfold in the group, members can convey to other members how their behaviors in social contexts affect others. Because members can tolerate differences among themselves, they can focus on the highly individualized and often sensitive issues that brought members into the group (MacKenzie, 1997).

Three other important features of Stage 4 concern the group's newfound ability to monitor and maintain healthy group norms, the emergence of a mature decision-making process, and a more complex and reality-based relationship with the therapist. Each of these features will be described in turn. In Stage 4 the group resembles Bion's work group more fully than it has in any prior stage. Because of this, members are able to keep in the forefront of awareness the goals of the group and recognize those behaviors that are not compatible with the pursuit of the goals. No longer is it typically the therapist who needs to point out to members how lateness or absence adversely affect the group's work. In exploratory groups members will often exhibit a reflective attitude toward behaviors that appear not to advance the group's work, as is illustrated in the interaction between two members in the following Putting It into Practice.

The group now acquires an ability to engage in mature decision making. Earlier in the life of the group, members make decisions with little consideration of the different positions of members on the issue at hand and the evidence for the merit of each position. Decisions are made precipitously and usually in conformity with the opinions of some especially assertive member. At this time in the group's life, members are far more able to give the diversity of views within the group their due and to make their decision after a period of slow and careful reflection. The therapist can nurture this ability by providing members with decision-making opportunities, such as by asking the group to make a deci-

Putting It Into Practice

An Illustration of Stage 4

The following exchange occurred between two members of a Stage 4 outpatient group in the beginning of the session.

Margaret: I had to miss last week. I just had the worst headache when I got home from work.

Sally: But you did go to work. It wasn't like you had the flu and couldn't do anything for several days. Maybe you wanted to avoid coming here because in the session two weeks ago you talked about feeling competitive with Joshua. You seemed a bit upset when you left.

Margaret: It's true that I was upset, because I felt I put myself out there and when you [Joshua] didn't acknowledge competing with me, I felt like a big fool. But my headache was real. . . . I didn't invent it.

Sally: I'm not doubting that. I just feel that it would have made you feel better and not worse to come to the group, because after the session was over I realized that I had been feeling that Josh did not really own up to having similar feelings toward you, and I wanted to let both of you know that. And I guess I felt kind of frustrated that I wasn't able to let you know what I was thinking.

Teaching note: In this exchange, Margaret begins to learn about a possible reason underlying her behavior and the effects of her behavior on others in the group. The fact that such learning can proceed without any intervention on the part of the therapist is very characteristic of a mature group. Also characteristic of a mature group is the relatively high level of risk taking. For example, Margaret acknowledges feeling like a fool, an admission that would typically be associated with the affect of shame.

sion about when a new member will be brought into the group (Agazarian & Peters, 1981).

A third dimension of difference is the way in which the group regards the therapist. In the earliest stages of group development, the members are preoccupied with what the therapist is or is not doing because of their belief that any help that is forthcoming will be received from the therapist. Later, the group members recognize that the therapist has a special role in the group based upon his or her specialized skills. Although the members welcome the therapist's input, they regard their relationships with one another as primary vehicles of change.

DON'T FORGET

The therapist supports the group's movement into a more mature mode of functioning by according the group the power to make decisions.

Stage 5: Termination

This stage is most evident when all group members begin and end therapy during the same sessions, although it occurs in more muted form when any member of the group leaves, including the therapist. Termination presents multiple tasks for the group members. The ending of the group is a loss for members. Often, individuals who participate in group treatment have had difficulty coping with prior losses (MacKenzie, 1997). In fact, it may have been difficulty in relation to a loss that brought many of the members into the group. The current loss can activate reactions associated with past losses; however, the ending of the group represents an opportunity for members to approach loss in a new and more constructive way. During this stage, members must also prepare themselves for their lives after the group. Reviewing insights and skills they have obtained in the group as well as anticipating obstacles to applying them are useful components of this preparation.

As members approach the ending of the group, it is not uncommon for them to begin to recollect and describe earlier losses that have occurred during their lives. These reactions can be understood as symbolic expressions of members' concern about termination. However, rarely will members on their own give more than fleeting acknowledgment that the group's ending is approaching. In many groups, it is only by dint of the therapist's reminders and interpretations of the group's preoccupation with external losses that members examine the current loss more thoroughly. This loss has multiple components. It is a loss of their relationship with one another and with the therapist. It is the loss of the supportive environment provided by the group. It is also the loss of the promise of what might have been accomplished that was not—members' unrealized fantasies of what the group could have been. All of these are potential areas of exploration for members.

Almost invariably, members will show difficulty engaging in this exploration. Often members will subgroup with one another on the basis of a given defense that they share in fending off one set of reactions to the loss. For example, some members will *deny* that the ending of the group constitutes a loss ("I don't understand what the big deal is here; I didn't even know any of you four months ago"). Other members will *idealize* the group as a way of ignoring negative feelings about the group experience. Still others fend off painful feelings by *devaluing* the group, focusing unduly on its limitations and imperfections. Some groups resort to the creation of an emergency that diverts the group from the loss. These and other defenses exist to spare members from having a comprehensive, richly textured experience of the ending of the group. The consequence of this defensive stance is that members fail to fully reconcile themselves to the losses in their lives and thereby prevent themselves from moving on to form new attachments. See the following Putting It into Practice for an illustration of Stage 5.

Putting It Into Practice

An Illustration of Stage 5

A group that had been meeting for two years with fairly stable membership was ending because the therapist was moving to another geographic area. Several members were going to continue with another therapist, whereas several others were terminating group treatment altogether. Bessy, a member who was transferring, began to interrogate another member, Dexter, about how he would handle difficulties with his overbearing mother. Dexter responded in an indecisive way. Other group members began to probe, only to get further equivocation from him. Finally, Bessy said to him in an imperious tone, "Are you quite sure you are ready to leave?"

Justin responded, "He's been here a long time. He's gotten about all he can."

"You don't want him to leave because that would bring your own decision into question," Bessy told Justin.

"I feel perfectly fine," he said. "I've been here three years, I've covered a lot of ground, and I just feel my time would be spent better going out and trying to meet someone."

Sebastian said, "You tell us you spend most nights not doing anything. . . . If you went with us to Dr. Calbert's, it probably would be easier for you to meet someone."

Nan added, "What don't you understand about he's had enough. Everything reaches its limit, and some of us can realize it and not hang on forever. This group thing has just dried up for him."

"And for you too, right?" Sebastian replied.

"Yeah," Nan said, "and I don't want to be hassled about it."

Teaching note: The group has created a subgrouping structure consisting of two subgroups: those who are and are not continuing with group treatment. The discontinuing subgroup is embracing the defense of devaluation, maintaining that group therapy is a medium that can be and has been depleted by members. They portray the members of the alternate subgroup as acting out of excessively intense dependency needs. The other subgroup is using another type of devaluation, the devaluation of the commitment of departing group members. For subgroups, devaluation occurs in the service of the denial of the ending of the group. Whether members are continuing with some other members in another group or leaving altogether, the present group is coming to an end. As the subgroups crystallize, the therapist's identification of the subgrouping structure and its possible function may enable these members to reckon with their feelings about this group's ending.

Typically in a short-term group (see Chapter 10) the therapist must take a very active role in helping members to achieve closure on the group experience. In an exploratory group, often this activity entails labeling both the defense that the group is using against a particular set of feelings and the warded-off contents themselves. In cognitive-behavioral short-term groups, the exploration may take the form of analyzing automatic thoughts and, ultimately, underlying schema in relation to loss events. For example, an automatic thought about the group might be "If I have any disappointment at all, it means I've wasted my time here." The underlying schema might be "I'm a failure no matter how hard I try." In longer-term groups, members may be able to make their own analyses, and to the extent that they can, the therapist should accord them the latitude to do so. Members, too, may take initiative in developing their own termination rituals (Shapiro & Ginzberg, 2002) that symbolize aspects of the group experience and their feelings about the group's ending. MacKenzie (1990) describes common rituals such as joining hands and forming a circle or initiating a go-around in which all members participate in describing what they will remember about each group member. By reflecting on the meaning of the specific ritual they have chosen, members can gain greater access to all of the thoughts and feelings connected to their departure from the group.

Preparation for the future can be achieved by reviewing accomplishments during the group. Sometimes members may be helped by recalling a critical incident (MacKenzie, 1990), an event in the group that was significant because it entailed successfully handling a stressor. For example, in the authors' experience, critical incidents have often involved expressing anger toward the therapist in a more effective way than had occurred with other authority figures prior to the group experience. This discussion sets the stage for the member to anticipate what impediments lie ahead and how the resources cultivated during the group can be marshaled to remove the impediments. A member might consider how success in expressing discontent toward the therapist can create a model for interacting with a difficult supervisor at work. Part of the prospective analysis involves identifying any remaining therapeutic needs. A member may recognize the importance of continuing therapy. For example, a member of a short-term group may decide that entering another short-term group experience would be beneficial.

HOW DO GROUPS DEVELOP?

We have seen that each stage of development affords members unique opportunities to do psychological work. Stage 1 enables members to approach issues pertaining to the establishment of relationships. Stage 2 offers an exploration of concerns about members' relationships with authority figures. In Stages 3 and 4, members can address conflicts related to connection and differentiation. Stage 5 allows an examination of loss and grief in members' lives. Yet not all groups afford members these rich opportunities for psychological growth; some instead remain fixed at a particular stage of development or regress to an earlier stage. What distinguishes those groups that develop from those that stagnate?

Certainly one factor is the therapist's skill in responding to the needs of the group at each stage. Because the needs of the group vary from stage to stage, the effective therapist will also show variation in style of intervention, much like a parent interacts differently with a child as he or she matures. For example, Kivlighan (1997) observed that a task orientation benefits a group more significantly early in its life whereas a relationship focus is more important later. This notion that the optimal leadership style is one that takes into account the needs of the group at the moment is referred to as the *situational leadership theory* (Hersey & Blanchard, 1977).

The members of the group also play a crucial role in whether or not the group develops. Wheelan (1997) suggests that to the extent that preparation for group therapy provides members with an understanding of group goals and member tasks, they are likely to interact in a way that contributes to the group's potential for growth. Based on her research, Wheelan suggests that members' knowledge that development is a phenomenon in the life of the group can itself facilitate group maturation. Wheelan and Podowski (1997) had work group members participate in a session in which they were educated about group dynamics and development and the roles both leaders and members play in the group's growth processes. Relative to control groups, the training groups showed greater improvement over time. Brabender (2000) suggests that during preparation members should also be helped to recognize that the unfamiliarity and disorder that often accompany members' encounter with a new set of developmental issues are in the service of their growth. Cultivating the expectation that rocky periods will occur in the group's life is an antidote to the tendency to revert to more familiar and comfortable terrain just as the group is progressing.

The five stages and the tasks associated with each are summarized in Rapid Reference 6.1.

Caution on the Use of Developmental Stage Concepts

As MacKenzie (1997) notes, the empirical evidence for the existence of developmental group phenomena is substantial. Studies that examine how different properties of a group change over time have been consistent with developmental theory. For example, MacKenzie (1983) used the Group Climate Questionnaire–Short Form to examine three dimensions of a group: engagement (or members' felt degree of involvement with one another), conflict or tension among members, and avoidance of personal responsibility. Monitoring the patterns of 12 therapy groups, he found that in accordance with development predictions, engagement increased over early sessions and conflict was at a low level. Later,

≡Rapid Reference 6.1

The Stages of Group Development

Stage	Tasks
Stage 1: Forming a group	• Resolve the conflict between isolation and involvement. • Develop a rudimentary sense of cohesion. • Achieve practice in using group processes. • Develop norms that support group goals.
Stage 2: Authority and power issues	• Make the transition from a leader-centered to a peer-centered group. • Have a safe experience of expressing negative feelings toward authority.
Stage 3: Intimacy	• Have an initial experience of a peer-centered group. • Achieve greater comfort at being known to others. • Experience diminished shame about the self and envy of others.
Stage 4: Dealing with differences	• Achieve closeness while recognizing differences. • Increase awareness of one's relational style through interpersonal learning. • Achieve greater experience in collaborative decision making.
Stage 5: Termination	• Experience a full range of reactions (thoughts and feelings) in relation to the group's ending and the loss of the relationships with the members and the therapist. • Consolidate gains made during the group. • Identify goals for the future and the means of pursuing them.

members showed a high level of conflict and avoidance and a lower level of engagement. This pattern was consistent with the notion of the group moving into a phase in which they confront their antagonism toward the leader and one another. Still later, engagement increased as avoidance and conflict diminished, suggesting that members were moving into a more intimate mode of relating.

If one compares the patterns among different groups, however, it becomes evident that variation is

CAUTION

The therapist's focus on stages of development should be accompanied by an attunement to what is unique about each group.

great. Brabender (1990), replicating MacKenzie's (1983) study with closed-ended eight-session inpatient groups, found that some inpatient groups showed an extremely high level of engagement very early on in the course of the group. Rather than manifesting the increases in engagement shown by MacKenzie's groups, these groups went on to enter a conflictual stage very quickly. However, by the group's end, the high level of engagement returned and exceeded that of other groups showing an increase in engagement over the early stages. This variability suggests that the composition of the group influences group development. Chapter 10 features an illustration of how the age of members in a group affects the way in which the group pursues the issues of a given stage. The therapist should not be so conceptually committed to the notion of an invariant set of stages to be blind to each group's singularity. As Elfant (1997) wrote, "The idealization of the developmental ideas . . . threatens to obliterate what is creative and original in this therapy group, with this unique configuration of particular individuals, and with this leader or leaders" (p. 313).

SUMMARY AND CONCLUSIONS

Like individuals, groups develop. The therapist must be attuned to the developmental status of the group in order to help the group take advantage of the opportunities at its particular developmental level and to understand the behavior of members within any given session. A five-stage model was presented. We saw how early in the life of the group, members deal with issues of joining a group and trust. They then move on to deal with conflict among themselves and ultimately with the authority member in the group, the therapist. Members leave this period of group life less reliant upon the therapist for help and more cooperative with one another. The later stages are what have been termed the working stages, much akin to Bion's work group (MacKenzie, 1990). Although initially members explore the intimate connections among themselves, later they examine the potential in relationships for being close to others while retaining their autonomy and sense of individuality. Termination provides an opportunity to approach the existential issues that will be outlined in Chapter 10. The individual confronts aloneness as he or she separates from other members, loss as the ending of the group and the relationships with members is faced, and the limit of time as the member sees that, like life, the group is finite.

🐠 TEST YOURSELF 🐠

A. Stage 1: Forming a group

B. Stage 2: Authority and power issues

C. Stage 3: Intimacy

D. Stage 4: Exploring differences

E. Stage 5: Termination

Questions 1–6: With what stages of development are each of the following behaviors most highly associated?

_____ 1. A member loudly cracks bubble gum during the session, making the other members laugh.

_____ 2. The group's motto might be "Love conquers all."

_____ 3. Some members worry that the therapist's feelings will be hurt by other members' comments.

_____ 4. Group members exercise care in not violating social conventions.

_____ 5. In this stage, members tend to either idealize or devalue the group.

_____ 6. Members diligently weighted the pros and cons of changing the meeting time for a particular session.

7. Generally, group cohesion increases steadily over the stages of development. True or False?

8. The situational leadership theory suggests that from stage to stage, different therapist behaviors are required. True or False?

Thought Question

9. Do cognitive-behavioral groups focus primarily on a different stage of group development than psychodynamic groups?

Answers: 1. b; 2. c; 3. b; 4. a; 5. e; 6. d; 7. False; 8. True

Seven

IS GROUP THERAPY AN
EFFECTIVE TREATMENT?

"How do you know that this treatment will be effective?" This question is routinely posed to group therapists by any number of parties in the service delivery system, such as third-party payers, referral sources, and prospective clients. This chapter will provide group therapists with the information they need to answer this question. We will examine whether group treatment is more effective than alternate treatments or no treatment. We will also show what psychological problems group therapy has been shown to ameliorate.

Although the early literature on group therapy was characterized by poorly designed studies, in the past two decades investigations of effectiveness have been characterized by greater rigor and have incorporated such features as random assignment of members to experimental, comparison, and control conditions; use of experienced group therapists; monitoring of therapists' adherence to the treatment; clear and operational definition of the independent and dependent variables; and attention to the *power* of the statistical tests (their likelihood of revealing an effect when there is one). Rapid Reference 7.1 outlines many of the features of methodological sound outcome studies that we employ in contemporary group therapy research.

The number of outcome studies done on group interventions is great. In order to see trends across studies, researchers have used *meta-analysis,* in which the statistical results of each of a group of studies are converted to a standard measure called an *effect size.* Effect sizes are then averaged across studies, which enables a comparison to be made between a given modality and control and comparison conditions. Although meta-analysis provides a statistical overview of a number of studies, it has various weaknesses, including the fact that it sometimes entails making comparisons between conditions that were not directly compared in the studies analyzed. Researchers continue to use less precise qualitative analyses of studies that avoid some of the difficulties created by meta-analysis.

In the picture we present of outcome findings, we will focus primarily on the results of large-scale meta-analytic and qualitative reviews. Our reason for this approach is practical: The number of studies is so large as to prohibit a study-by-study approach. Nonetheless, when we see that certain studies, especially those done recently, complete the picture offered by the reviews, we will cite them. Additionally, we cite many outcome studies throughout this text where their inclusion is relevant.

GLOBAL FINDINGS ABOUT GROUP THERAPY

Is group therapy more effective than no treatment at all? Review studies, both qualitative and meta-analytic, consistently

Rapid Reference 7.1

Characteristics of Methodologically Sound Studies

- Random assignment
- Contrasting treatment groups
- Explicit descriptions of the interventions
- Detailed analysis of client characteristics
- Multiple dependent measures
- Well-trained therapists

Other desirable features:

- Interventions using group-specific processes
- Consideration of pretreatment and posttreatment measures
- Clinical setting

reveal that group therapy is effective in producing positive changes. For example, in one meta-analytic study with adults, the average group member did better than 82 percent of the wait list patients (McRoberts et al., 1998). In another meta-analytic review of 15 studies of depressed individuals (Robinson, Berman, & Neimeyer, 1990), persons who participated in group therapy had more favorable outcomes than 80 percent of the controls. In a review of more than 700 group therapy studies, Fuhriman and Burlingame (1994b) conclude that the group modality reliably provides beneficial results across treatment models to individuals with a variety of disorders and problems.

Is group therapy equivalent or superior to other treatments? Despite the overwhelming evidence for the efficacy of group therapy, third-party payers seeking treatments that are maximally effective and economical are not likely to be satisfied: They want to know whether the group modality is superior to other well-known treatments. In general, group therapy has been shown to be comparable to individual therapy in its yield of favorable outcomes (see Rapid Reference 7.2). Although meta-analytic reviews (e.g., McRoberts et al., 1998) have generally revealed that group and individual therapy are of equivalent value, there are a few reviews that

≡ *Rapid Reference 7.2*

....

Reviews Comparing Group and Individual Psychotherapy

Studies concluding group and individual therapy equally effective:
- Luborsky, Singer, and Luborsky (1975)
- Hoag and Burlingame (1997; meta-analysis)
- McRoberts, Burlingame, and Hoag (1998; meta-analysis)
- Miller and Berman (1983; meta-analysis)
- Robinson et al. (1990; meta-analysis)
- Smith, Glass, and Miller (1980; meta-analysis)
- Tillitski (1990; meta-analysis)

Studies concluding individual superior to group therapy:
- Shapiro and Shapiro (1982)
- Dush et al. (1983)
- Nietzel et al. (1987)

Studies concluding group superior to individual therapy:
- Toseland and Siporin (1986)

show individual therapy to be superior (Dush, Hirt, & Schroeder, 1983; Shapiro & Shapiro, 1982). However, these reviews tend to focus on studies in which the group treatments were, essentially, individual therapy conducted in a group setting (McRoberts et al., 1998). Those factors that are unique to group, such as group cohesion, universality, and interpersonal learning, were not tapped. In fact, in many descriptions of the studies, the group aspect was mentioned only incidentally. Consequently, many of these interventions would not fit the definition of group therapy set forth in Chapter 1.

Two important implications of the pattern of findings from meta-analytic reviews are that (1) group treatment is more effective when the properties unique to group therapy are highlighted in the treatment and (2) in examining reviews of studies, the clinician must carefully consider the inclusion characteristics of the studies on which the review is based, lest important biases in the selection of studies be overlooked.

Using a qualitative analysis, Toseland and Siporin (1986) reviewed 32 studies in which individual and group treatments of members with heterogeneous problems and symptoms were compared. Group treatment was as effective as individual treatment in 75 percent of the studies and more effective in 25 percent. Notably, many of these studies involved short-term interventions, a finding that highlights the strengths of short-term group therapy (see Chapter 10).

DON'T FORGET

Group treatment is more effective when the therapist capitalizes on those properties that are unique to the modality.

How useful is group therapy when combined with other treatments? Although the study of *treatment combinations* (for example, group therapy and individual therapy) is an extremely important line of investigation, few investigations of such combinations have been undertaken. Smith, Glass, and Miller (1980) reported that most modalities are catalyzed when paired with other modalities. In Fuhriman and Burlingame's (1994a, 1994b) review of the research, they conclude that combining individual and group treatment results in superior outcomes when compared to the independent outcomes of either intervention. Although no studies have combined medication with group treatment, D. A. Shapiro and Shapiro (1982) have noted in their meta-analytic review that effect sizes of group and individual treatments are smaller when these treatments are combined with medications than when these treatments are used alone. Further contributions to this relatively slim literature are important.

The following Putting It into Practice describes how the therapist might use the material presented in this section to speak to a gatekeeper from a managed care organization.

Under what conditions does group therapy work best? The meta-analytic review by McRoberts et al. (1998) is particularly noteworthy in its extensive analysis of other potentially moderating variables. In their analysis of 23 peer-reviewed outcome studies of adults that directly compared group and individual therapy in the same study, they found the following:

- Treatment setting, size of group, and length of session did not differentially affect the efficacy of group or individual treatment.
- The presence or absence of a cotherapist did not affect the relative value of individual versus group therapy.
- Although more than half the studies used a cognitive-behavioral orientation, there was no difference in efficacy due to theoretical orientation.
- Groups categorized as psychoeducational or process did not yield differential efficacy.
- For studies that utilized a formal diagnostic classification, individual

Putting It Into Practice

Talking to a Managed Care Representative About Group Treatment

Representative: Dr. Smith, I don't see why there would be a need for group treatment. Mrs. Brown has been in individual therapy for six months, and she appears to intend to continue. We have approved her for eighteen more sessions. Why should we approve group treatment? Isn't it redundant?

Dr. Smith: In Mrs. Brown's case, the goals would be very different. Mrs. Brown has a great deal of anxiety in initiating social contact with others, and even when she does manage to get a relationship off the ground she is unable to sustain it due to fears of intimacy. Although her individual therapy has enabled her to learn about the underlying reasons for her fear, group therapy will provide her with the crucial opportunity to get feedback from other members and develop her social skills.

Representative: Is there any research to support that a person who has both individual and group therapy makes greater gains?

Dr. Smith: There have been a number of studies, and the trend is for individuals to show greater gains when group and individual therapies are used together than when either is used alone.

Representative: Is group therapy only effective when it is used with individual therapy?

Dr. Smith: No, the effectiveness of group therapy has been well established for the treatment of a wide variety of psychological problems.

Representative: I'm glad to hear that, because it's more cost effective, but tell me, is it really as good as individual therapy?

Dr. Smith: Well, as I said before, each modality has its own special contributions to make. However, it is also the case that in the number of studies in which group therapy and individual therapy are compared to one another, they produce comparable change in many. One review was done of thirty-two studies. In twenty-four, group and individual therapies were comparable. In eight, group surpassed individual therapy. However, there have been some studies showing that individual therapy clients surpassed group clients. It did seem, however, that these were studies in which the treatment was more of an individual therapy taking place in a group than a treatment capitalizing upon certain features that most group therapists perceive as most therapeutic.

therapy had significantly better outcomes than the group modality. However, when studies were categorized according to treatment focus, circumscribed symptoms, and problems (e.g., physical pain, Substance Abuse, obesity, parenting, etc.), the group modality showed superior results.

- When the therapist had a clear allegiance to group therapy, group therapy clients had more favorable outcomes than individual therapy clients.

In general, the McRoberts et al. (1998) meta-analysis supports the conclusion that many different forms of group therapy can lead to favorable outcomes.

CAUTION

The inclusion criteria for review studies of group therapy or any other intervention must be examined carefully to determine what biases are present.

SPECIFIC PROBLEMS OR DIAGNOSTIC CATEGORIES

Is group therapy effective with all kinds of disorders, in all types of settings, for all age groups, and for clients with diverse backgrounds? Does the model utilized differentially affect effectiveness? As sufficient numbers of high-quality outcome studies are completed, the meta-analytic technique is uniquely suited to answering many of these questions. Several areas have received sufficient attention to warrant a description of the findings. We will review therapy efficacy with respect to problem area/diagnosis and developmental stage. In the last section we examine the use of group therapy with those suffering from medical disorders.

Depression and Anxiety

Group therapy for the treatment of unipolar nonpsychotic depression has considerable empirical support (Truax, 2001). Treated participants improved substantially compared to nontreated individuals (e.g., Burlingame, Fuhriman, & Mosier, 2003). The average treated participant was better off than about 85 percent of the untreated participants (McDermut, Miller, & Brown, 2001). Meta-analyses yielded conflicting findings on whether group therapy was as useful as individual treatment, however. For instance, Nietzel et al. (1987) found that individual treatment had greater benefit than group treatment. However, outcome measures were limited to the use of the Beck Depression Inventory (BDI), which suggests that interventions were limited to cognitive-behavioral therapy. As mentioned earlier, studies utilizing this method often use group therapy as a convenient format in which to administer individual treatment. In another meta-analysis, Robinson et al. (1990) found that depressed individuals showed a comparable level of improvement in individual and group therapy.

Investigators are beginning to explore which types of groups are most useful with depressed individuals. The meta-analysis by McDermut et al. (2001) focused on a study utilizing a myriad of assessment instruments and representing a great variety of theoretical models, although most included group cognitive therapy. A separate analysis revealed that cognitive-behavioral therapy groups had a slight advantage over the more process-oriented groups. Studies were completed in a wide array of settings, although most were outpatient. McDermut et al. observed that the amount of improvement was greater in university research settings and was less dramatic in settings that are more typical of routine clinical practice (and in which a greater array of variables can operate to affect outcome). Therefore, the outpatient therapist should not expect to see the magnitude of change obtained under more controlled conditions. In many of these studies on depressed populations, severely depressed and suicidal individuals were often excluded from the studies. Most studies also eliminated potential participants with comorbid psychiatric conditions or medical problems. Therefore, whether findings are generalizable to populations with more complex difficulties is unclear.

Group therapy is also effective for the treatment of the symptoms of anxiety. In a meta-analysis of 10 studies, a significant level of improvement in anxiety symptoms was observed in group therapy participants in contrast to no improvement in the wait list group (Burlingame et al., 2003).

Grief Therapy

The effectiveness of the group modality in the treatment of grief reactions has received attention recently. Two analyses have produced contradictory results. Allumbaugh and Hoyt (1999), after reviewing 35 studies, concluded that the group modality is effective in treating grief reactions. Although individual treatment appeared to have a greater impact than did group therapy, therapists doing individual treatment tended to have greater experience. They also found that when clients self-selected (i.e., sought treatment) much larger effects were obtained compared to when an investigator recruited them. In contrast, Kato and Mann (1999) reviewed eight studies that examined the effects of group therapy on adjustment to loss. Most of the interventions consisted of support groups that featured lectures about the grieving process and open discussion (see Chapter 11). A few interventions focused on consciousness raising or cognitive restructuring. Several studies compared active interventions to organized social activities (the control condition). Seventy-five percent of the studies found no beneficial effects that were a direct result of the interventions; both those in the control condition and those in the intervention condition improved similarly. Kato and Mann suggest that many factors, such as time since death, whether death was expected, and study design problems, could have masked intervention effects. The high drop-out rate could also have obscured significant findings.

In a series of studies, Piper and colleagues investigated the use of psychodynamic treatment with individuals having pathological grief reactions. Piper, Mc-Callum, and Azim (1992) found that participants in a short-term psychodynamic group showed greater positive change than a control group in the areas of interpersonal behavior, self-esteem, and life satisfaction. Piper et al. (2001) compared interpretive group therapy with support group therapy and found that grief reactions were lessened through participation in either group format. However, members of the interpretive groups received greater relief from general symptoms than participants in the support groups. Ogrodniczuk, Piper, et al. (2003) found that the personality characteristics of the group members influenced the extent to which they would profit from different group formats. For example, the personality feature of agreeableness (the tendency to be trusting and open) was directly related to members' outcomes in interpretive group therapy (that is, the more agreeable the member, the greater the reduction in grief symptomotology) but not supportive group therapy. This study and many others show that it is not sufficient to examine the model of group treatment as it affects outcome; the personality characteristics of the group member must also be taken into account.

Substance Abuse

Despite the frequent use of group therapy in Substance Abuse settings, a surprising dearth of good outcome studies exists. Several qualitative reviews suggest the efficacy of group therapy for the treatment of Substance Abuse and other forms of addiction (Brandsma & Pattison, 1985; Miller & Hester, 1986). Although Burlingame et al. (2003) did not find significant effect sizes for group therapy compared to a control group, the number of studies included was small, thus reducing the statistical power of the analysis.

Barlow, Burlingame, Nebeker, and Anderson's review (2000) noted that self-help groups for alcohol, cocaine, or marijuana dependence produced larger effect sizes than those directed toward the treatment of physical or mental illness. Approaches known to be effective with this population include psychodynamic, interpersonal, interactive, rational emotive, Gestalt, and psychodrama (Brandsma & Pattison, 1985). The efficacy of behavioral and cognitive-behavioral groups has been more clearly established, although dynamically oriented groups have been shown to be effective with some patients (Holder, Miller, & Rubonis, 1991; Miller & Hester, 1986). The results of patient-matching studies indicate that patients

> **DON'T FORGET**
> ··
> The types of groups that are effective with persons with Substance Abuse depend on other diagnostic factors.

with less sociopathy and those with neurological impairment do better in interactional therapy, whereas those with higher levels of sociopathy and psychopathology improve more in cognitive-behavioral groups (Cooney, Kadden, Litt, & Getter, 1991; Litt, Baber, DelBoca, Kadden, & Cooney, 1992).

Investigators have considered whether persons with Substance Abuse disorders are able to benefit from group therapy when placed in groups with individuals with other types of disorders. This is a practical question because individuals with Substance Abuse disorders may have other psychiatric diagnoses. Moreover, in any locale, a group exclusively for persons with substance disorders may not be available. Fortunately, several individual studies (e.g., Albrecht & Brabender, 1983) suggest that persons with Substance Abuse derive as much benefit from participating in a group of members with heterogeneous diagnoses as individuals with other diagnoses.

Eating Disorders

Considerable empirical evidence for the efficacy of group treatment with eating disorders, particularly Bulimia Nervosa (e.g., Burlingame et al., 2003) and bulimia (Bacaltchuk, Trefiglio, de Oliveira, Lima, & Mari, 1999; Fettes & Peters, 1992) has been collected. Studies with pretreatment and posttreatment measures as well as those with control groups suggest that group treatment for bulimia is effective with a moderate effect size.

Little or no evidence that individual treatment has an advantage over group treatment exists. In one study, 40 percent of the participants in individual and in group therapy reported being completely abstinent from binging and purging at follow-up (Cox & Merkel, 1989). Most studies were short term with follow-up at 1 year. Greater improvement in symptoms was associated with more intensive treatment—that is, a greater number of therapy hours per week and the addition of other treatment components. There was no definite advantage of one theoretical approach over another, and inpatient and outpatient settings offered similar effect sizes (Fettes & Peters, 1992; Hartmann, Herzog, & Drinkmann, 1992).

> **DON'T FORGET**
> ··
> There is substantial evidence for the efficacy of group therapy in the treatment of eating disorders, particularly bulimia nervosa.

Should individuals with a particular type of eating disorder be in a group with individuals with the same eating disorders or a group in which the type of eating disorder is mixed? A review of the research (Moreno, 1994) suggests that there may be an advantage to groups that are heterogeneous for eating disorders, an advantage in terms of not only outcome but also perseverance. However, members benefit from being with individuals in their developmental stage (or age group).

Childhood Sexual Abuse

Although some evidence for the efficacy of group therapy with women who have been sexually abused as children has been obtained, the studies remain largely case studies and anecdotal reports (Marotta & Asner, 1999). Group treatments include individualized, psychoanalytic, psychodynamic, psychoeducational, and interpersonal process group therapies. Two reviews suggest that group work is beneficial in improving self-esteem and affect regulation (DeJong & Gorey, 1996; Marotta & Asner, 1999). Nonstandardized outcome measures (interview and participant surveys) and standardized instruments indicate that on average 75 percent of the group improves. The most frequent type of group was closed-ended, and the length varied from four sessions to 18 months, although there is no relationship between length and improvement in subjective well-being (Marotta & Asner, 1999). In general, gains are maintained at follow-up.

Psychotic Disorders

Kanas (1986) reviewed 40 outcome studies involving inpatient and outpatient schizophrenics. His conclusions about the usefulness of group therapy with this population were very favorable: Group therapy was superior to inert comparison control groups in 67 percent of the inpatients and 80 percent of the outpatients, with long-term therapy obtaining the most positive results. Kanas also noted that group therapy worked best when the leader worked in the here and now rather than in the there and then. A more recent meta-analytic review of 106 studies (26 of which involved a group intervention) (Mojtabi, Nicholson, & Carpenter, 1998) showed smaller effect sizes for group therapy than other modalities such as family and individual therapies.

THE DEVELOPMENTAL STAGE

Suppose you are planning to run a group for children and adolescents. Will the empirical literature provide you the same degree of backing as with an adult population? In fact, investigators have made considerable progress in delineating the types of group interventions that are effective for children and adolescents. Nascent efforts to establish usefulness in the treatment of elderly individuals are underway.

Children and Adolescents

Many outcome studies have been conducted on the population ranging in age from 4 to 18 years. Unfortunately, most of the reviews consider children and adolescents together, despite the considerable developmental differences between these groups. We will note where they have been separated and where they have been combined.

At least eight qualitative reviews of group outcome studies (Hoag & Burlingame, 1997a) and at least 11 meta-analyses that have included the group format as one of the several variables in assessing the child outcome literature are available. Collectively these studies provide evidence that group therapy with children and adolescents produces positive results compared with no treatment or placebo treatment.

With regard to differential effectiveness of the group and individual modalities, most of the qualitative reviews and meta-analyses suggest that individual therapy is no more effective than group therapy. However, age and venue may influence which modality is more effective. For example, Tillitski (1990) found that for adolescents group is more effective than individual treatment, whereas for children the opposite is true. Prout and De-Martino (1986) reported group treatment to be more effective than individual treatment for children and adolescents in a school setting.

Most of the reported group therapy outcome studies with children and adolescents take place in a school setting and, taken globally, suggest that these school-based groups are beneficial. This of course is in sharp contrast to the adult studies, in which the majority of the participants come

Rapid Reference 7.3

Group Therapy Outcomes for Children and Adolescents

Evidence exists that group therapy produces the following positive changes:

- Improved social skills and diminished social problems
- Enhanced self-esteem
- Greater sense of an internal locus of control
- Diminished negative consequences of parental divorce
- Diminished anxiety and depression in some groups
- Decreased antisocial and disruptive behaviors

from clinic- or university-based research settings. Some evidence exists that children and adolescents participating in the school-based studies have fewer and less severe problems than those in the clinical population. Therefore, the clinician must apply

> **DON'T FORGET**
> ....
> Treatment groups have been found effective for children and adolescents across different levels of structure.

the findings from school studies with caution to other populations. Various theoretical orientations as well as preventative programs, counseling, guidance, and training groups were assessed, with no clear advantage for any type of treatment. Less structured therapy-oriented groups as well as structured or didactic psychoeducational groups have been found to be effective (Hoag & Burlingame, 1997b).

Groups emphasizing problem solving, affect regulation, social skills training, and cognitive restructuring were equally effective (Hibbs, 2001). In the child and adolescent research, as in the adult outcome studies, the allegiance of the researcher was found to be a factor in outcome: When the therapist had a clear allegiance to the treatment being investigated, that treatment produced significantly greater improvement than when such an allegiance was lacking (Hoag & Burlingame, 1997b).

Evidence is accumulating that group therapy is effective in improving social skills and social problems, locus of control, and self-esteem/self-concept (Hoag & Burlingame, 1997b) and in assisting children of divorced parents (Dagley, Gazda, Eppinger, & Stewart, 1994; Hoag & Burlingame; see Rapid Reference 7.3). Empirical work on the use and outcome of group with children and adolescents who suffer from Obsessive-Compulsive Disorder, panic, and Schizophrenia is scanty.

The utility of group therapy with children and adolescents who exhibit symptoms of anxiety and depression has been most positive when the group was in the context of the school setting (e.g., Burns, Hoagwood, & Mrazek, 1999). Most of the school-based interventions were brief and usually more oriented toward cognitive-behavioral therapy. Follow-up studies indicate that fewer students developed depression than otherwise would have without the treatment, even after 2 years (Burns et al., 1999; Harrington, Whittaker, & Shoebridge, 1998). These interventions were effective with children as young as 7 and as old as 18, although the group intervention had a much larger effect upon elementary school children than upon those in middle school (Burns et al.; Hibbs, 2001; Prout & Prout, 1998). However, all of these studies indicated that they excluded children who would meet criteria for Major Depressive Disorder. The one review that included both clinical and school populations did not find group interventions to be effective for anxiety and depression (Hoag & Burlingame, 1997b), which raises questions about the sufficiency of group treatment in reducing symptoms at a moderate to high level of severity in children and adolescents.

Geriatric Clients

Work with geriatric clients is a relatively new area (see Chapter 9 on diversity), and the number of outcome research studies mirrors this recent development. Three areas warrant discussion. The first is the use of group therapy in facilitating the discharge of elderly patients from state hospitals and improving the medical condition of diabetics. In some of these early quasi-experimental studies, group therapy was found to be effective (Weiss & Lazarus, 1993).

The second significant effort is by Pinquart and Sorensen (2001), who conducted a meta-analysis of 122 psychosocial and psychotherapeutic intervention studies with adults older than 55. Individual interventions were found to be more effective than group interventions on most of the dependent variables. Although there is no difference in self-rated depression between the interventions, clients in the individual intervention reported better subjective well-being and had lower clinician-rated depression than those in the group intervention. The reviewers did acknowledge that many of the group interventions involved less effective forms of treatment (eclectic, activity promotion), which may have contributed to the lower effect size of the group interventions, particularly as it related to depression.

The third area that has yielded rather interesting results is the development of reality orientation. Reality orientation, which aims to improve the quality of life of confused elderly people, involves the presentation of orientation and memory information relating to time, place, and person. Spector, Davies, Woods, and Orrell (2000) conducted a meta-analysis on eight studies for demented patients, which showed that reality orientation had significant positive impact on cognition and behaviors, and those who received more intensive treatment had the highest cognitive scores.

Groups with Medical Patients

One of the most exciting areas of new development in the group psychotherapy literature is the use of group therapy with patients who suffer from chronic medical diseases. Although groups have been implemented with almost every kind of illness, published outcome research has been less forthcoming. However, a meta-analysis (Burlingame et al., 2003) of 23 studies covering a range of medical conditions yielded an effect size (ES) of .49 for treated individuals and .00 for un-treated individuals, showing a moderate-level effect. Three medical conditions that have shown promise in terms of patients' benefit from group treatment are heart disease, cancer, and gastrointestinal illness, which will be discussed in the following sections.

Heart Disease

One large study (Friedman et al., 1986) followed 1,000 patients who had had heart attacks for 4–5 years after the first event to monitor the reoccurrence of a myocardial infarction. Those patients who received group therapy had significantly fewer heart attacks at the end of the study than members of a control group: Among those who received group treatment, only 12.9 percent had an additional reoccurrence, compared with 28 percent of those in the control group. Further study will be helpful in delineating the essential features of the group structure that helped reduce the reoccurrence of a myocardial infarction.

Cancer

Although most of the outcome studies with a group intervention have focused on women with breast cancer, there has been investigation of group approaches for people with other forms of cancer, such as ovarian cancer, melanoma, lymphoma, and prostate cancer (Sherman et al., 2004). A variety of models have been found effective: behavioral (using specific techniques such as guided imagery, relaxation, biofeedback training), supportive expressive (Bloom, Ross, & Burnell, 1978; Gore-Felton & Spiegel, 1999), and cognitive-behavioral (Bottomley et al., 1996). The efficacy of the treatment is very much influenced by the specific outcome measure that is utilized. Reasonable evidence exists that group interventions are successful at decreasing depression, anxiety, and distress and enhancing adjustment, psychological well-being, and quality of life in this population (Andersen, 2002; Fawzy & Fawzy, 1998; Gore-Felton & Spiegel). In a recent study (Fukui et al., 2002) on Japanese women, investigators found that women with breast cancer who participated in a psychoeducational group treatment showed more active coping at a 6-month follow-up than those in a control group. However, control and experimental groups did not differ in changes in degrees of helplessness.

An emerging area of study is the group treatment of healthy individuals who are at high risk for cancer because of family history (see Sherman et al., 2004, for an extensive review of group therapy, cancer, and HIV). For example, Esplen et al. (2000) found that women at risk for breast cancer who participated in 12 sessions of supportive-expressive group treatment manifested diminished distress at the termination of the group.

DON'T FORGET

....

Therapy and support groups have been found to be effective in the treatment of the psychological symptoms associated with physical illness and, in some cases, the physical symptoms themselves.

More controversial and equivocal in terms of research findings are the efforts to link these psychological interventions to the course of the disease or physiological changes. A few studies have found that group therapy has boosted the immunological system, which presumably is likely to decrease morbidity (Cruess et al., 2000; Fawzy, Cousins, et al., 1990; Gruber, 1993). Some have even found that, compared with a control group, individuals who have participated in a group intervention have higher survival rates (Fawzy et al., 1993; Spiegel, Bloom, & Yalom, 1981). However, for every study that suggests an increased survival rate, there are two that have not found a difference. This will certainly be an exciting area to follow in the decades ahead.

Gastrointestinal Illness

Group therapy has been shown to be effective in the treatment of individuals with irritable bowel syndrome (IBS). Toner et al. (1998) randomly assigned individuals with IBS to a cognitive therapy group, a psychoeducational group, or conventional medical treatment. They found that only in the cognitive-behavioral group did participants show improvement in such physical symptoms as diarrhea, constipation, pain, and tenderness.

BIASES IN THE OUTCOME LITERATURE

The outcome literature on group therapy is biased in two important ways. The first is that the types of outcome variables investigated in studies predominantly concern symptoms. Although symptomatic change is often a goal of treatment, many approaches seek other types of changes. Perhaps most neglected is the study of interpersonal change, despite the fact that a variety of treatment approaches, most notably the interpersonal model, establish such change as a primary goal. A small collection of such studies does exist, and these studies have generally yielded favorable results. Burlingame et al. (2003), based on their analysis of eight studies, found that social adjustment measures produced the highest levels of improvement for group treatment. A meta-analysis (Morgan & Flora, 2002) on a set of six studies examining group therapy with incarcerated offenders yielded a moderate positive treatment effect: Inmates who participated in group therapy showed improved interpersonal functioning relative to controls. The research literature would be enriched by similar efforts on other populations.

The lack of research on interpersonal change may be a reflection of another bias in the research: the emphasis on short-term interventions (Piper, 1993). Short-term group interventions have been the primary focus of investigators for several reasons: (1) Short-term studies are easier to conduct (for example, member attrition is less of a problem); (2) they are less expensive; and (3) the findings are more attractive to third-party payers seeking economical therapies. Because of this bias, we have little information on the kinds of psychological changes that are unlikely to change over a brief interval, such as major changes in a person's style of relating.

ASSESSING THE EFFECTIVENESS OF GROUP THERAPY FOR THE INDIVIDUAL GROUP MEMBER

Group therapists should not only be aware of findings on group therapy but also attempt to ascertain whether their own groups are effective. Even if therapists use approaches that have demonstrated efficacy, local conditions may lead to outcome patterns that differ from those reported in the literature.

However, systematic efforts at data collection can provide other benefits. Dies and Dies (1993) identified the advantages of monitoring members' progress in the context of a short-term group therapy. For each of four phases of treatment, they specified how treatment monitoring might enhance members' progress.

In the *negotiation phase,* prior to treatment, the use of measures provides baseline data to which future data can be compared. Some measures can assist the member in concretizing goals. For example, the Target Goals Form (MacKenzie, 1990) requires the group member to list three goals and describe them in behavioral and interpersonal terms. These goals are then rated on a scale that reflects the extent to which each is bothering the group member. The member can return to these goals at the end of treatment or at some interval after treatment and indicate the extent to which the area still represents a problem for him or her.

In the *retention phase,* which occurs in the beginning of treatment, collection of data can aid in the early detection of potential dropouts, enhance the members' understanding of the therapy process, provide members with a medium in which to express concerns about the group, and convey the therapist's interest in members' progress. The *enhancement phase,* in which members have made a commitment to treatment, is characterized by the use of empirical measures to supplement the information available in the sessions, stimulate the members' reflection about the sessions, and expand the therapist's documentation of progress.

In the *evaluation phase,* which comprehends the termination and posttermination periods, measures can be compared to the baseline measures to assess the usefulness of the treatment. Measures administered during termination and at later intervals reciprocally show the short-term and long-term benefits of treatment. Measurement in the evaluation stage also enables the therapist to make an informed determination of members' continuing needs for further treatment. Data from some instruments may help members to transfer learning from the group to the outside world as they reflect on changes they observed in themselves outside the group.

Selection of Measures

What measures might the therapist use that would serve a number of the functions we have described? There are various criteria (see Rapid Reference 7.4), which the following sections will discuss.

Group Goals

The therapist should select measures that reflect the types of change that the group is designed to effect. For example, the Beck self-report scales—such as the Beck Depression Inventory II (A. T. Beck & Steer, 1993), the Beck Anxiety Inventory (A. T. Beck & Steer, 1990), and the Beck Hopelessness Scale (A. T. Beck et al., 1974)—are often used in cognitive-behavioral groups to assess targeted symptomatic changes. Broader symptom measures, such as the Symptom Checklist 90 (SCL-90-R; Derogatis, 1977), are also available and useful in the treatment of symptomatically heterogeneous groups. The Social Adjustment Scale—Self Report (SAS-SR; Horowitz et al., 1988; Weissman & Bothwell, 1976) provides a picture of the client's functioning in seven social roles such as work, social and leisure activity, and family unit roles. This instrument would be appropriate for groups designed to effect changes in interpersonal behavior. A brief form of this instrument is also available.

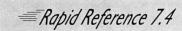

Rapid Reference 7.4

Factors to Be Considered in Selecting Measures of Progress/Outcome

- Goals of the group (what types of change is the group seeking to effect?)
- Use of multiple measures to obtain a comprehensive picture
- Use of measures with sound psychometric properties
- Brevity
- Reading level
- Cost

Overall adaptation can be assessed through service utilization statistics before and after the group experience (MacKenzie, 1990). For example, the number of visits to a medical practitioner or the number of days in the hospital over a defined period, such as 6 months, can reveal aspects of the individual's general functioning within the environment.

Use of Multiple Measures

To obtain a full picture of the effects of group treatment, the therapist should use different methods of measuring changes in the person (Maruish, 2002). First, different measures have built-in biases. For example, the therapist's assessment of the client's change is typically more favorable than that of a third party who knows the client's self-report (Lambert & Hill, 1994). Self-report measures are especially influenced by the test-taking set (e.g., the desire to present the self in a positive or negative light).

Second, often a group experience will be designed to produce change in a variety of areas such as symptom relief, increase in life satisfaction, and improvement in relational skills. For example, Piper (1995) described a short-term group for the treatment of individuals with problems related to loss. The broad goal was to help individuals achieve insight into their conflicts concerning loss. Among the more specific goals were a lessened intensity of symptoms related to loss, adaptive steps toward achieving satisfying relationships, and greater tolerance of ambivalence in relationships. To do justice to this array of goals, Piper and colleagues needed to have a variety of outcome measures. Among those they selected were the Social Adjustment Scale to investigate work, social, and sexual functions; the SCL-90-R (Derogotis, 1977) and the Beck Depression Inventory (A. T. Beck & Steer, 1987) to measure the intensity of symptoms; and the Interpersonal Dependency Scale (Hirshfield, Klerman, & Gouch, 1977) to measure the client's capacity for autonomous functioning.

Third, the use of different types of measures is desirable because different measures offer different information. For example, self-report measures (e.g., the SCL-90-R) should be complemented with behavioral measures, because whereas the former tell us how the person sees himself or herself the latter provide a more direct measure of the person's functioning.

Use of Measures with Sound Psychometric Properties

When possible, the group therapist should use measures that have been demonstrated to be valid and reliable (Anastasi & Urbina, 1997). If relevant measures do not exist with established psychometric properties, the therapist should regard their use as experimental and seek to determine their levels of validity and reliability.

Other Considerations

Among other important considerations is brevity. Particularly for those instruments that are used repeatedly during the course of the group, it is important that they can be taken in a brief interval so that the group member's cooperation is maintained. Moreover, in some treatment environments, there is a time limit on all of the activities associated with a session. A lengthy instrument could compromise the session itself. It may be possible to use instruments that involve a significant time commitment at the beginning and end of treatment.

An instrument's reading level should also be considered. Unless the therapist is using educational level as a selection variable, the therapist should assume that members' proficiency levels in different academic skills are variable. Therefore, selected instruments should have no higher than an eighth-grade reading level, and preferably a sixth.

Finally, if the therapist seeks to build in the careful monitoring of group members' progress as a feature of his or her group therapy practice, the expense of the measures should be taken into account. An instrument requiring a per-use charge for computer scoring and interpretation might become prohibitively expensive over time. Fortunately, there are a number of inexpensive and even no-cost reliable and valid instruments available on the market.

Use of Process Measures

Knowing how a group member is progressing over the course of the group is valuable information for the group therapist, but it is also helpful to know what experiences may be mediating the change. That is, how are the processes of the group, the change mechanisms, mediating outcome? Although the task of the therapist is to assess group processes continually, a number of formal instruments may aid the therapist in this task. Let us consider two examples.

Group Climate Questionnaire (GCQ-S)

This 12-item questionnaire (MacKenzie, 1983) assesses members' perceptions of three dimensions of the overall group atmosphere: *engagement,* or the extent to which there is a positive working environment; *conflict,* or the degree of negativity in the group associated with anger and mistrust; and *avoidance,* or the extent to which members refrain from assuming responsibility for their progress in the group. This scale can be completed in a very brief interval at the end of the session and can be completed by members, therapists, or observers. An advantage of this instrument is that it has been used with closed-ended groups, and its ability to show developmental trends has been demonstrated (e.g., MacKenzie, Dies, Coché, Rutan, & Stone, 1987). Therefore, a therapist can learn about his or her group by comparing how a particular group looks in relation to how groups often perform.

Critical Incidents

This questionnaire, which asks members to articulate the most important or crucial event of the session, can be used in at least two ways. The first is to see which therapeutic factors members perceive to be most important (see Chapter 4 for a listing of factors). For example, suppose a member writes, "Hearing Andrew talk about finally being capable of joyful moments a year after his father died." This statement would be categorized as signifying the member's use of the therapeutic factor of hope. If a group begins to shift in its use of different therapeutic factors, it may signify that the group has developed. Kivlighan and Mullison (1988) found that in early group sessions members emphasized cognitive factors such as universality whereas in later sessions members used interpersonal learning more extensively.

The second way in which the instrument can be used is qualitative. By reading each member's description of the most significant group event, the therapist can be privy to reactions that may not be evident from their behavior or comments in the session itself. For example, Joe may write, "I felt it was great how Dan stood up to the therapist. I wish I could do that with my mother." Although Joe may be benefiting from vicarious learning, this treatment may be catalyzed by more direct exploration of feelings toward authority figures.

Other Process Measures

A variety of other process measures exist, some of which are extremely complicated and beyond the scope of this text. For example, the Hills Interaction Matrix, which has been researched since the 1950s, entails an elaborate scoring that captures both the content and the form of group discussion (Hill, 1977). Although this system yields potentially valuable information, it may be impractical for everyday clinical use. The reader wishing to delve deeper is referred to A. P. Beck and Lewis's (2000) compendium of process measures.

Examining Outcome and Process Together

The group therapist should be a local scientist (Peterson, Peterson, Abrams, & Stricker, 1997) who strives to understand whether the group treatment he or she is providing is helpful and what about it works. By looking at process and outcome measures in concert with one another, therapists obtain the necessary information they need to maximize the benefit of group treatment. Suppose, for example, that upon tracking outcomes, the therapist realizes that there is one subgroup that shows large gains as a consequence of group treatment and another that shows minor or no gains. In looking back at the Group Climate Questionnaire, the therapist may discover that the latter subgroup perceived less engagement in the group, possibly a reflection of their own lack of enjoyment. The Critical Events Questionnaire responses may be sketchy and may reflect others' activities rather than their own. From this information the therapist could devise strategies to engage more fully all members. The therapist would then assess whether the implementation of these strategies was associated with an increase in the number of members who showed improvement over the course of the group.

Undoubtedly, the introduction of outcome and process measures poses difficulties and complications. However, for all of these, there are potential solutions. Both problems attendant upon the introduction of measures and potential solutions are listed in Rapid Reference 7.5.

≡Rapid Reference 7.5

Disadvantages of Measurement and Potential Solutions

Potential problems:
- Measurement arouses fear of exposure in members.
- Members may react with anger and anxiety out of a sense of being a guinea pig.
- Use of measurements can create tension between therapists and members.
- Measurement provides a mechanism for acting out by members (e.g., failing to fill out forms or doing so incorrectly).
- Use of measurements may be seen as taking the group's attention away from more important issues.

Solutions:
- Employ a careful, comprehensive informed consent form and provide an explicit statement about how confidentiality and anonymity will be preserved.
- Address potential sources of anxiety about the measures before using them.
- Be open about the purposes of the instrument.
- Explain the benefits of using measurement to the member.
- Indicate what feedback members will be given from the measures.

Source: MacKenzie and Dies (1982).

SUMMARY AND CONCLUSIONS

Recent narrative reviews and meta-analytic studies provide an abundance of empirical evidence that group treatment is better than no treatment at all for many problems and for many populations. Problems that appear particularly responsive to group treatment include depression, eating disorders, the psychological consequences of child sexual abuse, and particular medical conditions such as cancer. In most cases group therapy is as effective as individual interventions, and in some cases it is more effective. Insofar as group therapy is more cost efficient, it would seem to be the preferred modality when treatment must be limited.

One must, however, be wary of the extent to which these conclusions can be applied to a particular clinical situation. First, one must be cognizant of the inclusion and exclusion criteria of meta-analyses and qualitative studies for the studies from which conclusions are drawn. Second, many variables may moderate the efficacy of a given approach, such as group structure, therapist leadership style, and member characteristics. Third, persons in clinical situations may be lower functioning and may have more complex difficulties than individuals participating in research studies. Fourth, the research literature is biased in the direction of short-term interventions that emphasize symptomatic change. Greater exploration of long-term groups and the use of outcome measures reflecting other types of change, especially interpersonal, is needed. On an individual level, the therapist should have multiple means of assessing both the progress of individual members and the effectiveness of his or her own methods in the local clinical context.

 TEST YOURSELF

1. **The conclusions from a meta-analytic study are critically related to the selection criteria for the studies included in the meta-analysis.** True or False?

2. **The advantage of calculating the effect size is that it can be compared across studies.** True or False?

3. **Some meta-analyses claim that individual therapy is more effective than group therapy. Which is a valid criticism of these meta-analytic studies?**
   (a) The results obtained are only as good as the study designs.
   (b) In these studies, the group format is used as a convenient format to conduct individual therapy.
   (c) The effect size for group therapy is higher than it is for individual therapy.
   (d) These studies involved the treatment of depression.

(continued)

4. **Of the following psychiatric problems, which has little empirical evidence for the efficacy of group treatment?**

   (a) Depression

   (b) Grief

   (c) Eating disorders

   (d) Bipolar disorders

5. _____ **is the phenomenon whereby the results of the study are correlated with the beliefs of the author who published the paper.**

6. **The Group Climate Questionnaire is used**

   (a) to assess the individual members' perception of the overall group atmosphere.

   (b) to determine the vacation schedule of the therapist.

   (c) in the meta-analysis of the efficacy of group therapy.

   (d) to assess the interaction of psychopathology and group interaction.

7. **Most outcome research emphasizes _____ approaches and _____ change.**

   (a) short-term, symptomatic

   (b) long-term, symptomatic

   (c) short-term, personality

   (d) long-term, interpersonal

Answers: 1. True; 2. True; 3. b; 4. d; 5. allegiance effect; 6. a; 7. a

Eight

ETHICAL, LEGAL, AND GROUP MANAGEMENT ISSUES

The competent group therapist acts ethically and legally in conducting therapy groups. Achieving this type of competence requires more than good intentions. Many a well-intended practitioner has engaged in activity while lacking a solid ethical and legal foundation because of inadequate knowledge of ethical principles and guidelines, the ways they figure in different decisions, and the laws and court rulings that govern clinical practice. A high level of familiarity with the ethical codes of one's profession is a good starting point. Yet these codes necessarily are general: They do not address with specificity the problems characteristic of any particular form of practice, including group therapy. Therefore, the novice to any area of practice must make a special effort to learn what special problems or dilemmas are characteristic of that area, what ethical principles and legal issues they involve, and how experienced practitioners address them.

This chapter will aid the reader in this endeavor. The first section will highlight common ethical problems that arise in group therapy, and the second will focus on the group therapist as a manager of the group and the legal and ethical aspects of these managerial activities.

ETHICAL AND LEGAL PROBLEMS IN GROUP TREATMENT

This section will highlight some of the major issues with significant ethical dimensions, legal dimensions, or both that routinely occur in the conduct of a psychotherapy group.

Privacy: Confidentiality and Privileged Communication

When candidates interview for admission to a therapy group, often they express concern about the trustworthiness of the other members to hold the material they might share in utter confidence. Tacitly, they know that not being able to share what is of greatest significance to them will limit substantially what they can derive from the group. They realize, too, that the condition of such sharing is a sense of safety that those disclosures will not be communicated by the other members to parties outside the group. In fact, from their survey of experienced group therapists, Roback, Ochoa, Block, and Purdon (1992) found that, second only to anger toward the violator, the immediate effect of a breach of confidentiality is a lower level of self-disclosure.

The therapist has an ethical obligation to create the conditions in which confidentiality is likely to be preserved among members in order to safeguard each member's right to privacy and to enable the delivery of an effective therapeutic experience. There are many means the therapist can use to create a climate in which confidentiality is honored.

Establishing Expectations and Consequences

During member preparation the therapist should outline in very concrete terms what is meant by the requirement to observe confidentiality. Entering members must be told that observation of confidentiality means not only refraining from sharing what other members say in the group but also avoiding the disclosure of members' identities as group members (Luepker, 2003). Situations in which the new member may unwittingly violate confidentiality should be anticipated. For instance, members should be prepared for encountering other group members in the waiting room, where others may be present. How the member would respond when unexpectedly encountering a member outside the group should also be discussed, given that this situation is one in which violations most often occur. A member taken by surprise may unthinkingly identify another group member as such to a companion (e.g., "Oh, that's just someone in my therapy group"). In the preparation of the new member, alternate responses that do not create a confidentiality violation could be explored (see the following Putting It into Practice).

In group therapy with children, the therapist should inform prospective members whether and what information will be given to parents (Wagner, 2003). For example, children might be told that parents will receive a general description of the session but will be given specific information only if the child evidences an intent to harm others or self or if there is a clinical basis for suspecting abuse or neglect. Children should also be given explicit guidelines about what they can and cannot talk about with their parents.

The discussion about confidentiality should include an explicit acknowledgment that violation may lead to harm to the person whose confidence has been broken. This point bears emphasis because the new member may believe that the most negative effects would be shame or embarrassment. Although these nega-

Putting It Into Practice

Explaining Confidentiality

In explaining confidentiality, a conversation such as the following might take place.

Therapist: A most important rule of the group is that you observe confidentiality. This means that you do not share with anyone outside the group what another member shares in the group. Nor do you identify to anyone outside the group the identity of a member in the group.

New group member: Of course I wouldn't do that.

Therapist: Well, sometimes it might be tempting. Suppose you put two and two together and realized that a young man in the group once briefly dated your daughter. It might be very tempting to tell her, and yet you cannot. Can you commit to observing confidentiality under all circumstances, both easy and hard?

New group member: Yeah, I can see what you mean by it being tempting, but I'm certain that I can observe the rule.

Teaching note: This is merely a segment of the conversation about confidentiality that should occur. As noted in the text, both the dangers of confidentiality violations and the possible consequences for the violator must be spelled out.

tive experiences are bad enough, the new member should be made aware that jobs may be lost, relationships may be dissolved, or other tangible consequences may occur when confidential information is shared.

With the member's greater cognizance of these possible consequences of violations, the therapist can proceed to outline what might befall the member who violates confidentiality. One type of consequence consists of action taken by the therapist, often with the input of the other members. The most extreme sanction would be the member's removal from the group. Another sanction that is sometimes imposed is financial: The transgressor pays a prescribed fee to the violated member. Even the revelation of the violation to the entire group and a prolonged discussion of this event and its significance serves as a sanction. Violations of confidentiality vary in level of severity, and sanctions could be adjusted accordingly. A second type of consequence would be initiated by the group member who is the object of the violation. He or she might bring a civil suit against the violator, or, in parts of the United States where confidentiality violations are illegal, such as the District of Columbia, the violated member might even press charges.

Setting an Example

Another means by which the therapist can create an atmosphere in which confidentiality is maintained is through example. There are circumstances in which the therapist is legally required to break confidentiality, such as upon receiving a court order to submit documents or offer testimony. Other than these exceptions, which should be clearly outlined to a member before he or she begins the group, the therapist's behavior should be exemplary with respect to honoring confidentiality. If the therapist has obtained information about the member outside the group, the therapist should have an explicit agreement with the member about whether any or all of that information will be shared in the group sessions. For example, suppose a member calls the therapist the day before the session and says, "I can't attend the session tomorrow night because my child was hospitalized for an emergency appendectomy." The therapist should not share with the group the specific reason for the absence unless the member has agreed that such communication will occur. Likewise, the therapist must obtain specific written permission from the client before sharing information about the client with another professional who is treating the client.

Giving Reminders

Frequent reminders to the group about confidentiality are likely to bolster observation of this rule. Very often, these reminders can occur within the natural unfolding of events in the group as circumstances arise that might compromise confidentiality. The group therapist should take great interest in occasions on which members unexpectedly encounter one another outside of the group. If one of the members was accompanied by a party who was not a group member, the event is particularly demanding because members are likely to experience conflicting pressures. Hopefully, there is the pressure to preserve the other member's confidentiality by refraining from disclosing anything about the group member, including his or her status of being such. Yet there also is the pressure to avoid inflicting hurt upon the group member that might occur if he or she is not acknowledged. If the accompanied member acknowledges the other member, there also is the pressure not to appear oddly secretive if the companion asks who the other member is (particularly since secretiveness may arouse curiosity). The opportunity to share reactions accomplishes several functions:

- It rewards members for handling the situation well.
- It allows for the correction of mistaken impressions (for example, if a member construed a lack of acknowledgment as a rejection).
- It enables members to recognize other possible responses for handling this circumstance that might not occur to them spontaneously in the situation (for example, it might not occur to a member that he or she need not acknowledge the other member).
- It underscores the importance of all matters related to confidentiality.

Processing Violations

Any violations that do occur, no matter how minor, should be thoroughly processed within the group. Violations of confidentiality are not unusual. For example, in one survey, half of the experienced group therapists reported that there had been confidentiality violations in their groups (Roback et al., 1992). Most frequently reported was the violation in which a member identified another group member to someone outside the group (for example, a woman told her husband that one of his coworkers was in the group). Once trust has been shattered in the group, significant negative effects ensue—anger, caution, dropouts, fragmentation (Roback et al.). To both rebuild trust and also deter further violations, members should be given ample opportunities to verbalize their reactions. If the violating member is permitted to remain in the group, a commitment should be secured that he or she will avoid any further violations. Often a deepened level of trust follows a thoroughgoing exploration (Roback et al.).

In psychotherapy, the statutory right of *privileged communication* enables the patient to prevent the therapist from sharing confidential information in a court proceeding. Although privilege in the therapy relationship is recognized in all states, often there are exceptions. For example, some states specify that the mental health professional must be licensed in order for the communications in the therapy relationship to be regarded as privileged. Privilege has also been limited by court rulings. In some proceedings, the court has ruled that privilege does not exist in multiperson therapies such as group therapy. The reasoning has been that if a patient can share personal information with someone other than the therapist, then it is being shared with the world. In other proceedings, such as *State v. Andring*, the court has upheld that group therapy records are privileged on the premise that the presence of third parties is not incidental but integral to the delivery of the treatment.

Confronting the group therapist is a situation of ambiguity with respect to privilege. Whether privilege would be upheld in any particular legal circumstance would depend on a variety of factors, including the state in which the legal issue arose, the nature of the case (Slovenko, 1998), and the evidentiary value of the testimony. The therapist should respond to the ambiguous status of privilege in several ways. In the informed consent for group therapy, the prospective member should be apprised of the legal uncertainty surrounding privilege in group therapy. The therapist should explain to the new member that if a court ordered the member's records to be surrendered in a case involving either that member or another party in the group, the therapist might ultimately be compelled to surrender them. If a subpoena is received for a member's records and the member does not consent to have them released, the therapist should assert privilege. Often this step requires securing the services of an attorney. All of these interventions are made to protect the autonomy of each group member.

Informed Consent

The informed consent is the cornerstone of group therapy. It is an agreement between the therapist and group member that is a foundation for the member's constructive work within the group. Although *informed consent* is a singular term, each component has a separate meaning worthy of consideration. *Informed* refers to the right of the group member to know all of the crucial aspects associated with the group treatment. *Consent* refers to the entering member's agreement to participate in the group having cognizance of these crucial aspects. Each of these elements, *informed* and *consent,* will be described in turn.

An informed group member is one who understands the goals of the group and how his or her individual goals are congruent with the group goals. For example, suppose an individual in the interview for group therapy identifies a number of goals on which she might work. Among these is the achievement of the ability to be more assertive with authority figures in her life, such as her supervisor at work. This individual had been referred by her physician to a cognitive-behavioral group for the treatment of obsessive-compulsive symptoms. The therapist interviewing the candidate believes that although the group has another primary target, it nonetheless might provide the member with the means to make some headway on this interpersonal issue. At the same time, the therapist recognizes that there might be alternate groups that would provide the member with a more focal means to attend to this problem. To adequately inform the client, the therapist must share these conclusions with her. With this information, the client may then decide to pursue the group anyway because there are other personal goals she could address in the group, or she may instead decide to pursue the goal of becoming more assertive in another type of group. In either case, her decision will be rooted in accurate information about what this particular group can and cannot do.

An informed group member is also one who recognizes what processes and techniques are used in the group to effect change in members. Particularly important is apprising candidates for group about any techniques used in the group that would be unanticipated or that would raise members' level of anxiety. For example, although processes such as interpersonal learning, in which the member dwells within the here and now of the group, are highly familiar to the group therapist, they can seem quite strange and unexpected to the incoming group member. An individual whose cultural or ethnic background emphasizes the indirect expression of thoughts and feelings might be particularly likely to be fazed when the group's arena of operation differs from his or her anticipations. At minimum, such a surprise may cause the client needless anxiety. More important, it may lead the member to feel that a bait and switch has occurred and undermine the member's trust in the therapist, a particularly essential commodity early in the life of the group.

The incoming member must also be informed about the risks of the group. The standard that is typically used in determining disclosure is whether it is a risk that a reasonable person would want to know about before making the decision. Among the risks that have been identified are the following:

- Experiencing discomfort in the group sessions that may extend to life outside the group. Depending upon the goals and processes of the group, members may have negative reactions associated with receiving constructive feedback, recognizing certain psychological elements within themselves, or facing difficult behavioral tasks.
- Failing to benefit from the group. As noted in Chapter 2, the outcome literature on group therapy is very favorable, a fact that can be shared with the incoming member. Nonetheless, not every member benefits, and the entering member should be helped to understand that no guarantee of his or her progress can be made. This point applies to all forms of psychological treatment. However, some (Lakin, 1994) have argued that, relative to the practitioner of individual therapy, the group therapist has less control over the outcome of each member because group treatment is so crucially dependent on the contributions of other members.
- The member's confidentiality might be broken by another member, and harm could come to the member from this violation. As was discussed when the vantage of the violator was considered, members often fail to think through the possible consequences sufficiently to recognize that they could be very serious. Roback, Moor, Bloch, and Shelton (1996) suggest making the following kind of statement in the written informed consent:

  If you reveal secrets in the group, those secrets might be told outside the group by other members of the group. If your secrets are told outside the group, then people you know might learn your secrets. You could be hurt emotionally and economically if your secrets are told outside the group. (p. 135)

  Some practitioners may hesitate to acknowledge the possibility of harm out of fear that it may discourage the candidate from entering the group. An antidote to any overreaction on the part of the candidate to the disclosure of this risk is sharing the steps the therapist takes to prevent violations. However, as Roback et al. (1996) point out, research is needed to determine the effects of providing different types of information during the informed consent on the processes in the group (e.g., degree of self-disclosure) and outcome.

- The therapist or other group members may be required to share information about the member or vice versa in a legal situation if privilege is not upheld. This risk has been described in the prior section.

In order for the candidate to be adequately informed, each element of the informed consent must be discussed in depth, with plenty of opportunity for the candidate to ask questions and the therapist to discern any areas of confusion. In most instances, the presentation of the information should be given in verbal and written form and the consent should be obtained verbally and in writing. The therapist should document the conversation in which the elements of the informed consent are presented to the candidate.

There are some occasions on which treatment is not voluntary. For example, someone may be court committed to a group for anger management. The fact that consent is not required in order for treatment to proceed does not remove the therapist's responsibility to provide the information that has been specified. Sometimes, in fact, as the candidate is given the opportunity to understand how the group works, he or she may develop an internal motivation to participate even when treatment has been mandated. When treatment is not voluntary, it is necessary to apprise the entering member of any consequences that might ensue from his or her group behavior. For example, if the member's behavior in an anger management group was to be considered in the decision of whether he or she could have nonsupervised parental visits with his or her children, then the member must be apprised of this fact prior to his or her participation in the group.

The informed consent that has been described is separate from, and in addition to, the consent required by the *Health Insurance Portability and Accountability Act* (HIPAA), which was signed into law in August of 1996. The intent of this federal law is to provide a basic level of privacy protection for the recipients of health services (American Psychological Association Practice Organization & The American Psychological Association Insurance Trust [APAPO & APAIT], 2002). This law thereby takes precedence over state laws when the latter offer weaker protection. Although HIPAA's privacy law is activated when a health care provider or a party acting on behalf of the provider transmits electronic information such as health care claims, the likelihood of a provider's having some engagement with electronic forms of communication is so great that, realistically, all providers are well served by being HIPAA compliant. Moreover, even if electronic communication occurs in only one realm of a practitioner's practice, the law extends to the entirety of his or her practice (APAPO & APAIT, 2002).

The consent entailed by HIPAA is the client's agreement concerning the use of *protected health information*. Protected health information (PHI) includes material that identifies a person in terms of his or her physical or mental health status (past, present, and future), the care the individual is receiving, and payment information (past, present, and future; APAPO & APAIT, 2002). The consent form that the client signs prior to treatment describes the uses of PHI for particular purposes, such as treatment provision and payment. When the uses fall outside of the scope articulated in the consent form, specific written authorization must be obtained by the group member unless certain conditions obtain (for example, to avert a threat to the safety of the public; Schouten, 2003).

The HIPAA distinguishes between PHI and *psychotherapy notes*. In group therapy, the description of the contents of a member's communications and their analysis would be psychotherapy notes. If the therapist needs to send psychotherapy notes to a third party, specific written authorization is required from the group member. Moreover, under HIPAA, although group members have access to their PHI, they do not have the right to access psychotherapy notes (APAPO & APAIT, 2002).

The complexity of the HIPAA regulations requires that every group therapist carefully investigate how the privacy law would pertain to his or her practice. Generally, professional organizations and malpractice insurance carriers have developed the tools, such as model informed consent forms, to enable professionals within given disciplines to become HIPAA compliant. The practitioner must also be aware of statutory regulations to determine how they interface with the HIPAA privacy regulations.

The Use of Multiple Treatments

In Chapter 3, it was noted that clients can benefit from participation in treatment modalities simultaneous with the group therapy experience but that a patient's participation in multiple treatments creates the need for the coordination of each component. This section will outline some of the special legal and ethical problems that arise when group therapy is not the only intervention in the treatment package.

Concurrent Therapy

Both forms of concurrent therapy—conjoint therapy, in which a different therapist conducts the individual and group therapies, and combined therapy, in which the same therapist provides each treatment—require that the therapist carefully conceptualize whether, how, and what information will pass from one modality to the other and clearly articulate this conceptualization to the client entering the concurrent treatment. In conjoint therapy, there must be an explicit agreement on what the two therapists will share with one another and with the group. The following Putting It into Practice provides an illustration of therapists' failure to do this with sufficient thoroughness.

In combined therapy, the therapist receives information from two arenas: the group and the individual sessions. In the individual sessions, the therapist may be

Putting It Into Practice

Conjoint Therapist Confidentiality

Lupe had been in individual therapy for 2 years with Dr. James, who referred her to Dr. Sloan for group therapy. The group had been meeting for approximately 8 months with little membership change. The individual and group therapists had had a comfortable working relationship for many years and talked regularly about a host of professional concerns. In the informed consent, Lupe agreed that the two professionals would communicate regularly about her progress. However, no specific statement was made about how this information would be used.

Initially Lupe seemed at ease in the ongoing group, but after she had been in the group for 4 months she became reticent. Her change was puzzling to Dr. Sloan, and he consulted with Dr. James. Dr. James revealed that Lupe felt that a comment another member had made about obese people was directed at her. Because this was an area of great sensitivity to her, she was contemplating leaving the group. The two therapists agreed that it would be helpful to Lupe for her to give expression to her hurt feelings in the group.

In the next session, Dr. Sloan engineered the interaction in the group so that Lupe revealed the fact and the source of her distress. The member who had made the original offending comment was incredulous that Lupe found his comment objectionable. Lupe left saying that now he was putting her down for being crazy. She told Dr. James that it was obvious that Dr. Sloan was acting on information from Dr. James. Dr. Sloan had betrayed her trust by forcing her to talk about something she wanted to keep to herself. Her thought about leaving the group became even more fixed in her mind.

Teaching note: Although Dr. Sloan's behavior may have left much to be desired from a technical standpoint, a central problem is that he departed from what Lupe understood to be the basic agreement between them. Although he had not shared material directly with the group, his placement of pressure upon her to do so was in violation of her expectation regarding the boundaries that would be maintained between individual and group treatments. The burden falls squarely on the group and individual therapists to have a sufficiently clear, explicit discussion about the use of information so that the client's understanding is consonant with how the information is actually used.

privy to information not shared with the other group members or the cotherapist. The therapist must establish an agreement concerning how this information will be used. There are several alternatives. Therapists who see the group and individual treatments as two facets of a single therapy are likely to establish with the group member that the individual therapy would not be a safe harbor for the client's secrets from the group. The therapist would make clear that if there was something of importance that the client was withholding from the group, the therapist would encourage the client to share it. However, if the client refrained from doing so, ultimately the therapist would share this information with the group. This approach diminishes the extent to which the client can use individual treatment to resist particular work within the group.

An alternate approach is for the therapist to tell the client that he or she will not disclose in the group what is shared in individual therapy. The advantage of this approach is that it would lower the client's reluctance to share sensitive material. However, the therapist should not convey the notion that the modalities are entirely separate. The client should also be helped to recognize that the therapist's understanding of the client is going to be affected by both the individual and group work —after all, this is a major advantage of combined treatment—and this understanding will influence how the therapist works with the member in both contexts.

If a therapist is seeing a client in both individual and group therapy and wishes to share with the cotherapist information about the client's work in individual therapy, then the client's consent must be obtained. In the case in which the therapist seeing the client in both modalities has indicated that, in principle, he or she might share in the group sessions information obtained in individual treatment, it may seem less necessary to receive the client's consent in relation to the cotherapist. However, if the cotherapist receives information about the client outside of the group sessions (as one would expect the cotherapist would), then this disclosure would warrant its own specification in the informed consent.

An additional problem in combined therapy is the therapist's role as a referral source. Rarely do clients begin individual and group therapy simultaneously. When a therapist sees a person in one modality and recognizes the possible benefit the person might realize from participation in another, the therapist is in a potential conflict-of-interest situation. By referring the individual to him- or herself as a client in individual or group therapy, the therapist stands to profit financially (Gans, 1992). Yet a referral to another professional also creates risks. For example, the client may prefer working with the other professional, or the other professional may undermine the first therapist's work. What is important is that the therapist's primary motive for advocating combined therapy be the well-being of the client. A recommendation for combined therapy should be made only after the therapist has carefully weighed the advantages and disadvantages of it against those of other alternatives, particularly conjoint therapy.

In presenting his or her recommendation to the client, the therapist should discuss all relevant alternatives. The therapist should offer his or her reasons why combined therapy may be preferable but should also specify any risks it may entail. Because the therapist is referring the client to him- or herself, the therapist must exercise particular care in protecting the client's autonomy during the informed consent process. The client might have difficulty expressing doubts about combined therapy or lack of interest in pursuing another direction out of fear of offending the therapist. To guard against this possibility, the therapist could offer the client the opportunity to consult with another mental health professional who is knowledgeable about concurrent therapy.

Electronic Communication

Increasingly, mental health practitioners are using technology to provide psychological services, and group therapists are no exception. Certain uses of technology (such as the use of computers in generating process notes) have been long absorbed into the regular practices of group therapists, with some recognition of problems these uses entail as well as their possible solutions. The newest and most uncharted uses of technology are group treatment and education involving the use of cyberspace. In this section, two of the most recent applications will be identified, along with the special ethical dimensions of each.

Coordinator or Consultant to Online Group

Group therapists may participate in online groups as coordinators or consultants. For example, a group therapist may share his or her knowledge of interpersonal behavior and group dynamics on a web page or respond to questions about relationships. As Humphreys, Winzelberg, and Klaw (2000) note, a major problem for the professional serving in this capacity is that it is difficult to achieve role clarity with the participants, who may easily see the professional as having a role other than what he or she actually has. Specifically, rather than recognizing that the professional is serving as a coordinator or consultant, the participant may misconstrue the role as one of personal psychotherapy. What makes this medium so vulnerable to such misunderstandings is that the membership of such groups can fluctuate rapidly and the professional may not know who has entered the system when. Any role-clarifying statement the professional has made in the past may not be seen by a new group member.

Humphrey et al. (2000) suggest several safeguards that may eliminate or attenuate these problems: First, the group specialist should continually clarify his or her role. One way of doing so is to tag all messages to the group with a disclaimer that the relationship of the professional is to the group, is public, and does not constitute individual counseling (Humphreys et al., 2000). Second, the group professional should avoid individual personal or backchannel exchanges with subscribers, because such an extension of the e-mail relationship can easily be misconstrued by the member as constituting individual therapy. Third, the professional should use a separate e-mail account for participation in an online group so that the professional will not mistake a list-serve member's message for that of a party with whom the therapist does have an individual relationship.

Leader of Online Group

Therapists may consider running online therapy groups, although at present cybergroups may contain too many pitfalls to be ethically viable. One problem is that we do *not* have sufficient data to know that such groups are effective. Thus, they must be regarded, as one cybertherapist tells her group members in the informed consent, as "an experimental process" (Colon, 1997). Although there are indications that research efforts (e.g., Barak & Wander-Schwartz, 2000) are underway to study the effectiveness of cybergroups, there is not yet a sufficient accumulation of studies to determine the usefulness of this medium.

Moreover, the mechanisms of therapeutic action may function differently in a cybergroup than they do in a therapy group. For example, interpersonal learning requires that members observe one another. How does interpersonal learning occur in the absence of visual data? Although interpersonal learning also requires a balance between affect and cognition, the physical separation among members may have a liberating effect on affect that shifts the balance. Barak and Wander-Schwartz (2000) observed a higher level of aggression to be associated with brief chat room therapy in comparison with face-to-face therapy. If indeed the Internet has a disinhibiting effect on affect, is there greater risk for negative outcomes? We do not yet know how a therapist creates an environment in which work can get done in a cybergroup. For instance, in a therapy group the therapist has the responsibility of vigorously managing the group boundaries. However, in a cybergroup a member could leave or enter the group without its necessarily being detectable to the therapist or other members (Weinberg, 2001).

CAUTION

The effectiveness of cybertherapy groups in promoting healthy psychological change is yet to be established.

CAUTION

Cybergroups entail the following problems:

- Lack of outcome studies
- Lack of information about methods of action
- Difficulty for therapist in managing emergencies
- Possible confidentiality difficulties
- Difficulty for therapist in maintaining boundaries

How can the therapist maintain a positive working environment despite this fluidity?

Another problem area is confidentiality (Humphries et al., 2000). The therapist cannot be certain that it is actually the member who has logged on unless the group utilizes videoconferencing technology. Furthermore, unless information is encrypted, members cannot be assured that it is inaccessible to parties outside the group.

Special case management issues can also arise in cybergroups (Humphries et al., 2000). The wider the geographic area from which members are drawn, the greater the therapist's domain of responsibility. If a member is from a geographic area other than the therapist's, the therapist may need to know the mental health resources in that member's area in order to respond appropriately and promptly to any emergencies.

GROUP MANAGEMENT ISSUES

Group management issues that a therapist will have to confront are creating and enforcing group rules, arranging group fees. and keeping records of meetings.

Group Rules

For members to work productively in a group, they must engage in behaviors that are compatible with the group goals. There are certain behaviors whose presence or absence is so crucial to members' progress that the therapist establishes rules concerning them. Of course, because goals vary from group to group, there is variability in group rules across different types of groups. However, there are some behaviors whose presence or absence is important for virtually any group; hence, certain rules that are common to many groups. These will be discussed in the following sections.

Confidentiality

This rule, described earlier, is essential to members' right to privacy and members' sense of safety in the group. This rule has a special status in that the therapist has an obligation to protect members' confidences. Because of this, establishing a confidentiality rule and enforcing it is the standard of practice in the field. In some treatment environments such as inpatient groups the confidentiality rule may pertain not to the group sessions per se but to all transactions on the unit. Whatever the bounds of confidentiality are, the therapist must make them very explicit to members in the informed consent process.

Attendance

Members cannot benefit from group treatment unless they are present for the sessions and miss them only rarely. Consequently, group therapists often establish the rule of regular attendance. During member selection, the therapist should discern whether any impediments exist to the prospective member's regular attendance. For example, some members may have intermittent child care, elder care, or job responsibilities that could lead them to miss sessions more frequently than would be desirable. During the preparation, the therapist should help the entering member to understand the rationale for the attendance rule and the difficulties that ensue when members violate it (e.g., the group lacks continuity in its exploration of issues).

Translating Feelings and Impulses into Words

Both objectively and subjectively, safety must characterize the group member's experience. Thus, it is crucial that members refrain from engaging in physical actions that might be threatening to other members. Moreover, the ability to label affects and urges may be a significant achievement for many members. With some populations of group members, this rule would never be violated even if it were not explicitly articulated to incoming members. For other populations, especially those with impulse disorders, this rule must be given much emphasis and explanation.

No Socializing with Members Outside the Group

As members develop relationships with one another, a natural longing emerges to extend those relationships beyond the group (Rutan & Stone, 2001). In many types of groups, however, the therapist establishes a rule forbidding socialization, for several reasons. First, socializing among members interferes with the group's efforts to address successfully problems emerging within the group. This effect can occur in various ways. When two or more members socialize with one another, they may be tempted to pursue issues that have emerged within the sessions outside of the group. For example, two members who are friends on the outside might discuss some circumstance that led them to feel anger toward one another in the group. Having obtained some relief from an extragroup discussion of the event, they would be less motivated to continue its exploration in the group. Whatever resolution of the problem they had independently achieved would also be without the benefit of the therapeutic environment of the group. They would be depriving themselves of such resources as the many points of view that the group offers. At the same time, these members operating outside the group would be excluding other members from witnessing and participating in their own problem-solving efforts. These socializing members would thereby limit the learning opportunities of the other members of the group.

The other way in which socializing interferes with the group's problem-solving efforts occurs when members' social relationships become more important to them than their relationship as members of the therapy group. They may be hesitant to share negative feelings or provide one another with constructive feedback. Finally, when extragroup socializing occurs, members may have reactions to one another inside the group that are due to events on the outside. Yet, because the entire group did not witness these events, they will be less comprehensible to those group members who did not participate in them.

A second reason that therapists tend to forbid socializing outside of the group is that it may make it more difficult for members to observe other group rules, such as confidentiality. For example, suppose two members develop a friendship outside of the group and allow nongroup members into their social circle. They would then take on the burden of an even higher level of scrupulousness than is typically necessary in their conversation when in the presence of others because they must omit mention of their common frame of reference and their knowledge about others within the group.

Third, extragroup socializing can distract members from the original goals that brought them to group therapy. For example, suppose Andy enters the group to improve his ability to form relationships with others. Were he to develop friendships with group members, it might take the edge off the problem sufficiently to reduce his curiosity about the difficulties he has in forming relationships. Moreover, Andy may be less likely to do the hard work of applying the insights he acquired in the group to the task of forming new relationships outside the group. In other words, such friendships can create an easy but temporary solution to a complex problem.

Fourth, the prohibition of socializing outside the group may be a component of the therapist's risk management. To the extent that the therapist permits or even encourages members' involvement with one another outside of the group, others may see the extragroup encounters as an extension of the treatment and thereby hold the therapist responsible for any untoward consequences of the interactions. A no-socializing rule serves the function of defining the parameters of the treatment and, in doing so, establishes the boundaries of the therapist's responsibility.

Monetary Issues

The group therapist must decide what fee arrangement he or she will establish and how issues concerning payment will be addressed in the group. A basic question that the group therapist faces is what the group member is purchasing. Is the member paying for an individual session or for a seat in the group? If the therapist perceives the former to be the case, then the member pays when he or she has completed a session or set of sessions. Presumably, if the member were not present, he or she would not necessarily pay for the session. If the member pays for a seat in the group, then the member renders payment regardless of his or her attendance. This model is somewhat akin to a student taking an academic course: Payment occurs at the beginning of the semester, and whether the student attends all classes is irrelevant to the payment.

Although both of these arrangements have been used by group therapists, the literature suggests that the latter method is more common. Indeed, it has a number of advantages. First, it allows the therapist to have a stable income. Second, it discourages the use of absences as a means of acting out. Third, it enables the group to have the greatest stability, because members are more likely to attend consistently when they are required to pay for missed sessions. Therapists adopting this latter policy must make clear to members prior to their entry into the group that they will be unable to bill the insurance company for the missed sessions. Hence, a missed session may be more costly to the member than an attended session.

Another issue is whether to have a standard fee or determine fees with a sliding scale. The advantage of a standard fee is simplicity. When therapists charge different fees based upon ability to pay, they must grapple with the complexities of each member's financial situation. For example, two members may have roughly the same income, but one member may have greater debt. The therapist must consider whether to take this latter factor into account. The therapist must also monitor the member's financial situation to ensure that the member is paying the appropriate fee. The advantage of using differential fees is that it accords the therapist flexibility in selecting and retaining members. On the one hand, the therapist can take into the group individuals with low incomes or from managed care plans that permit only a certain fee for group sessions. On the other hand, the therapist can derive a reasonable level of remuneration from the group by setting higher fees for those who can pay more. The therapist can also lower the fee of a member who has had a significant decline in income. The consequence of this flexibility is that issues pertaining to money enter the group in a more salient way, so that, for example, the therapist might be perceived as valuing the members who pay more.

Whatever payment system the therapist uses, he or she must describe that system in detail in the informed consent process. The member should be apprised of the consequences of failure to remit fees. If the therapist anticipates raising fees at some future date, this possibility should be forecast for the prospective member as well as the interval between notice of the fee increase and the implementation of the new rate.

Apart from the therapist's financial arrangements with members is his or her stance on the discussion of money issues in the group. Most therapists are likely to recognize that money matters are sensitive. Within a Euramerican culture, few questions are experienced as more invasive than the query "How much money do you make?" The demand to provide information concerning income can elicit a sense of exposure, shame, or fear of others' envy, depending on one's circumstances. More difficult for therapists may be the recognition that they themselves are subject to this cultural prohibition and consequently may demur from taking up issues related to money even though they appear with considerable conspicuousness in the group. Yet, as Motherwell (2002) noted, "Payment for therapy delineates a boundary and defines the relationship between therapist and client. It can evoke powerful feelings, reactions, and meanings for clients. Each time fees are raised or lowered, negotiated, paid or unpaid, the boundary shifts and new feelings and meanings arise" (p. 51). Hence, a therapist who avoids exploring money issues with members deprives them of valuable learning opportunities. Moreover, as members sense the therapist's reluctance to pursue monetary issues in the group, it provides a ready means for members to act out conflict.

To facilitate the examination in the group of issues related to money, the therapist should take several steps. First, the therapist should prepare the new member for the fact that monetary issues, especially those related to payment for sessions, will be discussed in the group (Motherwell, 2002). The therapist might encourage the member to share a reaction to some money-related event in the group. The therapist might acknowledge the sociocultural prohibition against doing so while helping the member to recognize that through such explorations members can move toward their goals for joining the group. Such preparation can lessen the shame members may feel when monetary concerns are addressed.

Second, the therapist should conduct financial transactions within the group. Both bills and payment can be given within the sessions themselves. Third, the therapist must have a readiness to explore within the group any behaviors that depart from the agreement between the therapist and members. For example, the therapist should take note of early or late payments or payments of the incorrect amount. Fourth, if fees are increased or if any other changes are made by the therapist, he or she should have a heightened awareness of hidden member reactions to the change.

Record Keeping

Through a thorough interview for group therapy, the therapist develops a detailed treatment plan that specifies the long-term goals to which treatment should be directed, as well as the short-term objectives, which are the steps en route to the long-term goal (Jongsma & Peterson, 1999). The treatment plan should also include the processes that occur in the group that enable the individual to accomplish objectives and ultimately goals. Information at this level of specificity is crucial to satisfy the demands of third-party payers and other regulatory and review agencies. Of course, the treatment plan should be seen as dynamic: Through the group work itself, other goals and objectives may become evident to the therapist and group member.

An individual note should be written about every group member after each session. Many factors determine what types of observations the group therapist should include. The theoretical orientation and the goals established within that orientation are among these factors. Suppose a group were conducted within an interpersonal model with the goal of enhancing members' relational skills. The therapist's note would highlight members' interpersonal patterns and document any significant feedback given to the member about these patterns. For example, the therapist might write, "Paul was passive this evening as two members heatedly pursued a conflict between them. He appeared to want to distance himself lest he become a target of others' hostilities." The therapist might also note the relationship between this behavior and Paul's presenting problem by adding, "This behavior seems consistent with Paul's self-report that in certain life situations he isolates himself from others when the expression of anger toward him is a likelihood." Any significant feedback the member received might also be described. For instance, the therapist might write, "Members told Paul that he seemed aloof in the session and through his facial expression seemed to convey disdain for the issues that were so important to other members."

Other factors that are likely to determine the content of the note are the requirements of third-party payer or a regulatory group to whom the therapist must be responsive. For example, some managed care plans require that the therapist provide a Global Assessment of Functioning (GAF) rating for Axis V of the *Diagnostic and Statistical Manual of Mental Disorders* (4th ed., text revision; *DSM-IV-TR;* American Psychiatric Association, 2000) for each session or, more typically, a group of sessions. If so, the therapist should describe those indicators of functional impairment in the session that are related to the member's difficulties. For example, Paul's withdrawal upon the emergence of conflict in the group constitutes a type of functional impairment because the withdrawal substitutes for adaptive, constructive activities he might be pursuing with others.

In writing notes, the therapist should strive always to preserve the privacy and confidentiality of the group member. To this end, the therapist should write separate notes for each group member (Luepker, 2003) and refrain from writing in specific terms about one group member in another group member's notes. The therapist should also avoid identifying a group member in another group member's notes. Admittedly, it could be useful and convenient for the therapist to write a single comprehensive note about the entire group session, one that would incorporate a description of the participation of each member. However, such notes are likely to compromise the privacy and confidentiality of individual group members. For example, a therapist receiving a court order to submit to the court any notes concerning an individual member might be required to submit the comprehensive notes that would reveal material concerning all other members in the group. On the other hand, notes written about the entire group that capture such issues as the group-level conflict or theme and do not identify individuals would provide much greater protection of the confidentiality and privacy of the individual.

SUMMARY AND CONCLUSIONS

The group therapist can deliver effective treatment only by acting ethically and within the limits of the law. Doing so requires an awareness of areas in which ethical and legal issues often arise in a group therapy practice. Four areas were outlined in this chapter: privacy (confidentiality and privileged communication), informed consent, the use of multiple treatments, and the relatively new area of electronic communication. Ethical and legal difficulties can occur in many other domains. However, those that were discussed are ones in which the emergence of ethical dilemmas entailing the collision of two or more ethical principles is especially common. The related topic of group management issues was also covered in this chapter. The group management issues include the establishment of group rules such as confidentiality, monetary practices, and record keeping. By managing the group responsibly, the therapist creates an atmosphere in which ethical and legal dilemmas can be resolved constructively.

TEST YOURSELF

1. **Privacy issues in group therapy are the same as for individual therapy.** True or False?

2. **The most common consequence of confidentiality violations is anger toward the violator.** True or False?

3. **Conjoint and combined therapy each have a distinctive pattern of ethical issues.** True or False?

4. **Therapy groups conducted over the Internet entail the following ethical or legal problems:**
   (a) The effectiveness of such groups has not yet been established.
   (b) The therapist may be uncertain of who is logging into the group discussions.
   (c) The confidentiality of the information shared in the group may not be adequately protected.
   (d) all of the above

5. **The therapist can do all but which of the following to encourage members to observe confidentiality?**
   (a) Downplay the possibility of confidentiality violations
   (b) Model confidentiality himself or herself
   (c) Provide frequent reminders of the importance of confidentiality
   (d) Spell out the consequences of confidentiality violations in the informed consent

6. **The therapist may have a monetary policy in which the member pays for his or her seat in the group rather than individual sessions because**
   (a) such a policy is preferred by third-party payers.
   (b) the former method discourages absenteeism.
   (c) the former method safeguards a stable income for the therapist.
   (d) b and c only

(continued)

7. Which is NOT a rule common to many groups?

   (a) Stress the importance of socialization between group members outside the group setting

   (b) Establish the importance of regular attendance

   (c) Stress the importance of confidentiality

   (d) Encourage a safe environment for members to translate feeling and impulses into words

8. How often should a note be written about each member?

   (a) Once a month

   (b) After each session

   (c) At the end of treatment

   (d) Only upon request of the member

9. What are some consequences that may be enforced if a group member violates confidentiality?

10. Discuss some reasons why it is important to share reactions within the group when chance meetings occur between group members in an outside setting.

11. Define informed consent. Include what it means to be informed and to give consent.

12. With regard to fee arrangement, discuss the difference between a member's paying for an individual session as opposed to a seat in the group.

13. List some ways that a therapist can help to preserve the privacy and confidentiality of group members in record keeping.

Answers: 1. False; 2. True; 3. True; 4. d; 5. a; 6. d; 7. a; 8. b; 9. Removal from the group, financial sanction, and civil suit by the group member who was the object of the violation; 10. It rewards members for handling the situation well, it allows for the correction of mistaken impressions, it enables members to recognize other possible responses to handling the situation, and it underscores the importance of all matters related to confidentiality; 11. *Informed* refers to the right of the group member to know all of the crucial aspects associated with the group treatment, and *consent* refers to the entering member's agreement to participate in the group in cognizance of these crucial aspects; 12. When a member paying for an individual session misses a meeting he or she would not be required to pay; if you consider a member as paying for a seat in the group, then the member would pay regardless of attendance; 13. The therapist should write separate notes for each group member and should not write specific information about a group member in another group member's chart; notes that are written about the entire group should not contain identifying information.

Nine

THE DIVERSITY AMONG MEMBERS IN A THERAPY GROUP

Atherapist working in an outpatient facility organized a depression group for women. The eight women in the group ranged in age from 55 to 75. The therapist anticipated that the group members would instantly connect with one another because they shared many depressive symptoms, such as sadness, low self-esteem, appetite and sleep disturbances, and worry. Furthermore, for all of these women, the event precipitating these symptoms was the loss of a relationship. And yet the therapist found that her task was somewhat more difficult than she had imagined. Members did not immediately establish solid connections with one another. At times, certain members could not seem to grasp what others were saying. At other times, members found that remarks they had intended to be supportive were regarded as offensive by the recipients.

This chapter will provide the group therapist with tools to understand the challenge this therapist faced as well as other challenges that relate to diversity in the therapy group. It will address how we think about the identities of our group members and ourselves and how we factor these thoughts into planning and conducting our groups.

THE MYTH OF THE HOMOGENEOUS GROUP

When therapists speak of homogeneous versus heterogeneous groups, they are referring to the presenting problem. The homogeneous group is one in which members share a given psychological problem or malady that is the basis for the selection of members. Although therapists recognize that variability exists among members on other dimensions, the presumption is that this variability is not highly relevant to the workings of the group. This perspective has several roots. The first is the unfortunate tendency of some mental health professionals to treat individuals as if they were their problems, a posture manifested in the use of diagnostic labels as nouns rather than adjectives. If individuals are their problems, then all other features become at best secondary.

DON'T FORGET

The therapist's ability to constructively address differences within the group begins with the therapist's self-awareness.

Another root is the wish to avoid certain aspects of individuals' identities that may be associated with conflict. For example, religious or value differences can easily create tension among people. Still another cause is the person of the therapist him- or herself. Reckoning with all of the true heterogeneities in the group requires that therapists address them within themselves. Therapists may confront their own biases and prejudices and find them to be at odds with professional ideals. All of these factors conspire to lead therapists to limit permissible recognizable differences among members, and between members and therapist.

However, the homogenization of group members has a number of negative consequences. To have part of oneself ignored is to have part of oneself rejected. A member whose status on a certain variable is both unique and unrecognized is likely to feel that that status is in some way objectionable. Further, failure to attend to members in their singularity prevents the therapist from taking those factors into consideration in making interventions. How the therapist approaches termination in the group is likely to be influenced by the therapist's awareness of members' levels of functioning. But why is it less important to consider how members' cultural backgrounds affect how they approach relationship endings? The therapist's willingness to attend to all the differences among members creates the condition in which members can be understood by the therapist.

Group therapists are by no means alone in their failure to reckon with diversity. It is a shortcoming of the mental health field at large. One of the symptoms of this shortcoming is the lack of schemas by which practitioners can capture diversity in their clients. A change in the mental health field is suggested by the emergence over the last 15 years of a good number of scholarly works in which diversity is a focus. Often, however, the offerings focus on describing the characteristics of special populations. These works are extremely helpful to a therapist who enters a group that is different from him or her in important respects—for example, a young therapist conducting a group on the elderly or an African American therapist conducting a group with Latino group members. Yet these discussions of special populations are not as useful in characterizing the diversity that exists in the therapy group.

THE ADDRESSING FRAMEWORK

Pamela Hays (2001) has introduced a framework that holds potential utility for the group therapist who seeks to capture more fully the heterogeneity in his or her group. Her ADDRESSING system identifies nine dimensions that can be used to reveal the individual's identities. ADDRESSING is an acronym for each of these dimensions. Hays's system, outlined in Rapid Reference 9.1, should be used not only with the recipients of mental health services but also with providers. That is, the group therapist should use this system to develop greater awareness of his or her personal worldview. By looking at each participant in the group in relation to this system, therapists can understand (1) themselves more fully; (2) themselves in relation to the group members; (3) each member more fully; and (4) each member in relation to one another. Admittedly, the Hays framework does not capture every dimension relevant to diversity (for example, it does not include separate dimensions for urban, rural, suburban; biological ver-

≡ Rapid Reference 9.1

ADDRESSING Framework

Letter	Influence	Identified Minority
A	**A**ge and generational influence	Children, adolescents, elders.
D	**D**evelopmental and acquired	People with developmental, ac-
D	**D**isability	quired physical, cognitive, and/or psychological disabilities.
R	**R**eligion and spiritual orientation	People of Muslim, Jewish, Buddhist, Hindu, and other minority religions and faiths.
E	**E**thnicity	People of Asian, South Asian, Pacific Islander, Latino, African American, Arab, or Middle East heritage.
S	**S**ocioeconomic status	People of lower status by occupation, education, income, rural or urban habitat, or family name.
S	**S**exual orientation	People who are gay, lesbian, or bisexual.
I	**I**ndigenous heritage	North American Indians, Alaskan Natives, Inuit, Metis, Pacific Americans.
N	**N**ational origin	Immigrants, refugees, international students.
G	**G**ender	Women, transgender individuals.

Note: Adapted from Hays, P. A. (1996). Addressing the complexities of culture and gender in counseling. *Journal of Counseling and Development, 74*(March/April), 332–328. ©American Counseling Association. Reprinted with permission. No further reproduction authorized without written permission of the American Counseling Association.

sus adoptive; levels of education), but no framework possibly can. Nonetheless, use of such a framework attunes therapists to diversity in such a way as to assist them in recognizing other aspects of the members or of themselves that may be relevant to the immediate clinical situation.

We will consider each type of diversity covered by the ADDRESSING framework and explore its implications for the therapist's working more effectively in a therapy group. The reader should note that even though these dimensions are described sequentially, in clinical practice they should not be viewed in isolation from one another. They achieve their greatest descriptive power by being examined together. For example, the meaning of a person's age can be grasped far more completely if age is considered in relation to the person's ethnic group or socioeconomic status. Ultimately, we will be interested in groups that are heterogeneous on the dimensions we describe. However, we will also look at groups in which members share a status on a given dimension in order to (1) learn about the themes these members would bring to a heterogeneous group; (2) demonstrate the heterogeneity lying within homogeneous groups; and (3) identify the special challenges when the therapist differs from all or most of the members on one of the ADDRESSING dimensions.

Age and Generational Influences

Research studies and clinical reports on group therapy often characterize the population studied in broad-brush terms when it comes to age. For example, not uncommonly it is noted that the population is adult, which means it may range in age from, say, 21 to 65. This span encompasses enormous variability in developmental issues. The literature suggests that too infrequently are clinicians sufficiently attuned to this developmental variation. Even in groups in which the age span is far narrower, critical variation in developmental tasks corresponding to age differences is present. In the following Putting It into Practice, we have an example of how two members of the group described at the beginning of this chapter found communications between one another challenging because of this individual developmental variation.

Moreover, individuals of different ages have been affected by different historical events that influence their identity. For example, 25 years from now, groups in which some members have and some have not experienced the September 11, 2001, bombing of the World Trade Center will exist, and whether any given member has or has not lived through this event may well make a difference in how that member sees him- or herself and the world. The group therapist does well to grasp the significant historical events that have informed each member's life. In fact, Hays talks about the usefulness of making a timeline that lists important his-

Putting It Into Practice

Age Diversity in the Therapy Group

Ellen had been in the group for 6 months when Nikki entered. Ellen, a 75-year-old group member, had been suffering depressive symptoms in relation to chronic and serious health problems and a perceived lack of support from family members. Although she had been improving in terms of both health and spirits, she had recently received test results that were less encouraging than expected. Nikki was a 60-year-old woman who had held a managerial position and was forced to take early retirement. She entered the group energetically and spoke volubly about her confusion over whether to seek a new position or to immerse herself in avocational pursuits. Other group members questioned her extensively to help her make this decision. Although Ellen had typically been moderately active in the group, the therapist noticed that she appeared both withdrawn and pensive during this discussion.

Teaching note. Both members in this group are facing aging issues. However, for Nikki, the task is approaching constructively a new developmental era. Although the arrival of this era raises issues about mortality for Nikki, Ellen is forced to confront them in a much more immediate way. The developmentally minded therapist would recognize that each member could potentially pose a problem for the other. For Ellen, Nikki could be a symbol of opportunity that has passed; for Nikki, Ellen could be a reminder of a life event that is still far enough away to ignore. This awareness on the part of the therapist enables him or her to approach with sensitivity the concerns for which each member is a voice. Note that this disparity in developmental tasks will be most important in those groups that emphasize spontaneous interaction. It will be less important when the group's focus is educative, such as teaching relaxation, meditation, and guided imagery.

torical events. Although the relevance of such an enterprise may not be clear to the many group therapists who emphasize the here and now, to understand the symbolic value of members' recounting certain events requires a knowledge of their significance. For example, members may talk of September 11 as a derivative or symbol of their sense of danger within the session itself. By knowing something about September 11, the therapist can appreciate the horror and vulnerability that members may be feeling in relation to happenings within the group.

When members of the group are from the same cohort group, a shared understanding may be present that eludes the therapist who is not from that group. For example, the young therapist leading a group of veterans from World War II or survivors of the Great Depression may have difficulty understanding many of their allusions. He or she may fail to recognize esteem-bolstering aspects of their shared history and may attempt to take the group too quickly from the then and there to the here and now. Shared historical experiences constitute part of what S. H. Foulkes (1975/1986) referred to as the *foundation matrix,* the shared network of meaning that allows communication.

In some clinical environments, a need to include very different age ranges within the same group exists. In this circumstance, the group therapist must incorporate the techniques that are suited to each age group and consider the effect of the likely behaviors of each age group on the other. For example, suppose older adolescents and young adults are included in groups together. The older adolescents are likely to pose a greater problem in terms of volatility and impulsivity. So that the younger members do not undermine safety in the group, the therapist must have the skill to provide the necessary emotional containment.

Within each age group, there are typical sources of variation that should be anticipated by the therapist in designing the group. For example, illicit drug use is a more frequent problem in adolescent groups than adult groups. However, most adolescent groups will also include individuals who are not abusing drugs. The therapist should clearly specify the consequences of drug use during sessions prior to a member's entrance into the group so that nonusing youths feel safe.

Along the same lines, in groups of elderly members variations in the ability of members to remember the earlier proceedings of the group may exist. By building in a summary at various points in the session, the therapist accommodates the needs of members with diminished memorial capacities. Another example concerns the technique of reminiscence, which in many elderly groups increases members' potential for achieving group cohesion and, on an individual basis, attaining a sense of mastery over difficult life events such as illness (Leszcz, 1990). However, for some elderly persons reminiscing can exacerbate guilt, depression, and feelings of inadequacy and can further remove the elderly member from present relationships. The therapist should have the flexibility to move the group away from reminiscing—for instance, by highlighting the here-and-now implications of the memory. Hence, therapists who are working with a special age population must avoid stereotyping the members of that population and recognize that within each age group members are different from one another in a variety of ways.

Developmental and Acquired Disabilities

Disability is defined as "a physical, mental, emotional or sensory condition that limits a person in any major area of life such as self care, transportation, communication, mobility, activities of daily living and work" (Patterson, McKenzie, & Jenkins, 1995, p. 78). Individuals with disabilities (which can be developmental, physical, cognitive, and severe psychological) constitute the largest minority group in the United States. Group therapists have made significant contributions in developing groups to assist individuals with disabilities to adjust to their disability and in educating family members about the disability (e.g., Seligman & Marshak, 1990).

Persons with disabilities may enter groups that may or may not have a disability focus. In the former situation, members typically share a particular disability. Groups have been developed for individuals with most types of disability, including blindness (Krausz, 1980), mental retardation, stroke, spinal cord injuries and other neurological conditions (Alexopoulos, Raue, & Arean, 2003), learning disabilities (Salmon & Abell, 1996), and chronic mental illness (Plante, Pinder, & Howe, 1988), as well as for families with disabilities (Feigin, 2002). Disability-specific groups and disability focus groups for individuals who are attempting to adjust to the disability have been proven effective (Patterson et al., 1995). These groups provide a socialization experience that can foster friendships and help improve communication skills. They also can uncover basic threats to the sense of self, acknowledge and mourn the losses that accompany the disability, and strengthen self-esteem so that it is possible to incorporate the disability in the self-concept.

Nevertheless, therapists who conduct such groups must be sensitive to the fact that the disability is only one dimension of the individual. These individuals, like those without disabilities, experience marital difficulties, interpersonal isolation, career doubts, trauma, and adjustments to other life circumstances that warrant the group's attention. Attributing all of these life problems to the disability stereotypes the disabled individual. Also stereotyping is the tendency to assume that the disability has the same psychological consequences for all group members. Therapists, whether they share the disability or not, must be sensitive to the personal meaning of the disability for the individual member.

How does the therapist facilitate group members in realizing the opportunity that one member's disability creates? First, the therapist should be aware of his or her own attitudes and emotional reactions to disabilities in general and to the member's partic-

CAUTION

Group therapists leading groups of individuals who share a disability must recognize that the disability may have meaning for the group member that is different from the meaning ascribed to it by other members.

CAUTION

The language used in communicating about disabilities is important. For example, contrasting *normal* individuals with disabled individuals is derogatory: *Normal* implies that individuals with disabilities are not normal. *Able-bodied* is the preferred term when referring to individuals without physical disabilities. Also, using the term as a noun (e.g., *the disabled*) equates the individual with his or her disability rather than focusing on the feature as one aspect of a multifaceted human being.

ular disability. Prior to a disabled member's entrance into the group, therapists should educate themselves on the disability. Second, the therapist should open communication channels about the disability during the selection process. The therapist should convey a receptiveness to frank discussion about the disability. Third, the therapist should observe the rules of etiquette both in the interviewing process and in the group itself and model the observation of these rules for group members (see Rapid Reference 9.2 for a list of rules suggested by Patterson et al., 1995). At the same time, guidelines do not substitute for sensitivity to the unique reactions of a group member with a disability. The following Putting It into Practice shows how the therapist used a member's impression that she had violated a rule of etiquette to develop a norm of open communication about the disability.

Of particular note is the vulnerability experienced by adolescents with a disability. Like all adolescents, those with disabilities have an array of developmental tasks whose completion is critical to their later adjustment. These tasks include accepting one's body and physique, achieving emotional independence from the family, and forming mature, loving relationships with peers. The disability can constitute a challenge to one or more of these tasks. For example, a physical dis-

≡Rapid Reference 9.2

1. Acknowledge the disability. However, asking personal questions about the disability is inappropriate unless a comfortable relationship has already been established. If there are specific questions related to the individual's ability to participate in group, these should be addressed directly to the individual because he or she is likely to be the best source.

2. Look at and speak directly to the person with the disability even if an interpreter is present.

3. Use common words such as *look* and *see* even if the member is blind.

4. Offering assistance to the person with disability is fine, but you should take cues from the individual before actually providing the assistance.

5. The interview, when possible, should be held at the same place as the group sessions.

6. The group leader should initiate a brief educative discussion with able-bodied members, who may be uncomfortable with the member who has a disability. The therapist should consult with the entering member on whether this discussion should take place before the member enters or during an early session.

7. Each disability may require additional considerations. For example, individuals who are deaf and hearing impaired need to be able to see the speaker's mouth. The speaker should speak clearly with regular tone and speed.

Note: From Patterson et al., 1995.

Putting It Into Practice

Fostering Communication about Diversity

The therapist should foster a process in which members obtain direct feedback on their behavior. For example, in this exchange, a group member, Henrietta, addresses another group member, Sal. Henrietta immediately becomes apprehensive that a third group member, who is blind, will take offense:

Henrietta (to Sal): I think you're blind to the effect you're having on your daughter ... [turning to Dick] oh my God! I didn't mean ... I'm sorry. [Dick remains silent.]

Therapist (to Dick): Dick, how to do feel about Henrietta's apology?

Dick: Weary. People always do that. They use certain expressions and then get horrified and all apologetic. Maybe once every three days I go through this ... especially when I'm meeting new people. It's okay to use the word *blind* around me ... I use it myself in the way you do. I don't want you to change how you speak.

Henrietta: I know what you mean when you say you're weary. Remember when I told the group last week that I was adopted? Well, people are consistently saying irritating things to me, like "do you know who your real parents are?" And now I don't bother to explain anything any more ... I'm too tired. But, Dick, I still want to know from you how you're reacting. In here seems different from out there.

Dick (smiling): I think I can muster the energy.

Teaching note: This exchange was positive for both Henrietta and Dick. The therapist modeled for Henrietta how to go about obtaining information on what language is offensive and what is not. Dick was given an opportunity to see how he can be active in making his interpersonal world more comfortable. Henrietta was able to establish an identification with Dick regarding what it feels like not to be understood and to have assumptions made about oneself. The stage has been set for not only those two members but also others to discuss areas that they see as setting themselves apart from others.

ability can make more difficult the acceptance of one's bodily self. A contextual influence of paramount importance is the peer group: Adolescents weigh heavily the feedback of peers in the valuation of the self. In the environment outside the therapeutic group, however, the adolescent with a disability is at risk for being the victim of the needs of other adolescents to export their own self-disliked features. Others seeking to escape from their own physical selves and the features that they find difficult to accept can reject the adolescent with a physical disability. The same process can occur with psychological disabilities. The group setting can counteract many of these social experiences. In the controlled environment of the therapy group, members can learn about how they use others to defend against challenges to their self-esteem. The consequence of this process is that those with disabilities have an opportunity to receive feedback from others that is more holistic; that is, incorporating but not limited to the disability. Able-bodied adolescents are able to achieve greater self-acceptance, which leads to the affirmation of others' worth.

Religion and Spiritual Orientation

Recently, group therapists have begun to recognize that an individual's set of religious beliefs not only is an important element of a person's identity but also can be an adaptive resource. Consistent with this perspective are findings from research studies showing that individuals who participate in organized religion activities show superior health on a variety of indicators to those who do not (Myers, 2000). Among the benefits that religions offer are a system of meaning and conduct, opportunity for transformation, a sense of belonging, a variety of relationships with peers and authority figures, and, as noted earlier, assistance with some of life's existential challenges.

In the typical therapy group, members are likely to show great variability in terms of their involvement with organized religion, the content of their beliefs on such matters as the existence of God and an afterlife, and the centrality of religion or spirituality in their lives. Until very recently, group therapists tended to see members' engagement with religious topics as defensive. This stance toward religion made matters easy for members and therapists, even if this policy ran roughshod over an important element of members' personhood. Once religion enters the group room, the potential for conflict among members is great. Moreover, at times individuals do use notions of religion defensively or through them manifest aspects of their psychological difficulty. No substitute exists for a group therapist's modeling a stance that is accepting but also reflective or exploratory. For example, the therapist might observe that a particular group member espouses a religious view in such a doctrinaire way that others are alienated. The therapist can show a wholly accepting attitude toward the content of the belief but at the same time explore the interpersonal consequences of the individual's particular way of communicating it to others. When religion is allowed in the group door, members can move toward greater flexibility in a way that enhances their own life space (see the following Putting It into Practice).

Therapists sometimes lead groups in a setting such as a church or synagogue with a particular religious group. Here the challenges are some-

> **DON'T FORGET**
> ....
> One way to encourage members to share their religious and spiritual identities is to ask them about their religious beliefs in the interview for group therapy.

Putting It Into Practice

Religious Diversity in the Group

Eileen, a devout Catholic, did not hesitate to bring her religious beliefs into the group room. She very matter-of-factly described her expectation of seeing her father again after he died. She would speak of praying over a personal problem and occasionally alluded to praying for members. Liz Ann frequently showed exasperation when Eileen made these references and on one occasion castigated her for believing in an illusion. Eileen tended to shrug off these parries. One evening, Liz Ann came into the group session and said that she had had a positive biopsy result. She indicated that she would be missing the session the next few weeks due to emergency surgery. When the session neared its end, she turned to Eileen and said with the slightest note of sarcasm, "You've prayed for everyone else. Now it's my turn." Eileen simply said, "I will."

Teaching note: One of the strengths of group therapy is its ability to offer members a range of problem-solving strategies based upon each member's customary approaches that may not be serviceable for all situations but probably are useful in some.

what different. When the therapist is not a member of the group, the therapist carries the tremendous burden of educating him- or herself on the religion and its associated practices. The therapist must also establish through this education that there is a reasonable level of congruence between his or her beliefs and values and those of the religious group and that differences that do exist are tolerable to the therapist. For example, some group therapists may realize that their views on the role of women in society deviate sharply from those of a particular religious group for whom they are considering providing services. To agree to provide services as a group therapist with the hidden agenda of changing the community's views of women would be a violation of the ethical principles of fidelity (being faithful to one's agreements) and autonomy (providing clients with the essential information for decision making).

Ethnicity

This dimension includes both ethnicity and race (although Hays emphasizes the former). Although these terms have overlapping meanings, we will define them using the American Psychological Association's (2003) "Guidelines on Multicultural Education, Training, Research, Practice, and Organizational Change for Psychologists." According to these guidelines, *ethnicity* is "the acceptance of the group mores and practices of one's culture of origin and the concomitant sense of belonging" (p. 380). *Race* is defined as "the category to which others assign individuals on the basis of physical characteristics, such as skin color or hair type, and the generalizations and stereotypes made as a result" (p. 380). The latter definition sees race as socially rather than biologically based. Currently, more than one-third of the U.S. population consists of ethnic minorities, and it is predicted that within the next half-century ethnic minorities will become a majority (Sue & Sue, 1999). Currently, in some parts of the United States, White European Americans are no longer in the majority (U.S. Census Bureau, 2001). *Culture* comprehends both of the terms *ethnicity* and *race*.

Many groups are ethnically and racially diverse, and yet therapists may have little understanding of how to tap this resource. Most therapists have had no systematic training in how to approach the multicultural aspect of the group. However, the exploration of ethnic and racial differences can potentially help to solidify members' identities; diminish prejudice and stereotyping, thereby enhancing each member's openness to a greater range of relationships; and cultivate members' ability to respond sensitively to other human beings, regardless of how different they are from themselves. The following sections discuss suggestions for the creation of an atmosphere in which cultural differences can be safely addressed.

Preparing the Members for Group

Members' interest in multicultural exploration and cultural identity issues should be assessed in the screening interview. A detailed history that solicits information about a person's ethnic or racial identity conveys that these aspects of the prospective member are not irrelevant to his or her group work. Members with greater openness to a cultural focus can assist those who are less aware (Abernethy, 2002). Members should be informed that people with varying backgrounds will be attending (at this time, the therapist may wish to mention other differences as well, such as differences in values and religious beliefs) and that some of their interpersonal behaviors may be related to these backgrounds. The therapist might acknowledge that at times cultural and other differences may produce tension. However, the therapist should also develop the interviewee's awareness of the learning potential of these and other identities of the group member. More of a demand on screening and preparation exists when prospective members for inclusion in a group historically have had hostile relations with one another (e.g., Arabs and Israelis, Hindu Indians and Pakistani Muslims). Without care in the selection and preparation processes, conflict may break out so early in the group's life that members are discouraged from pursuing cultural issues further. To this end, the therapist might help members to think out how they would be likely to respond to a member from an ethnic group associated with conflict and identify the likely consequences of different ways of interacting with this member.

Opening the Discussion of Ethnic and Racial Issues

As members begin to disclose information about their backgrounds, they are often helped by the therapist's presentation of an organizing framework for discussion of ethnic and racial issues. A familiarity with racial identity theory is helpful (see Hays, 2001, for a detailed theoretical discussion). Often, a discussion early on of fears of being judged for one's prejudices or one's background and shame in relation to the anticipated judgment is helpful. The therapist's acknowledgment of the range of discomfort that exists as members talk about ethnic concerns will help members to modulate their anxiety (Abernethy, 1998).

Recognizing That Ethnic Composition Is Likely to Affect Many Aspects of Members' Group Behaviors

Group behaviors may be altered by ethnic composition in a number of ways. For example, Diener (2000) found that individuals from collectivist cultures base their expressions of satisfaction on their perception of the group's level of well-being ("If the group is fine, I must be fine"), whereas individuals from individualistic cultures consult their personal affects in making statements of satisfaction. Hence, the same verbalization from group members with different backgrounds may have very different meanings.

Addressing Racism, Privilege, and Oppression within the Here and Now of the Group

The most difficult part of this step can be addressing those events within the here and now of the group that suggest racist attitudes on the part of members, the willingness of members to oppress one another, or the greater privilege one member has relative to another. Typically, when members are relatively inexperienced in broaching the topic of racism, a member's view that a racist comment has been made will elicit denial on the part of other members. They may explain to that member that he or she is being too sensitive or is misinterpreting what the other member said. The member who made the charge of racism can be easily scapegoated, especially if he or she does not capitulate to the popular assumption that racism could not possibly exist in the group. A major source of resistance is members' own self-condemnatory tendencies (e.g., "If I did make a racist statement, it would mean that I am a bad person through and through"). Naturally, members would wish to defend against such a charge.

The therapist's role is important in laying bare members' self-indicting thinking and assisting them in finding goodness in their efforts to identify their own conscious and unconscious biases toward others. This is not to say that each time a member makes a charge of racism, it is accurate. However, when an atmosphere of defensiveness prevails, it is impossible for the group to engage in the necessary self-scrutiny to know if it is or not.

Privilege, which is the possession of advantage over others or being in a favored position, is also unlikely to be acknowledged by those members who hold it. Outside of group therapy, privilege is usually invisible in that people cannot easily see what they have always had and received merely by being a member of a larger group such as Euramericans (Hays, 2001). Of course, those who do not hold privilege cannot fail to recognize it because its absence makes life more difficult in innumerable ways. The group therapist, too, is likely to find privilege challenging to discern because therapists tend to hold membership in dominant groups such as the more highly educated and affluent sectors of society (Hammond & Yung, 1993; Hays, 2001). Yet the failure to acknowledge privilege comes with a great price: It renders the holder of privilege insensitive to the position and reactions of those who do not hold privilege.

Fortunately, group therapy is a modality that beyond all others can provide a venue for learning about the reactions of those different from oneself and hence about privilege. Within the group, privilege can operate to enable some members to take a more active role in the group, dominating the group's discussion, expressing strong opinions when group decisions are being made, or feeling free to express negative affects in the sessions. A first requirement for these here-and-now manifestations of privilege to be used effectively to raise members' awareness of others is for the therapist to have undergone the necessary self-examination to be cognizant of the privilege he or she holds. Areas in which the therapist experiences a sense of oppression are also usefully identified.

A second requirement is the therapist's skill in creating a safe climate in which privilege and oppression can be investigated. One highly useful technique is working with subgroups, a particularly viable route when there is more than one representative of an oppressed group. Encouraging members to subgroup based upon privilege and oppression provides a protective structure in that no member is individually on the line for the expression of a particular member. The subgroup structure provides a protection against the narcissistic hurt that can occur when other members fail to affirm one's reaction (Agazarian, 1997). Gradually, however, members of a subgroup begin to differentiate their positions from one another. A member of a subgroup may say to another, "I was more bothered by Mary's declaring that the fee hike in the group was no big deal for us than by her always being the first one in the group to speak." This differentiation sets the stage for members to identify with members of subgroups other than their own. Again, a member may say, "I realize that even though I often feel that I have a hard time speaking up, I know I am lucky and perhaps don't realize it—not to have to worry when the fees go up." Members representing a group that is dominant in society may begin to see areas in which they suffer oppression. For example, a member may say, "As an adopted child, I feel like I am on the outside looking in when people talk about tracing their ancestry."

Therapist Self-Examination
Dalal (1993) suggested a series of questions that leaders could ask themselves to facilitate their under-

Rapid Reference 9.3

Therapist's Self-Examination Questions (from Dalal, 1993)

a. What is gained or avoided by the patient by focusing on ethnicity or discrimination?

b. What is the underlying meaning of making this difference in ethnicity salient?

c. What does the leader acquire by focusing solely on an internal dynamic interpretation?

d. What might the leader be resisting by focusing on the internal dynamic interpretation?

e. Why could it be difficult for the leader to embrace what the patient is saying?

standing of racial content in a therapy group. These questions appear in Rapid Reference 9.3. The racial or ethnic content, of course, could have multiple meanings. Nevertheless, the therapist's ability to explore the content nondefensively provides the group with a role model for how to nonjudgmentally think about such emotionally provocative material. As part of this self-examination process, the leader must be mindful that many of our theoretical views of behavior are ethnocentric—that is, rooted in Western ways of thinking. For example, the theoretical foundation of transference is based on being brought up in a nuclear family. This perspective is less relevant to group members who were raised in an extended family.

Using Metaphor, Role Playing, and Group-as-a-Whole Statements
The therapist should use techniques that enable members to approach ethnic and racial issues despite their fear of doing so. An example of such a technique is *metaphor* (Abernethy, 2002), which entails working with the symbol of a thing rather than with the thing itself. Metaphors are less threatening than direct statements and have multiple levels of meaning (see the following Putting It into Practice for an example of metaphor). *Role reversal* is a particularly powerful technique to assist members in identifying with the position of individuals from an ethnic

Putting It Into Practice

Using Metaphor

A group held in a community mental health center had members representing two different ethnic groups. Members seemed to have difficulty gelling. The members representing one ethnicity appeared to take over the group, and the members of the other remained inactive and withdrawn. Members sensed that the group was floundering, and they tended to blame themselves. For example, one member of the less active group said she was not smart enough to be in the more active group. A member of the more active group talked about how bad she was at letting others talk. She wondered if she would do better in individual therapy. What members did not want to directly acknowledge was the ethnic difference among members and the connection between ethnicity and group behavior.

In one session, a member came in and initiated a discussion about the performance of a local sports team. Members talked about how team members playing defense and offense were not working together. The therapist not only allowed the discussion to continue but encouraged members to elaborate on their points. At one point, the therapist mentioned what an achievement it would be for team members to figure out how to work together. Notably, in this discussion, all members participated.

Teaching note: By working with the metaphor, members achieved a level of safety that enabled them to move beyond impasse to have a genuine dialogue with one another. In some cases, it is sufficient for members to discuss the issue at a metaphorical level. Often, however, the members can have a frank, open discussion of the previously avoided issue.

or racial group different from their own. This technique can be especially useful to assist individuals from a privileged group in developing empathy for oppressed individuals. *Group-as-a-whole* comments can also be helpful in taking the burden off a single member who may be providing a voice for others in the group. For example, if Janine says, "I feel very anxious about being here with Barry," the therapist can reframe this statement as "There is a sensitivity about members' having very different backgrounds from one another." Although "sensitivity" may not do full justice to Janine's anxiety, it does broaden her expression to encourage others' identifications with her expressed concern. Such articulated identifications increase the safety for each individual member, which in turn strengthens members' willingness to make disclosures about difficult topics.

In summary, this area of diversity can be one of the most challenging to explore. The trepidation that both members and therapist have leads many groups to avoid such discussions altogether. However, the cost of this recoiling is that members fail to recognize each other fully, cling to stereotypic notions that have little adaptive value, and neglect to develop the skills for living in a multicultural society.

Socioeconomic Status

In the beginning of the chapter, we introduced a group of eight women. Let us now consider that among these women, a fairly high level of variability in socioeconomic status existed. One woman was from an upper socioeconomic level, two women were from an upper middle socioeconomic level, four women were from a lower middle socioeconomic level, and one woman was from a lower socioeconomic level. The theme orientation of this group would make it attractive to individuals of varying socioeconomic levels. In most groups, however, the therapist is going to encounter some variability. Moreover, the therapist is likely to be from a socioeconomic class different from that of some members.

Like all of the forms of diversity we have discussed, socioeconomic diversity creates both special opportunities and challenges. Individuals from upper socioeconomic levels are frequently similar to the therapist in having a higher comfort level with therapy as a solution to psychological difficulties. Psychological concepts are likely to be fairly familiar to these individuals, both through their exposure to the broader milieu and through their formal education. Moreover, the value of self-reflection is established. These individuals have greater freedom than their counterparts from lower socioeconomic classes to pursue the goal that is at the top of Maslow's hierarchy of needs, self-actualization.

Individuals from lower socioeconomic strata tend to focus more intensively on basic survival needs that reside on the bottom of this hierarchy and must be socialized to therapy. They are less likely than their middle- and upper-class counterparts to understand what goals therapy can address and the processes it will involve (Heitler, 1973). Once they do begin therapy, they are less firmly supported by important people in their environment in securing such basic provisions as child care. These factors lead lower-class clients to drop out of treatment at higher rates than those from upper classes.

Hence, in a group of economically diverse members, the therapist must take into account the different levels of socialization members have received prior to treatment. Whatever resources members need in order to work productively within the group sessions must be cultivated either prior to the beginning of the group or in the very early sessions. For example, when Heitler (1973) randomly assigned lower-class clients to no preparation or to an anticipatory socialization interview to develop realistic expectations about inpatient group therapy, he found that members who had the benefit of a single preparation session communicated and engaged in self-exploration more frequently and were seen by therapists as being more dependable in keeping their commitment to the group.

Although certain socioeconomic levels seem to have a particular need for preparation, the research cited in Chapter 3 suggests that preparation is generally helpful. Indeed, members of higher social classes are likely to have their own set of misconceptions about group treatment in that they are likely to base their notions about it on individual therapy, a modality with which most people are more familiar. In thinking about how to conduct the preparation, the therapist would do well to take into account other aspects of diversity in the group. For example, there may be cultural effects at certain socioeconomic levels and not others. One cultural group may believe that entrance into therapy signifies moral weakness and another may associate it with extreme emotional instability. Age may be an additional moderating variable in that a certain belief may exist for a certain socioeconomic level within a particular culture but only for a given age group, such as the elderly. In designing the preparation, the therapist must have a sufficiently articulated sense of his or her constituency to encourage an airing and testing of the entire array of beliefs the members have.

The therapist must also exercise care to make certain that the privileges the therapist or other more affluent members of the group enjoy do not obscure the realistic problems other members have in fulfilling their commitment to the group. For example, members with fewer financial resources may be more dependent on public transportation. A therapist who is aware of this complication could interview members before establishing the time of the group meetings in order to ascertain what time arrangement would be most compatible with each member's life circumstance. Encouraging incoming members to talk about their practical problems during the preparatory phase accomplishes another goal: It conveys to them that they should bring into the treatment their total selves. The invitation for members to share all of their struggles—those related to symptoms and also those that are a part of life issues—creates an opportunity for all members. It fosters in members empathy for the real difficulties each faces, an empathy that is likely to increase their therapeutic investment in one another.

Sexual Orientation

Early work in group therapy assumed selection from a heterosexual population. Prior to the 1970s, the only effort to work with gay and lesbian clients occurred when some group therapists took on the project of attempting to change sexual orientation for homosexual individuals on the now-discarded assumption that homosexuality represents a form of psychopathology (Hawkins, 1993). The advent of the gay rights movement in the 1970s spawned the development of homogeneous support groups (Lenihan, 1985) and consciousness-raising groups (Masterson, 1983) to ease adjustment for gay and lesbian individuals in a heterosexual society. Homogeneous therapy groups of gay men were formed to explore how psychiatric problems are tethered to sexual orientation (Schwartz & Hartstein, 1986). A major recent development has been that men who are gay and women who are lesbian have been included in groups in which members are heterogeneous with respect to sexual orientation on the notion that there are unique benefits to be derived from this composition. We will discuss the special considerations to be made with respect to homogeneity or heterogeneity of sexual orientation in the next section.

Sexual Orientation and Homogeneous versus Heterogeneous Groups: Is One Better?

In making a decision about whether to refer an individual with a given sexual orientation to a homogeneous or heterogeneous group, the therapist should ask what the individual's goals are for the group. Suppose a lesbian woman came into group therapy to deal with feelings of loss associated with the death of her mother. The sexual orientation of the other members might not be nearly as important as the focus of the group. However, if the member states as a goal addressing sexual orientation issues either at the beginning or during the interviewing process, then other considerations must be factored into the decision. What is the person's position on the trajectory of recognizing and sharing his or her sexual orientation? *Coming out* is an extended developmental process of recognizing and coming to terms with one's personal and social identity as a person whose sexual and relational orientation is same sex and who has a choice whether to identify with the gay or lesbian culture (Hawkins, 1993). Coming out is both intrapsychic and social, "living on the outside what is real and honest on the inside" (Frost, 1996, p. 170).

Heterogeneous groups, by definition, present members with differences that create tensions among members. The tensions in turn provoke a process of self-examination as members struggle to ascertain what aspects of other members are similar to and different from themselves. In groups that are heterogeneous with respect to sexual orientation, all members are given the opportunity to discover their own sexual orientation. The therapist needs to be aware of the subtle pressure for conversion that a mixed group can exert so that no individual of a particular sexual orientation is scapegoated. This challenge may be particularly great if the individual has accepted a role of scapegoat prior to his or her group involvement, either by virtue of sexual orientation or by virtue of some other group membership, such as being in an oppressed racial or ethnic group. Here we see that sexual orientation cannot be examined independently of all of the other aspects of the person's identity.

At the earliest stages of self-identification, a homogeneous group may be too threatening because of the perceived or real pressure the person may experience to disclose sexual orientation. However, while in the midst of coming out, a closeted person is likely to be closeted in the group as well. The presence of another individual who is gay, lesbian, or bisexual would, in most instances, be essential in this process. This person would have the personal knowledge base to manifest understanding of what this individual is experiencing in the coming-out process. For this reason, the therapist should attempt to constitute the group with multiple members of different sexual orientations rather than having a member who is the sole representative of a given group. Nevertheless, heterosexual members have a contribution to make, too: They help the gay, lesbian, or bisexual individual recognize the universality of certain aspects of his or her struggle.

For example, in one group in which Bernice was well along in the coming-out process, Maryka talked about being able to identify with certain elements of Bernice's struggle. She was a middle-aged Ukrainian woman who had moved to a neighborhood of individuals of Russian descent. She did so with much trepidation, recognizing that historically there had been much conflict between the two ethnic groups. She had avoided socializing with others so that they would not discern her background. Gradually, however, her loneliness and isolation drove her to enter into contact with her neighbors. At the same time, she worried that she would experience oppression. On the one hand, the therapist should encourage such identifications. On the other hand, the therapist should assist members in making appropriate distinctions, since the experience of being in each minority culture invariably is unique. In our example, although Maryka faced a self-disclosure issue with her neighbors, Bernice's coming out may have affected the totality of her relationships.

Hawkins (1993) and Frost (1996) do not endorse groups that are homogeneous in sexual orientation for every stage of development. A homogeneous group is most appropriate for consciousness raising, for coming out, and for needs of normalization. It allows for early self-disclosure, mutual support for the isolated, rapid group identification, and the recogni-

CAUTION

In a group that is heterogeneous for sexual orientation, the therapist should avoid having a single representative of any one sexual orientation category.

tion of universality. It also provides a haven from external homophobia; in its absence, internalized homophobia can be acknowledged. New social skills can be developed for the establishment of friendship networks and connections in the gay community with the opportunity for a freer discussion of sexuality. Such groups help develop an appreciation of the diversity among individuals who share a sexual orientation (Schwartz & Hartstein, 1986). For those further along in their identity development, work on intrapsychic issues as they are manifested in intimate relationships is possible. One problem with the homogeneous group is that it may be used as a reference group or a substitute for other social relationships.

The therapist must consider a variety of factors in contemplating referring a member to one type of group or another. Among these are the other identity dimensions identified by Hays (2001). For example, if the person in need of group placement is an elderly individual and all available homogeneous groups are constituted of young individuals, the therapist must think carefully about the age heterogeneity. Might the age disparity be the basis of the member's being scapegoated in a homogeneous group? Other factors related to group design are also relevant. A heterogeneous group in which there are only 6 members may allow very different types of support to a coming-out person than a group of 10 members. Is the person already in a group that is heterogeneous with respect to sexual orientation? If the member has been in the group for a long duration and has achieved a fairly significant level of intimacy with the other members, might it be worth transferring the person to a group homogeneous for sexual orientation?

Are Gay Men and Lesbian Women Better Served by a Gay or Straight Therapist?

Gay and lesbian clients may prefer therapists of same-sex orientation because they fear judgment by their heterosexual counterparts. Indeed, negative biases toward lesbian, gay, and bisexual individuals are not at all unusual among straight therapists (Frost, 1998). Apart from being preferred by gay, lesbian, and bisexual group members, therapists of these sexual orientations enjoy other advantages. Disclosure by therapists of these orientations allows for positive role modeling. They understand at a deep, personal level members' intrapsychic and interpersonal struggles. Yet, as with therapists from every position and vantage, certain problems may present themselves. Depending on therapists' own identity evolution, they may not be wholly aware of any internalized homophobia and related shame, and this lack of awareness may skew their ways of listening to clinical material. Other countertransference issues may include avoiding overidentification (a potential issue whenever the therapist shares a characteristic of a group member that distinguishes both from the majority of the population) and managing group boundaries while existing in the same small community.

For short-term groups that focus on coming out or adjustment to life following coming out, many recommend a therapist with the same sexual orientation (e.g., Conlin & Smith, 1985). For longer-term groups, this factor may be less important. In fact, the experience of being understood by someone with a different sexual orientation (e.g., a straight member and a gay therapist, or vice versa) may have its own therapeutic value, providing a formative experience for acceptance from the broader society of those who not only are similar to, but also are different from, oneself. Whether the therapist be gay/lesbian/bisexual or straight, what is important is that the therapist engage in self-scrutiny, challenge personal homophobia and heterosexual bias, and accept all aspects of his or her sexual identity.

Indigenous Heritage

The group literature is sparse regarding the defining and distinctive characteristics of Native Americans (including Alaskan Natives) and the influence that these unique qualities have on the group therapy situation. When working with a group of individuals who espouse the traditional teachings of their ancestors, it is generally recommended that the therapist be a member of the community with knowledge of traditional methods of healing and teaching as well as training and familiarity with group therapy as endorsed by the larger academic community. Any successful group utilizing the scientific methods accepted by the larger Western culture must respectfully interface with traditional methods of healing. Given the limited number of qualified individuals capable of fulfilling such a role, knowledge of successful modifications is of paramount importance. Although no studies are available, we have a few clinical reports that are helpful in assisting us in understanding what occurs clinically when the therapist and group members are different from one another.

Fluency in the language has been regarded as essential for productive therapy. Yet Wolman (1970) reports a successful experience working with the Navajo in an inpatient alcoholic treatment program, despite her inability to converse in the Navajo language. This finding is important because alcohol addiction is a serious problem, affecting almost one-third of this population. The group, which was supportive in nature, centered on the drinking—identifying reasons for drinking and finding ways to solve the problems for which alcohol is seen as a solution. The group was conducted primarily in Navajo, with the aid of an interpreter, although some members had familiarity with English. As might be expected, the differences in linguistic knowledge accentuated the distance between the group and the leader. Misunderstandings sometimes occurred, which frequently reflected cultural differences, and the skill of the translator was essential to bridge the language gap.

Often, members in the group can to a small degree speak the language of the therapist even though a translator is needed. The particular language used and the switches between languages may be dynamically significant. For example, the members may speak the therapist's language when making a request of the therapist but switch to their primary language when they are expressing discontent with him or her. The therapist can use this variation to help members understand their behavior.

Native Americans who have chosen to reside in urban areas have the unique distinction of being foreigners in a land that once belonged to them, in addition to being subject to the pressure of acculturation. In such settings, Native Americans are most likely to find themselves as members of a group of mixed ethnicity. Although nothing specific has been written about this mixed composition, it is likely that some models appropriate for group work with other nationalities and ethnic groups might be applied appropriately to this population as well.

Whether forming a group of all Native Americans or one in which there is mixed ethnicity, it is important to remember that this group cannot be a homogeneous group. Two Native Americans in a mixed group may not help either feel more welcome, as language barriers and intertribal tensions make interpersonal connections more unlikely between them than with individuals of entirely different ethnicity. Nonetheless, when the entire group is composed of Native Americans, although they may be quite diverse, the diversity need not impair efficacy. McDonald (1975) formed a group of eight Native American women from assorted tribes who were participating in a government-funded project that aided women with education and placement in urban settings. Using a here-and-now Gestalt approach, he was able to help most of the women focus on their feelings and associated problems of social isolation, vulnerability to American men, alcohol abuse, and anxieties related to acculturation. Although members had significant differences in background, they were united by the immediate focus of the group. At the same time, McDonald was sensitive to the importance of the traditional healing arts and supported the group norm of individual members' returning to the reservation to receive the benefits of a ceremony performed by a medicine man.

National Origin

Social isolation, multiple actual and psychological losses (e.g., of relatives, country, language, and social position), cultural conflicts, and the shared experience of living in a foreign country would seem to make the group setting ideal for persons who have recently immigrated to a new country. Indeed, there have been a number of efforts to use group therapy with immigrant populations, including work with Indochinese (Kinzie et al., 1988), Mexican and South American women (Hynes & Werbin, 1977; Leon & Dziegielewski, 2000), and Greeks (Dunkas & Nikelly, 1975). Most endeavors have required modification of the more traditional group therapy in order to accommodate the particular immigrant culture. Besides the level of psychopathology, developmental stage of the population, and goals to be accomplished, several aspects of the group may require unique consideration: appreciation of the relationship of therapy to the notions of traditional healing, language barriers, the degree of distrust of the leader and/or group members, and the impact of cultural norms on the psychotherapy process.

The Relationship of Therapy to the Notion of Traditional Healing

Some immigrants may be somewhat suspicious of mental health interventions and reluctant to commit themselves in traditional expressive group therapy. Revealing personal information in the group setting is often against the accepted mores of the member's particular culture. For example, in Asian culture, a formalistic style of communication with a hesitancy to speak publicly about oneself dominates. Even within traditional healing methods, nothing comparable to the level and kind of disclosure frequently endorsed in an expressive group therapy exists. With most immigrants from Asian and Latino cultures, somatic complaints are a much more acceptable expression of psychological distress than is the direct acknowledgment of anxiety and depression (Nakkab & Hernandez, 1998). The therapist or doctor is viewed as a strong authority figure who is imbued with magical healing powers. As we learned from Chapter 7, it is common in the initial phases of group therapy for all participants to view the therapist as the authority with answers. However, this attitude is even more deeply ingrained in immigrant cultures. At its extreme, disagreement with the leader is not even permitted.

Language Barriers

Many immigrants and refugees have little or no ability to converse in English. There is some debate over the language that should be spoken in the group. It is often difficult to communicate complex events and emotional material if the individual has very little mastery of English. Consequently, the examination of old traumas and the healing of psychological scars may most successfully be accomplished in a member's native language. Conversely, speaking in English may aid with acculturation. Brooks, Gordon, and Meadow (1998) suggested that if the group goals are to provide a cultural orientation, further the acculturation process, cope with cultural conflict, learn to access resources of the new country, or some combination of these, then an attempt should be made to encourage the use of the new language. Groups with at least one cotherapist who was bilingual in the relevant languages have been most successful.

CAUTION

Cultural paranoia should be explored in the group prior to paranoia associated with individual pathology.

Lack of Trust

Trust, an essential element of a cohesive and successive group, is often something that is particularly difficult to establish in groups with immigrants. Many members appear on the surface to be paranoid. The group therapist, however, must differentiate individual pathology from cultural (societal attitudes) pathology. Cultural paranoia needs to be acknowledged and explored first before individual pathology (e.g., history and traits) can be examined (Fenster & Fenster, 1998). Two factors contribute to cultural paranoia:

- A distrust of the host culture that is projected onto group therapists, who serve as agents of the host culture. Refugees fleeing from real or imagined threats are very reluctant to reveal current discontents or problems or even speak about friends and relatives because they worry that such information may be used to harm people still living in their native country. They also worry that such self-disclosures could adversely affect their current status. Conflict and war discourage listening and encourage the search for facts to support one's previous notions. Hence, notions about present dangers are not instantly amenable to modification from information in the group that is discrepant with these notions. Moreover, an unwillingness to reveal current distress makes it impossible to work through the likely traumas that are part of their experiences.
- A lack of trust of other group members. Our ethnocentrism often leads us to assume that the group is homogeneous if members originate from the same country. However, centuries of conflict within the native country can leave those from the same country mistrustful of one another. A classic contemporary example is thinking that groups composed of people from Ireland will share a special bond or trust. In fact, Irish Catholics and Irish Protestants in the same group are likely to be so mistrustful of one another that the subjects of religion and politics are often avoided (Rice & Kapur, 2002). A naïve therapist may sense the uneasiness, but without the knowledge of the differences and deep conflict he or she would be perplexed as to the reasons. Of course, the

therapist using the ADDRESSING framework would have the information about the two religious subgroups and could go into the group with a plan for how to approach it.

Cultural Mores Altering Group Process

Patterns of accepted communication, respect for authority, and social relationships are always culture bound. Individual characteristics, such as age and sex, often determine communication patterns. For example, with regard to age, Kinzie et al. (1988) found that younger Asian refugees would not offer an opinion without first hearing from their respected elders. Likewise, in some cultures, men do most of the talking while women embrace a passive posture and are unlikely to voice their views unless given permission by men (Dunkas & Nikelly, 1975). In these instances, prudence dictates separating men and women for group treatment. In some cultures, open disagreement is unacceptable, whereas in others an emotional display is acceptable and does not signify disrespect.

Effective Models and Suggested Technical Modifications for Groups That Are Homogeneous versus Heterogeneous with Respect to National Origin

Whether all or only a subset of the members of a group have immigrated, the therapist working with immigrants must be sensitive to the accepted practices of the individual's culture of origin in designing suitable techniques. As the individual who has immigrated comes to trust the other members, the group achieves the potential to bridge the gap between old and new cultures, decrease the immigrated member's isolation, and increase the likelihood that the immigrant will come to recognize the value of aid outside the traditionally culturally accepted methods.

If the therapist is treating a group of individuals all of whom are recent immigrants, injecting a component of activity can reduce isolation and aid in the acculturation process. Kinzie et al. (1988) found that a professionally led group that incorporated an activity such as cooking ethnic food, sharing traditional stories, or teaching practical skills was beneficial for immigrants of Indochinese descent. Activities from the traditional culture are likely to lead to positive cohesive group experiences. Often more personal material—such as symptoms, losses, and cultural conflict—will emerge from the activity than from a formal group experience.

In mixed groups in which not all members are immigrants, employing a mechanism by which the member's background can be introduced into the group is helpful. In the interview, the therapist should make an effort to learn about the individual's immigration history and how life has changed, especially in a social way, since the immigration. Once the group begins, the therapist might use techniques to enable the person to share his or her background. For example, in a short-term, closed-ended group, in the first session, the therapist might organize an icebreaker in which members interview one another and proceed to introduce their interviewee to the larger group. This step is likely to give formal recognition to the immigrant's background and even nurture members' curiosity about this special aspect of the group member. Finally, the therapist should be sensitive to role expectations that are violated by virtue of the culture of the group that reflects the culture of the new society. For example, suppose an elderly woman from another country enters the group and speaks dogmatically on a number of issues. Group members, who are mostly younger, gradually become irritated by her doctrinaire style of communicating. In this woman's country, achieving advanced age was respected. The individual became an elder whose responsibility it was to share wisdom. In her new country, however, age is not seen as providing an individual with any special entitlement to respect. Hence, this woman's expectation of what her role should be was violated. Helping both the woman and the group appreciate the cultural clash fosters mutual empathy and tolerance.

Gender

The vast majority of therapy groups include both men and women, although often women are present in greater numbers (e.g., Russo, 1990). Men and women are affected by one another's presence in the group. For example, when men and women are present in a group, men appear to be more engaged in the group and less preoccupied with competition and aggression than when they are in an all-male group (e.g., Aries, 1976). On the other hand, women tend to be less engaged and more passive when men are present than when they are not (e.g., Aries, 1976; Carlock & Martin, 1977).

These findings and clinical observations consistent with them have led clinicians to ponder whether all-male and all-female groups or mixed groups are more desirable. Particularly for women, the argument has been made that an all-female group frees women from the pressure to engage in stereotypic behavior. Holmes (2002) noted that in the mixed group men frequently presented problems for women to solve, and when women performed this service they were reinforced for doing so. In contrast, in the all-female group, Holmes observed, "With no masculine object present to compulsively play subject to, they seemed to carve out the time and the space they needed to begin to know themselves" (p. 176). A different argument is made concerning all-male groups because men seem to be less stereotypically masculine when women are present. The argument is that when women are present, men find greater difficulty in making themselves vulnerable as difficult issues are raised (McPhee, 1996).

> **DON'T FORGET**
> ....
> Mixed groups provide a real-world environment for dealing with gender-based stereotypes.

Yet many argue that a strength of group therapy is its power to function as a microcosm of society. Limiting the group to one gender creates an artificial world for members. In contrast, the mixed group is an ideal social context for examining gender-related attitudes and behaviors and then making conscious choices concerning sex role stereotypes. The mixed group offers a corrective experience for reworking socialized stereotypic interpersonal and intrapersonal responses (Schoenholtz-Read, 1996). However, this corrective experience requires the therapist's awareness that men and women may enter the group with different needs. Often men require help in dealing with fears of entrapment and engulfment, while women benefit from addressing fears related to aggression and loss of relationships (Holmes, 2002). Sexual stereotypes are in part efforts to allay these fears. By being sensitive to these fears and helping members to recognize them, the therapist can assist both male and female members in becoming emancipated from these stereotypes. Empirical support for the usefulness of mixed-gender groups was found in Burlingame et al.'s (2003) meta-analysis, which indicated that mixed-gender groups showed greater improvement than all-female or all-male groups.

Once again, though, we can see the limitations of examining one dimension in isolation. Gender differences are shaped by environment, yet environments vary. The individual's socioeconomic status (not only in adulthood but also in childhood, when gender differences are established), level of education, ethnicity and race, and all of the other factors we have considered will bear upon how men and women in the group relate to one another. The therapist cannot take refuge in general trends observed by the therapists of other groups such as the gender differences described in this section. Rather, the therapist must be alive to the uniqueness of his or her group, a uniqueness that emerges in part from the concatenation of variables defining each member's identity.

EFFECTIVELY WORKING WITH DIVERSITY

Although this chapter has focused in large part on the group members themselves, the therapist must come to the group ready to work with the diversities each group presents. How can the therapist prepare him- or herself to do so? We offer the following guidelines:

- Develop an appreciation of the multifaceted nature of your identity. This task can be accomplished using a system such as the ADDRESS-ING framework (Hays, 2001). For each aspect of your identity, explore its status and how it might affect your worldview. Strive to develop awareness of your attitudes toward each of the majority and minority groups on each dimension, and develop an understanding of how these attitudes have been formed. This exploration may best be accomplished in personal therapy or with supervision.

- Using the ADDRESSING framework, recognize your own privilege and minority status for each aspect of your identity. In the United States, the majority of therapists are Americans of White European descent. Appreciating the impact that privilege has on one's perception of self and others is essential. Minorities seem to be more aware of their race or ethnicity, whereas White Euro-Americans appear to have difficulty seeing and identifying themselves as racial beings (Sue & Sue, 1999). If therapists cannot identify themselves as privileged, they are unlikely to appreciate the many ways in which others struggle with oppression.

- Familiarize yourself with the resources on diversity. For example, the 2001 surgeon general's report focused on mental health and minority issues and provides a substantial bibliography (*http://www.surgeongeneral.gov/library/mentalheath/cre/*). There are many web sites providing diversity-related information, such as the following: *http://www.diversityrx.org*, which contains abundant information on many aspects of diversity and health care, and *http://www.apa.org/division/div 45/publications.html*, which is maintained by Division 45, the Society for the Psychological Study of Ethnic Minority Issues, and contains issues of the journal *Cultural Diversity and Ethnic Minority Psychology*.

- Seek consultation and training. Attempting to develop competency as a therapist who is sensitive to group diversity is a humbling experience because it reveals one's limitations in knowledge and experience. Relying too heavily on written material may give you a false sense of security. Seek out consultants who share the same identity as the member. Training experiences that enable exposure to a particular population with supervision, through either occupational training or continuing education, will help you to develop self-awareness as well as knowledge about the particular population.

- Have a readiness to communicate respect genuinely even if understanding is lacking. Keep in mind that members are in a position to teach you about themselves. Part of the humility of this process is the willingness to betray your own ignorance.

- Recognize that part of working with group diversity is raising issues that are seen as taboo areas within your life outside the group. To increase your comfort level, role-play with other therapists how you would introduce the discussion of particular areas of diversity. Obtain feedback on your efforts.
- Be familiar with your discipline's ethical and practice guidelines on working with diversity in groups. For example, psychologists should be conversant with the "Guidelines on Multicultural Education, Training, Research, Practice, and Organizational Change for Psychologists" (American Psychological Association, 2003).

SUMMARY AND CONCLUSIONS

Heterogeneity abounds in the therapy group. The competent group therapist recognizes that diversity is created not only by variation in psychological problems or diagnoses but also by members' individual characteristics that define their identities. To the extent that the recognition of these characteristics is comprehensive, the therapist can communicate empathically with group members, identify tensions that are likely to emerge in the group, marshal resources created by the differences, and adapt his or her techniques to the unique needs of the membership of the group. In order to assist the therapist in appraising group diversity, Hays's ADDRESSING framework was presented. This framework consists of the following dimensions: age and generational influences, developmental and acquired disabilities, religion and spiritual orientation, ethnicity and race, socioeconomic status, sexual orientation, indigenous heritage, national origin, and gender. The therapist undoubtedly will be able to identify other dimensions that may have importance for his or her group. Guidelines were offered to enable the therapist to respond most helpfully to the diversities the group presents.

🐾 TEST YOURSELF 🐾

1. **Hays's ADDRESSING framework can be used to**
   (a) identify the cultural influences of a client.
   (b) identify the cultural influences of a therapist.
   (c) determine areas where an individual can hold privilege or minority status.
   (d) all of the above

2. **Why is the group model ideally suited for an elderly population?**

3. **With increasing age, children will increasingly benefit from**
   (a) more structured activities.
   (b) verbal commentary.
   (c) incorporating the aid of props.
   (d) all of the above

4. **This group constitutes the largest minority group in the United States:**
   (a) Hispanic Americans
   (b) Elderly individuals
   (c) African Americans
   (d) Individuals with disability

5. **Generally, mixed-gender therapy groups are beneficial for Hispanic American but not African American populations.** True or False?

6. **What is the most essential prerequisite for a therapist working with longer-term mixed-sexuality or homogeneous-sexuality groups?**

7. **Which group may have difficulty benefiting from ethnically mixed group therapy?**
   (a) African Americans
   (b) Asian Americans
   (c) Native Americans
   (d) Hispanic Americans

8. **What does it mean to hold privilege for a particular identity?**

9. **What steps can a therapist take to become more culturally competent in his or her work?**

10. **Therapists working with groups of mixed composition should introduce differences in identity early on in the group process.** True or False?

Answers: 1. d; 2. In an elderly population, an appropriate group experience can buffer against stressors such as loss and isolation, the universality of aging, a diminished sense of utility, and fears of disability or illness; 3. b; 4. d; 5. False; 6. Self-awareness and comfort with one's own sexuality and lifestyle; 7. c; 8. To have an advantage due to membership or identity in a dominant group; 9. Exploring one's own multicultural heritage and identify and examine the patient's background through direct questions; reading literature, seeking consultation, additional training, and/or supervision; 10. True.

Ten

SHORT-TERM GROUP THERAPY

This chapter will discuss an increasingly popular type of group format in the contemporary practice of group therapy: the short-term group. In the literature, short-term groups have been described functionally and practically. The temporal or practical definition of short-term therapy is a group experience lasting, by design, 6 months or less. According to the functional definition, the member's group experience is planned to be neither longer nor shorter than what is necessary for the treatment of a psychological problem. Within short-term groups, MacKenzie (1995), a leading writer on short-term groups, makes a distinction between *brief* groups, which meet for up to eight sessions, and *time-limited* groups, whose life span ranges from 6 weeks to 6 months. Whereas the former groups are tailored to help individuals successfully negotiate crisis, the latter are designed to treat persons with more severe or complicated problems or move them to a higher level of psychological functioning. MacKenzie's distinction between brief and short-term groups will be used in this chapter.

The short-term therapy group is currently flourishing because of many factors, but two are particularly significant. The first is the revolution in health care treatment. Skyrocketing health care costs in the United States led to the emergence of managed care programs that entail the application of controls on the provision of health care services. Currently over 60 percent of Americans are enrolled in some managed care plan (Spitz, 2001). Most other Western countries have been operating under managed care for many years (MacKenzie, 1995). The managed care movement has had a positive effect on the utilization of therapy groups. Group treatment is more economical than individual treatment because it enables a group of individuals to be treated simultaneously by one or two professionals. This advantage is particularly significant given the outcome literature showing, that generally, group treatment is at least as effective as individual therapy (see Chapter 7). At the same time, just as short-term individual therapy has been regarded more favorably by managed care groups than treatment that extends indefinitely, so is short-term group treatment with well-defined goals and processes leading to those goals seen as preferable to time-unlimited group therapy. Group therapists, like practitioners of all modalities, are asked by reimbursers, "What are the goals? How are you going to get there? How long will it take?"

Another influential factor has been the increased knowledge of how clients utilize therapy due to studies that track attendance in sessions. What has been learned is that regardless of how long clients intend to remain in treatment when they begin, the vast majority remains only briefly. For example, Sledge, Moras, and Hartley (1990) followed 69 clients who entered long-term treatment and discovered that the mean number of sessions in which members participated was 15.4. However, the investigators also found that when the therapist specified in advance an ending point to treatment, the client tended to remain for the entire course of treatment. Findings from other modalities have been obtained in group treatment as well: What the therapist designs as a long-term group, the member converts into short-term treatment. For example, Klein and Carroll (1986) found that of 200 clients who were referred to long-term groups in a university setting, 40 percent dropped out before their participation began. Of those who entered a group, approximately half had 12 or fewer sessions. Forty-two percent remained between 3 months and a year, and only 8 percent remained beyond a year.

Only 15 years ago, the prevailing notion was that the only effective group therapy was long-term treatment. However, accumulating evidence has disputed this belief. MacKenzie (1995), describing the pattern emerging across a large number of psychotherapy outcome studies, noted that most patients show rapid improvement over the first 2 months of treatment, with continued marked improvement over the next 4 months. Although improvement continues beyond 6 months, the rate of improvement is much slower. A review (Piper & Joyce, 1996) of outcome studies on short-term groups provided impressive evidence of the efficacy of short-term groups run from a great variety of orientations directed toward the treatment of a wide range of psychological problems. Out of 50 studies, 48 showed greater benefit from participation in short-term groups relative to the control comparison. Moreover, this greater benefit was demonstrated across nine categories of psychological problems. These include lifestyle problems (e.g., smoking, social skills), medical conditions, affective disorders, trauma, eating disorders, and others. In six studies comparing short-term group with individual therapy, one study favored group, another individual, and the remaining four failed to show a difference between the modalities. Recent studies (e.g., Kush & Fleming, 2000; Piper et al., 2001) have provided additional support for the benefits of short-term group therapy.

Both attendance patterns and efficacy findings suggest that community needs require the availability of a large number of brief therapy groups of 10 or fewer sessions, a lesser but still substantial number of time-limited therapy groups, and a much smaller number of long-term therapy groups that extend beyond 6 months. Even though the need for short-term groups is great, practical factors may impede many therapists from conducting them. Short-term groups (especially brief groups) require a continuous and plentiful flow of potential group members, a demand that cannot be accommodated in many private practice situations. Brief and time-limited groups are most feasible in large health care organizations. Nonetheless, all group therapists must be knowledgeable about short-term therapy in order to recognize when a referral to a short-term group is appropriate.

COMMON FEATURES OF SHORT-TERM GROUPS

Although there are a great variety of short-term groups being conducted in contemporary practice, most share a number of characteristics. When evaluating any approach for application in the short-term situation, the therapist should look for these features.

Specificity of Goals

Historically in long-term treatment, goals were often vague and diffuse. A member may enter knowing that his or her relationships were unfulfilling and plan to learn from the group experience itself what were the particular deficiencies that should be addressed during the course of the group. In the short-term group, the goals are clearly demarcated prior to the member's entrance into the group. For example, in an interpersonally oriented group, the specific relational goal the member would pursue would be understood by the therapist and member prior to that member's entrance into the group. Hence, rather than intending to work on relationship difficulties, a member might enter the short-term group with the goal of handling more constructively his or her anger toward authority figures.

As implied, the long-term group provides more of an opportunity for the discovery of one's areas of difficulty than the short-term group. Yet there is no group experience—regardless of how brief—in which the member is unable to acquire insights about the self that suggest goals for future group work. What if a member discovers a potential goal yet lacks the time to pursue it? An important fact about short-term groups is that they rarely occur in isolation. As Budman, Simeone, Reilly, and Demby (1994) noted, "there are indications that between 50 and 60% of patients who terminate at any given time seek additional care within the following year (Budman & Gurman, 1988). Thus, viewing the index episode of therapy as being brief treatment is, in some ways, misleading" (p. 321).

Whatever new goals are identified during the course of a short-term group can be used in several ways. First, the identification of a new goal may position a member well for any future therapy experiences. Second, a goal may be pursued within the context of any concurrent therapies. Third, some short-term groups carry the option for renewal. As members approach termination, they take stock of their progress. If there is further work to be done on current goals or if new goals have emerged, then the member can recontract for a new stint in a group. Practitioners (Hardy & Lewis, 1992) who have incorporated this feature have found that having veterans in the group is useful to the group in that their positive report about their prior group experience fosters optimism in other members. Moreover, senior members are able to model appropriate group behaviors and reinforce other members' constructive behaviors. Their presence enables the group to develop healthy norms more quickly and thereby develop a higher level of functioning than would have existed were they to be absent.

Careful Screening and Preparation

In short-term group treatment, screening and preparation are even more important than in long-term therapy. Screening is crucial because the presence of inappropriate individuals can derail a group from its intended focus and undermine its effectiveness. Yalom (1995) emphasizes the necessity of the individual pregroup interview rather than a screening conducted over the telephone or through some other means. The criteria the therapist uses relate to the goals of the group in that the goals must have appropriateness for the person and the person must have an interest in working on those goals. As noted in the prior section, the goals of a short-term group are often more specific than those of a long-term group and thereby serve as more of a basis for selection.

When members in a group share goals, several important benefits accrue. Commonality of goals facilitates the establishment of a consistent focus in the sessions, enables time to be used efficiently, and catalyzes members' identification with one another. As the therapist discusses the candidate's goals, those goals are likely to become more precisely defined. This process not only is useful in ensuring his or her suitability, but also may help in the member's installation in the group. Research has shown that relative to pretherapy dropouts, clients who enter treatment are more likely to state goals that are clearer and more detailed (Garfield, 1986).

Although some similarity among members' goals is beneficial, members need not have identical goals. Research has shown that short-term groups can accommodate some heterogeneity in members' presenting complaints. An example is

Piper, McCallum, and Azim's (1992) psychodynamic approach for the group treatment of persons experiencing pathological grief reactions in relation to losses. Despite this significant commonality, members differed from one another in terms of the concrete aspects of their presenting complaints and the conflicts underlying the complaints. Nevertheless, this variability did not hinder members from participating in the group in such a way as to produce positive changes symptomatically and interpersonally. Such variability can benefit the group work because it enables members to have a level of neutrality about one another's problems that is more difficult to achieve when problems are shared. At the end of this chapter, we will see two models, one inpatient and one outpatient, that can accommodate great heterogeneity in symptoms.

There are other characteristics of an individual that should be evaluated in determining his or her appropriateness for short-term group. The therapist should consider the member's history of relationships to ascertain how the member is likely to interact with others in the group. For example, a particular person may have difficulty being trusting of others. Examination of history may show that the person forms relationships very slowly. In a short-term time frame the person's wariness may lead the person to be disengaged and thereby fail to derive benefit from the group. For another person, also with a difficulty trusting others, history may show that the person is better able to relate actively in short-term relationships because he or she perceives them as providing a measure of safety. For that member, short-term group treatment may be an effective prelude to a longer-term investment.

Another consideration is whether the prospective member is able to use the processes on which the group depends to move members toward their goals. For example, if the group depends on members' ability to give feedback to one another, the therapist might assess whether a prospective member has a capacity to make observations of other people and to verbalize those observations. Even if a candidate lacks the skills and behaviors needed to take full advantage of the group, he or she need not be excluded from the group provided the requisite capabilities are cultivated either in pretraining or in the initial group sessions.

Preparation is an essential component of the short-term group as it is for longer term groups. As noted in Chapter 3, preparation reduces dropouts, improves attendance, and facilitates the manifestation of behaviors that move members toward the therapeutic goals. This last effect is especially significant for the short-term group situation. Because time is limited, it is crucial that members make full use of all of the sessions. They have little time to learn to work, so ideally they will be prepared to work upon entrance into the group. Budman and Gurman (1988) describe a format for a preparatory workshop for short-term group therapy that fosters constructive group behaviors. In Part 1, a common group exercise is used in which members divide into pairs, interview one another, and introduce their interviewees to the group. In Part 2, members divide into subgroups of three or four and complete a task that relates to the group's orientation. For example, in an interpersonally oriented group, members might observe a videotape of a group and discuss their observations of each member and how they might verbalize those observations in ways that would be sensitive and helpful. In Part 3, a whole-group exercise occurs in which members work together on another task that pertains to the focus of the group. For example, in a psychodrama group for teen-agers working on anger management, the therapist could offer a scenario in which a protagonist confronted an anger-arousing stimulus, which members could then enact and discuss.

Such a progression from dyadic to whole-group exercises enables members to master the anxiety that typically attends joining a group. It also provides practice in behaviors that are important for a successful group experience. Finally, such a preparation provides more opportunity for screening clients and additional information on which the client can base his or her consent.

Sometimes, when logistical factors make it difficult to have the preparation prior to the group, the preparation can occur during the first group session. Whether preparation occurs before the group begins or in the first session, what is crucial is that the therapist carefully considers what the member needs in his or her repertoire to function effectively in the group and then organize experiences to cultivate these elements if members are not fully in possession of them.

Emphasis on the Development of Group Cohesion

In all types of groups, cohesion is crucial to members' work in the group. For example, cohesion appears to catalyze the activation of many of the other therapeutic factors described in Chapter 4 (MacKenzie, 1990). What distinguishes a short-term from a long-term group is that the former does not afford the luxury of allowing cohesion to develop gradually, as in the normal course of group development. The therapist must be more active in fostering group cohesion. There are many ways in which the therapist can encourage the development of a cohesive group (Klein, 1993). One way is in the selection of members. Members who can easily identify with one another—that is, who see one another as similar in important respects—more readily come together as a cohesive group. For this reason, the therapist may compose a group with individuals who are likely to see themselves as being similar. For example, the therapist may select the members of a group from persons in a limited age range. Whereas in a long-term group people in a broader age range could learn how to identify with one another, and in fact such an experience could have a great deal of therapeutic usefulness in its own right, in a short-term group the broad age range could impede the group from cohering. One of the authors has had the experience of having a single elderly patient in a group with young adults and middle-aged persons. The elderly member often said in the first session, "I don't belong here," and other members agreed and asked if the member could be moved to a group of older individuals.

In many settings, the size of the pool of candidates for group therapy precludes limits on how selective the therapist can be in composing the group. Fortunately, there are other means by which group cohesion can be established. Thorough preparation can be extremely instrumental in giving members a shared sense of purpose and fostering cohesiveness.

Once the group gets underway, the most effective way of promoting cohesion will depend upon the maturity of the group (Budman et al., 1994). Early in the life of the group, the members' sense of being a group, or cohesion to the group as a whole, is extremely important (Kipnes, Piper, & Joyce, 2002). However, when ambiguity exists about the focus of the group, members can be stymied in coalescing as an effective working unit. At any time, group cohesion can be fostered in the following ways:

- Create as many sources of constancy early in the life of the group as you can so that the group has an identity with recognizable features. To this end, the therapist should be meticulous in beginning and ending on time and holding the group meetings in the same location. The therapist should emphasize the importance of regular, punctual attendance so that norms develop supporting constancy of membership.
- Encourage all members to actively participate. Studies have shown that members' high levels of engagement with one another early in the group are associated with favorable outcomes (Kivlighan & Lilly, 1997; Ogrodniczuk & Piper, 2003). The therapist should monitor each member's level of participation and invite silent members to join in the conversation. Because silence is often a reflection of anxiety about being in the group, the therapist must be skilled in involving these reticent members in a way that will be as nonthreatening as possible.
- Help members to focus on one another. Early in the group's development, members' focus on the therapist is natural. The therapist is the authority figure whom they see as having the resources to alleviate suffering. Because this focus is almost inevitable, the therapist must actively work to enlarge members' view of the group to encompass the other members. There will be many opportunities to support members'

attending to one another. For example, when a member questions the therapist, the therapist can ask the member posing the question to direct it to other members of the group. The therapist might ask, "From which member would you like a response?"

As the group increases in maturity and moves into its middle phase, members' interest in one another and capacity to see each other in a differentiated way will increase. At this point, the therapist's effort should be in helping participants to deepen their member-to-member relationships. For example, the therapist can find opportunities for members to share their full range of feelings toward one another and offer one another highly detailed feedback on their behavior in the group.

Toward the end of the life of the group, the connection both with the group as a whole and with individual members is important. The therapist's effort at this time should have a dual focus, aiding members in processing both their responses to the loss of the group as an entity and the ending of the relationships between individual members.

Time as a Therapeutic Force

In long-term therapy, members have the luxury of believing that whatever problems are not being addressed in the present will be pursued in the near or remote future. Such a belief can operate in the service of members' resistance: Like anyone facing work that might be arduous or threatening, members are glad to put it off, and the lack of a time pressure fosters this procrastination.

The short-term group has the advantage over long-term group therapy in that there is less room for procrastination (see Rapid Reference 10.1). Members' awareness of the time limit has the potential to exert a positive effect on members' motivation to work, even if that work entails an acceptance of discomfort. In order for this potential to be realized, the therapist must keep the time limit in the forefront of members' awareness. The therapist may remind members at the beginning of each session how many sessions remain in the life of the group. The therapist may ac-

Rapid Reference 10.1

How Time Is Used as a Resource in Short-Term Group Therapy

- To encourage members to take responsibility for their difficulties
- To motivate members to work vigorously
- To stimulate loss-related conflicts so they can be explored and more adequately resolved
- To inspire members to address existential factors

knowledge to members that they will continue to work after the group has ended and may indicate the nature of that work.

The time limit of the short-term group provides a stimulus for members to address issues related to loss. This stimulus is especially potent and rich in a closed-ended format in which all members begin and end the group at the same time. The ending of the group constitutes a loss for the entire group. Because the loss can be anticipated, members' customary ways of responding to loss can not only emerge but be explored. This opportunity is useful because for many members who find themselves in group therapy, the event of loss is a challenge to their capacity to maintain a state of well-being. Rather than reckoning with the full range of feelings associated with the loss, these individuals often engage in defensive activity designed to remove from awareness some part of their loss-related reactions. For example, they may simply deny them, or they may act them out in destructive behaviors. When these individuals do not grapple with the diverse emotions that loss brings, they remain tied to that psychological experience, unable to move on to enjoy new, fulfilling experiences. The short-term group provides an opportunity to examine both the defenses that interfere with members' having a full experience of loss and the feelings, impulses, and ideas against which the defenses are erected. The fact that these elements are shared with other group members enables them to be accepted more readily than if the individuals were to experience them in isolation. Through this exploration, members are able to learn a new and more adaptive way of coping with the inevitable losses that life brings. The following Putting It into Practice illustrates this process.

Loss, however, is merely one type of limit. The limit in time is evocative of members' reactions to limits of all sorts—limits in relationships, limits in opportunities, and ultimately the limit of life itself. Yalom (1995) described the existential factors that correspond to the fundamental realities of human existence such as death, aloneness, and individuals' own responsibility for their destinies. As discussed in Chapter 2 in relation to existential therapy, the affirmation of these realities enables members to live more authentically as they liberate themselves from engagement in trivial, empty pursuits merely to hide from themselves these existential facts. The finitude of time in short-term therapy provides a stimulus for members to grapple with the existential facts of life.

Actively Moving a Group Toward Its Goals

In long-term groups, different theoretical orientations are associated with highly different levels of observable activity on the part of the therapist. Some theoretical approaches, such as cognitive-behavioral therapy, require frequent interventions by the therapist, who implements a highly structured format, directs the

Putting It Into Practice

Confronting Issues of Loss

Rita entered a 10-session group in a large community mental health center 6 months following the death of her mother. She had found that she was having difficulty performing everyday chores such as caring for her three children. She also had sleep and appetite disturbances. She was perplexed by her reaction to her mother's death because she never felt herself to be particularly close to her mother: She thought of their relationship as having been friendly but distant.

The group was not specifically designed for individuals who were experiencing pathological grief reactions. Nonetheless, during the first session, Rita noticed that many members reported various losses that they had had over the past year. For example, one man, Abraham, had lost a high-level administrative job and was unable to find a comparable position. A female member, Kirby, had lost her husband.

During the initial sessions, Rita experienced tremendous relief, as she was able to talk about her disappointment in herself in not being able to rebound after her mother's death. She also appreciated the feedback she received from other members of the group on her positive ways of relating to them. For example, several members had commented that they felt she listened to them carefully and they felt understood by her. In the seventh session, the therapist reminded the group that there were three more sessions remaining. Abraham asked the therapist if it would be possible to extend the life of the group by five sessions or so. He noted that members were just getting "warmed up." Several other members responded to this suggestion enthusiastically. The therapist indicated that it would not be possible to extend the group. Kirby expressed annoyance at this idea, exclaiming that a 10-session group made no sense whatsoever. She revealed that it had been difficult for her to join the group; she had to overcome great trepidation. Now that she was comfortable in the group, she was facing its end. She then berated the agency for organizing the group in this manner. One other member looked at the therapist and sarcastically said, "Yeah, and you'll probably be glad to be rid of us!"

Rita noted that it was not the therapist's fault that the group was coming to an end. Abraham irascibly responded, "Who said it was?" Rita said she did not want the therapist to feel hurt, thinking that the group had been a failure. She went on to extol the agency, noting that staff had responded quickly and supportively when she had been in crisis. Several other members shared similar reactions. Kirby expressed irritation with this subgroup of members, calling them "goody-goodies."

The therapist commented, "The impending ending of the group has evoked various feelings from group members. For some, there is anger about this ending. The anger is directed both at the agency and also at me; after all, I'm the agency's representative here in the room. Others feel protective of me—that somehow if there is anger directed toward me, I will be harmed by it." The group went on to explore members' different stances toward the reaction of anger in relation to loss and reality testing the belief that the therapist would be injured by the expression of anger. On her own Rita made the connection that she could never get angry with her mother because she feared that she would become even more distant. Group members pointed out that other people, like the therapist, may be different than her mother and may even appreciate her getting angry if that is her genuine feeling.

Teaching note: In this session, Rita took advantage of one of the features of a closed-ended short-term group, the prominence of the ending of the group, an event that activates loss-related conflicts. Rita was able to make a beginning in addressing her apprehension about recognizing negative feelings associated with the loss, such as anger and the fantasies associated with this apprehension (e.g., damaging the other person). This awareness may make it easier for her to find more bearable her full range of reactions associated with past and future losses.

CAUTION

Inactive therapists may allow a destructive pattern of group dynamics to take hold.

group's activities, and interacts extensively with members on an individual level. Other approaches, such as psychodynamic therapy, tend to involve a more sparing therapeutic style, although not because of a lack of therapist zest. Rather, psychodynamic therapists are less active behaviorally, relative to other approaches, for the following reasons: (1) to encourage members' independence and interdependence; (2) to create an atmosphere in which group dynamics can develop and crystallize; and (3) to allow for the emergence of each member's characteristic style of relating.

In short-term therapy, however, all therapists must consider the drawbacks of a low level of activity on their parts. With the absence of a highly active therapist, some members could participate minimally and derive little from the experience. Destructive group dynamics might take hold of the group for its duration. The group might fail to utilize the therapeutic factors that the therapist sees as key to their progress. To minimize these possibilities, therapists of all orientations generally adopt an active posture.

At the same time, therapists have found ways both to maintain a high level of activity and to preserve the benefits of a less active and nondirective stance when the theoretical orientation requires the presence of these features. In the next section, we will consider two models that strike a balance between therapist activity and member spontaneity. There are several means by which balance is achieved. One is that the therapist may use different levels of activity with different segments of the group. One segment may be highly structured, and members' interactions may be highly orchestrated by the therapist. Another segment may allow for a freer exchange among members. The structured segment primes the member to use the unstructured segment as profitably as possible. We will see the application of this method in Yalom's interactional agenda group. Another means is through the therapist's willingness to accept less evidence for making interpretive statements. As Piper, McCallum, and Azim (1992) noted, "The therapist must be ready and able to offer interpretations based upon considerable inference" (p. 69). The therapist is assisted by knowledge of common themes and conflicts that appear in the population from which group members are drawn.

A Present and a Future Temporal Orientation

When the group's attention is drawn to the here and now (i.e., to the immediate interactions among members), members derive a variety of benefits. A first benefit is that a here-and-now focus engages members emotionally and intellectually. Engagement is a requirement for members' deriving any benefit from the group experience. A second benefit is that a focus on the here and now is efficient. Whereas a focus on an individual's past has a high level of relevance for one member of the group, the here and now includes all members. A third benefit is that the here and now maximally utilizes the special resources of the group, such as the opportunity to receive a multiplicity of perspectives on oneself.

≡Rapid Reference 10.2

Special Features of Short-Term Groups

- Specificity of goals
- Careful screening and preparation
- Development of rapid group cohesion
- The use of time as a therapeutic force
- A highly active therapist
- A present and future temporal orientation and a focus on the here and now

The therapist must also prepare the members to leave the group, that is, to ready themselves for their futures. This preparation occurs in the following ways:

- By helping members to anticipate the obstacles they will encounter in applying the learning and insights from the group outside of the group.
- By establishing linkages between in-group experiences and members' struggles outside the group. In fact, research has shown that interventions linking members' behaviors in the group to those outside produce enhanced outcomes relative to interventions that refer exclusively to members' group behaviors (Flowers & Booraem, 1990a, 1990b).
- By providing members with homework assignments so that they can practice learning in their natural environments and see what impediments lie in their way.

The special features of short-term groups are summarized in Rapid Reference 10.2.

MODELS OF SHORT-TERM GROUP THERAPY

In this text, we have covered theoretical approaches that are employed primarily in a short-term time frame. These approaches include cognitive-behavioral therapy, redecision therapy, and psychodrama. In this section, we will describe two short-term group models based on theoretical orientations that have been historically associated with long-term applications. These models are instructive in showing us how the principles of short-term group therapy described in the prior section can be taken into account at the same time that the integrity of the theoretical orientation is preserved. We will also show how each approach can be used in different types of clinical venues, such as inpatient and outpatient.

Yalom's Interactional Agenda Model

The interpersonal approach, described in Chapter 2, has as its goal the modification of an individual's style of relating in a way that increases the person's ability to derive fulfillment from relationships. In his original description of this approach, Yalom (1970) envisioned a long-term treatment situation in which members would come to know one another intimately in the context of mature relationships. In the early 1980s, Yalom (1983) proposed a version of the interpersonal approach adapted to inpatient groups, in which members may remain for as little as one session. This approach is now widely used in inpatient partial hospitalization settings and could easily be used with short-term outpatient groups.

With an extremely brief period of participation, how is it possible for a group member to make substantial changes in his or her style of relating, a style that may have been present from a very early age? Yalom (1983) acknowledges that more modest goals should be set for brief groups. For inpatients, Yalom identified one goal that he believes can be realistically pursued: developing in members a positive attitude toward treatment so that they continue with therapy upon leaving the hospital. This goal is an extremely worthy one given that many inpatients fail to obtain follow-up treatment upon being discharged, and whether they do will influence their need for further hospitalizations. Moreover, members can learn about psychotherapeutic processes and specific goals that could be addressed in a longer-term therapy so that outpatient treatment gets off the ground quickly and effectively. An important factor of these goals is that they are not likely to duplicate the contributions of other modalities in the inpatient setting.

A Typical Session

The interactional agenda approach entails a formatted session consisting of five steps. Orientation and preparation, the first step, is built into the session itself, a practical inclusion given that new members enter the group throughout the group's life. At this time, the therapist explains what members can accomplish in the group and what processes members can use to achieve their goals.

The second step is the agenda go-around. Each member has a turn in formulating an agenda that is clear and specific, interpersonally focused, and capable of being accomplished during the confines of a session. Typically, members produce agendas lacking these properties. So that their work during the session will be productive, the therapist must help each member to sculpt the agenda initially offered so that it effectively organizes the member's work during the session.

For example, the member may say, "I want to stop leaving places because I get really scared all of a sudden." The therapist would work with the member to develop the interpersonal component, which may be, "When people begin to focus on me, I leave the situation." However, the agenda still has not been made relevant to the immediate situation. The therapist would go on to help the group develop the following: "When a member asks me a question, if I feel frightened I will tell the group I am frightened rather than running out of the room."

The achievement of a workable agenda is therapeutically useful because it helps members to understand how the here and now of the group is a resource for identifying these areas of difficulty. This understanding is one that can catalyze any posthospital therapeutic endeavor. It also increases members' hope in that it makes their problems more circumscribed and hence more manageable. The agenda focuses the work of the session so that the time members spend with one another is both productive and felt to be productive by them. Members' positive valuation of the session contributes to the development of a positive attitude toward therapy, the achievement of which fulfills the overarching goal of the treatment.

Agenda fulfillment is the third step of the treatment. This segment allows for the most spontaneous interaction among the group members although the therapist continues to be very active in identifying for members opportunities to fulfill their agendas through their interactions with one another. In the following Putting It into Practice, the reader will see an example of how a therapist helped a group member, Leo, fulfill his agenda. To ensure that all group members have an opportunity to make some progress on their agendas, the therapist will assist members in addressing together complementary agendas. For example, a member who has planned to work on taking initiative in social situations may be directed to query a member who has established the session goal of more openly disclosing his feelings. Members may be given homework assignments that they may complete in collaboration with one another. For example, two withdrawn members may be directed to have a conversation with one another on the unit.

As the agenda fulfillment process unfolds, the therapist attends to both the affective and cognitive elements of interpersonal learning to ensure that they are in balance with one another. The therapist monitors the level of anxiety to ensure

Putting It Into Practice

Helping Leo Fulfill His Agenda

Leo is a 40-year-old man who was admitted to a psychiatric hospital for a serious suicide attempt. A precipitant to the suicide attempt was his wife's leaving him following the death of their child. The child was under his supervision at the time of a tragic accident, and his wife blamed him for the child's death. Shortly after his hospitalization, he was placed in an inpatient group. We will follow Leo through the segments of an interactional agenda session to see how he derived benefit from group participation.

Orientation and preparation. As this was Leo's first session, he benefited from hearing the ground rules. He commented, "I don't feel like I can be of use to anyone here," and Polly, a member who had been in the group for four prior sessions, assured him that she had had similar feelings. She said she was surprised that others did seem to be helped by what she had to say and that it was a relief to realize that she could focus on someone else.

Agenda go-around. Initially, Leo said, "I want to stop being depressed." The therapist responded that although this goal was an understandable and important one, it might be difficult to reach in that session. The therapist then encouraged Leo to talk about an aspect of this goal in interpersonal terms. Eventually, Leo said, "I want to be able to initiate conversations with people I don't know." The therapist worked with Leo further to specify this goal in a way that would enable its accomplishment during the session. This work resulted in the agenda "I want to initiate an interaction with one or more members of the group during this session."

Agenda fulfillment. As this segment got underway, Leo stared at the floor and refrained from any sort of overt participation until one member of the group made a humorous remark and Leo chuckled. Bernice said to him, "I didn't think you were with us. It's nice to see you laugh." Leo responded, "Oh, I'm here all right. I'm following everything right along and I'm thinking about it all." Bernice responded, "Well, I wish you'd share some of your thoughts with us!" Linda added, "Yeah, what were you thinking right before you laughed? I was noticing as Tom and I were speaking, you seemed amused."

"Well, I just was thinking that it's amazing how you think no one else has been through what you're going through . . . like yours is worse . . . but it's just because you don't know what's in someone else's head." The therapist then interjected, "Leo, I'm thinking about your agenda and how you wanted to start an exchange with a member of the group. As you look around, is there anyone here with whom you think you could establish some common ground if only you could learn more about that member?" Leo answered, "Well, yeah, I notice Violet is quiet like I am." The therapist then suggested that Leo speak directly to Violet. Leo took this suggestion and said, "Violet, I think you're sort of like me. You listen to everything but feel kind of shy about speaking up."

Observation. In a conversation between the observers and the therapist, one of the observers noted that once Leo began to participate, he was able to continue to do so without prodding. The therapist also pointed out that Leo appeared to be more and more relaxed the more he participated.

Final reflection. Leo remarked that what the observer had noticed about his being able to continue to involve himself once he initially made contact was generally true. He said, "I just have to get the ball rolling. Then I'm okay." Another member said, "That's like the difference between having to get your fan belt repaired instead of your engine."

Teaching note: In only a single session, Leo derived benefit from group participation. He learned how to think about his difficulties in concrete, immediate, and interpersonal terms so that they are both manageable and addressable. This more focused approach to his problems could catalyze his posthospital treatment. During the agenda fulfillment stage, he had the experience of making progress on his agenda and having it noted by others. This success will be likely to enhance his motivation to pursue treatment in the future.

that it remains within limits that are tolerable for members. Whereas in a long-term outpatient group therapy, members' leaving the group with a heightened level of anxiety may be useful, in a short-term inpatient group, members' dominant reaction upon leaving the group should be one of satisfaction.

As the session progresses, members move into a more reflective mode. The next step entails the group therapist's offering his or her impressions of the events of the group. If there have been observers of the group session, as there often are in inpatient settings (especially teaching hospitals), they participate in the conversation with the therapist in fishbowl style (in which the observers and therapist sit in a small circle surrounded by the larger circle of members). In this way, the observers who are often present in a learning capacity not only take something from the group members but also give something back. During this exchange, the positive steps taken by members can be acknowledged. Sometimes the achievements of group members will be more evident to the observers than they are to the members themselves. The discussion participants might also identify those members who may benefit from some additional work or attention in the group's final moments. For example, an observer may notice that a given member looked downcast after an exchange with another member. The therapist might check in with this person to determine whether there were any reactions that would be important to acknowledge or explore.

The group's last segment is reflective in nature. Members may respond to any observations made in the prior session. The therapist may check in with members for whom the session was especially intensive. The reader can get a sense of a member's odyssey through the steps of a session by following the progress of Leo in the previous Putting It into Practice.

Characteristics of the Approach

This model bears many of the features of short-term group therapy. The goals of the approach are highly specified and establish a unique role for the group intervention in the client's treatment package. The therapist works vigorously within the sessions to ensure that the goals of the group are met. The approach encourages the formation of as cohesive a group as it is possible to have when the membership may be changing daily. A key element that contributes to cohesion is the preparation segment of the session that gives members a shared sense of purpose. Cohesion is nurtured also by the progress members see as they develop and fulfill these agendas. The temporal orientation is primarily within the present. Probably more than any other approach, this model is firmly grounded within the here and now of the group. However, the homework assignments provide some future focus as they demand members' engagement in new behaviors outside of the group session itself. This component of the approach is one that could be developed further so that its presence is a more regular aspect of each member's participation.

Short-Term Developmental Model

Budman and colleagues discovered an effective approach to short-term group therapy somewhat serendipitously. In order to efficiently treat large groups of patients, this clinical research team placed clients in short-term groups according to the variable of chronological age. They discovered that this compositional strategy held two benefits. First, groups of like-aged members establish cohesiveness very quickly. As we noted earlier, cohesion is all-important to the effectiveness of short-term groups. Individuals in an age group share a set of developmental tasks. As members recognize that they share both the tasks and the struggles to accomplish these tasks, an esprit de corps develops that catalyzes the group's work. Budman and colleagues discovered that even in the midst of highly varied symptoms, relatively high-functioning members could hone in on common developmental ground.

Second, the developmental processes of the group varied somewhat from age group to age group. Whereas the young adult group closely resembled the developmental sequence described in Chapter 7, groups for individuals in older age ranges showed some departures from the ways in which the stages have been commonly described. Budman and colleagues discovered that when the unique developmental processes of different age groups were made foci of the treatment, they provided important therapeutic opportunities for group members.

These and other discoveries enabled Budman and colleagues to solve the problem that presents itself to every short-term therapist: how to establish the clear focus that is neither too restrictive nor too vague for any type of short-term work. They believed that the foci of greatest relevance to many patients have three important dimensions. The *interpersonal* dimension acknowledges that we are social beings and that the problems we encounter in life in some way involve other humans. The *developmental* dimension recognizes that our experience occurs in the context of where we are on the continuum from birth to death. The *existential* dimension captures the fact that our awareness of our finitude and the limitations of our lives and those of others colors our experience. They labeled this framework the interpersonal-developmental-existential (I-D-E) approach, which is "an attempt to capture and understand the core interpersonal life issues that are leading the patient to seek psychotherapy at a given moment in time, and to relate these issues to the patient's stage of life development and to his or her existential concerns" (Budman & Gurman, 1988, p. 27).

The developmental groups organized by Budman and colleagues are the following: (1) young adults from early 20s to early 30s; (2) early midlife groups from mid-30s to early 50s, and (3) later midlife groups from early 50s to early 70s. We will focus on the early midlife age range as we show how this developmental model is applied. The reader is referred to Budman, Bennett, and Wisneski (1981) to learn about groups with the other age ranges.

The members selected for the early midlife group are individuals who are not actively psychotic, suicidal, or substance abusing. Persons who have pronounced schizoid or paranoid features are also excluded. Among the inclusionary criteria are adequate communication skills and the requirement that candidates' acceptance of problems have an internal locus. Despite variability in diagnoses and symptoms, selected group members, by virtue of their developmental status, have had some significant life event, often involving loss, that motivates their entrance into treatment. The individual recognizes that he or she has hit a plateau because of certain internal obstacles that hinder him or her from making potentially desirable life choices. Feelings of stagnation and ennui are common. In the preparation, entering members are told that these sorts of issues are developmentally expectable and that the group will help members to cope more effectively with them. Members are also prepared to work on identity and self-esteem issues through the here-and-now dimension of the group.

There are several features that typify the midlife group and distinguish it from at least some other age groups. The first is that members proceed rather quickly through the group's introductory phase, spending little time on demarcating the group from the outside world. A second feature is that conflicts with authority are more muted than with younger age groups. The feeling in the group is that members are prepared to take responsibility for their work and have a lessened expectation of the therapist's providing magical solutions. A third feature is the group's distinctive use of time. The temporal limit of the group creates a stimulus for midlife individuals to address the core developmental issues of accepting the impermanence and imperfections in self and others and making optimal use of their remaining time on earth by combating successfully those obstacles to their continued development. The midlife individual's awareness that his or her lifetime is quickly passing is mirrored in the awareness of the group's hourglass. According to Budman et al. (1981),

> The time limit ultimately forces, during the termination phase, a confrontation with universal, depressive issues: the inevitable disparity between what is wished for and what is possible, the fact that everything ends, and the need to come to grips with one's own anger and disappointment in

order to make new, positive choices in the face of an imperfect self that operates in an imperfect world. (p. 325)

A typical midlife group would progress as follows. In a closed-ended group, members are asked what brought them to the group. In an open-ended group, this question is typically posed by one of the prior group members. In very early sessions, members' responses to one another are positively toned rather than judgmental and confrontational. Members' initial descriptions of the problems are followed by an exploration of the historical and situational factors that led up to the problem, and then there is an increasing focus on the member's role in the problem's origin, perpetuation, and, where applicable, exacerbation.

As the sessions progress, typically around the third or fourth session, the limits of positive input are recognized by members: They see that supportive responses alone will not suffice to alter the problem. Members' frustration increases because they have lost faith in what they have done thus far but feel uncertain about how to proceed. It is at this juncture that the midlife group distinguishes itself from younger age groups. Whereas younger members would question why the therapist is not being more helpful, older members tend to examine themselves and explore what they might do together to make their time more productive. Members' intensified commitment to work leads them to begin to question each other's pat explanations for their troubles, which in turn leads those questioned to erect their character defenses. As members challenge the defenses, an argument ensues. A benefit of cohesion in the group is that the challenged member is likely to take very seriously the disparity between his or her self-perception and how others perceive him or her. Rather than simply continuing to defend him- or herself, the individual has the opportunity to examine the defense itself. However, for the outcome to be positive change rather than mere acrimony, that member must feel supported by the group throughout the process. The therapist can assist greatly with this process by helping the member to recognize the group's positive intent.

As the member recognizes the defenses that have been obstacles to growth, he or she typically examines those early experiences with parents that are associated with the need to erect defenses. This step, referred to as *the confession,* entails confronting the shame and self-criticism that are connected to the early memories. The memories that are unearthed may not be clearly tied to the member's presenting problem. Nonetheless, their exploration is important because they constitute, at least in part, the core depressive image, which is the wellspring of the person's adaptive difficulties. As elements of this negative memory emerge, the member can engage in personal reevaluation of their legitimacy. These elements can also be shared with the group for their evaluation. These activities enable the individual to integrate the shameful part of the self that had previously been banished from awareness and from the more tolerable aspects of the personality. With this integration, those defenses that so tenaciously had kept these elements out of awareness are relaxed.

The group's work with depressive issues often coincides with the approach of the group's ending. The limitations of time become salient for members who use it as a stimulus for mourning not only the ending of the group but also the finiteness of their own lives (a theme less poignant with groups of younger members). Budman and colleagues refer to this period as *getting unstuck* because members recognize their need to take advantage of the time remaining both in the group and in their lives. At this time, members experiment with new behaviors, obtain feedback, and make refinements. The final step of *termination* entails members' mourning both their loss of other members and old losses, the memories of which have been activated by the group's ending. Because of the work members have done earlier in becoming more aware of and integrating diverse aspects of themselves, they can approach this loss with an openness and availability to one another that constitute for some members a new and healthier approach to loss. For example, Budman et al. (1981) described one female member who dealt with disappointment in relationships by keeping herself apart from others, often through her biting wit. During the termination, she managed to remain with the group through the final session and share her feelings of loss and her appreciation of the other members. She went on to enter a relationship that held more fulfillment than those in her past.

THE LIMITATIONS OF SHORT-TERM GROUP THERAPY

Short-term group therapy can enable members to make gains in a variety of arenas. Changes in symptomatology, level of adjustment, interpersonal relations, and capacity for conflict resolution have been demonstrated to occur as a consequence of participation in short-term group therapy. Nonetheless, the reader should not be led to conclude that short-term group treatment is an adequate substitute for long-term group therapy. Relationships that have longevity have different characteristics from those that are short-lived. Members' capacity in a long-term group to see one another over a great range of situations confers upon members knowledge that is broader or deeper than that which can be achieved over a brief period. Processes such as interpersonal learning that rely upon such knowledge can be delivered more effectively than when members' observations and understanding are more superficial. As Yalom (1995) notes, the research on short-term therapy is at a relatively early stage. Much more research is needed to enable us to know what goals can be successfully pursued in different time frames.

SUMMARY AND CONCLUSIONS

Short-term groups are an increasingly important part of the group therapy landscape. They offer individuals the opportunity to pursue psychological change in a way that is both time and cost effective. Although short-term treatment is still a relatively new application of group therapy, sufficient knowledge exists to enable the identification of the characteristics of those applications that are most successful. These characteristics include the following: (1) specificity of goals; (2) careful screening and preparation; (3) emphasis on the development of group cohesion; (4) use of time as a therapeutic force; (5) energetic movement of the members toward their goals; and (6) a present and future temporal orientation. Two models of short-term therapy were presented: Yalom's interactional agenda model and Budman and colleagues' developmental approach. Although short-term group therapy has great usefulness in many clinical arenas, the limit of time precludes the depth and breadth of psychological work performed in the effective long-term group.

 TEST YOURSELF

1. **Most people who enter long-term group therapy remain at least for a 6-month period.** True or False?

2. **Individuals who enter therapy will tend to do so again at some future date.** True or False?

3. **Short-term groups have been demonstrated to be effective on only a very limited type of psychological problems.** True or False?

4. **The ways different age groups pursue the tasks of the group developmental stages are variable.** True or False?

5. **The emergence of short-term models has eliminated the need for long-term group therapy.** True or False?

6. **Which theoretical element of Budman and colleagues' short-term approach pertains to members' awareness of the limitation of their life?**

7. **What is the goal of the interactional agenda model?**

Thought Question

8. **What personality characteristics might distinguish the therapist with an affinity for long-term group as opposed to short-term group work?**

Answers: 1. False; 2. True; 3. True; 4. True; 5. False; 6. Existential; 7. To help members develop a positive attitude toward therapy.

Eleven

SELF-HELP AND SUPPORT GROUPS

Special kinds of therapeutic groups exist that are not strictly therapy groups yet whose influence on society has been profound. These groups are referred to as self-help and support groups. Our discussion of the terms *support* and *self-help* will lay bare the fact that the literature characterizing these formats has failed to offer a concensus on what constitutes the essential distinguishing and therapeutic features of these types of groups. Several factors have clouded these definitions: (1) the methodological difficulties of conducting research, especially in the domain of self-help groups; (2) the varying leadership styles that have been represented across a wide range of these specialty groups; and (3) the heterogeneity of groups that occur within these categories, many of which have distinct cultures, ideologies, and technologies of delivering help to their memberships. Nonetheless, our description is congruent with much of the most recent literature on these formats.

We use the term *support group* to refer to a routinized meeting of people, always with a common problem, usually one that has caused them to feel ill or in some way socially stigmatized. This meeting, as opposed to the meeting of a self-help group, is often led by a professional, whose theory about the etiology of the problem shapes the treatment method. These meetings are generally not free of cost, they are usually held at a locale that is more the turf of the professional than of the member, and they may be time limited or open ended in duration. The appellation *support* is not accidental: The theoretical orientation of the leader, and thus the atmosphere of the group, places a relative emphasis on the shoring up of the patient's defenses, and not on an analytic, deconstructive approach (Yalom, 1995). Of course, this emphasis is relative; there is usually room in these groups for some deeper psychological work and for ego-supportive techniques.

We define the *self-help group*, also referred to in the literature as the *mutual-support group*, as a routinized meeting of people who are brought together by a common problem, symptom, heritage, or situation and who talk and learn from one another new perspectives on that identified problem. Central to the definition is that professional involvement, although more common than was once recognized (Lieberman, 1990a), is peripheral; that is, the group members own and control the setting, determine the cost of the help delivered (always minimal or nonexistent), and have developed the methods by which the aid is provided. Several other important elements follow from these concepts, elements having to do with the appropriate role of the professional, the question of leadership, the therapeutic factors that operate in such a setting, and the member characteristics that draw them to such a setting. We will proceed to describe the core characteristics of these groups and give clinical examples of such groups in the following pages.

SELF-HELP GROUPS

The following sections describe the characteristics of self-help groups.

Epidemiology and Research

Epidemiologic figures on self-help in the United States indicate a prevalence rate of approximately 3 to 4 percent of the population over a 1-year period, and lifetime participation rates are estimated at around 25 million (Kessler, Mickelson, & Zhao, 1997; Lieberman & Snowden, 1993). The most comprehensive analysis of self-help groups found that the leading reason for participation in groups was the presentation of physical illness (Lieberman & Snowden). Kililea (1976) provides an extensive review of the wide range of self-help groups registered in this country; they include support systems, social movements, systems of consumer involvement, caregiving adjuncts to professional services, community groups, populations seeking mental health services, and organizations of the stigmatized. Many have considered Alcoholics Anonymous (AA), and its well-established approach to treating alcoholism, the sine qua non of the self-help group, but for reasons we will go on to explain, AA is a complex system that is difficult to study by conventional, well-controlled methods, and may not be a typical example of a self-help group.

Several explanations for the rise of the self-help movement have been proposed. The functionalist framework suggests that new institutions arise when there are meaningful needs that are not being met by existing institutions; for example, if the traditional medical system were not attending to the full range of its patients' needs, the patients would create a forum for more optimal response (Tracy & Gussow, 1976). Another view is that the growth and emergence of such institutions is best explained by individuals' need for affiliation and community with others in similar conditions; cultural trends have moved away from such communal units, so people attempt to create them (Lieberman, 1990a). Social comparison theory would argue that affiliative behaviors increase under conditions of high anxiety (Davison, Pennebaker, & Dickerson, 2000), with the exception of highly embarrassing or humiliating affective states, which discourage affiliation (Sarnoff & Zimbardo, 1961). This theory will be discussed in greater detail when we describe a study (Davison et al., 2000) that explores the patient characteristics that propel people to join self-help groups.

Much of the literature on self-help groups is limited to anecdotal reports of its members and to books about social movements and the ideology that provides the impetus for formation of the groups. Goodman and Jacobs (1994) point out that the emphasis of these articles and books is contextual and experiential, and not process oriented, which would be of greater interest to group therapists and scholars. Examples of this trend are the numerous books about the impact of AA on the life course of many of its members.

Research on the self-help group has been limited by several obstacles. For one, the self-help group culture, by definition, excludes professionals as organizers, thus diluting the professional's control. Recruitment of participants to self-help groups is by definition random, anonymous, and member determined, making it impossible for the researcher to design a standard, controlled, scientific research experiment. Moreover, the research that does exist is largely time limited, and by dint of the professional's manipulation of the setting, it creates a deviation from the customary self-help atmosphere. Levy (1988, as cited by Goodman & Jacobs [1994]) also points out an interesting "intrinsic positive bias effect," in which he argues that dropout patterns create group compositions of more socially competent, adjusted, and active members, causing the groups to appear more effective than they are. Moreover, since the leaders are actually ongoing members, the therapeutic intervention cannot be separated easily from the objects of the intervention, thus contaminating the outcome measures of the groups' effectiveness (Goodman & Jacobs, 1994). Barlow et al. (2000) summarize the many limitations of studies that attempt to demonstrate the effectiveness of self-help groups.

Despite these artifacts and restrictive conditions, research has generally demonstrated the effectiveness of self-help groups (for a full review of these outcome studies, see Barlow et al., 2000; Goodman & Jacobs, 1994; and Lieberman, 1990b). An interesting study by Lieberman (1993a) suggests that some aspects of adaptation to bereavement may be dealt with more effectively by the self-help setting, while other aspects—such as irrational guilt or intense anger at the deceased—are dealt with more effectively by individual psychotherapy. This is probably explained by the fact that such irrational feelings are usually influenced by unconscious conflicts, which are more directly addressed in individual psychotherapy than in a self-help group setting. Lieberman (1990a) asserts that the aforementioned methodological limitations should not discourage group therapists from becoming involved in this research, but these limitations should temper our expectations and influence our designs accordingly.

Self-Help Groups and Traditional Groups: Commonalities

What do self-help groups have in common with traditional groups? It would be of help to begin our answer by defining what, more specifically, self-help groups have in common with traditional group therapy methods. For one, both are small, face-to-face interactive units aiming to help their constituents. In both cases, individuals enter during a high state of personal need and are required to share with others feelings that are considered personal. This shared sense of suffering creates a sense of belonging and high levels of cohesiveness. An atmosphere of relative unconditional acceptance evolves, and it becomes possible for members to take risks and share precious feeling states that have been hidden. The feeling of "we-ness" that develops from this feeling of safety can cross over to a feeling of hostility toward nonmembers; if members have suffered a change in functioning that has left them feeling deviant from the rest of society, they may become increasingly isolated from nonmembers (Lieberman, 1990a).

Lieberman (1990a) points out that in both psychotherapy groups and self-help groups the most therapeutic factors are support, acceptance, and normalizing of perceived affliction. The most notable affects expressed are pain, anger, and profound sadness. He identifies another important area of overlap: cognitive modeling. In both types of groups, members engage in social comparison, exchanging different perspectives on what to think and feel and how to approach dilemmas that have arisen in relation to the identified problem (Lieberman, 1993b). The relative significance of this mechanism is probably greater in self-help groups than in psychotherapy groups, where this comparative component is usually then integrated with intrapsychic understanding.

Self-Help Groups versus Traditional Therapy: Differences

How are self-help groups different from traditional psychotherapy groups? Antze (1976) suggests that each self-help group he studied had a specific ideology closely linked to the underlying psychological problem associated with the group's problem. Self-help groups provide an instillation of hope, much like in traditional groups, but often with more dramatic impact. One other significant difference is the emphasis on social linkage: Traditional groups utilize interpersonal communication to help members learn about themselves, and the leaders often limit communication to what can be observed during the group meeting time. On the other hand, self-help groups view the social networking that occurs during their meetings as only the first step toward bolstering members' social supports. Members are encouraged to continue and deepen their communication outside of group, even using this contact to recruit new members who could also be helped by the group work.

The kind of interventions applied by psychotherapy group leaders and patients is different from those commonly observed among members of self-help groups. A less skeptical or challenging response on the part of the self-help group member to a fellow member's disclosure occurs; fewer interpretations of defense or character style are made (Toseland, Rossiter, Peak, & Hill, 1990). Empathic responses are greater in number, and "me-too" self-disclosures often bridge the dialogue. Consequently, less learning about the intrapsychic realm and less emphasis on psychological insight are possible. Much greater value is placed on problem solving and managing the outside forces impinging on each member. A member's resistance to attempting new coping strategies is confronted, but without delving much into his or her personal past or established patterns of resistance (Biegel & Yamatani, 1987). Advice and information—sometimes in the form of written material, tapes, or media communications—are given freely, and progress is explicitly encouraged (Goodman & Jacobs, 1994).

One result of not having a professional leader regularly placed within a self-help group is that the power gradient is reduced (Riessman, 1990). This has several important consequences. For one, it gives members the opportunity to feel like leaders, usually episodically. This experience promotes a feeling of altruism within that member, and in some kinds of self-help groups this feeling of altruism may be the main curative factor (Klass, 1984–1985; Lieberman & Videka-Sherman, 1986). For another, this experience also may lend a feeling of power and mastery to members, which is clearly essential to the therapeutic experience within AA (Galanter, Castaneda, & Franco, 1991) and also to members of other self-help groups (Dube, Mitchell, & Bergman, 1986). The leveling of the power gradient present in traditional groups also reduces the dependency that is often nurtured within the transference to the leader. Because transference exploration is not a vehicle for therapeutic change within self-help groups, space is left for members to trade reciprocal positions, at times benefiting from the other and at times giving to the other.

Nevertheless, hierarchical difference is a regulating factor within the matrix of the self-help group. Maton's study (1988) suggests that group organization components, such as role differentiation and competent leadership, are positively associated with outcome. In Lieberman's (1990b) study of 36 self-help groups, those that failed to help most of their members were low on cohesiveness, saliency of discussion, and methods for reframing common concerns. There are other accounts in the literature of self-help movements that have faded, and most seem to have lacked a well-established culture populated with experienced members who could serve as unofficial leaders. This kind of leadership extends beyond the self-help group unit per se; it permeates the organization. We should emphasize, for example, the sophisticated system of organization that has been established by AA, which includes a clear hierarchy and multiple dependencies, reflected by its 12-step program and sponsorship relationships, both of which are essential to AA's philosophy of what is therapeutic.

One complication of the research conducted on self-help groups is that many of the studies compare outcomes of groups led by professionals with those led by peers. Rioch, Elkes, and Flint (1963) demonstrated that housewives without prior professional training could be taught psychotherapeutic techniques and could apply them successfully. However, as has been demonstrated by Lieberman and Bliwise (1985), peer leaders may not be representative of the typical self-help participant, for they have been trained to some degree by professionals, and therefore one of the basic therapeutic components of self-help groups is contaminated. In fact, Lieberman points out that training peers to lead groups may be deleterious on two counts: It robs self-help groups of their self-determined technology of cure, and it provides the group with less effective leadership than could be provided by a professional (1990a).

In describing this problem, Lieberman expounds on several other dimensions of the helping method that is different in self-help groups: He calls these factors the continuum of technological complexity, the continuum of psychological closeness between helper and helpee, the specificity of help methods exhibited, and the degree of differentiation among participants. For example, traditional psychotherapy groups have a high degree of technological complexity, and self-help groups a low level. The psychological distance between members in a self-help group is low, and the reciprocal identification and trust that result are thought to facilitate productive therapy. The helping methods in self-help groups have been refined by the organization and are highly specific to the particular problem at hand, much more so than in a traditional psychotherapy group. Finally, the low degree of differentiation among members in a self-help group discourages focus on individual psychology but allows for peer identification and the therapeutic mechanisms such as altruism, empowerment, and shared mastery that were described earlier (Lieberman, 1990a).

Although we have labeled common therapeutic factors that operate within self-help groups, different organizations, even those dedicated to the same problem, often have slightly different cultures of cure (for a study of these differences, see Lieberman, 1983). For example, the extent to which factors such as cognitive reworking, altruism, externalization of anger, catharsis, diminution of guilt, and existential considerations are given salience varies. In general, the particular factors given highest priority do have significant correlation with the kind of problem fueling formation of the group. For example, for parents who have lost a child, existential considerations such as hope, learning to accept their tragic reality, and anger at society appear to be crucial; for members of Mended Hearts, survivors of cardiac surgery, altruism, apparently in response to survivor guilt themes, seems more therapeutically significant.

Alcoholics Anonymous as Self-Help Group

Alcoholics Anonymous has been the most widely observed self-help group (Emrick, 1987; Lieberman, 1990a). However, the same methodological problems that we have already described apply to AA; in addition, nearly all measurements of sobriety are biased by surveys drawn from more active members, and many respondents are also in professional treatment, which confounds the results (Bebbington, 1976). Some have argued that examining AA has been even more difficult because the powerful social identity of fellowship that has become inextricably woven into AA's treatment philosophy has excluded nonmembers and has indirectly prevented the development of other treatment modalities (Tournier, 1979). There are several other valid criticisms of AA as the optimal treatment approach: Only between 46.5 and 62 percent of the active members achieve at least 1 year of continuous sobriety (Emrick); it is not clear that sobriety as a treatment goal is the best measure of improvement, nor is it clear that the goal of sobriety is optimal for all subgroups of alcoholics (Ogborne & Glaser, 1981). Moreover, research has demonstrated that alcoholics participating in additional treatment modalities fare better than those in AA alone (Emrick).

Ogborne and Glaser (1981) describe the prominent characteristics of members drawn to the fellowship of AA. Frank's work (2001) suggests an association between adult attachment style and alcohol dependence: A greater percentage of patients presenting for substance abuse treatment were insecurely attached than in the non-substance-abusing population, and avoidant subtypes, specifically, had higher baseline levels of addiction severity. Relational components are other crucial elements of AA that may affect whom it draws and may influence the process of AA as a self-help group experience. These include the social networking that extends before and after the actual meetings, the emphasis on the sponsorship relationship, and the explicit hierarchy of experience among participants in the treatment program. Gordon and Zrull (1991) suggest that social supports who do not drink regularly, and who exert a positive influence on the alcoholic attempting sobriety, have an important influence on recovery. The presence of these formal sponsorship relationships within the wider self-help milieu, and the consequent multiple dependencies of members on each other that result, yield a self-help environment more complex than the model described earlier in the chapter.

Characteristics of Self-Help Group Members

Davison et al. (2000) performed an interesting study in which they sought to discern which illnesses galvanize formation and maintenance of self-help groups, and what social and personal factors propel people to join them. They measured the formation of groups for 20 medical conditions in four metropolitan areas, and they also measured the contributions to online forums by participants in Internet newsgroups and America Online bulletin boards over a 2-week period (see Chapter 8 for further discussion of online groups). Despite some methodological complications, they determined (by measuring group counts per million people) that alcoholism mobilized the greatest live participation, followed by HIV, then by cancers, depression, and diabetes; participation for cardiovascular disease was notably low. In contrast, online participation (measured by the number of postings, and adjusted for prevalence of illness) was high for cancer and HIV, relatively high for chronic fatigue and for multiple sclerosis, and much lower for alcoholism. The authors conclude that the long tradition of AA probably causes in vivo treatment for alcoholism to be popular, while the physical disabilities in illnesses such as multiple sclerosis may render online communication preferable. They also point out that social factors, such as ethnicity and physical and vocal characteristics, are neutralized by online communication.

The authors then attempted to determine which sources of anxiety contribute to patients' seeking support. Referring to Leventhal, Meyer, and Nerenz's (1980) model of illness schema, the authors divided patients' anxiety into three areas: patient characteristics (both psychological and demographic), health care burden (aspects of illness that increase medical care usage), and social burden (the interpersonal dimensions of the illness experience). They found that the most notable associations between support seeking and illness pivot around the social ramifications of illness: Factors such as social embarrassment, stigma, and disfigurement were associated with high levels of support for both actual and online contact. Psychological characteristics did not correlate with patients' reaching out for support. They also found that aspects of illness associated with the high cost of treatment and with mortality are associated with support seeking for actual group contact. Online support is correlated with importance of patient's attitude to outcome; that is, online support occurs at higher rates

> **DON'T FORGET**
> ....
> Whether a group is properly designated a self-help group depends upon its characteristics (goals, membership criteria, processes), not the name affixed to it.

among patients with conditions that are debilitating in ways that are less responsive to conventional medical care.

Davison et. al (2000) conclude that people pursuing live self-help groups seek company with fellow sufferers as a refuge from the social stigma caused by serious illness and/or its treatment. They also raise questions about the nature of certain illness-sufferers—such as patients with cardiovascular disease—and what about their temperament causes them to be less willing to accept help.

The following Putting It into Practice provides an example of a self-help group.

Roles for Professionals in Self-Help Groups

Professional practitioners have been skeptical of the self-help movement for several reasons. For one, they fear that self-help groups will attempt to treat patients with serious pathology, thus derailing them from obtaining the help they need (Henry & Robinson, 1978). Empirical evidence in support of this suspicion is lacking. Professionals also have doubts, probably not warranted, about the general effectiveness of self-help groups. Finally, they feel threatened by the competition posed by self-help groups and are afraid patients will elect not to receive professional treatment. However, Lieberman (1993b) points out that self-help group members are eager consumers of other mental health services; Powell (1987) also writes about the augmentation of professional programs that has resulted from the growth of the self-help movement.

The pure self-help group, one devoid of professional participation, is actually in the minority (Lieberman, 1990a). Professionals have been connected with the self-help movement in four roles. First is the professional who contributes validation to the modality. This can take the form of the professional's referring a patient to a self-help group or supporting a referral made by a fellow practitioner. Second is the professional who extends his or her theoretical orientation to a self-help program. This has taken the form of the professional who trains a member of a self-help program, or peer, to behave as a leader of the group. This approach, however, runs the risk of the professional's creating a hybrid group, one without

Putting It Into Practice

Illustration of a Self-Help Group

Five mental health professionals, two of whom are female and three male, meet on a weekly basis in the same office, over lunch, to discuss difficulties that arise in their professional therapeutic work. Two of the five work from a psychoanalytic orientation, and the other three from a cognitive-behavioral point of view. Two of the five are senior clinicians, and three are of moderate experience. There is no particular leader of this group; each week, one of the therapists chooses a case to present, one that is causing him or her particular difficulty. Sometimes, the difficulty involves complicated or conflictual feelings on the part of the therapist toward the patient; sometimes, the difficulty involves a stalemated treatment course; and sometimes it involves a controversy about optimal clinical approach.

The clinical material conveyed during the hour is confidential. The feelings on the part of the therapist presenting the case are often raw; he or she may talk about feeling helpless or frustrated by the patient and may admit to feeling conflicted or ashamed because of such feelings. The psychogenetic origins of such feelings are rarely discussed; the members of the study group know a bit about each other's family histories and likely transference reactions to patients, but only offer observations about them incrementally, over time, at the volition of the member. The challenges and shortcomings of ongoing therapeutic work are reviewed, with members often supporting each other and validating the efforts of the struggling therapist.

There are interesting and complex dynamics noted particularly by the psychodynamically oriented members. For example, there is a competitive undercurrent percolating between the two represented theoretical orientations. In addition, two of the males often vie for space to offer their contributions. When one of the females is absent, the men tend to behave differently, presumably to gain the attention of the remaining female. Some of the members are annoyed at another member, who seems to offer the same advice no matter what the details of the case discussed in a particular session. However, no member ever comments on these dynamics during the study group meeting. Attention is restricted to the clinical matters at hand.

Teaching note: This study group is an excellent example of a self-help group. The exercise is conducted free of cost, on the terrain of the group, and at a regular meeting time. The structure and function of the group were founded by its members and are determined, in a continuous way, by them. The group is vitally important to its members, as they rarely miss a meeting; they feel safe in each other's presence with the depth of material discussed, they derive invaluable help from the meetings, and they have developed a feeling of belonging and esteem from membership. Learning is both cognitive and affective; feelings from their work, notably difficult and conflictual ones, are revealed, although the full depth of their origins is shared only selectively. There is no dominant leader of the group. Presenters of clinical material rotate, so that a member will largely be in the role of offering advice to the presenter to facilitate his or her clinical work one week and in the next week will be in the role of receiving such advice from fellow members. Empathic, validating interventions dominate the group experience; one member noted one week that most of the group's comments, independent of the unique circumstances of the clinical presentation, usually supported the fine efforts of the therapist trying to help a difficult patient. It is interesting to note that the members of this study group would probably not consider themselves a self-help group; this echoes Goodman and Jacobs's (1994) point that self-help groups are an omnipresent social institution, often not recorded by formal data collections.

the benefit of solid professional leadership or of the self-help ideology that has evolved within the self-help environment (Lieberman, 1993b). Third is the professional who serves as consultant. Professionals are often invited as guest speakers or are available to group members who may need additional mental health services. Lieberman (1993b) emphasizes that professional group therapists can be particularly helpful if called upon to advise a group on managing a difficult patient or on reversing an atypically high dropout rate. The fourth role is the professional who teaches general group therapy skills to new self-help programs. The professional should be mindful not to interfere with the program's specific helping ideology (Lieberman, 1993b).

Because professional participation in self-help programs is common, it should be obvious that the boundary between the self-help group and the support group is thin. The difference between the two paradigms—largely around the locus of leadership and its impact on group process—may be more theoretical than practical.

SUPPORT GROUPS

We will now describe the salient features of the support group in contemporary practice.

Epidemiology

Barlow et al.'s meta-analysis of medical self-help groups (2000) concludes that the majority have significant professional involvement; a survey of 2,000 self-help groups on California Self-Help Center's statewide database found that mental health professionals were leaders in 32 percent of the groups (Gradman, 1985). In fact, Barlow had difficulty separating self-help groups from support groups, given the significant involvement of professionals in many of the studies.

A significant expansion in psychosocial interventions for the medically ill has occurred over the last 10 to 15 years. Support group psychotherapy is effective for patients through the experience of universality in reducing the feelings of stigma and isolation often associated with medical illness. Across many medical diagnoses, outcome studies have demonstrated a reduction in psychological morbidity and, in some, a change in the primary disease process. We will discuss some of these specific support group programs in more detail over the course of the chapter.

Other kinds of support groups are well known to group psychotherapists, who have provided leadership for them traditionally. These include staff support groups such as T-groups for mental health professional trainees, support groups for professionals of other disciplines, support groups for the chronically psychiatrically ill, and support groups for families of psychiatric patients. Some of these groups are structured for short-term duration, and some for the long term; some have closed memberships from the outset, and some are open ended. These groups are generally less thoroughly studied than support groups for medical illnesses.

Support Groups and Traditional Psychotherapy: Commonalities

Support groups have much in common with the traditional group. Like self-help groups, they are relatively small units that aim to reduce the suffering of their members, all of whom share some affliction. In the case of T-groups or staff support groups, they aim to reduce suffering indirectly; the leader of a process group for trainees attempts to teach group principles and to help the group to function more cohesively, while the staff support group leader hopes to improve the cohesiveness of the team so it can function more effectively and efficiently. Support group members usually enter during states of high personal need, particularly if they are suffering from illness. As in the case of self-help groups, the atmosphere of unconditional acceptance is crucial: This allows for the group to cohere relatively quickly, which in turn paves the way for the exchange of educational information, coping strategies, and the revelation of painful affects related to the identified problem.

Support groups, similar to traditional psychotherapy groups, explicitly identify professional leadership. Several technical considerations follow from this fact: There is a professional theory of etiology of illness that shapes the treatment approach, there is a clear power gradient between the leader and the members, there is a tendency for issues of dependency to be played out between patient and leader, and there is a readily available transference object on which members' conflicts and wishes can be projected. The trust members have in the leader's power and knowledge will be a potential issue for the group: Some members will test the leader's authority relatively quickly, and others will invest inordinate faith in the leader's symbolic strength (Yalom, 1995; Rutan & Stone, 2001). How the leader manages this tension is a thorny technical matter, and this is one of the important distinctions between support groups and traditional psychotherapy groups.

Support Groups versus Traditional Psychotherapy: Differences

How are support groups different from traditional psychotherapy groups? For a start, the leader begins with a very different assumption from that of the traditional therapy group leader: The leader assumes that the psychological symptoms causing distress to the patient follow from the illness contracted by the patient, and not vice versa. Although this may seem obvious, the traditional psychodynamic perspective, which emphasizes theories of psychopathology such as masochism and the negative therapeutic reaction, can run the risk of blaming the patient for his suffering. On the other hand, the assumptions underlying support groups may not do justice to the contribution of character and personality features to a person's psychological difficulties. There is no controversy, however, about the support group leader's orientation: He or she must first empathize with the patient's condition, and must first address the patient's functional concerns, before addressing emotional sequelae (Leszcz, 1998; Spira, 1997b). This tenet holds not only for patients suffering from medical illness, who are already prone to blaming themselves for developing an illness, but also for patients suffering from chronic psychiatric illness and for professionals struggling to work together in a staff support group. This is not to suggest that the leader cannot comment on the unique psychologies of the members of the group, but he or she must not do so too early in the group's development, and only to a limited extent. The leader may arrange to meet with an individual separately if he or she has reason to recommend additional mental health services to that patient.

Second, the leader must have knowledge not just about group process but also about the particular issue at hand. If the group is focused around a specific medical diagnosis, for example, the leader should know a fair amount about that illness, its etiology, its treatment options and their effects, and its potential lethality. The leader should also be in communication with colleagues from other disciplines relevant to that illness; the leader may be called upon to facilitate contact with ancillary professional services, such as pain managers, social workers, or additional medical specialists (Abbey & Farrow, 1998; Allan & Scheidt, 1998; Kelly, 1998; Leszcz & Goodwin, 1998). A leader of a support group for professionals will be required to have a close working knowledge of the larger system in which the working unit is embedded (Lederberg, 1998). This part of the leader's role involves technical measures relied upon to a greater degree by the support group leader than by the traditional group leader: dissemination of education, imparting of advice, and provision of resources that will directly reduce suffering.

Existential concerns—defined by Yalom (1995) as personal struggle with death, isolation, meaning in life, and freedom—will become the focus of discussion in support groups as an environment of safety is established. The leader must not be too frightened to grapple with these subjects. He or she must also be careful to encourage discussion of these subjects at the appropriate time. If the group is organized around a potentially lethal diagnosis, for example, the leader must help to overcome the group's resistance to discussing death, but must not do so prematurely, for this may frighten members away. Such emphasis on mortality, and the possibility that members will die during the life of the group, may be taxing for the leader; Abbey and Farrow (1998) recommend coleadership so the leaders can help each other manage these ongoing losses.

The leader must also negotiate the restriction placed on his or her therapeutic zeal. If he or she has been trained psychodynamically and has run more traditional psychotherapy groups, he or she will quickly recognize phenomena such as transference distortions, power struggles among members, and manifestations of members' pathologic character styles. He or she must keep sight of the group's larger therapeutic goals, however, and must tailor his or her interventions according to those priorities.

Finally, although the power gradient between patient and therapist—and the transferences that may follow from this divide—is sure to be present within the matrix of the support group, the therapist must be careful about his or her use of this phenomenon. Gabbard (1990) sets a standard for the psychoanalyst's judicious use of positive transference in promoting the process of supportive individual psychotherapy, and the same principles apply to support groups. The leader should employ the knowledge he or she has about group process, and about the particular problem at hand, to endorse a high level of functioning for the members of the group. In keeping with this principle, the leader may be more transparent about his or her thoughts or feelings, particularly when existential issues are broached.

Idealization of the leader's healing powers should be confronted if it interferes with the group's goals. Rebellion, inevitable disappointment in the leader's shortcomings, and threats to the leader's authority need to be addressed aggressively, but less from the point of view of understanding an individual member's psychology and more from the vantage point of preserving the group's integrity. Although important in traditional groups, this protective function is still more important here, for the group is more vulnerable and can withstand less of a threat to its leader. The following Putting It into Practice provides an illustration of a support group.

Characteristics of Specific Support Groups

Spira (1997b) has summarized three fundamental approaches with medically ill populations: (1) the deductive approach, in which the therapist acts as health educator and patients pose questions to the therapist; (2) the interactive approach, in which the therapist introduces a theme and the group discusses the theme more generally; and (3) the inductive approach, in which the floor is open for members to raise themes. Many of the support group programs combine these different formats, with some moving along a continuum, first initiating patients with a deductive atmosphere, then allowing them to shift, as they grow comfortable, toward an inductive setting (Abbey & Farrow, 1998; Allan & Scheidt, 1998).

It is beyond the scope of this chapter to describe in detail the unique group set-

Putting It Into Practice

Illustration of a Support Group

The head psychiatrist of an inpatient unit served as leader of a support group for family members of schizophrenics. He met with the family members once weekly in an open-ended support group format and had several clearly articulated group goals: to impart education about the illness, to provide distraught family members with a sense of hope, and to provide a forum in which family members could commiserate with each other and with the doctor about the impact of schizophrenic illness on their families. Gradually, over several sessions, one patient's mother became increasingly angry, first seemingly at her ill son for disrupting her life, and then at the doctor for failing to cure her son quickly. She began to criticize the doctor, pointing out that he did not spend enough time with her son, that he seemed too young to know about the best available treatments, and that his indecisiveness had already been reflected by his having changed her son's medications twice.

The doctor intervened quickly. He sensed that the other members were becoming anxious, and rather than allowing the angry member more room to explore her doubts about him, he interrupted her. He said to her directly that he understood how sad and angry she felt about her son and that he understood how much she wished that he could fix her son quickly. He emphasized that he did have the requisite skills to help her son. He also added that it would take time, and that although there were no guarantees about outcome, he was optimistic about the treatments offered to the patients. He then turned to other members, said that feeling angry toward an ill family member was normal but difficult to admit, and asked if any others felt the same way. Other members began to talk, at first reluctantly but then more freely, about how angry they felt toward their ill, and sometimes violent, family members.

Teaching note: In this example, the leader kept in mind that although expression of a negative transference was expectable, it was essential that it be limited. The leader had to preserve his authority, to a significant degree, if most members were to trust him and benefit from the group process. He utilized one member's expression of anger to broach the subject of anger within other members. Moreover, although he acknowledged that member's angry feelings, he did not explore them; he attempted instead to contain them within the context of broader group goals.

ting created for each diagnosis. Some of the features described for some of these groups will be highlighted in an attempt to link technical approach to the underlying cause of suffering. This is parallel to Antze's (1976) point, described earlier, that the ideology of a self-help group was an extension of the psychological conflicts related to its affliction.

Abbey and Farrow (1998) note that in their organ transplantation support groups, particularly with patients affected by liver failure and renal failure, they expect to attend to cognitive dysfunction and its effect on the group process. They also point out that leaders must be comfortable with high rates of absenteeism and the experimental nature of parts of the medical treatment process. Allan and Scheidt (1998) highlight the strong link between medical risk factors,

≡Rapid Reference 11.1

Differences Between Traditional Therapy Groups, Self-Help Groups, and Support Groups

Therapeutic Issues	Traditional Therapy	Self-Help	Support
Payment	Yes	No	Sometimes
Regular attendance	Yes	No	Sometimes
Outside subgroup socializing	No	Yes	Usually
Personal intrapsychic goals	Yes	No	Usually not
Therapeutic use of anxiety	Yes	No	Limited
Members' associations brought into group process	Yes	No	Limited
Encouragement of member-to-member confrontation	Yes	No	Limited
Interpretation of transference to leader	Yes	No	Only to reinforce positive transference
Tolerance of regression in the transference	Yes	No	No
Leader stance/activity in group	Less directive	Very directive	Moderately directive
Transparency	Limited	Often	Moderate
Communication with other disciplines as part of group process	Limited	Moderate	Yes
Training of other leaders as part of role	No	Yes	Sometimes
Methodology of empirical research	Strict standards	Looser standards	Strict standards

Note: Adapted with permission of The Guilford Press. From M. S. Lederberg's (1998) staff support groups for high-stress medical environments. *International Journal of Group Psychotherapy,* 48(2), 275–304.

premorbid psychological functioning, and the development of cardiovascular disease, and the goal of increasing awareness of this link among patients. Helping patients to manage their anger, and thus their cardiovascular reactivity (Siegman & Snow, 1997), is a focus of the group work. Allan and Scheidt emphasize the resistance of many cardiac patients to changes in lifestyle and to psychologically mediated treatments. They also point out that the failure of mental health professionals to develop relationships with physicians greatly reduces the possibility of introducing the cardiac patient to psychological treatments.

Kelly (1998) describes group work with patients suffering with HIV. What distinguishes this patient population from others with life-threatening illnesses is its association with homosexuality and therefore its greater degree of social stigma, the long-standing hysteria associated with its transmission, the young age of its sufferers, the sense of personal responsibility and guilt experienced by its patients, and the loss of many peers from the same illness. Support group treatment is especially aimed at reducing stigma and guilt. Also of importance are reduction in behaviors of high risk for transmission, an enlargement of social supports, compliance with medical care, and emphasis on coping with the uncertainty of the treatment course.

Leszcz and Goodwin (1998) attempted to replicate earlier studies by Spiegel, Bloom, Kraemer, and Gottheil (1989) and Fawzy et al. (1993) that demonstrated that psychosocial interventions increased the survival rate of cancer patients. Fawzy et al. noted a significant correlation between lower emotional distress at baseline and poorer survival, which led them to suggest that patients in denial did less well than those who could aggressively meet the threat to their life. Leszcz and Goodwin describe the backbone of their brand of supportive expressive group therapy: (1) social support and integration; (2) acquisition of adaptive coping skills, including a desire to defeat the disease (described by Greer, 1995, as a "fighting spirit"), balanced by the limitations of treatment; (3) effective communication with health care providers; and (4) existential coping with the possibility of death. In accordance with the possibility of death, they endorse a long-term, open-ended approach, one less likely to avoid its being raised as a therapeutic issue. They also emphasize that their group sessions end with 5 to 10 minutes of relaxation and self-hypnosis exercises, intended to develop physical mastery and to help manage pain. This explicit inclusion of body awareness exercises is a feature of support groups not often encouraged in traditional psychotherapy groups.

Lederberg (1998) describes a model for staff support groups. The leader is called upon to have a comprehensive grasp of the medical system, including the social stresses on the modern health care worker, and the likely reactions of the health care worker to the patients' suffering. The leader must validate the health care worker's feelings of helplessness and frustration in the face of a high volume of loss. Ledergerg highlights succinctly the differences between support groups and therapy groups, noting, as we have noted here, differences in the management of transference, member-to-member interactions, analysis of each member's psychological conflicts, and overall group goals. The following Putting It into Practice provides a vignette concerning leader activities in a support group.

Putting It Into Practice

The Role of the Leader in a Support Group

A support group for hospice staff has been meeting weekly for many years. The new leader is an experienced group therapist and, as a physician, is familiar with medical issues, but he is fresh to the existential intensity of regular work with dying patients. He notes that the staff, which has worked together closely for many years, has an unusual, black sense of humor they employ often to mute their despair. He also notes a hostile tension between one of the nurses and the chaplain, one that seems long standing and disruptive to the interdisciplinary care given to several patients. Finally, he is curious about the staff's feelings about him, as they allude during early meetings to two prior leaders, a long-standing one who died of HIV, and his successor, whom they dismissed quickly for her quirky style and ineffectiveness.

The leader has met several times with the director of the program, and, although she does not attend the weekly group sessions, she strongly endorses its utility. The leader emphasizes the importance of her conveying confidence in him to the members of the team. He then attempts to address in group sessions some of the issues he has observed with the group, namely their use of humor as a defense, the tension between two of the members, and the group's feelings about him as the new leader. All of these attempts go badly; they explain that their humor is something they have always been able to share only with each other and has always been a vital strand of their cohesiveness. Moreover, they demand, how else can they muster the courage to deal with the series of losses they experience, even when they do their job well? The tension between the two members, at the urging of the therapist, boils over into an open exchange of anger. Although this confrontation is not too destructive, the therapist learns that the two members have had these conversations before and have always clashed but have learned to work acceptably together on shared cases. Finally, the group members say they do not really want to explore their feelings about the new leader; this is what the prior leader tried, and they really need help immediately with the impact that institutional changes are having on their case management.

After learning from his errors, and admitting them, the leader settles into a more supportive role. He tries to help the group with their stated concerns. He tries to learn to laugh with them and to appreciate the pain of their losses. He learns to accept their tolerance of each other and the difficulty of their struggles with the health care system. In time, the members do discuss their feelings about him, but to a limited degree, and mostly in the context of their disappointment with their director.

Teaching note: This case example illustrates the leader's attempts to intervene with techniques not appropriate for support group work. For one thing, he seeks to analyze a defense before understanding its function in the group culture. This defense should probably not be challenged, especially given the losses the group has suffered recently. Then he facilitates the opening up of angry feelings between two long-standing members without inquiring about the history between the two. Moreover, he has not really established that the tension between the two interferes with care. Finally, his curiosity about the nature of the transference, following close in time to their having lost two leaders, proves to be too much too soon. He probably could have ascertained this by learning more from the director of the program or from the clues dropped by the group when they described his predecessor as "quirky."

SUMMARY AND CONCLUSIONS

In this chapter, we have described the qualities, mostly from a perspective of group process, of self-help and support groups. We have tried to distinguish some of the therapeutic factors that operate in these groups from those that operate in traditional psychotherapy groups. These include, in the case of self-help groups, an emphasis on unique self-help cultures, on the benefits of social comparison and connection, and on the absence of professional leadership. In the case of support groups, the professional has a well-defined role, one that requires him or her to combine knowledge of group process with other tasks. These tasks may include discussion of medical risk factors and treatments, review of pain management, and advice about handling the patient-doctor relationship. The leader must at times keep his or her awareness of certain process phenomena to him- or herself, revealing it when it helps to promote larger group goals.

Many questions remain. What is the role of these group formats in the long-term treatments of certain conditions? When is a self-help group just as effective as a professionally led group? Are certain patients better suited to one frame of treatment than another? What is the optimal way to combine these methods with individual psychotherapy? We can be hopeful that future research will provide more insight into these and other questions.

🐟 TEST YOURSELF 🐟

1. **Which of the following does not represent a methodologic limitation to conducting research on self-help groups?**
   (a) The intrinsic positive bias effect
   (b) Member recruitment of participants
   (c) Professional manipulation of the treatment setting
   (d) none of the above
2. **How does self-help group process compare with that of traditional groups?**
   (a) Groups typically explore individual members' personal histories behind expressed painful affects.
   (b) Members present for treatment in a greater state of personal need.
   (c) They explore transferences to the leader within the group process to a greater degree than do traditional groups.
   (d) They employ a greater degree of supportive, validating interventions.

(continued)

3. **How is AA different from the typical self-help group?**
   (a) Research on its methods has been methodologically problem-free.
   (b) Its groups employ professional leaders.
   (c) Its sponsorship relationships have a unique influence on its therapeutic impact.
   (d) It is time limited in format.

4. **Which is not among the possible roles for the professional in the world of self-help groups?**
   (a) The professional can validate the modality in referring patients to a group.
   (b) The professional can teach group techniques to a prospective peer leader.
   (c) The professional can lecture to a self-help organization.
   (d) The professional can convince a self-help organization that its theory of cure does not comport with current group object relational theory.

5. **Which of the following is unique to support group process, relative to the process observed in traditional group psychotherapy?**
   (a) Professional leadership
   (b) Exploration of transferences to the leader
   (c) Emphasis on existential concerns
   (d) Careful selection of members

6. **Which of the following is not a therapeutic emphasis in its accompanying medical support group?**
   (a) Attention to cognitive dysfunction in organ transplantation support groups
   (b) Attention to anger management in cardiovascular support groups
   (c) Attention to issues of stigma and guilt in HIV support groups
   (d) Exploration of the negative transference in staff support groups

7. **Which is not a technique employed in staff support groups?**
   (a) Awareness of issues outside the boundary of the group
   (b) Tempering of transference exploration
   (c) Requirement of members to expose their feelings about other members
   (d) Exploration of members' existential concerns

Answers: 1. c; 2. d; 3. c; 4. d; 5. c; 6. d; 7. c

Twelve

TRAINING GROUP THERAPISTS FOR CURRENT AND FUTURE PRACTICE

Having covered the rudiments of group therapy, we are now able to consider what additional training steps should be taken to be competent in delivering this treatment modality. Surveys reveal that often the training mental health professionals in group therapy receive is haphazard and superficial. In many programs, the attention group therapy receives in the curriculum is far less than the coverage of individual therapy. Depending upon the discipline (Fuhriman & Burlingame, 2001), a typical graduate program may offer only a single introductory course on group treatments. Internships and residencies fail to compensate for these training deficiencies. Based on their survey of fully accredited predoctoral psychology internship programs, Marcus and King (2003) concluded that "predoctoral internship programs continue to fall short of providing psychology trainees with sufficient depth and breadth of clinical skills in the area of group psychotherapy" (p. 207). Institutions that had given interns and residents systematic training experiences in group therapy (and other modalities as well) now place primary emphasis upon billable hours.

In view of this situation, the individual aspiring to be an effective group therapist must often do considerable work on his or her own knowledge base, skills, and attitudes that will qualify him or her to conduct groups. In this chapter, we will outline those core components that are critical to the success of any training program in group therapy. We will also address the issue of credentialing of the senior group therapist. We will then anticipate certain emerging areas that should be of interest to any new or experienced group therapist who wishes to be competent not only in the present but also in the future.

TRAINING AND CREDENTIALING

The following sections will discuss the training and credentialing requirements for the group therapist.

The Essential Components of a Training Program

Professional organizations such as the American Group Psychotherapy Association and the Association for Specialists in Group Work have come to the rescue of the clinician who seeks to structure an individual educational program. These organizations both specify the essential elements of a training program and offer the needed experiences at the national and regional levels. These organizations and individual group therapy practitioners have identified four areas of particular importance in the training of a group therapist: (1) didactic instruction, (2) experience in conducting groups, (3) supervision of group work, and (4) personal experience in training groups, personal group therapy, or, preferably, both (see Rapid Reference 12.1). We will discuss each area in this chapter.

Didactic Instruction

Development as a group therapist requires the integration of two realms: knowledge and experience. To organize and find meaning in his or her group experiences, the aspiring group therapist must have exposure to the body of knowledge concerning how groups operate. Texts of this nature provide the beginning group therapist with the rudiments of group work. However, trainees should not merely read but also actively process this material within a learning community. Ideally, additional opportunities to explore these topics will be available in a course or a study group. Doing so provides the opportunity to share examples of group phenomena described in this text, such as scapegoating or subgrouping, that are aspects not only of therapy groups but also of groups in everyday life. As the learner is exposed to abundant and varied examples, the capacity to recognize these phenomena when sitting in a group therapy session is enhanced.

Learning is abetted by witnessing groups in action. One of the most accessible means by which students can observe groups is by watching one or more of the excellent series of videotapes currently available. Videotapes offer the advantage over live groups of being able to be not only viewed but also reviewed. By seeing a seg-

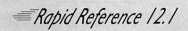

Rapid Reference 12.1

Components of Group Therapy Training Program

Didactic instruction. Learning about the theory, technique, and research base of group therapy
Experience in conducting groups. Leading different types of groups with various populations in a range of settings
Supervision of group work. Reflecting on one's group work under the guidance of a highly experienced group therapist
Personal experience in therapy or growth groups. Participating in a therapy group or experiential group

ment of a group session multiple times, students are able to discern increasingly subtle aspects of members' responses and thereby have a greater appreciation of the complexity of group life. Students also benefit from critiquing the behavior of the therapist. When students become aware that even experienced therapists may not always respond optimally in the sessions, they are able to be more tolerant of their own fledgling efforts. Initially, students in this modality are presented with the task of distinguishing group therapy from individual therapy. However, once they achieve an understanding of the special features of this medium, they are in a position to explore different theoretical approaches to group work. Videotapes are useful in illustrating how theoretical differences give rise to differences in intervention style. For example, by comparing Yalom's (1990) demonstration of an interpersonal approach with Piper and colleagues' application of a psychodynamic model (1992; see Swillel, 1996, for a review), the viewer will recognize the influence that theory has on therapist activity.

For those individuals who do not have easy access to training opportunities, the Internet represents a viable option. For example, in response to the September 11 attack, the American Group Psychotherapy Association developed an online symposium on the group treatment of traumatized individuals.

Experience Conducting Groups

In order for students of this modality to appreciate fully the concepts they encounter in formal didactic instruction, it is extremely helpful for them to have beginning experiences in conducting groups. Otherwise elusive concepts such as projective identification (see Chapter 2) come to life when the student is sitting in an actual session with group members. When classroom instruction is separated in time from actual group work, students are deterred from fully integrating theory, research, and practice.

When is a student ready to lead a group? The answer to this question depends on the leadership structure and the context of the group. Ideally, a student's experience of leading a group would be in collaboration with a senior group therapist. Initially, the student should have an opportunity merely to observe the senior therapist. Over time, the student could take a progressively more active role. This arrangement necessitates less prior didactic instruction than a circumstance in which the student is required to lead the group either alone or with another new group therapist (albeit under supervision in both circumstances). Context is another important factor. In a training setting in which the student has a great deal of support (e.g., access to senior clinicians), the student is able to begin functioning as the therapist of a group at an earlier point than in settings in which such support is lacking. Co-leading a group with another trainee also can be a valuable experience. C. A. Rice (1995) found that out of 28 trainees who had co-led a group with another new group therapist, 86 percent expressed a high level of satisfaction, and most indicated that they would choose to work with that cotherapist again. Rice stressed the importance of a shared orientation and supportive training milieu as helpful in enabling trainees to derive the most benefit from their cotherapy work.

Diversity of group experiences is helpful to the developing group therapist for several reasons. First, certain group phenomena become more evident when they are seen across different types of groups with different compositions. For example, we noted in Chapter 6 that the stages of group development can be recognized more readily as the beginning group therapist has experienced different groups over time. Second, experiences with groups of varying composition enable the group therapist to learn at a very early point the necessity of taking into account individual differences in how the therapist conducts the group. Such a therapist is more likely to do the necessary preparation and show the requisite sensitivity when working with a group that differs in important ways such as race, social class, or ethnicity from ones he or she has encountered in the past. Third, varied group experiences require that trainees practice different leadership styles. For example, short-term versus long-term groups or cognitive-behavioral versus interpersonal groups place differential demands on the leader for what types of goals are established, which therapeutic processes are activated, and what degree of structure the therapist builds into the group session. Unfortunately, although trainees such as psychology interns may gain experience in leading therapy groups, often the experience is restricted to a particular theoretical orientation or time frame (Marcus & King, 2003).

Supervision of Group Work

Supervision of the new therapist's group work by a senior group therapist is an essential component of any training program and an ethical requirement until the new group therapist achieves competence. Supervision entails not only the supervisor's provision of direction and feedback to the supervisee but also the assumption of legal responsibility for the supervisee's work and the well-being of the group members. The supervisor may also serve as an advocate for the neophyte group therapist who is providing group therapy in a larger treatment context such as in a psychiatric hospital. For example, the trainee may

> **DON'T FORGET**
> ....
> The group therapist's supervisor assumes responsibility for the supervisee's work and the well-being of the members.

require the supervisor's assistance in explaining to the treatment team why it is not helpful to a member's group work to pull the member from a session for another involvement on the unit. In performing such advocacy, the supervisor can provide valuable modeling for the trainee on how to foster an environment that is supportive of the group.

There are many formats in which supervision can occur, each of which has a distinctive set of strengths and weaknesses (Bernard, 2000). Dyadic supervision occurs when a single supervisee meets with a supervisor. Compared to other formats, this arrangement has the advantage of logistical ease. The supervisee is afforded the security of knowing that there will be ample opportunity for his or her work to be evaluated as regularly as the supervision is scheduled. Some supervisees may also be more disclosing about their group work in individual supervision in contrast to group supervision insofar as the former affords freedom from being judged by their peers (Day, 1993). With certain types of groups in which major case management decisions (e.g., whether or not to hospitalize individual members) are regularly made, the exclusivity of the supervisor's focus is an asset.

The supervisor and supervisee may conduct the group together, although this relationship is regarded by some writers as not being a true cotherapy relationship because the parties do not have equal expertise and responsibility in the group. Roller and Nelson (1993) refer to this training situation in which a master and an apprentice are paired as *nequipos*. An advantage of this involvement in and outside of the group is that the supervisor is privy to a wealth of information about both the supervisee and the group, far more than if the supervisor were to rely exclusively on the supervisee's account of the events of the session.

Insofar as both of the former formats are dyadic, they fail to use maximally a significant resource in supervision: parallel process (Ekstein & Wallerstein, 1963). *Parallel process* occurs when unconscious elements within the therapy situation emerge within the supervisory situation. The exploration of parallel process is a great resource to the supervisee because it serves as a signpost to aspects of the therapy relationship that may otherwise be inaccessible. For example, a passive-dependent stance on the part of the supervisee toward the supervisor may reflect group members' longing for the therapist to provide cures without their having to exert themselves. Although parallel process can occur in any supervisory relationship, a dyadic supervisory relationship is not conducive to its emergence. More facilitative of parallel process are formats involving a supervision group. For example, a group of therapists in training could meet with a supervisor. In some cases, the supervision group might consist of pairs of cotherapists. Members of the supervisory group could take turns presenting material from their group sessions. At the same time, the group members and supervisor might examine how aspects of their own interactions might parallel the dynamics of the presenter's group. Indeed, a role of the supervisory group is to process the emotional elements of the parallel process. The containment and processing of conflictual elements allow for a *reverse parallel process* (Friedman & Handel, 2002; Searls, 1962), by which the work accomplished in the supervision group is exported back to the therapy group and exerts a transforming effect on the latter.

Tschuschke and Greene (2002) provided some support for the importance of a training group's attendance to its own processes. Participants in training groups reported that the level of emotional engagement of the group and members' willingness to explore conflict predicted the extent of learning occurring in the groups. Perhaps unsurprisingly, the investigators also found that the greater the skill level of the leader in the perception of the members, the more favorable the outcome.

Group supervision has additional advantages. Just as in therapy groups, supervisory groups offer members a number of points of view. Moreover, given that many issues that therapists face are shared, particularly when they are at roughly the same developmental level, universality has great opportunity to operate in the supervision group. As each supervisee sees, for example, that others fear their group members' anger, then the examination of this reaction becomes more tolerable.

Although group supervision provides rich opportunities for exploration, a major disadvantage is that participants must share the supervisor's time (Altfeld & Bernard, 1999). When supervisees are sufficiently inexperienced to be unable to practice independently, or if they are not independently licensed, it is important that they present regularly. Some group supervisions are structured so that one individual is slated to provide an extensive, detailed presentation of one or more sessions and other individuals offer a more abbreviated account of their recent group work.

To remain competent, group therapists must engage in lifelong learning about their modality. Seasoned group therapists who are able to function as independent practitioners may enter a *peer supervision group* in which members serve as consultants to one another. These groups differ from the type of groups described previously for newer group therapists in that in the peer supervision group each member retains full responsibility for his or her group and for any case management deci-

---

CAUTION

To remain competent, the group therapist must engage in lifelong learning about the modality.

sions made about individual members. Such groups also can use parallel process as a way of enhancing understanding of each member's respective group.

Personal Experience in a Group

The experience of being a group member prepares one for the task of leading a group. This experience can take various forms. An individual may participate in an actual therapy group, attend a training group, experience a Tavistock weekend (a large-group marathon in which members have the goal of studying their own group process), or utilize a variety of other mediums. As Bernard (2000) noted, "What is crucial is the experience of working on one's personal issues in a group context. Such experience helps immeasurably in developing empathy for the challenges and difficulties our patients will experience in the treatment groups we will be conducting both during our training and after our training is completed" (p. 170).

Each type of involvement in groups contributes a special form of learning on the part of the group therapist. Particularly in a long-term interpersonally oriented group, the therapist has the opportunity to discover many aspects of his or her relational style that will affect how he or she interacts with group members. The training group, while also presenting manifold opportunities for personal exploration, may offer a clearer focus on group dynamics and provide intellectual tools to the therapist to describe and explain these dynamics. Both types of experiences enable the participant to experience both the vulnerabilities that attend group membership and the many sources of support for personal growth.

Credentialing of the Advanced Practitioner

The senior group therapist may be interested in establishing his or her expertise through a credentialing process. Such credentialing may be helpful in presenting one's qualifications to prospective group members, third-party payers, employers, or any other person or entity seeking to ascertain the training, competence, or both of a group practitioner. Currently, there are various options available. The American Group Psychotherapy Association (AGPA) has sponsored the creation of a credentialing organization called the National Registry of Certified Group Psychotherapists (NRCGP). For those individuals with certain designated licenses, fulfillment of the following criteria leads to membership in this organization: 12 hours of didactic course work, 300 hours of clinical experience, and 75 hours of clinical supervision. To maintain membership, participants must obtain ongoing continuing education in group therapy.

An alternative type of credentialing is available to professional psychologists. The American Board of Professional Psychology (ABPP) has established a diplomate examination in group psychology. What is distinctive about this credential relative to the NRCGP certification is the fact that it is based on an actual evaluation of competence in group therapy (Bernard, 2000). In the application, the candidate must provide evidence of having had two graduate or postgraduate courses in group psychology or group therapy, at least 2 years and 150 hours of supervised group contact, and at least 3 years and 600 hours of unsupervised group experience. The applicant must then submit a work sample that includes a tape and transcript of a session. If this material receives a favorable evaluation, the candidate then sits for an oral examination.

As Bernard (2000) noted, the NRCGP is establishing minimal credentials for competence in group treatment, whereas the ABPP is recognizing those individuals who have achieved truly advanced status in the use of this modality. In defending the need for different types of credentialing, Bernard writes:

> We owe it to the consuming public to develop ways to determine who should be certified as a competent group practitioner. The alternative is to shirk our duty, thereby leaving us vulnerable to being associated with incompetent practitioners, and leaving the public vulnerable to charlatanism and other forms of unethical practice. (p. 174)

Beyond establishing the qualifications of the individual practitioner, credentialing communicates to society at large that clear standards of training and practice define the modality of group therapy.

THE FUTURE OF GROUP THERAPY

For what type of future should group therapists be prepared? Although it might seem that to even pose this question reveals foolhardiness, arrogance, or possibly both, it is nonetheless true that there are identifiable forces currently afield that will indubitably shape group practices to come. This last section of our text will describe some emerging trends in the field, the full flowering of which will define the future practice of this modality.

Broader Application of the Modality

In the future, group therapy will be used in a greater diversity of conditions. There are three types of diversity that characterize group applications. First, group therapy will be used to address a greater array of problems in living. In the early 1900s, group therapy originated to treat individuals with physical diseases such as tuberculosis. Today, group therapy applications exist for the treatment of many different psychological and physical problems, yet for the most part group treatment is instigated only after a problem has been identified in an individual. In the future, group treatment will also be used preventatively. For example, Stamatogianni (2003) notes that when entering college, students encounter a variety of challenges to self-esteem, both academic and social. Precipitous losses in self-esteem lead to substance abuse, a phenomenon now pervasive on college campuses. Stamatogianni's group format is designed to enable beginning college students to discover resources to regulate self-esteem in healthy ways so as to diminish the likelihood of their resorting to substance abuse.

Beyond prevention, therapy groups will also work toward goals that are focused not merely on problem areas but also on the promotion of health and happiness. For example, group therapists may be more likely to work toward goals such as developing optimism in group members. There is a burgeoning literature on the connection between optimism and good mood, physical health, and achievement (Peterson, 2000). How optimism rather than rigid defense can be used in the service of healthy adaptation is a question that future group therapy scholars might address.

Second, group therapy interventions will be used not merely to treat or prevent individual problems but also to address issues occurring among societal-level groups of individuals. Jacob Moreno devised sociodrama as a method to address intragroup tensions. Sociodrama was ultimately eclipsed by psychodrama, a method for the treatment of individuals. Yet events in today's world make clear the critical need for responses to societal tensions. Events such as those of September 11 are, in essence, a problem among the subgroups of the larger group called humanity. Although our group concepts and techniques need refinement, they nonetheless possess utility for intervening in systems that are more complex and have longer histories than the traditional therapy group. An example of a group approach to the treatment of ethnic conflict rooted in historical events is provided in the following Putting It into Practice.

Third, if group therapists will not only treat but also prevent problems and if their target of intervention is the group in all sizes, then group therapists must have a readiness to intervene wherever people have formed a group. One evident example of such a new venue is the Internet. According to an estimate by the U.S. Department of Commerce, as of 2002 there were over 85 million Internet users in the United States. Among these users are individuals who may have no or limited access to face-to-face therapy groups because of location, infirmity, or any number of other factors. There are undoubtedly other individuals who would feel

Putting It Into Practice

Group Storytelling to Address Ethnic Conflict

Maoz and Bar-On (2002) describe the TRT (To Reflect and Trust) approach to effecting social change by altering individuals' perceptions through use of the group process to work through traumatic and posttraumatic experiences. This method brings together groups who have historically had a conflictual relationship with one another (either in the past or present), with one group perpetrating violence and oppression and the other group occupying the victim role. A storytelling process occurs in which members of each group, in the presence of the other, reflect upon their personal, family, and collective histories. When narratives are shared in a supportive emotional environment, members are able to achieve greater empathy with the alternate group and see their own experiences from a fresh perspective. Bar-On (1995) has reported extremely positive results in applying the TRT method to group work with children of Nazi perpetrators and descendants of Nazi survivors.

greater comfort joining an Internet therapy group than a traditional one. Although face-to-face group therapy is still the norm, ultimately the community of group therapists will need to grapple with the complexities of group treatments that involve interactive, real-time communication media or *telehealth* (Nichelson, 1998). Questions such as whether Internet groups are effective in moving individuals toward their goals, how Internet groups compare to face-to-face groups, how the confidentiality of the group member can be protected, and how the group therapist can provide emergency coverage for members representing a large geographic area must be answered so that this new form of service delivery can be used responsibly.

Fourth, the use of group treatments to pursue a greater variety of goals in a greater range of settings with groups of widely varying sizes will be facilitated by continued work on effective brief or short-term interventions. The following Putting It into Practice describes such a short-term format that utilizes many of the processes of the small group while also capitalizing upon the distinctive features of larger groups such as anonymity in order to assist members in coping constructively with problems in the workplace.

Eidelson and Eidelson (2003) identify five beliefs that are often held among groups embroiled in conflict. Although these beliefs generally do have grounding in an individual's experiences, they often are extreme, fail to do justice to the person's full range of experiences, and do not serve either the individual's or the group's ability to achieve a state of well-being. These beliefs are that one's group is superior and entitled, one's group has legitimate grievances against another group, the group is in a perpetually vulnerable position, one or more other groups

Putting It Into Practice

A Short-Term Group Intervention in the Workplace

An example of an innovative use of group treatment in a brief time frame was provided by Nuttman-Schwartz and Shay (2000), who noted that in today's world the workplace is characterized by greater uncertainty and ambiguity than ever before. They point to technological developments and the knowledge revolution that these developments have spawned as leading to a fiercely competitive environment, resulting in "rapidly changing tasks and roles, constant movement of employees from place to place, and loss of jobs" (p. 279). The consequence of the features of this landscape is that workers experience a tremendous degree of fear and apprehension that undermines their well-being and that of the organization in which they work.

In response to this, Nuttman-Schwartz and Shay developed a large-group format to assist workers in diminishing their anxiety levels and in making more adaptive responses to stressful work environments bearing these features. Their intervention, which could be applied over the course of a single-day workshop, entailed seating participants in the shape of a snail, an arrangement commonly used in large-group interventions. The group leaders sit in the first and third rows. This configuration, as well as the large size of the group, limits the access members can have to one another's reactions. The features of the group environment parallel those of the work environment in their capacity to challenge participants' sense of identity and cohesion and to elicit anxiety. The goal of the workshop is to enable the members to establish a dialogue despite the impediments to doing so. The leader opens the workshop by reading the following statement (which could be modified depending on the group):

> You are social workers in a factory. Recently, there have been rumors that the factory is going to be sold to new owners. It is clear to you that the sale will lead to changes in the organization, including changes in the workforce. Workers may have to change jobs in the organization. People may be forced to take early retirement. Others may be fired, and so on. You, as social workers, have not yet received any official notice. Place yourself in the situation and respond to it. (Nuttman-Schwartz & Shay, 2000, p. 284)

Nuttman-Schwartz and Schay observed that in the midst of this ambiguous, uncertain situation, participants feel many of the uncomfortable feelings of fear, hopelessness, and helplessness that characterize their professional lives outside the group. They look to the group leaders to rescue them from this predicament. If the group leaders allow the members to experience these reactions but then assist them in reflecting on their group behaviors, they move onto a greater sense of cohesion. Aided by the group leaders' efforts to direct the group toward the here and now, the members are able to move from feelings to words and from words to thoughts. These transformations enable them to have a dialogue with one another wherein they can connect their reactions to the structure of the situation. As they became active in dialogue, they also recognize the possibility of becoming active in the work setting rather than abjectly dependent upon authority figures.

are untrustworthy and malignant, and one's group is helpless to improve its lot. Groups designed to address ethnic conflicts would create a safe environment for members by allowing a process to develop in which these so-called dangerous beliefs could emerge and be identified, be tested to assess the extent of the grounding in experience, and ultimately be altered through the use of both interpersonal learning (Yalom, 1995) and cognitive restructuring (J. S. Beck, 1995). Using the principles of general systems theory, we might anticipate that changes in group participants could lead to broader societal shifts.

The Empirical Study of Therapy Groups

As noted in Chapter 7, there will be continued demands for research that demonstrates the effectiveness of group therapy. Although meta-analytic reviews have resoundingly established the usefulness of the modality, additional research is needed to determine the generalizability of positive findings. Furthermore, research is needed to shed light on the comparative benefits of particular models applied to specific populations in a given setting and time frame. For example, although we know that cognitive-behavioral groups work for a variety of psychological problems, we do not yet know whether the cognitive-behavioral approach (relative to other approaches) is optimal for hospitalized patients exhibiting a mixture of symptoms of depression and anxiety and who are available for only brief treatment. Given the continued pressure of managed care, of particular importance is research that shows what types of changes are possible in short-term versus long-term time frames.

No matter how much research accrues, there will always be the question of whether a particular approach is useful in one's own clinical context. Although some approaches may be shown to be serviceable across a broad range of conditions, the individual clinician still has the responsibility of establishing that a considered approach works within his or her own unique setting. Many group therapists function in situations in which conducting a controlled experiment is either impossible or impractical. Ethical considerations may preclude assigning group members to a condition that the therapist anticipates will be less than optimally beneficial. Despite these impediments, therapists are nonetheless obligated to ensure that treatment is working. As noted in Chapter 7, therapists increasingly will function as local scientists (Peterson

CAUTION

Although the benefits of group therapy have been established through controlled studies, the generalizability of these findings to specific clinical conditions (combinations of patient populations, settings, time frames, and so on) has not.

et al., 1997). Rather than operating within an *efficacy paradigm* in which variables are carefully controlled, thereby enabling inferences about causality, therapists will use the more practical *effectiveness paradigm,* wherein data is collected at various points, especially at the beginning and end of treatment (Howard et al., 1996). Over time, the therapist will be able to discern a pattern in the direction and degree of change group members undergo over the course of the group. Although data yielded from the effectiveness paradigm may not in all cases be suitable for a published study, they may provide crucial information to the therapist in determining the contextual appropriateness of his or her approach.

Another area in which continued study is needed is the phenomenon of adverse outcomes. Like any medical treatment or form of therapy, group therapy can produce negative outcomes. So that adverse effects can be avoided to the greatest extent possible, knowledge of when they are most likely to occur is essential. Roback (2000) points out that past research has focused on individual factors such as leadership style, the personality of the therapist, selection errors, and the characteristics of the individual members. He notes that although each of these factors has been shown to be influential, a more complete picture can be obtained through the examination of possible interactions among these sets of variables. As an example of such an interaction, Roback cites a study by Patterson (1984) in which patients with chronic lung disease exhibited an intensification of their breathing problems during emotionally intense segments of the group sessions. However, once the treatment approach changed from exploratory to didactic, these adverse physical effects disappeared. Were the therapist to examine only a single variable, such as the medical status of the patient, an erroneous conclusion could be drawn about dangers and benefits of group therapy.

Support groups and self-help groups are now ubiquitous. Although the benefits of these groups have been established through many outcome studies, further work is needed to enable practitioners to demarcate as clearly as possible what psychological problems are most effectively treated within group therapy, support groups, or self-help groups. This information is crucial to the practitioner's ability to make appropriate referrals to each type of group (Ettin, 2000). Also needed is an understanding of whether the usefulness of these types of group is enhanced through a more active incorporation of the knowledge base that has developed from the study of therapy groups (Bernard, 1993).

All of the aforementioned efforts concern, in some way, the study of outcomes. Nevertheless, to know that a particular approach works, and even to know with whom and under what conditions it works, is not sufficient. The furtherance of the modality and the capacity of the practitioner to use it to its fullest depend upon an understanding of what particular processes within the group therapy session produce certain results. As we discussed in Chapter 7, the field has recently undergone the development of process measures capable of capturing the complexity of events within the session both at the individual and group levels (A. P. Beck & Lewis, 2000). The identification of process-outcome patterns for each theoretical approach will enable us to use these approaches to their best advantage.

A Focus on Diversity

As implied in the previous section, now that the hard work has been done of establishing the general usefulness of group therapy, it is time to look at the particulars of who is receiving group treatment, where, and for how long. With respect to the question of who is receiving group treatment, the history of the modality has largely been focused on the diagnosis and level of functioning of the group member. Although these variables have importance, there are many other characteristics of the group member that need to be considered. Variables such as race and ethnicity, socioeconomic status, ableness, religion, and sexual orientation, which were explored in Chapter 9, all bear investigation. Groups that are homogeneous versus heterogeneous on these dimensions require study of what approaches are most suitable for these varying compositions.

Greater attention to the characteristics of the therapist is also warranted, particularly as they interact with the characteristics of the group members. For example, what are the effects of having a middle-class therapist in a group of individuals who are all lower class as opposed to a group of members who are heterogeneous in socioeconomic status? In the literature, there has been an increasing number of theoretical pieces and anecdotal reports focusing on individual differences among both members and therapists. However, there is not yet adequate research on this topic. Those few studies that have focused on variables other than psychiatric diagnoses suggest that the sets of variables outlined in Hays's ADDRESSING framework (Chapter 7) are well worth exploration. An example is Heitler's (1973) study of social class, which showed that first-admission inpatients from lower socioeconomic levels have different attitudes toward participation in psychotherapy groups than what has been documented in the literature based upon the study of upper- and middle-class groups. He demonstrated that these class-based attitudes were important to consider in preparing members for group treatment.

To a large extent, the areas of neglect in the theoretical and research literature are reflective of areas of neglect in the therapy groups themselves. As Abernethy (1998) points out, therapists have a much easier time addressing issues that arise from gender differences than they do taking up issues connected to differences in race, sexuality, and religion. The cost of neglecting these areas appears at both the individual and group levels. On the individual level, members are denied opportunities for the psychological growth that would occur were the therapist able to facilitate the exploration of difficult (and sometimes painful) issues associated with each member's unique identity. The therapist who is insensitive to all that defines the member may easily misinterpret the member's meaning (given the embeddedness of meaning in sociocultural context), leaving the member to feel still again misunderstood. On the group level, a therapist's unwillingness to approach issues relating to members' race, religion, gender preference, and so on detracts from the atmosphere of openness so critical to a group's work. On both the group and the individual level, the therapist who is unable to recognize countertransference responses tied to aspects of members' identities is at risk for acting them out in a way that will be detrimental to the group and individual members. Fenster (1996) provides the example of the therapist whose guilt prompts him or her to show hypercuriosity about the member's culture in a way that prevents the member from doing the most critical therapeutic work. Conversely, to the extent that the full range of variables is addressed sensitively, in the words of Montero and Colman (2000) both therapists and members can "feel competent and comfortable rather than terrorized in multiplicity and diversity" (p. 212).

SUMMARY AND CONCLUSIONS

This chapter has addressed the topic of the training of the group therapist, an ongoing enterprise for as long as the practitioner utilizes this modality. Among the elements of a group therapy training program are didactic instruction, experience in leading a group, supervision, and personal experience in a training or treatment group. Opportunities for the credentialing of the senior group therapist were also outlined.

Future directions, both probable and desirable, were outlined. Group therapy is likely to be used in a greater variety of settings and with groups of highly varying sizes. Technology will have a marked impact on how group therapy is delivered. Treatment approaches will address individual mental health issues, prevention, and societal problems. Future research efforts will utilize both effectiveness and efficacy paradigms. Particular areas of interest are (1) the continued study of process-outcome connections; (2) increased knowledge about the types of changes that can occur through participation in brief groups, short-term groups, and long-term groups; and (3) systematic observations on outcome differences between self-help, support, and therapy groups. Further efforts in the study of individual differences relating to both group members and therapists will stimulate group therapy's vitality as a modality.

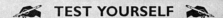

TEST YOURSELF

1. *Parallel process* refers to the identification of similar dynamics in different group members. True or False?

2. The most important aspect of a supervision group is the clarity of the conceptualization that is achieved about each participant's group. True or False?

3. The leader's skill is a determinant of members' gains from participating in a training group. True or False?

4. Most graduate programs that educate mental health professionals provide substantial training opportunities in group therapy. True or False?

5. Why is it helpful for the neophyte group therapist to have a diversity of group experiences?

6. What are the advantages of group supervision?

7. Factors that enable trainee cotherapists to have a productive and satisfying relationship with one another include

   (a) a common or similar theoretical orientation.

   (b) a supportive milieu for the group work.

   (c) a shared distaste for competition.

   (d) a and b only

   (e) a, b, and c

8. Future research on adverse effects of group therapy should focus on

   (a) the race or ethnicity of the group members.

   (b) the theoretical approach.

   (c) the race or ethnicity of the therapist.

   (d) the personality of the therapist.

   (e) all of the above in interaction with one another.

9. The following areas of member variability have been researched minimally:

   (a) Religion

   (b) Gender preference

   (c) Race

   (d) all of the above

Answers: 1. False; 2. False; 3. True; 4. False; 5. Greater salience of group phenomena; emphasis on the importance of individual differences among members; opportunity for the therapist to practice different leadership style; 6. Facilitates the emergence of parallel processes; creates greater opportunity for feedback; shows supervisees that they share certain reactions to their groups; 7. d; 8. e; 9. d

References

Abbey, S., & Farrow, S. (1998). Group therapy and organ transplantation. *International Journal of Group Psychotherapy, 48*(2), 163–185.

Abernethy, A. D. (1998). Working with racial themes in group psychotherapy. *Group, 22,* 1–13.

Abernethy, A. D. (2002). The power of metaphors for exploring cultural differences in groups. *Group, 26*(3), 219–231.

Agazarian, Y. M. (1997). *Systems-centered therapy for groups.* New York: Guilford Press.

Agazarian, Y. M., & Carter, F. B. (1993). Discussions on the large group. *Group, 17*(4), 210–234.

Agazarian, Y. M., & Janoff, S. (1993). Systems theory and small groups. In H. I. Kaplan & B. J. Sadock (Eds.), *Comprehensive group psychotherapy* (3rd ed., pp. 32–44). Baltimore: Williams & Wilkins.

Agazarian, Y. M., & Peters, R. (1981). *The visible and invisible group: Perspectives on group psychotherapy and group process.* London: Routledge & Kegan Paul.

Albrecht, E., & Brabender, V. (1983). Alcoholics in inpatient, short-term interactional group psychotherapy: An outcome study. *Group, 7*(2), 50–54.

Alexopoulos, G. S., Raue, P., & Arean, P. (2003). Problem-solving therapy versus supportive therapy in geriatric major depression with executive dysfunction. *American Journal of Geriatric Psychiatry, 11*(1), 46–52.

Allan, R., & Scheidt, S. (1998). Group psychotherapy for patients with coronary heart disease. *International Journal of Group Psychotherapy, 48*(2), 187–214.

Allen, J. R., & Allen, B. A. In C. E. Lennox (Ed.) *Redecision therapy: A brief, action-oriented approach* (pp. 255–271). Northvale, NJ: Jason Aronson.

Allison, T. G. (1996). Identification and treatment of psychosocial risk factors for coronary artery disease. *Mayo Clinic Proceedings, 71*(8), 817–819.

Allumbaugh, D. L., & Hoyt, W. T. (1999). Effectiveness of grief therapy. *Journal of Counseling Psychology, 46*(3), 370–380.

Alonso, A., & Rutan, J. S. (1990). Common dilemmas in combined individual and group treatment. *Group, 14*(1), 5–12.

Alonso, A., & Rutan, J. S. (1993). Character change in group psychotherapy. *International Journal of Group Psychotherapy, 43*(4), 439–451.

Altfeld, D. A., & Bernard, H. S. (1999). Experiential group psychotherapy supervision. *Group, 23*(1), 1–17.

American Psychiatric Association. (1995). Practice guideline for the treatment of patients with substance use disorders: Alcohol, cocaine, opioids. *American Journal of Psychiatry, 152*(11), 5–59.

American Psychological Association. (2003). Guidelines on multicultural education, training, research, practice, and organizational change for psychologists. *American Psychologist, 58*(5), 377–402.

American Psychological Association Practice Organization & American Psychological Association Insurance Trust. (2002). *Getting ready for HIPAA: What you need to know now—A primer for psychologists.* Washington, DC: Authors.

Anastasi, A., & Urbina, S. (1997). *Psychological testing.* Upper Saddle River, NJ: Prentice Hall.

Anderson, B. L. (2002). Biobehavioral outcomes following psychological interventions for cancer patients. *Journal of Consulting and Clinical Psychology, 70*(3), 590–610.

Anderson, C. A. (1989). Temperature and aggression: Ubiquitous effects of heat on occurrence of human violence. *Psychological Bulletin, 106,* 74–96.

Anthony, J. (1972a). Comparison between individual and group psychotherapy. In H. I. Kaplan & B. J. Sadock (Eds.), *The evolution of group therapy* (pp. 83–96). New York: Dutton.

Anthony, J. (1972b). The history of group psychotherapy. In H. I. Kaplan & B. J. Sadock (Eds.), *The evolution of group therapy* (pp. 1–26). New York: Dutton.

Antonuccio, D. O., Danton, W. G., & DeNelsky, G. Y. (1995). Psychotherapy versus medication for depression: Challenging the conventional wisdom with data. *Professional Psychology, Research and Practice, 26*(6), 574–585.

Antze, P. (1976). The role of ideologies in peer group organizations: Some theoretical considerations and three case studies. *Journal of Applied Behavioral Science, 12,* 300–310.

Arean, P. A., Perri, M. G., Nezu, A. M., Schein, R. L., Christopher, F., & Joseph, T. X. (1993). Special populations: Comparative effectiveness of social problem-solving therapy as treatment for depression in older adults. *Journal of Consulting and Clinical Psychology, 61*(6), 1003–1010.

Aries, E. (1976). Interaction patterns and themes of male, female, and mixed groups. *Small Group Behavior, 7*(1), 7–18.

Bacaltchuk, J., Trefiglio, R. P., de Oliveira, I. R., Lima, M. S., & Mari, J. J. (1999). Antidepressants versus psychotherapy for bulimia nervosa: A systematic review. *Journal of Clinical Pharmacy and Therapeutics, 24,* 23–31.

Baird, J. (1997). Contracting for change. In C. E. Lennox (Ed.). Redecision therapy: A brief action-oriented approach. Northvale, NJ: Aronson.

Barak, A., & Wander-Schwartz, M. (2000). Empirical evaluation of brief group therapy conducted in an internet chat room. *The Journal of Virtual Environments, 5.* Retrieved October 16, 20002, from http://www.brandeis.edu/bups/jobe/html/v5/cherapy3.htm

Barlow, S. H., Burlingame, G. M., Nebeker, R. S., & Anderson, E. (2000). Meta-analysis of medical self-help groups. *International Journal of Group Psychotherapy, 50*(1), 53–70.

Bar-On, D. (1995). Encounters between descendants of Nazi perpetrators and descendants of Holocaust survivors. *Psychiatry, 58*(3), 225–245.

Bebbington, P. E. (1976). The efficacy of Alcoholics Anonymous: The elusiveness of hard data. *British Journal of Psychiatry, 128,* 572–580.

Beck, A. P., Dugo, J. M., Eng, A. M., & Lewis, C. M. (1986). The search for phases in group development: Designing process analysis measures of group interaction. In L. S. Greenberg & W. M. Pinsof (Eds.), *The psychotherapeutic process: A research handbook* (615–705). New York: Guilford Press.

Beck, A. P., & Lewis, C. L. (2000). *The process of group psychotherapy: Systems for analyzing change.* Washington, DC: American Psychological Association.

Beck, A. T. (1976). *Cognitive therapy and the emotional disorders* (4th ed.). Madison, CT: International Universities Press.

Beck, A. T., & Steer, R. A. (1987). *Manual for the Revised Beck Depression Inventory.* San Antonio, TX: Psychological Corporation.

Beck, A. T., & Steer, R. A. (1990). *Beck Anxiety Inventory Manual.* San Antonio, TX: Psychological Corporation.

Beck, A. T., & Steer, R. A. (1993). *Manual for the Beck Depression Inventory.* San Antonio, TX: Psychological Corporation.

Beck, A. T., Weissman, A., Lester, D., & Trexler, M. (1974). The measurement of pessimism: The Hopelessness Scale. *Journal of Consulting and Clinical Psychology, 42,* 861–865.

Beck, J. S. (1995). *Cognitive therapy: Basics and beyond.* New York: Guilford Press.

Bennett, D. S., & Gibbons, T. A. (2000). Efficacy of child cognitive-behavioral interventions for antisocial behavior: A meta-analysis. *Child & Family Behavioral Therapy, 22*(1), 1–15.

Bennis, W. G., & Shepard, H. A. (1956). A theory of group development. *Human Relations, 9,* 415–437.

Bernard, H. S. (1993). Future of group psychotherapy. In H. I. Kaplan & B. J. Sadock (Eds.), *Comprehensive group psychotherapy* (3rd ed., pp. 724–732). Baltimore: Williams & Wilkins.

Bernard, H. S. (2000). The future of training and credentiality in group psychotherapy. *Group, 24*(2/3), 167–175.

Berne, E. (1972). *What do you say after you say hello?* New York: Gione.

Bernstein, B. H. (1990). "A current look at transference in combined analytic therapy": Discussion. *Group, 14*(1), 25–26.

Berzon, B., Pious, C., & Farson, R. E. (1963). The therapeutic event in group psychotherapy: A study of subjective reports by group members. *Journal of Individual Psychology, 19*(2), 204–212.

Biegel, D. E., & Yamatani, H. (1987). Self-help groups for families of the mentally ill: Roles and benefits. *International Journal of Family Psychiatry, 8,* 151–173.

Billow, R. M. (2000). Relational levels of the "Container-contained" in group therapy. *Group, 24*(4), 243–259.

Billow, R. M. (2001). The therapist's anxiety and resistance to group therapy. *International Journal of Group Psychotherapy, 51*(2), 225–242.

Bion, W. (1959). *Experiences in groups.* New York: Basic Books.

Bion, W. (1961). *Experiences in groups* (2nd ed.). New York: Basic Books.

Blatner, A. (1996). *Acting-in: Practical applications of psychodramatic methods* (3rd ed.). New York: Springer.

Bloch, S., & Crouch, E. (1985). *Therapeutic factors in group psychotherapy.* London: Oxford University Press.

Bloom, J. R., Ross, R. D., & Burnell, G. (1978). The effect of social support on patient adjustment after breast surgery. *Patient Counseling Health Education, 1*(2), 50–59.

Bonds-White, F. (1996). Working with men in groups: A female therapist's perspective. In M. P. Andronico (Ed.), *Men in groups: Insights, interventions, and psychoeducational work* (pp. 181–213). Washington, DC: American Psychological Association.

Bostwick, G. (1987). "Where's Mary?" A review of the group treatment outcome literature. *Social Work with Groups, 10,* 117–131.

Bottomley, A., Pitkethly, M., Hunton, S., Roberts, G., Jones, L., & Bradley, C. (1996). Social support and cognitive behavioral therapy with cancer patients: A pilot study of group interventions. *Journal of Psychosocial Oncology, 14,* 65–83.

Bourgeois, L., Sabourin, S., & Wright, J. (1990). Predictive validity of therapeutic alliance in group marital therapy. *Journal of Consulting and Clinical Psychology, 58*(5), 608–613.

Brabender, V. (1990, February). Short-term group therapy. In R. MacKenzie (Chair), *Therapeutic strategies in brief group therapy.* Symposium conducted at the meeting of the American Group Psychotherapy Association, Boston, MA.

Brabender, V. (1997). Chaos and order in the psychotherapy group. In F. Masterpasqua & P. A. Perna (Eds.), *The psychological meaning of chaos* (pp. 225–252). Washington, DC: American Psychological Association.

Brabender, V. (2000). Chaos, group psychotherapy, and the future of uncertainty and uniqueness. *Group, 24*(1), 23–32.

Brabender, V. (2001). The future of group psychotherapy: Expanding the conversation. *International Journal of Group Psychotherapy, 51*(2), 181–189.

Brabender, V. (2002). *Introduction to group therapy*. New York: Wiley.

Brabender, V., & Fallon, A. (1993). *Models of inpatient group psychotherapy*. Washington, DC: American Psychological Association.

Brandes, N. S., & Moosbrugger, L. (1985). A 15-year clinical review of combined adolescent/young adult group therapy. *International Journal of Group Psychotherapy, 35*(1), 95–107.

Brandsma, J., & Pattison, E. M. (1985). The outcome of group psychotherapy in alcoholics: An empirical review. *American Journal of Drug and Alcohol Abuse, 11,* 151–162.

Bright, J. I., Baker, K. D., & Neimeyer, R. A. (1999). Professional and paraprofessional group treatments for depression: A comparison of cognitive-behavioral and mutual support interventions. *Journal of Consulting and Clinical Psychology, 67*(4), 491–501.

Brook, D. W., Gordon, C., & Meadow, H. (1998). Ethnicity, culture, and group psychotherapy. *Group, 22,* 53–80.

Budman, S. H., Bennett, M. J., & Wisneski, M. (1981). An adult developmental model of group psychotherapy. In S. H. Budman (Ed.), *Forms of brief therapy* (pp. 305–342). New York: Guilford Press.

Budman, S. H., Demby, A., Solde, S., & Merny, J. (1996). Time-limited psychotherapy for patients with personality disorders: Outcomes and dropouts. *International Journal of Group Psychotherapy, 46*(3), 357–377.

Budman, S. H., & Gurman, A. S. (1988). *Theory and practice of brief therapy*. New York: Aronson.

Budman, S. H., Simeone, P. G., Reilly, R., & Demby, A. (1994). Progress in short-term and time-limited group psychotherapy: Evidence and implications. In A. Fuhriman & G. M. Burlingame (Eds.), *Handbook of group psychotherapy: An empirical and clinical synthesis* (pp. 319–339). New York: Wiley.

Budman, S. H., Soldz, S., Demby, A., Feldstein, M., Springer, T., & Davis, M. S. (1989). Cohesion, alliance and outcome in group psychotherapy. *Psychiatry: Journal for the Study of Interpersonal Processes, 52*(3), 339–350.

Burlingame, G. M., Fuhriman, A., & Johnson, J. E. (2001). Psychotherapy: Theory, research, practice, training, 38(4), 373–379.

Burlingame, G. M., Fuhriman, A., & Mosier, A. (2003). The differential effectiveness of group psychotherapy: A meta-analytic perspective. *Group Dynamics: Theory, Research and Practice, 7,* 2–13.

Burns, B. J., Hoagwood, K., & Mrazek, P. J. (1999). Effective treatment for mental disorders in children and adolescents. *Clinical Child and Family Psychology Review, 2*(4), 199–254.

Burrow, T. (1928). The basis of group analysis, or the analysis of the reactions of normal and neurotic individuals. *British Journal of Medical Psychology, 8,* 198–206.

Caine, T. N., & Wijesinghe, B. (1976). Personality, expectancies, and group psychotherapy. *British Journal of Psychiatry, 129,* 384–387.

Caligor, J. A. (1990). A current look at transference in combined analytic therapy. *Group, 14*(1), 16–24.

Carlock, C. H., & Martin, P. Y. (1977). See composition and the intensive group experience. *Social Work, 22,* 27–32.

Clarke, G. N., Rohde, P., Lewinsohn, P. M., Hopson, H., & Seeley, J. R. (1999). Cognitive-behavioral treatment of adolescent depression: Efficacy of acute group treatment and booster sessions. *Journal of the American Academy for Child and Adolescent Psychiatry, 38*(3), 272–279.

Cohen, S., & Weinstein, N. (1981). Nonauditory effects of noise on behavior and health. *Journal of Social Issues, 37*(1), 36–70.

Colon, Y. (1997). Chatter(er)ing through the fingertips: Doing group therapy online. *Women and Performance, 17*. Retrieved October 16, 2002, from http://www.echonyc.com/~women/Issue17/public-colon.html

Conlin, D., & Smith, S. (1985). Group psychotherapy for gay men. In J. C. Gonsiorek (Ed.), *A guide to psychotherapy with gay and lesbian clients* (pp. 105–112). New York: Harrington Park Press.

Connelly, J. L., & Piper, W. E. (1989). An analysis of pretraining work behavior as a composition variable in group psychotherapy. *International Journal of Group Psychotherapy, 3*(2), 173–189.

Cooney, N. L., Kadden, R. N., Litt, M. D., & Getter, H. (1991). Matching alcoholics to coping skills or interactional therapies: Two-year follow-up results. *Journal of Consulting and Clinical Psychology, 59,* 598–601.

Corsini, R. J., & Rosenberg, B. (1955). Mechanisms of group psychotherapy: Processes and dynamics. *Journal of Abnormal & Social Psychology, 51,* 406–411.

Cox, G., & Merkel, W. (1989). A qualitative review of psychosocial treatments for bulimia. *The Journal of Nervous and Mental Disease, 177*(2), 77–84.

Cruess, D. G., Antoni, M. H., McGregor, B. A., Kilbourn, K. M., Boyers, A. E., Alferi, S. M., et al. (2000). Cognitive-behavioral stress management reduces serum cortisol by enhancing benefit finding among women being treated for early stage breast cancer. *Psychosomatic Medicine, 52,* 304–308.

Curry, L. A., Snyder, C. R., Cook, D. L., Ruby, B. C., & Rehm, M. (1997). The role of hope in academic and sport performance. *Journal of Personality and Social Psychology, 73*(6), 1257–1267.

Dagley, J. C., Gazda, G. M., Eppinger, S. J., & Stewart, E. A. (1994). Group psychotherapy with children, preadolescents, and adolescents. In A. Fuhriman & G. M. Burlingame (Eds.), *Handbook of group psychotherapy* (pp. 340–369). New York: Wiley.

Dalal, F. N. (1993). "Race" and racism: An attempt to organize difference. *Group Analysis, 26*(3), 277–290.

Davison, K. P., Pennebaker, J. W., & Dickerson, S. S. (2000). Who talks? The social psychology of illness support groups. *American Psychologist, 55*(2), 205–217.

Day, M. (1993). Training and supervision in group psychotherapy. In H. I. Kaplan & B. J. Sadock (Eds.), *Comprehensive group psychotherapy* (3rd ed., pp. 656–668). Baltimore: Williams & Wilkins.

Deffenbacher, J. L., Thwaites, G. A., Wallace, T. L., & Oetting, E. R. (1994). Social skills and cognitive-relaxation approaches to general anger reduction. *Journal of Counseling Psychology, 41,* 386–396.

DeJong, T. L., & Gorey, K. M. (1996). Short-term versus long-term group work with female survivors of childhood sexual abuse: A brief meta-analytic review. *Social Work with Groups, 19*(1), 19–27.

De Mare, P. B. (1989). The history of large group phenomena in relation to group analytic psychotherapy: The story of the median group. *Group Analysis, 4,* 79.

Derogatis, L. R. (1977). *SCL-90-R: Administration scoring and procedures manual I.* Baltimore: Clinical Psychometric Research.

Dewey, J. (1900). Psychology and social practice. *Psychology Review, 7,* 105–124.

Diener, E. (2000). Subjective well-being: The science of happiness and a proposal for a national index. *American Psychologist, 55*(1), 34–43.

Dies, R. R. (1985). Leadership in short-term group therapy: Manipulation or facilitation? *International Journal of Group Psychotherapy, 35*(3), 435–455.

Dies, R. R. (1992a). The future of group therapy. *Psychotherapy, 29,* 58–64.

Dies, R. R. (1992b). Models of group psychotherapy: Sifting through confusion. *International Journal of Group Psychotherapy, 42*(1), 1–17.

Dies, R. R. (1994). Therapist variables in group psychotherapy research. In A. Fuhriman and G. M. Burlingame (Eds.), *Handbook of group psychotherapy: An empirical and clinical synthesis* (pp. 114–154). New York: Wiley.

Dies, R. R., & Cohen, L. (1976). Content considerations in group therapist self-disclosure. *International Journal of Group Psychotherapy, 26*(1), 71–88.

Dies, R. R., & Dies, K. R. (1993). The role of evaluation in clinical practice: Overview and group treatment illustration. *International Journal of Group Psychotherapy, 43*(1), 77–105.

Dies, R. R., & Teleska, P. (1985). Negative outcome in group psychotherapy. In D. Mays & C. Franks (Eds.), *Negative outcome in psychotherapy* (pp. 118–142). New York: Springer.

Dube, B. D., Mitchell, C. A., & Bergman, L. A. (1986). Uses of the self-run group in a child-guidance setting. *International Journal of Group Psychotherapy, 30*(4), 461–479.

Dugo, J. M., & Beck, A. P. (1984). A therapist's guide to issues of intimacy and hostility viewed as group-level phenomena. *International Journal of Group Psychotherapy, 34,* 25–45.

Dunkas, N., & Nikelly, A. G. (1975). Group psychotherapy with Greek immigrants. *The International Journal of Group Psychotherapy, 25,* 403–449.

Dush, D., Hirt, M., & Schroeder, H. (1983). Self-statement modification with adults: A meta-analysis. *Journal of Consulting and Clinical Psychology, 94,* 408–422.

Eidelson, R. J., & Eidelson, J. I. (2003). Dangerous ideas. *American Psychologist, 58*(3), 182–192.

Eifert, G. H., & Craill, L. (1989). The relationship between affect, behaviour, and cognition in behavioural and cognitive treatments of depression and phobic anxiety. *Behaviour Change, 6*(2), 96–103.

Ekstein, R., & Wallerstein, R. S. (1963). *The teaching and learning of psychotherapy.* New York: Basic Books.

Elfant, A. B. (1997). Submergence of the personal and unique in developmental models of psychotherapy groups and their leaders. *Group Dynamics: Theory, Research, and Practice, 1*(4), 311–315.

Emrick, C. D. (1987). Alcoholics Anonymous: Affiliation processes and effectiveness as treatment. *Alcoholism: Clinical and Experimental Research, 11*(5), 416–423.

Erikson, E. H. (1994). *The life cycle completed.* New York: W. W. Norton.

Esplen, M. J., Toner, B., Hunter, J., Glendon, G., Liede, A., Narod, S., et al. (2000). A supportive-expressive group intervention for women with family history of breast cancer: Results of a phase II study. *Psycho-Oncology, 2,* 243–252.

Ettin, M. F. (2000). Fostering a "group ethos": Truth or dare! *Group, 24*(2/3), 229–240.

Ettin, M. F. (1997). A brief history of group-as-a-whole models and twenty sets of questions for comparing them. *International Forum of Group Psychotherapy, 6,* 3–8.

Ettin, M. F., Cohen, B. D., & Fidler, J. W. (1997). Group-as-a-whole theory viewed in its 20th-century context. *Group dynamics: Theory, Research, & Practice, 1*(4), 329–340.

Fawzy, F. I., Cousins, N., Fawzy, N. W., Kemeny, M. E., Elashoff, R., & Morton, D. (1990). A structured psychiatric intervention for cancer patients, I: Changes over time in methods of coping and affective disturbance. *Archives of General Psychiatry, 47,* 729–735.

Fawzy, F. I., & Fawzy, N. W. (1998). Psychosocial treatment of cancer: An update. *Clinical Psychology and Behavioral Medicine, 11*(6), 601–605.

Fawzy, F. I., Fawzy, N. W., & Canada, A. L. (1998). Psychosocial treatment of cancer: An update. *Current Opinion in Psychiatry, 11*(6), 601–605.

Fawzy, F. I., Fawzy, N. W., Hyun, C. S., Elashoff, R., Guthrie, D., Fahey, J. L., et al. (1993). Malignant melanoma: Effects of an early structured psychiatric intervention, coping, and affective state of recurrence and survival 6 years later. *Archives of General Psychiatry, 16,* 149–192.

Fawzy, F. I., Kemeny, M. E., Fawzy, N., Elashoff, T., Morton, D., Cousins, N., et al. (1990). A structured psychiatric intervention for cancer patients: Changes over time in immunological measures. *Archives of General Psychiatry, 47,* 729–735.

Feigin, R. (2002). Group therapy with individuals and families coping with illness or disability in Israel. *Group, 26*(1), 61–80.

Feindler, E. L., Ecton, R. B., Kingsley, D., & Dubey, D. R. (1986). Group anger-control training for institutionalized psychiatric male adolescents. *Behavior Therapy, 17*(2), 109–123.

Fenster, A. (1996). Group therapy as an effective treatment modality for people of color. *International Journal of Group Psychotherapy, 46*(3), 399–416.

Fenster, A., & Fenster, J. (1998). Diagnosing deficits in "basic trust" in multiracial and multicultural group: Individual or social psychopathology? *Group, 22*(2), 81–93.

Fettes, P. A., & Peters, J. M. (1992). A meta-analysis of group treatments for Bulimia Nervosa. *International Journal of Eating Disorders, 11*(2), 97–110.

Flowers, J. V., & Booraem, C. D. (1990a). The effects of different types of interpretation on outcome in group psychotherapy. *Group, 14*(2), 81–88.

Flowers, J. V., & Booraem, C. D. (1990b). The frequency and effect of different types of interpretation in psychodynamic and cognitive-behavioral group psychotherapy. *International Journal of Group Psychotherapy, 40*(2), 203–214.

Forsyth, D. R. (2000). One hundred years of group research: Introduction to the special issue. *Group Dynamics, 4*(1), 3–6.

Forsyth, D. R. (1990). *Group dynamics* (3rd ed.). Belmont, CA: Brooks/Cole.

Forsyth, D. R., & Corazzini, J. G. (2000). Groups as change agents. In C. Snyder & R. Ingram (Eds.), *Handbook of psychological change: Psychotherapy processes and practices for the 21st century* (pp. 309–336). New York: Wiley.

Foulkes, S. H. (1975/1976). *Group analytic psychotherapy: Methods and principles.* London: G. Kamos.

Foulkes, S. H. (1975/1986). *Group analytic psychotherapy methods and principles.* London: H. Karnac.

France, D. G., & Dugo, J. M. (1985). Pretherapy orientation as preparation for open psychotherapy groups. *Psychotherapy, 22,* 256.

Frank, J. P. (2001). Adult attachment and its association with substance dependence treatment outcome. *Dissertation Abstracts International, 62*(5-B), 2482.

Frankel, B. (2002). Existential issues in group psychotherapy. *International Journal of Group Psychotherapy, 52*(2), 215–231.

Fried, L. (1972). Basic concepts in group psychotherapy. In H. I. Kaplan & B. J. Sadock (Eds.), *The evolution of group therapy* (pp. 27–50). New York: Jason Aronson.

Friedman, R., & Handel, O. (2002). Facilitating individual processes in supervision groups comprised of co-therapists conducting group therapy with bereaved parents. *Group, 26*(1), 95–105.

Friedman, M., Thorensen, C. E., Gill, J. J., Ulmer, D., Powell, L. H., Price, V. A., et al. (1986). Alteration of type A behavior and its effect on cardiac recurrences in post myocardial infarction patients: Summary results of the Recurrent Coronary Prevention Project. *American Heart Journal, 156,* 745–752.

Frost, J. C. (1990). A developmental keyed scheme for the placement of gay men into psychotherapy groups. *International Journal of Group Psychotherapy, 40,* 155–167.

Frost, J. C. (1996). Working with gay men in psychotherapy groups. In M. P. Andronico (Ed.), *Men in groups: Insights, interventions, and psychoeducational work* (pp. 163–179). Washington, DC: American Psychological Association.

Frost, J. C. (1998). Countertransference considerations for the gay male when leading psychotherapy groups for gay men. *International Journal of Group Psychotherapy, 48,* 3–24.

Fuhriman, A., & Burlingame, G. M. (1994a). Group psychotherapy, research, and practice. In A. Fuhriman & G. M. Burlingame (Eds.), *Handbook of group psychotherapy: An empirical and clinical synthesis* (pp. 3–41). New York: Wiley.

Fuhriman, A., & Burlingame, G. M. (Eds.). (1994b). *Handbook of group psychotherapy: An empirical and clinical synthesis.* New York: Wiley.

Fuhriman, A., & Burlingame, G. M. (2001). Group psychotherapy training and effectiveness. *International Journal of Group Psychotherapy, 51*(3), 399–416.

REFERENCES

Fukui, S., Kugaya, A., Okamura, H., Kamiya, M., Koike, M., Nakanishi, T., et al. (2000). A psychosocial group intervention for Japanese women with primary breast carcinoma. *Cancer, 89,* 1026–1036.

Gabbard, G. (1990). *Psychodynamic psychiatry in clinical practice.* Washington, DC: American Psychiatric Press.

Galanter, M., Castaneda, R., & Franco, H. (1991). Group therapy and self-help groups. In R. J. Frances & S. I. Miller (Eds.), *Clinical textbook of addictive disorders* (pp. 521–546). New York: Guilford Press.

Gans, J. S. (1992). Money and psychodynamic group psychotherapy. *International Journal of Group Psychotherapy, 42*(1), 133–152.

Garfield, S. L. (1986). Research on client variables in psychotherapy. In S. L. Garfield & A. E. Bergin (Eds.), *Handbook of psychotherapy and behavior change* (3rd ed., pp. 213–256). New York: Wiley.

Garland, J. A., Jones, H. E., & Kolodny, R. L. (1965). A model for stages of development in social work groups. In S. Bernstein (Ed.), *Explorations in group work* (pp. 17–71). Boston: Milford.

Garrison, J. (1978). Written vs. verbal preparation of patients for group psychotherapy. *Psychotherapy: Theory, Research and Practice, 15,* 130–134.

Gladfelter, J. (1992). Redecision therapy. *International Journal of Group Psychotherapy, 42,* 319–334.

Gladfelter, J. (2000). One-session group therapy with six clients (real) from the audience & brief therapy—Redecision model [Review of videos]. *International Journal of Group Psychotherapy, 50*(1), 130–132. (One-session group therapy with six clients (real) from the audience by Mary Goulding; Brief therapy—Redecision model)

Goodman, G., & Jacobs, M. K. (1994). The self-help, mutual support group. In A. Fuhriman & G. Burlingame (Eds.), *Handbook of group psychotherapy: An empirical and clinical synthesis* (pp. 489–526). New York: Wiley.

Goodman, M., & Weiss, D. (2000). Initiating, screening, and maintaining psychotherapy groups for traumatized patients. In R. H. Klein & V. L. Schermer (Eds.), *Group psychotherapy for psychological trauma* (pp. 47–63). New York: Guilford Press.

Gordon, A. J., & Zrull, M. (1991). Social networks and recovery: One year after inpatient treatment. *Journal of Substance Abuse Treatment, 8*(3), 143–152.

Gore-Felton, C., & Spiegel, D. (1999). Enhancing women's lives: The role of support groups among breast cancer patients. *Journal for Specialists in Group Work, 24*(3), 274–287.

Gotlib, I. H., & Schraedley, P. K. (2000). Interpersonal psychotherapy. In C. R. Snyder and R. E. Ingram (Eds.), *Handbook of psychological change: Psychotherapy processes & practices for the 21st century* (pp. 258–279). New York: Wiley.

Goulding, M., & Goulding, R. (1979). *Changing lives through redecision therapy.* New York: Branner/Magel.

Gradman, T. (1985). *Leader and member perception of communication problems in self-help groups.* Unpublished manuscript, University of California–Los Angeles.

Gray, J. J., & Hoage, C. M. (1990). Bulimia Nervosa: Group behavior therapy with exposure plus response prevention. *Psychological Reports, 66*(2), 667–674.

Greer, S. (1995). Improving quality of life: Adjuvant psychological therapy for patients with cancer. *Supportive Care in Cancer, 3,* 248–251.

Gruber, B. L., Hersh, S. P., Hall, N. R., Walettszky, L. R., Kunz, J. F., Kverno, K. S., et al. (1993). Immunological responses of breast cancer patients to behavioral interventions. *Biofeedback Self Regulation, 18,* 1–22.

Hall, E. T. (1966). *The hidden dimension.* New York: Doubleday.

Hammond, W. R., & Yung, B. (1993). Minority student recruitment and retention practices among schools of professional psychology: A national survey and analysis. *Professional Psychology: Research & Practice, 24*(1), 3–12.

Hardy, J., & Lewis, C. (1992). Bridging the gap between long- and short-term group psychotherapy: A viable treatment model. *Group, 16*(1), 5–17.

Harrington, R., Whittaker, J., & Shoebridge, P. (1998). Psychological treatment of depression in children and adolescents. *British Journal of Psychiatry, 173,* 291–298.

Hartmann, A., Herzog, T., & Drinkmann, A. (1992). Psychotherapy of Bulimia Nervosa: What is effective? A meta-analysis. *Journal of Psychosomatic Research, 36*(2), 159–167.

Hawkins, D. (1993). Group psychotherapy with gay men and lesbians. In H. I. Kaplan & B. J. Saddock (Eds.), *Comprehensive group psychotherapy* (3rd ed., pp. 506–515). Baltimore: Williams & Wilkins.

Hays, P. A. (2001). *Addressing cultural complexities in practice: A framework for clinicians and counselors.* Washington, DC: American Psychological Association.

Heitler, J. B. (1973). Preparation of lower-class patients for expressive group therapy. *Journal of Consulting and Clinical Psychology, 41*(2), 251–260.

Henry, S., & Robinson, D. (1978). Understanding Alcoholics Anonymous. *Lancet, 1,* 372–375.

Herman, J. (1992). *Trauma and recovery.* New York: Basic Books.

Hersey, P., & Blanchard, K. (1977). *Management of organizational behavior: Utilizing human resources* (3rd ed.). Englewood Cliffs, NJ: Prentice Hall.

Hibbs, E. D. (2001). Evaluating empirically based psychotherapy research for children and adolescents. *European Child & Adolescent Psychiatry, 10*(1), 3–11.

Hill, W. F. (1977). Hill Interaction Matrix (HIM): The conceptual framework, derived rating scales, and an updated bibliography. *Small Group Behavior, 8,* 251–268.

Hirshfield, R. M. A., Klerman, G., Gough, H., Barrett, J., Korchin, S. J., & Chodoff, P. (1977). A measure of interpersonal dependency. *Journal of Personality Assessment, 46,* 610–618.

Hoag, M. J., & Burlingame, G. M. (1997a). Child and adolescent group psychotherapy: A narrative review of effectiveness and the case for meta-analysis. *Journal of Child and Adolescent Group Therapy, 7*(2), 51–68.

Hoag, M. J., & Burlingame, G. M. (1997b). Evaluating the effectiveness of child and adolescent group treatment: A meta-analytic review. *Journal of Clinical Child Psychology, 26*(3), 234–246.

Holder, H. D., Miller, W. R., & Rubonis, A. V. (1991). The cost effectiveness of treatment for alcoholism: A first approximation. *Journal for the Study of Alcoholism, 52,* 517–540.

Holmes, L. (2002). Women in groups and women's groups. *International Journal of Group Psychotherapy, 52,* 171–188.

Honey, K. L., Bennett, P., & Morgan, M. (2002). A brief psycho-educational group intervention for postnatal depression. *British Journal of Clinical Psychology, 41,* 405–409.

Hope, D. A., & Heimberg, R. G. (1993). Social phobia and social anxiety. In D. H. Barlow (Ed.), *Clinical handbook of psychological disorders* (2nd ed., pp. 99–136). New York: Guilford Press.

Hopper, E. (2001). I am I: AIM—The therapist as personification of Hopper's fourth basic assumption. *Group, 25*(3), 139–171.

Horne, A. M., Jolliff, D. L., & Roth, E. W. (1996). Men mentoring men in groups. In M. P. Andronico (Ed.), *Men in groups: Insights, interventions, and psychoeducational work* (pp. 97–112). Washington, DC: American Psychological Association.

Horowitz, L. M., Rosenberg, S. E., Baer, B. A., Ureno, G., & Villasenor, V. S. (1988). Inventory of interpersonal problems: Psychometric properties and clinical applications. *Journal of Consulting and Clinical Psychology, 56,* 885–892.

Horwitz, L. (1993). Group-centered models of group psychotherapy. In H. I. Kaplan & B. J. Sadock (Eds.), *Comprehensive group psychotherapy* (pp. 156–165). Baltimore: Williams & Wilkins.

Horwitz, L. (2000). Narcissistic leadership in psychotherapy groups. *International Journal of Group Psychotherapy, 50*(2), 219–235.

Howard, K. I., Moras, K., Brill, P. L., Martinovich, Z., & Lutz, W. (1996). Evaluation of psychotherapy: Efficacy, effectiveness, and patient progress. *American Psychologist, 51*(10), 1059–1064.

Humphreys, K., Winzelberg, A., & Klaw, E. (2000). Psychologists' ethical responsibilities in Internet-based groups: Issues, strategies, and a call for dialogue. *Professional Psychology: Research and Practice, 31*(5), 493–496.

Hynes, K., & Werbin, J. (1977). Group psychotherapy for Spanish-speaking women. *Psychiatric Annuals, 7*(12), 52–63.

Jacobs, A. (1974). The use of feedback in groups. In A. Jacobs & W. Spredlin (Eds.), *The group as agent of change* (pp. 408–445). New York: Behavioral Publications.

James, W. (1907). *Pragmatism: A new name for some old ways of thinking.* Oxford, England: Longmans.

Jones, D. E. (1981). Interpersonal cognitive problem-solving training—A skills approach with hospitalized psychiatric patients. *Dissertation Abstracts International, 42*(5), 2060.

Jongsma, A. E., & Peterson, L. M. (1999). *The complete adult psychotherapy planner* (2nd ed.). New York: Wiley.

Kadden, R. M., Cooney, N. L., Getter, H., & Litt, M. D. (1989). Matching alcoholics to coping skills or interactional therapies: Posttreatment results. *Journal of Consulting and Clinical Psychology, 57,* 698–704.

Kanas, N. (1986). Group therapy with schizophrenics: A review of controlled studies. *International Journal of Group Psychotherapy, 36,* 339–351.

Kaplan, H. I., & Sadock, B. J. (1993). Structured interactional group psychotherapy. In H. I. Kaplan & B. J. Sadock (Eds.), *Comprehensive group psychotherapy* (3rd ed., pp. 324–338). Baltimore: Williams & Wilkins.

Kapur, R., Miller, K., & Mitchell, G. (1988). Therapeutic factors within in-patient and out-patient psychotherapy groups: Implications for therapeutic techniques. *British Journal of Psychiatry, 152,* 229–233.

Kato, P. M., & Mann, T. (1999). A synthesis of psychological interventions for the bereaved. *Clinical Psychology Review, 19*(3), 275–296.

Kaufman, W. (1975). *Existentialism from Dostoevsky to Sartre.* New York: Penguin.

Kellermann, P. F. (1992). Processing in psychodrama. *Journal of Group Psychotherapy Psychodrama & Sociometry, 45*(2), 63–73.

Kellner, M. H., & Bry, B. H. (1999). The effects of anger management groups in a day school for emotionally disturbed adolescents. *Adolescence, 34,* 645–651.

Kelly, J. A. (1998). Group psychotherapy for persons with HIV and AIDS-related illnesses. *International Journal of Group Psychotherapy, 48*(2), 143–162.

Kessler, R. C., Mickelson, K. D., & Zhao, S. (1997). Patterns and correlates of self-help group membership in the United States. *Social Policy, 27,* 27–46.

Kibel, H. D. (1987). Contributions of the group psychotherapist to education on the psychiatric unit: Teaching through group dynamics. *International Journal of Group Psychotherapy, 37*(1), 3–29.

Kibel, H. D. (1993). Inpatient group psychotherapy. In A. Alonso & H. I. Swiller (Eds.), *Group therapy in clinical practice* (pp. 93–111). Washington, DC: American Psychiatric Press.

Kililea, M. (1976). Mutual help organizations: Interpretations in the literature. In G. Caplan & M. Killilea (Eds.), *Support systems and mutual help.* New York: Grune & Stratton.

Kilmann, P. R., Laughlin, J. E., Carranza, L. V., Downer, J. T., Major, S., & Parnell, M. M. (1999). Effects of an attachment-focused group preventive intervention on insecure women. *Group Dynamics: Theory, Research, and Practice, 3*(2), 138–147.

Kinzie, J. D., Leung, P., Bui, A., Ben, R., Keopraseuth, K. O., Riley, C., et al. (1988). Group therapy with Southeast Asian refugees. *Community Mental Health Journal, 24*(2), 157–166.

Kipnes, D. R., Piper, W. E., & Joyce, A. S. (2002). Cohesion and outcome in short-term psychodynamic groups for complicated grief. *International Journal of Group Psychotherapy, 52*(4), 483–509.

Kipper, D. A. (1992). Psychodrama: Group psychotherapy through role playing. *International Journal of Group Psychotherapy, 42*(4), 495–521.

Kipper, D. A. (1998). [Review of the book *Acting-In: Practical applications of psychodramatic methods*]. *International Journal of Group Psychotherapy, 48*(1), 129–131.

Kipper, D. A., & Matsumoto, M. (2002). From classical to eclectic psychodrama: Conceptual similarities between psychodrama and psychodynamic and interpersonal group treatments. *International Journal of Group Psychotherapy, 52*(1), 111–120.

Kipper, D. A., & Ritchie, T. D. (2003). The effectiveness of psychodramatic techniques: A meta-analysis. *Group Dynamics: Theory, Research, and Practice, 7*(1), 13–25.

Kivlighan, D. M. (1997). Leader behavior and therapeutic gain: An application of situational leadership theory. *Group Dynamics: Theory, Research, and Practice, 1*(1), 32–38.

Kivlighan, D. M., & Lilly, R. L. (1997). Developmental changes in group climate as they relate to therapeutic gain. *Group Dynamics: Theory, Research, and Practice, 1*(3), 208–221.

Kivlighan, D. M., McGovern, T. V., & Corazzini, J. G. (1995). Effects of content and timing of structuring interventions on group therapy process and outcome. *Journal of Counseling Psychology, 31*(3), 363–370.

Kivlighan, D. M., & Mullison, D. (1988). Participants' perception of therapeutic factors in group counseling: The role of interpersonal style and stage of group development. *Small Group Behavior, 19,* 452–468.

Klass, D. (1984–1985). Bereaved parents and the compassionate friends: Affiliation and healing. *Omega—Journal of Death and Dying, 15,* 353–373.

Klein, R. H. (1993). Short-term group psychotherapy. In H. I. Kaplan & B. J. Sadock (Eds.), *Comprehensive group psychotherapy* (3rd ed., pp. 256–269). Baltimore: Williams & Wilkins.

Klein, R. H., & Carroll, R. A. (1986). Patient characteristics and attendance patterns in outpatient group psychotherapy. *International Journal of Group Psychotherapy, 36,* 115–132.

Krausz, S. L. (1980). Group psychotherapy with legally blind patients. *Clinical Social Work Journal, 8*(1), 37–49.

Kush, F. R., & Fleming, L. M. (2000). An innovative approach to short-term group cognitive therapy in the combined treatment of anxiety and depression. *Group Dynamics, 4*(2), 176–183.

Lakin, M. (1994). Morality in group and family therapies: Multiperson therapies and the 1992 ethics code. *Professional Psychology: Research and Practice, 25*(4), 344–348.

Lambert, M. J., & Hill, C. E. (1994). Assessing psychotherapy outcomes and processes. In A. E. Bergin & S. L. Garfield (Eds.), *Handbook of psychotherapy and behavior change* (4th ed., pp. 72–113). New York: Wiley.

Lederberg, M. S. (1998). Staff support groups for high-stress medical environments. *International Journal of Group Psychotherapy, 48*(2), 275–304.

Leichtentritt, J., & Schechtman, Z. (1998). Therapist, trainee, and child verbal response modes in child group therapy. *Group Dynamics: Theory, Research, and Practice, 2,* 36–47.

Lenihan, G. O. (1985). The therapeutic gay support group: A call for professional involvement. *Psychotherapy, 22,* 729–739.

Lennox, C. L. (1997). Introduction: Redecision therapy, a brief therapy model. In C. E. Lennox (Ed.), *Redecision therapy: A brief, action-oriented approach* (pp. 1–14). Northvale, NJ: Jason Aronson.

Leon, A. M., & Dziegielewski, S. F. (2000). Engaging Hispanic immigrant mothers: Revisiting the time-limited psycho-educational group model. *Crisis Intervention & Time-Limited Treatment, 6*(1), 13–27.

Leszcz, M. (1990). Towards an integrated model of group psychotherapy with the elderly. *International Journal of Group Psychotherapy, 40*(4), 379–399.

Leszcz, M. (1992). The interpersonal approach to group psychotherapy. *International Journal of Group Psychotherapy, 42*(1), 37–62.

Leszcz, M. (1998). Introduction to special issue on group psychotherapy for the medically ill. *International Journal of Group Psychotherapy, 48*(2), 137–141.

Leszcz, M., & Goodwin, P. J. (1998). The rationale and foundations of group psychotherapy for women with metastatic breast cancer. *International Journal of Group Psychotherapy, 48*(2), 245–273.

Leventhal, H., Meyer, D., & Nerenz, D. (1980). The common sense representation of illness danger. In S. Rachman (Ed.), *Contributions to medical psychology* (pp. 7–30). New York: Pergamon Press.

Levy, L. H. (1988). *Self-help groups.* Unpublished manuscript.

Lieberman, M. A. (1983). Comparative analyses of change mechanisms in groups. In H. H. Blumberg, V. Kent, & M. Davies (Eds.), *Small groups in social interaction* (pp. 239–252). London: Wiley.

Lieberman, M. A. (1985). Comparative analysis of change mechanisms in groups. In R. R. Dies & K. R. MacKenzie (Eds.), *Advances in group psychotherapy: Integrating research and practice* (pp. 159–170). Madison, CT: International Universities Press.

Lieberman, M. A. (1989). Group properties and outcomes: A study of group norms in self-help groups for widows and widowers. *International Journal of Group Psychotherapy, 39*(2), 191–208.

Lieberman, M. A. (1990a). A group therapist perspective on self-help groups. *International Journal of Group Psychotherapy, 40,* 251–278.

Lieberman, M. A. (1990b). Understanding how groups work: A study of homogeneous peer group failures. *International Journal of Group Psychotherapy, 40*(1), 31–52.

Lieberman, M. A. (1993a). A reexamination of adult life crises: Spousal loss in mid- and late life. In G. H. Pollock & S. I. Greenspan (Eds.), *The course of life* (pp. 69–110). Madison, CT: International Universities Press.

Lieberman, M. A. (1993b). Self-help groups. In H. I. Kaplan & B. J. Sadock (Eds.), *Comprehensive group psychotherapy* (3rd ed., pp. 292–309). Baltimore: Williams & Wilkins.

Lieberman, M. A., & Bliwise, N. G. (1985). Comparisons among peer and professionally directed groups for the elderly: Implications for the development of self-help groups. *International Journal of Group Psychotherapy, 35*(2), 155–175.

Lieberman, M. A., & Snowden, L. R. (1993). Problems in assessing prevalence and membership characteristics of self-help group participants. *Journal of Applied Behavioral Science, 29,* 166–180.

Lieberman, M. A., & Videka-Sherman, P. R. (1986). The perils of borrowing: Role of the professional in musical help groups. *Journal for Specialists in Group Work, 11,* 68–73.

Lieberman, M. A., Yalom, I. D., & Miles, M. B. (1973). *Encounter groups: First facts.* New York: Basic Books.

Linehan, M., & Wagner, A. (1990). Dialectical behavior therapy: A feminist-behavioral treatment of borderline personality disorder. *Behavior Therapist,* 9–14.

Litt, M. D., Babor, T. F., DelBoca, F. K., Kadden, R. M., & Cooney, N. I. (1992). Types of alcoholics: Application of an empirically derived typology to treatment matching. *Archives of General Psychiatry, 49,* 609–614.

Lomonaco, S., Scheidlinger, S., & Aronson, S. (2000). Five decades of children's group treatment: An overview. *Journal of Child and Adolescent Group Therapy, 10*(2), 77–96.

Lonergan, E. C. (1982). *Group intervention: how to begin and maintain groups in medical and psychiatric settings*. New York: Aronson.

Lonergan, E. C. (1994). Using theories of group therapy. In H. S. Bernard & K. R. MacKenzie (Eds.), *Basics of group psychotherapy*. New York: Guilford Press.

Luborsky, L., Singer, B., & Luborsky (1975). Comparative studies of psychotherapy. *Archives of General Psychiatry, 32*, 995–1008.

Luepker, E. T. (2003). *Record keeping in psychotherapy and counseling: Protecting confidentiality & the professional relationship*. New York: Brunner-Routledge.

MacKenzie, K. R. (1983). The clinical application of the group climate measure. In R. R. Dies & K. R. MacKenzie (Eds.), *Advances in group psychotherapy: Integrating research and practice* (pp. 159–170). Madison, CT: International Universities Press.

MacKenzie, K. R. (1990). *Introduction to time-limited group psychotherapy*. Washington, DC: American Psychiatric Press.

MacKenzie, K. R. (1994). Where is here and when is now? The adaptational challenge of mental health reform for group psychotherapy. *International Journal of Group Psychotherapy, 44*(4), 407–428.

MacKenzie, K. R. (1995). *Effective use of group therapy in managed care*. Washington, DC: American Psychiatric Press.

MacKenzie, K. R. (1997). Clinical application of group development ideas. *Group Dynamics: Theory, Research, and Practice, 1*(4), 275–287.

MacKenzie, K. R., & Dies, R. R. (1982). *CORE battery clinical outcome results*. New York: American Group Psychotherapy Association.

MacKenzie, K. R., Dies, R. R., Coché, E., Rutan, J. S., & Stone, W. N. (1987). An analysis of AGPA Institute groups. *International Journal of Group Psychotherapy, 37,* 55–74.

MacNair-Semands, R. R. (2002). Predicting attendance and expectations for group therapy. *Group Dynamics, 6*(3), 219–228.

Maoz, I., & Bar-On, D. (2002). From working through the holocaust to current ethnic conflicts: Evaluating the TRT group workshop in Hamburg. *Group, 26*(1), 29–48.

Marcus, M., & Bernard, H. (2000). Group psychotherapy for psychological traumata of prolonged, severe, and/or terminal illness. In R. H. Klein & V. L. Schermer (Eds.), *Group psychotherapy for psychological trauma* (pp. 188–208). New York: Guilford Press.

Marcus, H. E., & King, D. A. (2003). A survey of group psychotherapy training during predoctoral psychology internship. *Professional Psychology: Research and practice, 34*(2), 203–209.

Marotta, S. A., & Asner, K. K. (1999). Group psychotherapy for women with a history of incest: The research base. *Journal of Counseling and Development, 77*(3), 315–323.

Marshall, J. E., & Heslin, R. (1975). Boys and girls together: Sexual composition and the effect of density and group size on cohesiveness. *Journal of Personality and Social Psychology, 31*(5), 952–961.

Maruish, M. E. (2002). *Essentials of treatment planning*. New York: Wiley.

Marziali, E., Munroe-Blum, H., & McCleary, L. (1997). The contribution of group cohesion and group alliance to the outcome of group psychotherapy. *International Journal of Group Psychotherapy, 47*(4), 475–497.

Masterson, J. (1983). Lesbian consciousness-raising discussion groups. *Journal for Specialists in Group Work, 8,* 24–30.

Maton, K. I. (1988). Social support, organizational characteristics, psychological well-being, and group appraisal in three self-help group populations. *American Journal of Community Psychology, 16,* 53–77.

McDermut, W., Miller, I. W., & Brown, R. A. (2001). The efficacy of group psychotherapy for depression: A meta-analysis and review of the empirical research. *Clinical Psychology: Science and Practice, 8,* 98–116.

McDonald, T. (1975). Group psychotherapy with Native-American women. *International Journal of Group Psychotherapy, 25*(4), 410–420.

McDougall, W. (1923). *Outline of psychology.* New York: Scribner.

McLean, P. D., Whittal, M. L., Thordarson, D. S., Taylor, S., Sochting, I., Koch, W. J., et al. (2001). Cognitive versus behavior therapy in the group treatment of Obsessive-Compulsive Disorder. *Journal of Consulting and Clinical Psychology, 69*(2), 205–214.

McNary, S. W., & Dies, R. R. (1993). Cotherapist modeling in group psychotherapy: Fact or fantasy? *Group, 17*(3), 131–142.

McPhee, D. M. (1996). Techniques in group psychotherapy with men. In M. P. Andronico (Ed.), *Men in groups: Insights, interventions, and psychoeducational work* (pp. 21–34). Washington, DC: American Psychological Association.

McRoberts, C., Burlingame, G. M., & Hoag, M. J. (1998). Comparative efficacy of individual and group psychotherapy: A meta-analytic perspective. *Group Dynamics: Theory, Research, and Practice, 2*(2), 101–117.

Mendlowitz, S. L., Manassis, K., & Bradley, S. (1999). Cognitive-behavioral group treatments in childhood anxiety disorders: The role of parental involvement. *Journal of the American Academy of Child and Adolescent Psychiatry, 38*(10), 1223–1229.

Miller, R., & Berman, J. (1983). The efficacy of cognitive behavioral therapies: A quantitative review of research evidence. *Psychological Bulletin, 94,* 39–53.

Miller, W. R., & Hester, R. K. (1986). Inpatient treatment for alcoholism: Who benefits? *American Psychology, 41,* 794–805.

Mojtabai, R., Nicholson, R. A., & Carpenter, B. N. (1998). The role of psychosocial treatments in management of schizophrenia: A meta-analytic review of controlled outcome studies. *Schizophrenia Bulletin, 24,* 569–587.

Montero, P., & Colman, A. D. (2000). Collective consciousness and the psychology of human interconnectedness. *Group, 24*(2–3), 203–219.

Moreno, J. L. (1940). Mental catharsis and psychodrama. *Sociometry, 3,* 209–244.

Moreno, J. L. (1959). The scientific meaning and the global significance of group psychotherapy. *Acta Psycotherapeutica, 42*(7), 148–167.

Moreno, J. L. (1992). Psychodrama. In K. R. MacKenzie (Ed.), *Classics in group psychotherapy* (pp. 47–60). New York: Guilford Press.

Moreno, J. K. (1994). Group treatment for eating disorders. In A. Fuhriman & G. M. Burlingame (Eds.), *Handbook of group psychotherapy: An empirical and clinical synthesis* (pp. 416–457). New York: Wiley.

Morey, L. C. (1991). *The Personality Assessment Inventory professional manual.* Odessa, FL: Psychological Assessment Resources.

Morey, L. C. (1999). Personality assessment inventory. In M. E. Maruish (Ed.), *The use of psychological testing for treatment planning and outcomes assessment* (2nd ed., pp. 1083–1121). Mahwah, NJ: Erlbaum.

Morgan, R. D., & Flora, D. B. (2002). Group psychotherapy with incarcerated offenders: A research synthesis. *Group Dynamics: Theory, Research, and Practice, 6*(3), 203–218.

Morran, D. K., Robison, F. F., & Stockton, R. (1985). Feedback exchange in counseling groups: An analysis of message content and receiver acceptance as a function of leader versus member delivery, session and valence. *Journal of Counseling Psychology, 32,* 57–67.

Motherwell, L. (2002). Women, money, and psychodynamic group psychotherapy. *International Journal of Group Psychotherapy, 52*(1), 49–66.

Mullan, H. (1992). Existential therapists and their group therapy practices. *International Journal of Group Psychotherapy, 42,* 452–468.

Muller, E., & Scott, T. (1984). A comparison of film and written presentations used for pre-group training experiences. *Journal for Specialists in Group Work, 9,* 122–126.

Myers, D. G. (2000). The funds, friends, and faith of happy people. *American Psychologist, 55*(1), 57–67.

Nakkab, S., & Hernandez, M. (1998). Group psychotherapy in the context of cultural diversity. *Group, 22*(2), 95–103.

Nichelson, D. W. (1998). Telehealth and the evolving health care system: Strategic opportunities for professional psychology. *Professional Psychologist: Research and Practice, 29*(6), 527–533.

Nicholas, M., & Forrester, A. (1999). Advantages of heterogeneous therapy groups in the psychotherapy of the traumatically abused: Treating the problem as well as the person. *International Journal of Group Psychotherapy, 49*(3), 323–342.

Nietzel, M. T., Kelly, R., Hemmings, A., & Gretter, M. L. (1987). Clinical significance of psychotherapy for unipolar depression: A meta-analytic approach to social comparison. *Journal of Consulting and Clinical Psychology, 55*(2), 156–161.

Nitsun, M. (2000). The future of the group. *International Journal of Group Psychotherapy, 50*(4), 455–472.

Nuttman-Schwartz, O., & Shay, S. (2000). Large group interventions to encourage dialogue between directors and workers in the context of organizational ambiguity. *Group, 24*(4), 279–288.

Ogborne, A. C., & Glaser, F. B. (1981). Characteristics of affiliates of Alcoholics Anonymous. *Journal of Studies on Alcohol, 42*(7), 661–675.

Ogrodniczuk, J. S., & Piper, W. E. (2003). The effect of group climate on outcome in two forms of short-term group therapy. *Group Dynamics, 7*(1), 64–76.

Ogrodniczuk, J. S., Piper, W. E., Joyce, A. S., McCallum, M., & Rosie, J. S. (2003). NEO-Five factor personality traits as predictors of response to two forms of group psychotherapy. *International Journal of Group Psychotherapy, 53*(4), 417–442.

O'Hearne, J. J. (1993). Transactional analysis in groups. In H. I. Kaplan & B. J. Sadocks (Eds.), *Comprehensive group psychotherapy* (4th ed., pp. 195–205). Baltimore: Williams & Wilkins.

Ormont, L. (1991). Use of the group in resolving the subjective countertransference. *International Journal of Group Psychotherapy, 41*(4), 433–447.

Palmer, K. D., Baker, R. C., & McGee, T. F. (1997). The effects of pretraining on group psychotherapy for incest-related issues. *International Journal of Group Psychotherapy, 47*(1), 71–89.

Pattison, E. M. (1984). Chronic lung disease. In H. Roback (Ed.), *Helping patients and their families cope with medical problems* (pp. 190–215). San Francisco: Jossey-Bass.

Patterson, J. B., McKenzie, B., & Jenkins, J. (1995). Creating accessible groups for individuals with disabilities. *Journal for Specialists in Group Work, 20*(2), 76–82.

Perls, F. (1969). *Gestalt therapy with children.* Lafayette, CA: Real People Press.

Peterson, R. L., Peterson, D. R., Abrams, J. C., & Stricker, G. (1997). The National Council of Schools and programs of professional psychology education model. *Professional Psychology: Research and Practice, 28*(4), 373–386.

Pine, F. (1990). *Drive, ego, object, & self: A synthesis for clinical work.* New York: Basic Books.

Pine, C. J., & Jacobs, A. (1991). The acceptability of behavioral and emotional feedback depending upon valence and structure in personal growth groups. *Journal of Clinical Psychology, 47*(1), 115–122.

Pinquart, M., & Sorenson, S. (2001). How effective are psychotherapeutic and other psychosocial interventions with older adults? A meta-analysis. *Journal of Mental Health and Aging, 7*(2), 207–243.

Piper, W. E. (1993). Group psychotherapy research. In H. I. Kaplan & B. J. Sadock (Eds.), *Comprehensive group psychotherapy* (3rd ed.). Baltimore: Williams & Wilkins.

Piper, W. E. (1994). Client variables. In A. Fuhriman & G. M. Burlingame (Eds.), *Handbook of group psychotherapy: An empirical and clinical synthesis* (pp. 83–113). New York: Wiley.

Piper, W. E. (1995). Brief intensive group psychotherapy for loss. In K. R. MacKenzie (Ed.), *Effective use of group therapy in managed care* (pp. 43–59). Washington, DC: American Psychiatric Press.

Piper, W. E., Debbane, E., Bienvenu, J., & Garant, J. (1982). A study of group pretraining for group psychotherapy. *International Journal of Group Psychotherapy, 32,* 309–325.

Piper, W. E., Debbane, E., Garant, J., & Bienvenu, J. (1979). Pretraining for group psychotherapy. *Archives of General Psychiatry, 36,* 1250–1256.

Piper, W. E., & Joyce, A. S. (1996). A consideration of factors influencing the utilization of time-limited, short-term group therapy. *International Journal of Group Psychotherapy, 46*(3), 505–512.

Piper, W. E., & McCallum, M. (1994). Selection of patients for group interventions. In H. S. Bernard & K. R. MacKenzie (Eds.), *Basics of group psychotherapy* (pp. 1–34). New York: Guilford Press.

Piper, W. E., McCallum, M., & Azim, H. F. A. (1992). *Adaptation to loss through short-term group psychotherapy.* New York: Guilford Press.

Piper, W. E., McCallum, M., Joyce, S. C., Duncan, J., Bahrey, F., & members of the short-term group psychotherapy seminar. (1992). *Helping people adapt to loss: A short-term group therapy approach* [film]. New York: Guilford Press.

Piper, W. E., McCallum, M., Joyce, A. S., Rosie, J. S., & Ogrodniczuk, J. S. (2001). Patient personality and time-limited group psychotherapy for complicated grief. *International Journal of Group Psychotherapy, 51*(4), 525–552.

Piper, W. E., & Perrault, E. L. (1989). Pretherapy preparation for group members. *International Journal of Group Psychotherapy, 39*(1), 17–34.

Plante, T. G., Pinder, S. L., & Howe, D. (1988). Introducing the Living with Illness Group: A specialized treatment for patients with chronic schizophrenic conditions. *Group, 12*(4), 198–204.

Pollack, H. B., & Slan, J. B. (1995). Reflections and suggestions on leadership of psychotherapy groups. *International Journal of Group Psychotherapy, 45*(4), 507–519.

Porter, K. (1993). Combined individual and group psychotherapy. In A. Alonso & H. I. Swiller (Eds.), *Group therapy in clinical practice* (pp. 309–341). Washington, DC: American Psychiatric Press.

Powell, T. J. (1987). *Self help organizations and professional practice.* Silver Spring, MD: National Association of Social Workers.

Price, J. R., Hescheles, D. R., & Price, A. R. (1999). *A guide to starting psychotherapy groups.* New York: Academic Press.

Prout, H. T., & DeMartino, R. A. (1986). A meta-analysis of school-based studies of psychotherapy. *Journal of School Psychology, 24,* 285–292.

Prout, S. M., & Prout, T. H. (1998). A meta-analysis of school-based studies of counseling and psychology: An update. *Journal of School Psychology, 36*(2), 121–136.

Rachman, A. W. (1990). Judicious self-disclosure in group analysis. *Group, 14*(3), 132–144.

Racker, H. (1972). The meanings and uses of countertransference. *Psychoanalytic Quarterly, 41,* 487–506.

Radomile, R. R. (2000). Obesity. In J. R. White & A. S. Freeman (Eds.), *Cognitive-behavioral group therapy for specific problems and populations* (pp. 99–125). Washington, DC: American Psychological Association.

Reid, F. T., & Reid, D. E. (1993). Integration and nonintegration of innovative group methods. In H. I. Kaplan & B. J. Saddock (Eds.), *Comprehensive group psychotherapy* (pp. 244–255). Baltimore: Williams & Wilkins.

Rice, A. K. (1969). Individual, group and intergroup processes. *Human Relations, 22,* 565–584.

Rice, C. A. (1995). The junior-junior team. *Group, 19*(2), 87–99.

Rice, C. A., & Kapur, R. (2002). The impact of the "Troubles" on therapy groups in Northern Ireland. *Group, 26,* 247–264.

Rice, C., & Rutan, S. (1981). Boundary maintenance in inpatient therapy groups. *International Journal of Group Psychotherapy, 31*(3), 297–309.

Riessman, F. (1990). Restructuring help: A human services paradigm for the 1990s (An invited address to Division 27 of the American Psychological Association). *American Journal of Community Psychology, 18,* 221–230.

Rioch, M., Elkes, D., & Flint, A. (1963). *A pilot project in training mental health counselors.* Washington, DC: U.S. Government Printing Office, no. 1254.

Riva, M. T., Lippert, L., & Tackett, M. J. (2000). Selection practices of group leaders: A national survey. *Journal for Specialists in Group Work, 25*(2), 157–169.

Roback, H. B., Ochoa, E., Block, F., & Purdon, S. (1992). Guarding confidentiality in clinical groups: The therapist's dilemma. *International Journal of Group Psychotherapy, 42,* 81–103.

Roback, H. B., Moore, R. F., Waterhouse, G. J., & Martin, P. R. (1996). Confidentiality dilemmas in group psychotherapy with substance-dependent physicians. *American Journal of Psychiatry, 153*(10), 1250–1260.

Roback, H. R. (2000). Adverse outcomes in group psychotherapy: Risk factors, prevention, and research directions. *Journal of Psychotherapy, Practice and Research, 9*(3), 113–122.

Roback, H. R., Moore, R. F., Bloch, F. S., & Shelton, M. (1996). Confidentiality in group psychotherapy: Empirical findings and the law. *International Journal of Group Psychotherapy, 46*(1), 117–135.

Robinson, L. A., Berman, J. S., & Neimeyer, R. A. (1990). Psychotherapy for the treatment of depression: A comprehensive review of controlled outcome research. *Psychological Bulletin, 108*(1), 30–49.

Rogers, C. R. (1957). The necessary and sufficient conditions of therapeutic personality change. *Journal of Consulting Psychology, 21,* 95–103.

Roller, B. (1997). *The promise of group therapy: How to build a vigorous training and organizational base for group therapy in managed behavioral healthcare.* San Francisco: Jossey-Bass.

Roller, B., & Nelson, V. (1993). Cotherapy. In H. I. Kaplan & B. J. Sadock (Eds.), *Comprehensive group psychotherapy* (3rd ed., pp. 304–312). Baltimore: Williams & Wilkins.

Rollock, D. A., Westman, J. S., & Johnson, C. (1992). A black student support group on a predominantly white university campus: Issues for counselors and therapists. *Journal for Specialists in Group Work, 17*(4), 243–252.

Rose, S. (1990). Putting the group into cognitive-behavioral treatment. *Social Work with Groups, 13,* 71–83.

Rose, S. D. (1993). Cognitive-behavioral group psychotherapy. In H. I. Kaplan & B. J. Sadock (Eds.), *Comprehensive group psychotherapy* (3rd ed., pp. 205–214). Baltimore: Williams & Wilkins.

Rosenbaum, M. (1993). Existential-humanistic approach to group psychotherapy. In H. I. Kaplan & B. J. Sadock (Eds.), *Comprehensive group psychotherapy* (3rd ed., pp. 235–243). Baltimore: Williams & Wilkins.

Rosenthal, L. (1992). The new member: "Infanticide" in group psychotherapy. *International Journal of Group Psychotherapy, 42*(2), 277–286.

Roth, B. (2002). Some diagnostic observations of post-September 11, 2001 crisis groups. *Group, 26*(2), 155–161.

Rouchy, J. C. (2002). Cultural identity and groups of belonging. *Group, 26*(3), 205–217.

Russo, N. F. (1990). Overview: Forging research priorities for women's mental health. *American Psychologist, 45*(3), 368–373.

Rutan, J. S. (1993). Psychoanalytic group psychotherapy. In H. I. Kaplan & B. J. Sadock (Eds.), *Comprehensive group psychotherapy* (3rd ed., pp. 138–146). Baltimore: Williams & Wilkins.

Rutan, J. S., & Stone, W. (2001). *Psychodynamic group psychotherapy* (3rd ed.). New York: Guilford Press.

Sacks, J. M. (1993). Psychodrama. In H. E. Kaplan & B. J. Sadock (Eds.), *Comprehensive group psychotherapy* (3rd ed., pp. 214–235). Baltimore: Williams & Wilkins.

Salmon, G., & Abell, S. (1996). Group therapy for adults with learning disability: Use of active techniques. *Psychiatric Bulletin, 20*(4), 221–223.

Salvendy, J. T. (1993). Selection and preparation of patients and organization of the group. In H. I. Kaplan & B. J. Sadock (Eds.). *Comprehensive group psychotherapy* (3rd ed., pp. 72–84). Baltimore: Williams & Wilkins.

Samide, L. L., & Stockton, R. (2002). Letting go of grief: Bereavement groups for children in the school setting. *Journal for Specialists in Group Work, 27*(2), 192–204.

Santarsiero, L. J., Baker, R. C., & McGee, T. F. (1995). The effects of cognitive pretraining on cohesion and self-disclosure in small groups: An analog study. *Journal of Clinical Psychology, 51*(3), 403–409.

Sarnoff, I., & Zimbardo, P. G. (1961). Anxiety, fear, and social facilitation. *Journal of Abnormal and Social Psychology, 62,* 597–605.

Schamess, G. (1993). Group psychotherapy with children. In H. I. Kaplan & B. J. Sadock (Eds.), *Comprehensive group psychotherapy* (3rd ed., pp. 560–577). Baltimore: Williams & Wilkins.

Scheidlinger, S. (1985). Group treatment of adolescents: An overview. *American Journal of Orthopsychiatrists, 55*(1), 102–111.

Scheidlinger, S. (1993). History of group psychotherapy. In H. I. Kaplan & B. J. Sadock (Eds.), *Comprehensive group psychotherapy* (3rd ed., pp. 2–10). Baltimore: Williams & Wilkins.

Scheidlinger, S. (1994). An overview of nine decades of group psychotherapy. *Hospital and Community Psychiatry, 45*(3), 217–225.

Scheidlinger, S. (2003). Freud's group psychology revisited: An opportunity missed. *Psychoanalytic Psychology, 20*(2), 389–392.

Schoenholtz-Read, J. (1996). Sex-role issues: Mixed-gender therapy groups as treatments of choice. In B. DeChant (Ed.), *Women and group psychotherapy: Theory and practice* (pp. 223–241). New York: Guilford Press.

Schouten, R. (2003). Legal Ease: HIPAA displeasure. *Curbside Consultant, 2*(5), 3.

Schroeder, D. J., Bowen, W. T., & Twemlow, S. W. (1982). Factors related to patient attrition from alcoholism treatment programs. *International Journal of the Addictions, 17*(3), 463–472.

Schwartz, R. D., & Hartstein, N. B. (1986). Group psychotherapy with gay men: Theoretical and clinical considerations. In T. S. Stein & C. J. Cohen (Eds.), *Contemporary perspectives on psychotherapy with lesbians and gay men* (pp. 159–177). New York: Plenum.

Searls, H. F. (1962). *Collected papers on Schizophrenia and related subjects.* New York: International Universities Press.

Seligman, M., & Marshak, L. E. (Eds.). (1990). *Group psychotherapy: Interventions with specific populations.* Newton, MA: Allyn & Bacon.

Shaffer, J. B., & Galinsky, M. D. (1974). *Models of group therapy and sensitivity training.* Englewood Cliffs, NJ: Prentice Hall.

Shapiro, D. A., & Shapiro, D. (1982). Meta-analysis of comparative therapy outcome studies: A replication and refinement. *Psychological Bulletin, 92*(3), 581–604.

Shapiro, E. W., & Ginzberg, R. (2001). The persistently neglected sibling relationship and its applicability to group therapy. *International Journal of Group Psychotherapy, 51*(3), 327–341.

Shapiro, E. W., & Ginzberg, R. (2002). Parting gifts: Termination rituals in group therapy. *International Journal of Group Psychotherapy, 52*(3), 319–336.

Sherman, A. C., Mosier, J., Leszcz, M., Burlingame, G. M., Ulman, K. H., Cleary, T., Simonton, S., Latif, U., Hazelton, L., & Strauss, B. (2004). Group interventions for patients with cancer and HIV disease: Part I. Effects on psychosocial and functional outcomes at different phases of illness. *International Journal of Group Psychotherapy, 54*(1), 29–82.

Siegman, A. W., & Snow, S. C. (1997). The outward expression of anger, the inward experience of anger and CVR: The role of vocal expression. *Journal of Behavioral Medicine, 20,* 29–45.

Simoni, J. M., & Perez, L. (1995). Latinos and mutual support groups: A case for considering culture. *American Journal of Orthopsychiatry, 65*(3), 440–445.

Skolnick, M. R. (1992). The role of the therapist from a social systems perspective. In R. H. Klein, H. S. Bernard, & D. L. Singer (Eds.), *Handbook of contemporary group psychotherapy* (pp. 321–369). Madison, CT: International Universities Press.

Sledge, W. H., Moras, K., Hartley, D., & Levine, M. (1990). Effect of time-limited psychotherapy on patient dropout rates. *American Journal of Psychiatry, 147*(10), 1341–1347.

Slovenko, R. (1998). *Psychotherapy & confidentiality: Testimonial, privileged communication, breach of confidentiality, and reporting duties.* Springfield, IL: Charles C. Thomas.

Smith, M., Glass, G., & Miller, T. (1980). *The benefits of psychotherapy.* Baltimore: Johns Hopkins University Press.

Snyder, D. R., Cheavens, J., & Sympson, S. C. (1997). Hope: An individual motive for social commerce. *Group Dynamics, 1*(2), 107–119.

Snyder, K. V., Kymissis, P., & Kessler, K. (1999). Anger management for adolescents: Efficacy of brief group therapy. *Journal of the American Academy of Child and Adolescent Psychiatry, 38,* 1409–1416.

Spector, A., Davies, S., Woods, B., & Orrell, M. (2000). Reality orientation for dementia: A systematic review of the evidence of effectiveness from randomized controlled trials. *The Gerontologist, 40*(2), 206–212.

Spiegel, D., Bloom, J. R., Kraemer, H. C., & Gottheil, E. (1989). Effect of psychosocial treatment on survival of patients with metastatic breast cancer. *Lancet, 2,* 888–891.

Spiegel, D., Bloom, J. R., & Yalom, I. (1981). Group support for patients with metastatic cancer. *Archives of General Psychiatry, 38,* 527–533.

Spira, J. L. (1997a). Existential group therapy for advanced breast cancer and other life-threatening illnesses. In J. L. Spira (Ed.), *Group therapy for medically ill patients* (pp. 165–222). New York: Guilford Press.

Spira, J. L. (1997b). Understanding and developing psychotherapy groups for medically ill patients. In J. L. Spira (Ed.), *Group therapy for medically ill patients* (pp. 3–51). New York: Guilford Press.

Spitz, H. I. (1997). Brief group therapy. In S. Sauber (Ed.), *Managed mental health care: Major diagnostic and treatment approaches* (pp. 103–132). Philadelphia: Brunner/Mazel.

Spitz, H. I. (2001). Group psychotherapy of substance abuse in the era of managed mental health care. *International Journal of Group Psychotherapy, 51*(1), 21–41.

Stamatogianni, D. M. (2003). Prevention of alcohol abuse on college campuses: A systemic view. Doctoral Dissertation. Chester, PA: Widener University.

State v. Andring Supreme Court of Minnesota. 342 N. W. 2d 128.

Sue, D. W., & Sue, D. (1999). *Counseling the culturally different: Theory and Practice.* New York: Wiley.

Sullivan, H. S. (1953). *Conceptions of modern psychiatry: The first William Alanson White memorial lectures* (2nd ed.). New York: W. W. Norton.

Swillel, S. I. (1996). Review of *Helping people adapt to loss: A short-term group therapy approach. International Journal of Group Psychotherapy, 46*(4), 563–564.

Taylor, R. E., & Gazda, G. M. (1991). Concurrent individual and group therapy: The ethical issues. *Journal of Group Psychotherapy Psychodrama & Sociometry, 44*(2), 51–59.

Tillitski, C. J. (1990). A meta-analysis of estimated effect sizes for group versus individual versus control treatments. *International Journal of Group Psychotherapy, 40*(2), 215–224.

Toner, B. B., Segal, Z. V., Emmott, S., Myran, D., Ali, A., DiGasbarro, I., et al. (1998). Cognitive-behavioral group therapy for patients with irritable bowel syndrome. *International Journal of Group Psychotherapy, 48*(2), 215–243.

Toseland, R. W., Rossiter, C. M., Peak, T., & Hill, P. (1990). Therapeutic processes in peer-led and professionally led support groups for caregivers. *International Journal of Group Psychotherapy, 40*(3), 279–303.

Toseland, R., & Siporin, M. (1986). When to recommend treatment. *International Journal of Group Psychotherapy, 36,* 172–201.

Tournier, R. E. (1979). Alcoholics Anonymous as treatment and as ideology. *Journal of Studies on Alcohol, 40*(3), 230–239.

Tracy, G., & Gussow, Z. (1976). Self-help groups: A grass-root response to a need for services. *Journal of Applied Behavioral Science, 12,* 381–396.

Truax, P. (2001). Review: Group psychotherapy is effective for depression. *Evidence-Based Mental Health, 4*(3), 82.

Truax, C. B., & Carkhuff, K. B. (1967). *Toward effective counseling and psychotherapy.* Chicago: Aldine.

Tschuschke, V., & Dies, R. R. (1994). Intensive analysis of therapeutic factors and outcome in long-term inpatient groups. *International Journal of Group Psychotherapy, 44*(2), 185–208.

Tschuschke, V., & Green, L. R. (2002). Group therapists' training: What predicts learning? *International Journal of Group Psychotherapy, 52*(4), 463–482.

Tylim, I. (1982). Group psychotherapy with Hispanic patients: The psychodynamics of idealization. *International Journal of Group Psychotherapy, 32*(3), 339–350.

Ulman, K. H. (2002). The ghost in the group room: Countertransferential pressures associated with conjoint individual and group psychotherapy. *International Journal of Group Psychotherapy, 52*(3), 387–407.

U.S. Census Bureau. (2001). *Population profile of the United States of America and the close of the 20th century.* Washington, DC: U.S. Department of Commerce.

Vannicelli. (2002). A dualistic model for group treatment of alcohol problems: Abstinence-based treatment for alcoholics, moderation training for problem drinkers. *International Journal of Group Psychotherapy, 52*(2), 189–213.

Van Schoor, E. P. (2000). A sociohistorical view of group psychotherapy in the United States: The ideology of individualism and self-liberation. *International Journal of Group Psychotherapy, 50*(4), 437–454.

Vinodagrav, S., & Yalom, I. (1989). *A concise guide to group psychotherapy.* Washington, DC: American Psychiatric Press.

Von Bertalanffy, L. (1950). The theory of open systems in physics and biology. *Science, 3,* 23–29.

Waelder, R. (1960). *Basic theory of psychoanalysis.* New York: International Universities Press.

Wagner, W. G. (2003). *Counseling, psychology, and children: A multidimensional approach to intervention.* Upper Saddle River, NJ: Merrill Prentice Hall.

Weber, R. L., & Gans, J. S. (2003). The group therapist's shame: A much undiscussed topic. *International Journal of Group Psychotherapy, 53*(4), 395–416.

Weinberg, H. (2001). Group process and group phenomena on the Internet. *International Journal of Group Psychotherapy, 51*(3), 361–378.

Weinstein, I. P. (1971). Guidelines on the choice of a co-therapist. *Psychotherapy: Theory, Research & Practice, 8*(4), 301–303.

Weiss, L. J., & Lazarus, L. W. (1993). Psychosocial treatment of the geropsychiatric patient. *International Journal of Geriatric Psychiatry, 8,* 95–100.

Weissman, M. M., & Bothwell, S. (1976). Assessment of social adjustment by patient self-report. *Archives of General Psychiatry, 33,* 111–115.

Weisz, J. R., Weiss, B., Han, S. S., Granger, D. A., & Morton, T. (1995). Effects of psychotherapy with children and adolescents revisited: A meta-analysis of treatment outcome studies. *Psychological Bulletin, 117*(3), 450–468.

Wheelan, S. (1997). Group development and the practice of group psychotherapy. *Group Dynamics: Theory, Research, and Practice, 1*(4), 288–293.

Wheelan, S., & Podowski, C. (1997). *Enhancing group effectiveness and productivity.* Manuscript submitted for publication.

White, J. R., & Freeman, A. S. (Eds). (2000a). *Cognitive-behavioral group therapy for specific problems and populations.* Washington, DC: American Psychological Association.

White, J. R. (2000b). Introduction. In J. R. White & A. S. Freeman (Eds.), *Cognitive-behavioral group therapy for specific problems and populations* (pp. 3–25). Washington, DC: American Psychological Association.

Wolman, C. (1970). Group therapy in two languages, English and Navajo. *American Journal of Psychotherapy, 24*(4), 677–685.

Wood, A., Trainor, G., & Rothwell, J. (2001). Randomized trial of group therapy for repeated deliberate self-harm in adolescents. *Journal of American Academy of Child and Adolescent Psychiatry, 40*(11), 1246–1253.

Yalom, I. (1970). *The theory and practice of group psychotherapy.* New York: Basic Books.

Yalom, I. (1983). *Inpatient group psychotherapy.* New York: Basic Books.

Yalom, I. (1990). *Understanding group psychotherapy: Process and practice* [Film]. Pacific Grove, CA: Brooks/Cole.

Yalom, I. (1995). *The theory and practice of group psychotherapy* (4th ed.). New York: Basic Books.

Yalom, I., & Vinodagrav, S. (1993). Interpersonal group psychotherapy. In H. I. Kaplan & B. J. Sadock (Eds.), *Comprehensive group psychotherapy* (3rd ed., pp. 185–195). Baltimore: Williams & Wilkins.

Young, J. (1990). *Cognitive therapy for personality disorders: A schema-focused approach.* Sarasota, FL: Professional Research Exchange.

Yuksel, S., Kulaksizoglu, I. B., Turksoy, N., & Sahin, D. (2000). Group psychotherapy with female-to-male transsexuals in Turkey. *Archives of Sexual Behavior, 29,* 279–290.

Zarit, S. H., & Knight, B. G. (Eds.). (1996). *A guide to psychotherapy and aging: Effective clinical interventions in a life-stage context.* Washington, DC: American Psychological Association.

Annotated Bibliography

Brabender, V. (2002). *Introduction to group therapy*. New York: Wiley.

In addition to serving as a primer of group therapy, this text offers an extended discussion of four theoretical approaches: interpersonal, psychodynamic, cognitive-behavioral, and problem-solving.

Fuhriman, A., & Burlingame, G. (Eds.). (1994). *Handbook of group psychotherapy: An empirical and clinical synthesis*. New York: Wiley.

Although this text does not contain the most recent research, it nonetheless provides the most extensive compendium of research done on group therapy to date. It also provides a number of excellent discussions of methodology in group studies.

Price, J. R., Hescheles, D. R., & Price, A. R. (Eds.). (1999). *A guide to starting psychotherapy groups*. New York: Academic Press.

A number of noted authors provide practical suggestions for getting a therapy group off the ground.

Rutan, J. S., & Stone, W. (2001). *Psychodynamic group psychotherapy* (3rd ed.). New York: Guilford Press.

This text provides a discussion of all of the basic topics concerning group therapy—such as mechanisms of change, member selection and preparation, and leadership—from a psychodynamic perspective.

White, J. R., & Freeman, A. S. (Eds.). (2000). *Cognitive-behavioral group therapy for specific problems and populations*. Washington, DC: American Psychological Association.

This text provides coverage of cognitive group treatment for an array of psychological problems including depression, panic and phobia, obesity, dissociative disorders, adult attention deficit disorder, and so on. A variety of special populations (e.g., older adults, medical patients, and latinos) are also featured.

Yalom, I. D. (1995). *The theory and practice of group psychotherapy* (4th ed.). New York: Basic Books.

Yalom's book is a classic in the area and provides many wonderful clinical illustrations of group treatment. The theoretical framework presented in this text is the interpersonal approach.

Index

Breinigsville, PA USA
09 May 2010
237624BV00002B/15/P